THE HISTORY OF AL-ṬABARĪ

AN ANNOTATED TRANSLATION

VOLUME XXXII

The Reunification of the ʿAbbāsid Caliphate

THE CALIPHATE OF AL-MAʾMŪN

A.D. 812–833/A.H. 198–213

The History of al-Ṭabarī

Editorial Board

Ihsan Abbas, American University of Beirut

C. E. Bosworth, The University of Manchester

Jacob Lassner, Wayne State University, Detroit

Franz Rosenthal, Yale University

Ehsan Yar-Shater, Columbia University (*General Editor*)

SUNY

SERIES IN NEAR EASTERN STUDIES

Said Amir Arjomand, Editor

Bibliotheca Persica
Edited by Ehsan Yar-Shater

The History of al-Ṭabarī

(Ta'rīkh al-rusul wa 'l-mulūk)

VOLUME XXXII

The Reunification of The 'Abbāsid Caliphate

translated and annotated
by
C.E. Bosworth
THE UNIVERSITY OF MANCHESTER

State University of New York Press

The preparation of this volume was made possible by a grant from the Translation Program of the National Endowment for the Humanities, an independent federal agency; and in part by the Persian Heritage Foundation.

Published by
State University of New York Press, Albany

Printed in the United States of America

For information, address State University of New York Press, State University Plaza, Albany, N.Y. 12246

Library of Congress Cataloging in Publication Data

Ṭabarī, 838?–923.
The Reunification of the ʿAbbāsid Caliphate.

(SUNY series in Near Eastern studies) (The History of al-Tabari ; v. 32)
Bibliography: p.
Includes index.
1. Islamic Empire—History—750–1258. 2. Iraq—History—634–1534. I. Bosworth, Clifford Edmund.
I. Title. III. Series. IV. Series: Ṭabarī, 838?–923.
Tārīkh al-rusul wa-al-mulūk. English ; v. 32.
DS38.6.T328 1985 909′.097671 84-16311
ISBN 0-88706-058-7
ISBN 0-88706-057-9 (pbk.)
10 9 8 7 6 5 4 3 2 1

Acknowledgements

In 1971 the General Editor proposed to the UNESCO to include a translation of al-Ṭabarī's *History* in its Collection of Representative Works. UNESCO agreed, but the Commission in charge of Arabic works favored other priorities. Deeming the project worthy, the Iranian Institute of Translation and Publication, which collaborated with UNESCO, agreed to undertake the task. After the upheavals of 1979, assistance was sought from the National Endowment for the Humanities. The invaluable encouragement and support of the Endowment is here gratefully acknowledged.

The General Editor wishes to thank sincerely also the participating scholars, who have made the realization of this project possible; the Board of Editors for their selfless assistance; Professor Franz Rosenthal for his many helpful suggestions in the formulation and application of the editorial policy; and Dr. Susan Mango of the National Endowment for the Humanities for her genuine interest in the project and her advocacy of it.

Preface

THE HISTORY OF PROPHETS AND KINGS (*Ta'rīkh al-rusul wa'l-mulūk*) by AbūJaᶜfar Muhammad b. Jarīr al-Ṭabarī (839-923), here rendered as the *History of al-Ṭabarī*, is by common consent the most important universal history produced in the world of Islam. It has been translated here in its entirety for the first time for the benefit of non-Arabists, with historical and philological notes for those interested in the particulars of the text.

Ṭabarī's monumental work explores the history of the ancient nations, with special emphasis on biblical peoples and prophets, the legendary and factual history of ancient Iran, and, in great detail, the rise of Islam, the life of the Prophet Muḥammad, and the history of the Islamic world down to the year 915. The first volume of this translation will contain a biography of al-Ṭabarī and a discussion of the method, scope, and value of his work. It will also provide information on some of the technical considerations that have guided the work of the translators.

The *History* has been divided here into 38 volumes, each of which covers about two hundred pages of the original Arabic text in the Leiden edition. An attempt has been made to draw the dividing lines between the individual volumes in such a way that each is to some degree independent and can be read as such. The page numbers of the original in the Leiden edition appear on the margins of the translated volumes.

Al-Ṭabarī very often quotes his sources verbatim and traces the chain of transmission (*isnād*) to an original source. The chains of transmitters are, for the sake of brevity, rendered by only a dash (—) between the individual links in the chain. Thus, according to Ibn Ḥumayd—Salamah—Ibn Isḥāq means that al-Ṭabarī received the report from Ibn Ḥumayd who said that he was by Salamah, who said that he was told by Ibn Isḥāq, and so on. The numerous subtle and important differences in the original Arabic wording have been disregarded.

The table of contents at the beginning of each volume gives a brief survey of the topics dealt with in that particular volume. It also includes the headings and subheadings as they appear in al-Ṭabarī's text, as well as those occasionally introduced by the translator.

Well-known place-names, such as, for instance, Mecca, Baghdad, Jerusalem, Damascus, and the Yemen, are given in their English spellings. Less common place-names, which are the vast majority, are transliterated. Biblical figures appear in the accepted English spelling. Iranian names are usually transcribed according to their Arabic forms, and the presumed Iranian forms are often discussed in the footnotes.

Technical terms have been translated wherever possible, but some, such as qāḍā'and imām, have been retained in Arabic forms. Others that cannot be translated with sufficient precision have been retained and italicized as well as footnoted.

The annotation aims chiefly at clarifying difficult passages, identifying individuals and place-names, and discussing textual difficulties. Much leeway has been left to the translators to include in the footnotes whatever they consider necessary and helpful.

The bibliographies list all the sources mentioned in the annotation.

The index in each volume contains all the names of persons and places referred to in the text, as well as those mentioned in the notes as far as they refer to the medieval period. It does not include the names of modern scholars. A general index, it is hoped, will appear after all the volumes have been translated.

Ehsan Yar-Shater

Contents

Abbreviations employed / xvii
Translator's Foreword / 1
Genealogical table of the 'Abbāsids (with special reference to those members of the family mentioned in this section of al-Ṭabarī's *History*) / 4
Maps. 1. Al-'Irāq in the Caliphate of al-Ma'mūn / 5
2. Baghdad and its environs / 6

The Caliphate of al-Ma'mūn / 9

[The Remainder of the Events of the Year 198 (813/814)]

The Events of the Year 199 (814/815) / 12

Various events in al-ʿIrāq / 12
The revolt in al-Kūfah of Muḥammad b. Ibrāhīm, called Ibn Ṭabāṭabā, under the military leadership of Abū al-Sarāyā / 13
The spread of the revolt to Mecca under Ḥusayn b. Ḥasan al-Afṭas / 19

The Events of the Year 200 (815/816) / 24

Harthamah b. Aʿyan's recapture of al-Kūfah, and the defeat and execution of Abū al-Sarāyā / 25
The revolt in the Yemen of the ʿAlid Ibrāhīm b. Mūsā al-Jazzār / 28

The proclamation in Mecca of the ʿAlid Muḥammad b. Jaʿfar al-Ṣādiq as Caliph / 30
The overthrowing of Muḥammad b. Jaʿfar's rule by the ʿAbbāsid forces, and his renunciation of power / 34
The abortive attempt to seize power in Mecca by a member of the ʿAqīlī branch of the Ṭālibids / 37
Harthamah b. Aʿyan's journeying to al-Ma'mūn's court at Marw and his fate there / 39
The civil strife in Baghdad between the troops of the Ḥarbiyyah quarter and those of al-Ma'mūn's representative in al-ʿIrāq, al-Ḥasan b. Sahl / 42

The Events of the Year 201 (816/817) / 46

The expulsion from Baghdad of al-Ḥasan b. Sahl's representative in the city, ʿAlī b. Hishām; the fighting between the Sahlid forces and the leader of the Baghdad rebels, Muḥammad b. Abī Khālid; the proclamation in Baghdad of the ʿAbbāsid prince Manṣūr b. al-Mahdī as al-Ma'mūn's *amīr* and *khalīfah* / 46
The breakdown of social order in Baghdad, and the movement there of the volunteers and vigilantes under Khālid al-Daryūsh and Sahl b. Salāma al-Anṣārī / 55
Al-Ma'mūn's designation of the Eighth Imām of the Shīʿah, ʿAlī al-Riḍā, as his heir and the adoption of the ʿAlid green colour / 61
The proclamation in Baghdad of Ibrāhīm b. al-Mahdī as anti-caliph / 621
Various items of information / 641

The Events of the Year 202 (817/818) / 66

Ibrāhīm b. al-Mahdī's assumption of power in central al-ʿIrāq / 66
The revolt in al-Kūfah of the ʿAlid al-ʿAbbās b. Mūsā al-Kāẓim, and its suppression by Ibrāhīm b. al-Mahdī's forces / 69
Ibrāhīm b. al-Mahdī's arrest and jailing of the vigilante leader in Baghdad Sahl b. Salāma / 75

Al-Ma'mūn's decision to leave Marw and to travel westwards and secure al-ʿIrāq; the murder of his minister al-Faḍl b. Sahl; Ibrāhīm b. al-Mahdī's preparations to withstand al-Ma'mūn's forces / 78
Various items of information / 82

The Events of the Year 203 (818/819) / 84

The death of the Imām ʿAlī al-Riḍā; al-Ḥasan b. Sahl's nervous breakdown / 84
Ibrāhīm b. al-Mahdī's despairing attempt to retain his caliphal power in Baghdad; his loss of the people of Baghdad's allegiance; his disappearance underground in the city / 86
Various items of information / 92

The Events of the Year 204 (819/820) / 94

Al-Ma'mūn's arrival in Baghdad and assumption of authority there; the abandonment of the ʿAlid colour of green and restoration of the traditional ʿAbbāsid colour of black / 94
Various items of information / 97

The Events of the Year 205 (820/821) / 99

Al-Ma'mūn's appointment of Ṭāhir b. al-Ḥusayn as governor of Khurasan and the East; Ṭāhir's suspicions of al-Ma'mūn's good faith towards him and his scheming with the Caliph's minister Aḥmad b. Abī Khālid / 99
Various appointments to governorships in the outlying part of the empire / 106

The Events of the Year 206 (821/822) / 108

Various items of information / 108
Al-Ma'mūn's appointment of ʿAbdallāh b. Ṭāhir as governor of al-Jazīrah and Syria with the task of suppressing the revolt there of Naṣr b. Shabath / 109
Ṭāhir b. al-Ḥusayn's epistle of advice to his son ʿAbdallāh on the latter's taking up his post / 110
The epistle's immediate fame / 128

The Events of the Year 207 (822/823) / 130

The revolt in Yemen of the ʿAlid ʿAbd al-Raḥmān b. Aḥmad / 130
The mysterious death in Khurasan of Ṭāhir b. al-Ḥusayn / 131
The appointment of his son Ṭalḥah as successor over Khurasan and the East; a variant account of this episode / 133
Various items of information / 135

The Events of the Year 208 (823/824) / 136

Al-Ḥasan b. al-Ḥusayn al-Muṣʿabī's revolt in Khurasan; various appointments to official positions / 136

The Events of the Year 209 (824/825) / 138

ʿAbdallāh b. Ṭāhir's lengthy campaigns against Naṣr b. Shabath; ʿAbdallāh's letters to Naṣr inviting his submission and guaranteeing his safety; Naṣr's final submission and the demolition of his fortress Kaysūm / 138
Military operations in Azerbaijan against the rebel Bābak al-Khurramī / 144

The Events of the Year 210 (825/826) / 145

Al-Ma'mūn's execution of the conspirator Ibn ʿĀ'ishah / 145
The capture of Ibrāhīm b. al-Mahdī, dressed in woman's clothing, in the streets of Baghdad; Ibrāhīm's ode addressed to al-Ma'mūn seeking the Caliph's forgiveness / 146
Al-Ma'mūn's consummation of his marriage to al-Ḥasan b. Sahl's daughter Būrān and the sumptuous celebrations at Fam al-Ṣilḥ / 153
ʿAbdallāh b. Ṭāhir's march into Egypt to combat the rebel ʿUbaydallāh b. al-Sarī; his capture of Alexandria and expulsion thence of the Andalusians to Crete / 159
The revolt of the people of Qumm against tax burdens / 166

The Events of the Year 211 (826/827) / 168

ʿUbaydallāh b. al-Sarī's submission to ʿAbdallāh b. Ṭāhir / 168

Anecdote in which ʿAbdallāh is cleared of suspected sympathies for Shīʿism / 169
Aḥmad b. Yūsuf's letter of congratulation to ʿAbdallāh on his restoration of order in Egypt / 172
Various items of information / 174

The Events of the Year 212 (827/828) / 176

Various items of information / 176

The Events of the Year 213 (828/829) / 178

Various items of information / 178
Ghassān b. ʿAbbād's appointment as governor of Sind / 179

The Events of the Year 214 (829/830) / 181

Various items of information / 181

The Events of the Year 215 (830/831) / 184

Al-Ma'mūn's journey to the Byzantine frontier and his campaigning there / 184

The Events of the Year 216 (831/832) / 187

Al-Ma'mūn's further campaigns against the Byzantines / 187
Various items of information / 188

The Events of the Year 217 (832/833) / 191

Al-Ma'mūn's execution at Adana of ʿAlī and Ḥusayn, the two sons of Hishām / 192
Al-Ma'mūn's campaigns in the Byzantine lands; his correspondence with the Emperor Theophilus / 194

The Events of the Year 218 (833/834) / 198

Al-Ma'mūn's fortifications at Tyana and his troop levies for the Byzantine wars / 198
Al-Ma'mūn's orders to his governor in Baghdad, Isḥāq b. Ibrāhīm al-Muṣʿabī, to interrogate the judges and traditionists on the question of the createdness of the Qur'ān: the Caliph's first letter / 199

Al-Ma'mūn's interrogation at al-Raqqah of certain scholars, and his second letter to Isḥāq b. Ibrāhīm / 204
Isḥāq's interrogation at Baghdad of a further group of scholars / 210
Al-Ma'mūn's third letter to Isḥāq after receiving the scholars' replies / 214
Isḥāq's despatch of the remaining recalcitrants to the Caliph at Tarsus / 220
Al-Ma'mūn's letters to his governors appointing his brother Abū Isḥāq al-Muʿtaṣim and his successor and commending him to their obedience / 222
Al-Ma'mūn's fatal illness at al-Budandūn; his last testament and commendation to al-Muʿtaṣim; his death on 18 Rajab 218/9 August 833 and burial at Tarsus / 224

Anecdotes about al-Ma'mūn and his conduct: / 232

Al-Ma'mūn's answer to Ibrāhīm b. ʿĪsā b. Burayhah's request to be admitted into the circle of the Caliph's travelling companions / 232
Al-Ma'mūn's suspicious attitude towards the Syrians / 233
His reverence for a document emanating from the Prophet himself / 234
His generosity with the revenues collected in Syria / 234
Al-Ma'mūn and the poet of Tamīm from al-Baṣrah / 236
Al-Ma'mūn and the exigent boon companion from Syria / 240
Al-Ma'mūn's dismissal of a poet-judge of Damascus for his jesting attitude towards the Islamic faith / 241
The singer ʿAllawayh's defence of the Umayyads before his master al-Ma'mūn / 243
Stories illustrating al-Ma'mūn's own poetic talent and aesthetic judgement; his relations with his court poets and the hostile one Diʿbil / 244
Al-Ma'mūn and Kulthūm al-ʿAttābī / 253
More stories about al-Ma'mūn's relations with his court poets / 255

Abbreviations Employed

BGA	Bibliotheca geographorum arabicorum
EI[1]	*Encyclopaedia of Islām*, first edition
EI[2]	*Encyclopaedia of Islām*, new edition
GAS	F. Sezgin, *Geschichte des arabischen Schrifttums*
GMS	Gibb Memorial Series
IC	*Islamic Culture*
IJMES	*International Journal of Middle East Studies*
Isl.	*Der Islam*
JA	*Journal Asiatique*
JAOS	*Journal of the American Oriental Society*
JESHO	*Journal of the Economic and Social History of the Orient*
JNES	*Journal of Near Eastern Studies*
JRAS	*Journal of the Royal Asiatic Society*
JSAI	*Jerusalem Studies in Arabic and Islam*
JSS	*Journal of Semitic Studies*
MW	*The Muslim World*
REI	*Revue des Etudes Islamiques*
RSO	*Rivista degli Studi Orientali*
SI	*Studia Islamica*
WZKM	*Wiener Zeitschrift für die Kunde des Morgenlandes*
ZDMG	*Zeitschrift der Deutschen Morgenländischen Gesellschaft*

In citations from the Qur'ān, where two different numbers are given from a verse, the first is that of Flügel's text and the second that of the official Egyptian edition.

Translator's Foreword

The section of Ṭabarī's history devoted to the caliphate of al-Ma'mūn concentrates essentially on events in Iraq and, to a lesser extent, on events in Mecca and the Hijaz insofar as the struggles for political and religious control of the Holy Places were reflections of those going on in the heartland of Iraq. Nevertheless, Ṭabarī was a chronicler of the history of the caliphate as a whole, hence he could not entirely neglect the regions outside Iraq. A fair amount of attention is paid to Egypt, where al-Ma'mūn's governors had to cope with various rebellions of both the local Muslim Arabs and the Copts, and to events in northern Syria, the Jazīrah and the Byzantine marches in eastern Anatolia, which formed the backdrop to the Caliph's last illness and death. But events in the Maghrib beyond Barqah are totally ignored; and the laconic references to Khurasan, Transoxiana and Sind rarely go beyond the noting of changes of governors there.

The main theme of the annalistic narrative of the earlier years of the reign, from al-Ma'mūn's succession to rule over the united empire on al-Amīn's death in 198(813) until al-Ma'mūn's decision to come westwards from Marw and establish firmly for the first time his authority in Iraq in 204(819), is of violent conflict in Iraq. At the outset the conflict focused on three contending groups: Abū al-Sarāyā's pro-Shī'ī revolt; the representatives of al-Ma'mūn's authority there under al-Ḥasan b. Sahl; and the old Arab and Iranian families of Iraq like the Hāshimites and their allies the Khurasanian Abnā' or guards of the first ʿAbbāsids, now settled mainly in Baghdad, above all in the Ḥarbiyyah quarter to the north of al-Manṣūr's Round City. This last group resented the Persophile policies of al-Ma'mūn exemplified, as they saw it, by his favor to the Sahl brothers; hence they took the lead in raising to power at Baghdad other members of the ʿAbbāsid family, notably in 201(817) al-Manṣūr b. al-Mahdī as amīr or nominal deputy for the Caliph, and then in 202(817) Ibrāhīm b. al-Mahdī as an explicit anti-Caliph. The military maneuvers of the respective groups, covering an area between Baghdad and Baṣrah, are treated in great detail, as are domestic events within the capital itself, including the fascinating episode of the attempt of the local representatives of Sunnī orthodox piety, Khālid al-Daryūsh and Sahl b. Salāmah, to take advantage of the deep yearning for public order after the social chaos and strife of the Civil War years and to establish in Baghdad a theocratic society with the secular power made more conformable to the moral imperatives of the Qur'ān and sunnah.

This period of storm and stress comes to an end with al-Ma'mūn's migration from Khurasan to assume the throne of his forefathers in their traditional capital; the collapse of Ibrāhīm b. al-Mahdī's anti-caliphate; and the latter's subsequent ignominious capture in the streets of Baghdad wearing female guise. The death—most probably accidental—of the Eighth Imām of the Shīʿa, ʿAlī al-Riḍā, conveniently brought about the abandonment of al-Ma'mūn's policy of endeavoring to reconcile the two wings of Islam, Sunnī and Shīʿī, by making the Imām his heir, though a similar policy was sustained on the intellectual plane with the enforcement by al-Ma'mūn and his two successors of Muʿtazilī theological doctrines. The most serious grievances of the anti-Iranizing forces in Iraq were removed by the murder of al-Faḍl b. Sahl in 202(818) and the illness and retirement shortly afterwards of al-Ḥasan b. Sahl.

Hence Ṭabarī's narrative for the last decade-and-a-half of al-Ma'mūn's reign is taken up with such episodes as the final quelling of Naṣr b. Shabath's prolonged uprising amongst the

Arabs of the Jazīrah; the story of Ṭāhir b. al-Ḥusayn's appointment as governor of Khurasan and his apparent repudiation of caliphal authority just before his sudden death in 207(822); the munificent ceremonies attending al-Ma'mūn's consummation of his marriage to Būrān, daughter of al-Ḥasan b. Sahl, at Fam al-Ṣilḥ; the abortive rebellion in Baghdad of the ʿAbbāsid Ibn ʿĀ'ishah; the restoration of caliphal authority in Egypt; and the last campaigns of al-Ma'mūn against the Byzantine emperor Theophilus, in the course of which he was to die near Tarsus in 213(833). Above all, we find inserted here, under the events of the year 213(833), the story of the beginnings of the *miḥnah* or inquisition by means of which al-Ma'mūn endeavored to impose on the leading religious dignitaries of the empire acquiescence in the Muʿtazilī doctrine of the createdness of the Qur'ān. The annals proper of al-Ma'mūn's caliphate close with a selection of anecdotes about the Caliph and his conduct, relating to his stay in Syria or to his presence at the court in (normally) Baghdad.

A feature of the post-204(819) part of Ṭabarī's account of al-Ma'mūn's caliphate is his insertion of the apparently complete texts of various chancery or *inshā'* documents, such as Ṭāhir b. al-Ḥusayn's admonition to his son ʿAbdallāh, itself an early example of the "Mirrors for Princes" genre in Arabic; letters from al-Ma'mūn and ʿAbdallāh b. Ṭāhir summoning the rebel Naṣr b. Shabath to obedience; the letter from Aḥmad b. Yūsuf to ʿAbdallāh b. Ṭāhir congratulating him on receiving the surrender of the Egyptian rebel ʿUbaydallāh b. al-Sarī; the public proclamation made on the occasion of al-Ma'mūn's execution of ʿAlī b. Hishām; the correspondence between al-Ma'mūn and the Emperor Theophilus; al-Ma'mūn's *waṣiyyah* or dying testament to his brother Abū Isḥāq al-Muʿtaṣim; and above all, the series of three lengthy letters sent by al-Ma'mūn, en route for the Byzantine front, to his lieutenant in Baghdad, the Ṭāhirid Isḥāq b. Ibrāhīm al-Muṣʿabī, requiring subscription by the theologians and canon lawyers to the doctrine of the createdness of the Qur'ān.

For some three-fifths of Ṭabarī's section on al-Ma'mūn's caliphate we have a parallel text, that of the surviving part of Aḥmad b. Abī Ṭāhir Ṭayfūr's *Kitāb Baghdād*; the parallelism

GENEALOGICAL TABLE OF THE ʿABBĀSIDS
(with special reference to those members of the family mentioned in this section of al-Ṭabarī's *History*)

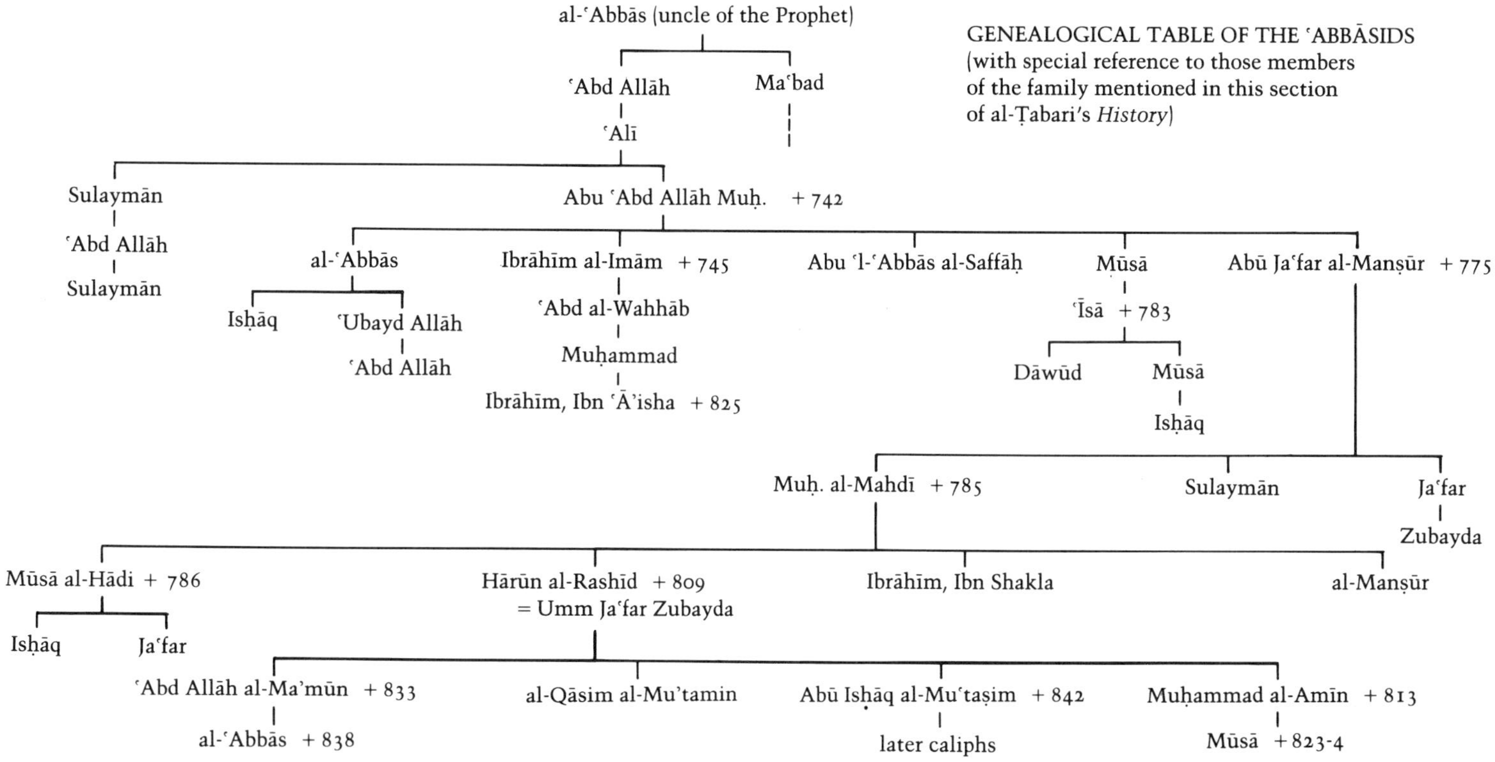

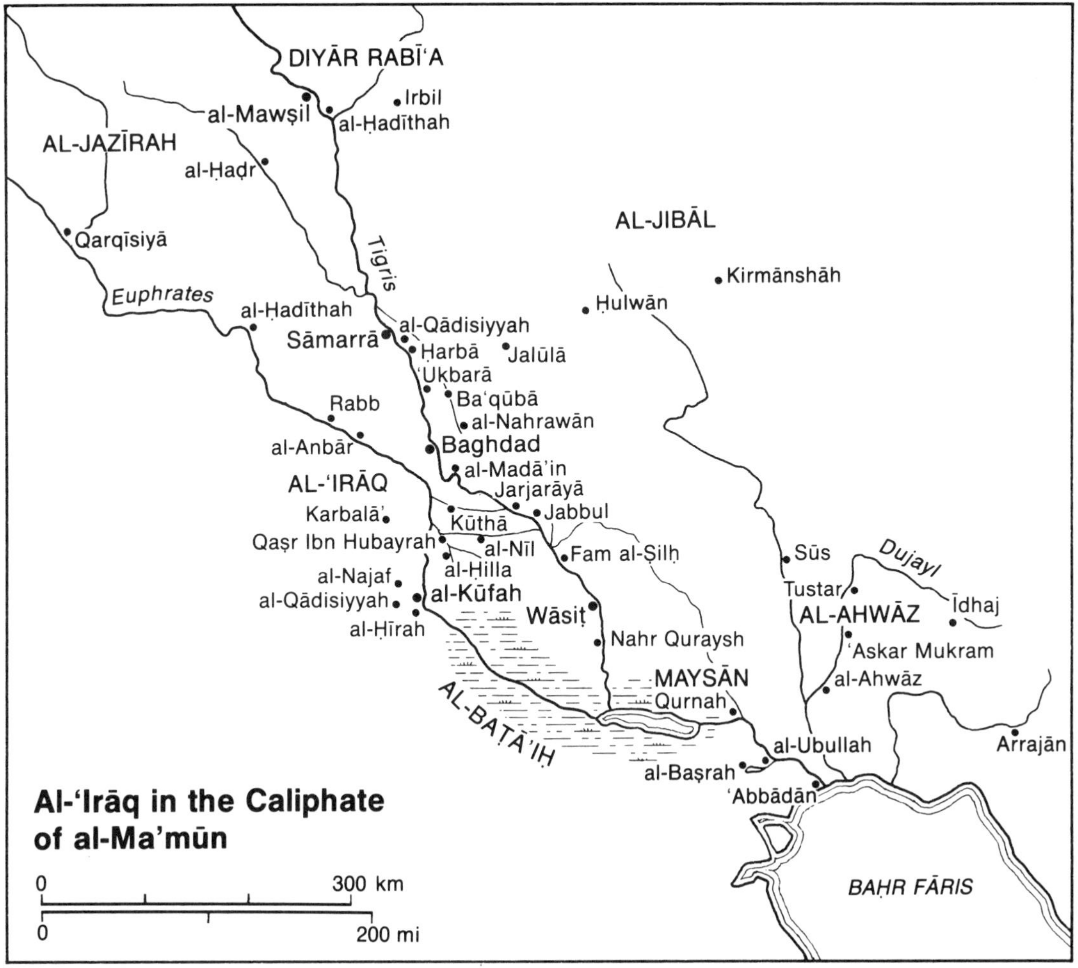

Al-ʿIrāq in the Caliphate of al-Maʾmūn

Farn-al-Ṣarāt

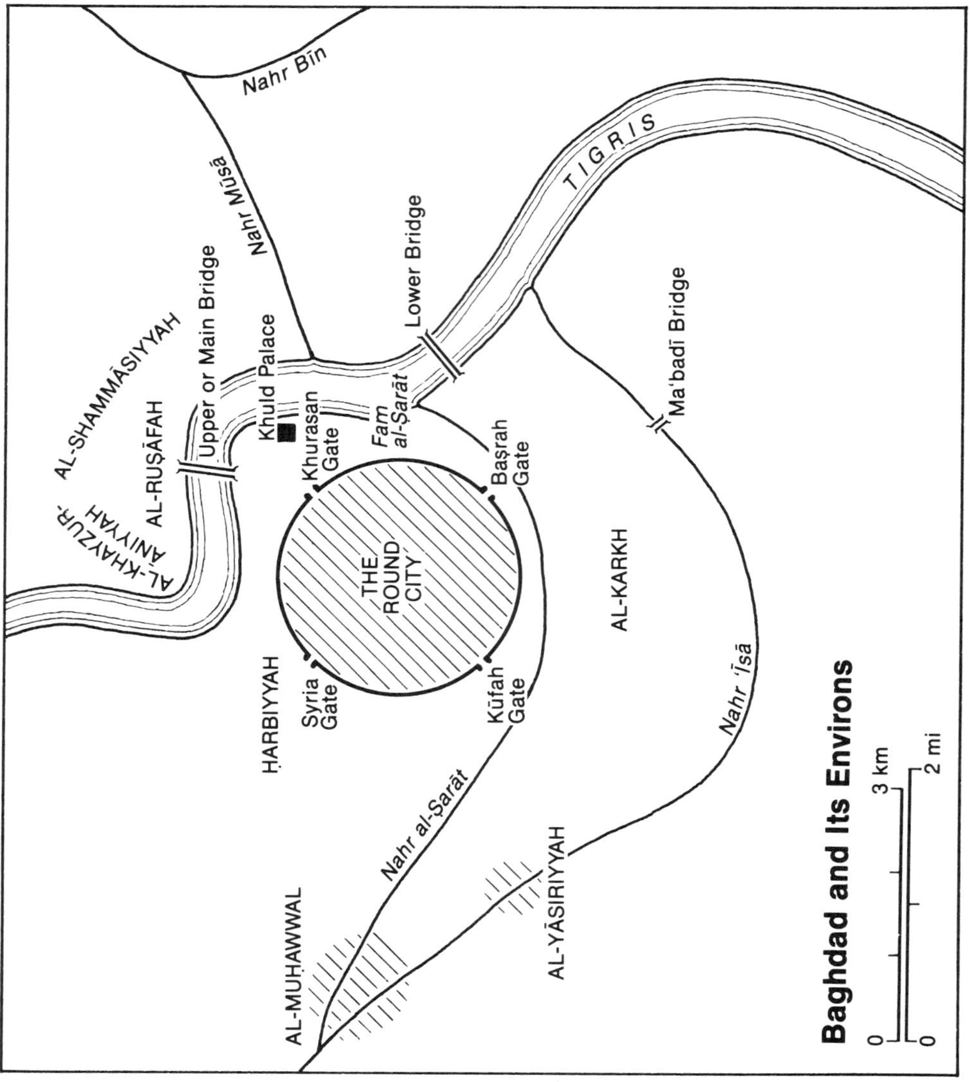

begins in Ṭabarī at III, 1036, with the events of the year 204(819/20), but excludes a part of the extensive section (III, 1118–33) on the *miḥnah*, where several folios of the corresponding text of Ibn Abī Ṭāhir seem to have been lost. There is no doubt that Ṭabarī followed the older historian (who died in 280[893], according to al-Masʿūdī and Ibn al-Nadīm), even though he only mentions Ibn Abī Ṭahir once by name (in III, 1516, quoting him, citing Ibn al-Ṣūfī al-Ṭālibī on the rebellion of the Ḥusaynī ʿAlid Yaḥyā b. ʿUmar b. Yaḥyā in Kūfah in 250[864]). Yet Ṭabarī copied intelligently; thus Keller, the editor and translator of Ibn Abī Ṭāhir, has pointed out that he omitted two verses of the ode to al-Ma'mūn by which Ibrāhīm b. al-Mahdī made his submission to the Caliph because Ibn Abī Ṭāhir's text rendered them faultily. He was also, as an annalist, less interested in literary and cultural history, hence he omitted some of the anecdotes which Ibn Abī Ṭāhir gives at the end of his narrative about al-Ma'mūn's stay in Damascus and about the poets and singers at his court; but it seems certain that the passage on the *miḥnah* mentioned above as unique to Ṭabarī stemmed also from Ibn Abī Ṭāhir. However, Ibn Abī Ṭāhir's concentration on affairs in Iraq and Syria meant that Ṭabarī could not, as a conscientious annalist, entirely pass by events in other parts of the caliphate comprising the Islamic heartlands, and so had to find other sources for, e.g., the events in Egypt. Here, two sources are specifically mentioned: Aḥmad b. Muḥammad b. Makhlad, who was personally in Egypt at the time of ʿAbdallāh b. Ṭāhir's quelling of the revolt of Ibn al-Sarī (III, 1087); and, more vaguely, several of the indigenous people of Egypt (III, 1091). Other items of information, e.g., the sparse ones relating to events in Khurasan and on the far eastern fringes of the caliphate, must have come from (to us) unknown chronicles, *kutub al-ta'rīkh.* The whole question of the relationship between Ibn Abī Ṭāhir and Ṭabarī has been discussed in a highly detailed and masterly fashion, so as to require no further discussion here, by Keller in the Introduction to his German translation of the *Kitāb Baghdād*, II, pages XIII-XXVI.

Although Ibn Abī Ṭāhir's history is a parallel text and source and, therefore, provides a control for much of Ṭabarī's text, Stanislas Guyard, who edited pages 459–1163 of the *Tertia se-*

ries of Ṭabarī's history, faced peculiar difficulties in his task. Like Ibn Abī Ṭāhir's history (which Guyard utilised in the then still unedited British Museum manuscript), much of this section, from page 755 l. 14 onwards, rests on a unicum in the Istanbul manuscript Köprülü 1041 (C) copied in 651(1253). From page 1068 l. 11 onwards, it is true, he had a second manuscript, located in the Oxford Bodleian, Pococke 354 (O), but this has a lacuna from page 1101 l. 16 to page 1112 l. 14 (see the general editor de Goeje's *Introductio*, page LXV). That the text which Guyard finally produced for the period of al-Ma'mūn's caliphate reads as intelligibly as it mostly does is a tribute to his sagacity and insight; the obscure passages which remain would not appear to be capable of complete elucidation unless fresh good manuscripts turn up.

There remains only the pleasant task of thanking those who have given valuable advice on problems connected with the text or have lent me necessary books: my colleague Dr. Norman Calder; my former student Dr. Yūsuf Abū al-ʿAddūs; and my friends Dr. Martin Hinds, Dr. Patricia Crone and Dr. Carole Hillenbrand. I am particularly indebted to Dr. Hinds, who has read through the whole of my translation and accompanying notes, and has indicated many useful references, corrections and improvements; but for any remaining shortcomings, the responsibility is mine alone.

C.E. Bosworth
Manchester, April 1984

The Caliphate of ʿAbdallāh b. Hārūn al-Maʾmūn

[*The Remainder of the Events of the Year 198 (September 1, 813–August 21, 814)*]

In the year 198 (September 1, 813–August 21, 814), the war between the two sons of Hārūn al-Rashīd, Muḥammad (al-Amīn) and ʿAbdallāh (al-Maʾmūn), came to an end, and the people in the eastern lands, in Iraq and the Hijaz, came together and gave their obedience to ʿAbdallāh al-Maʾmūn.

In this year, al-Ḥasan al-Hirsh came out in revolt in Dhū al-Ḥijjah (July–August 814) with a group of the dregs of the people and a large number of tribesmen, proclaiming, or so he asserted, the cause of "the one well-pleasing [to God] from the house of Muḥammad [*al-Riḍā min al-Muḥammad*]." He came as far as Nīl,[1] and then exacted taxes, practised extortion on the merchants, plundered the villages (of the neighborhood) and drove off herds.[2]

In this year, al-Maʾmūn granted to al-Ḥasan b. Sahl,[3] brother

1. Town of central Iraq to the south-southeast of Baghdad, near a transverse canal, the Greater Ṣarāt, which connected the Euphrates with the Tigris; see G. Le Strange, *The lands of the Eastern Caliphate*, 72–3.

2. Ibn al-Athīr, *al-Kāmil*, VI, 301.

3. Secretary and financial official for al-Maʾmūn, detested, like his brother, by the Abnāʾ, the Khurasanian military class of Baghdad, for his Zoroastrian background (see below, 52) and Iranian sympathies; see D. Sourdel, *Le vizirat ʿabbāside*, I, 215–18; id., *EI*[2] s.v.

of al-Faḍl b. Sahl,[4] the governorship of all the districts of Jibāl, Fārs, Ahwāz, Baṣrah, Kūfah, the Hijaz and the Yemen which Ṭāhir b. al-Ḥusayn[5] had conquered, this being after the killing of the deposed one Muḥammad (al-Amīn) and the people's general submission to al-Ma'mūn.[6]

In this year, al-Ma'mūn wrote to Ṭāhir b. al-Ḥusayn, who was at that moment established at Baghdad,[7] ordering him to hand over the whole of the tax revenues in his possession, collected from all the provinces, to the representatives of al-Ḥasan b. Sahl, and that he should leave and make his way to Raqqah.[8] He handed over to him responsibility for the war against Naṣr b. Shabath[9] and appointed him governor of Mosul, the Jazīrah, Syria and the western provinces (al-Maghrib).[10]

In this year, ʿAlī b. Abī Saʿīd[11] came to Iraq as al-Ḥasan b. Sahl's representative for collection of the land tax there. However, Ṭāhir refused to hand over the land tax to ʿAlī until he had paid in full the army's pay allowances. When he had fulfilled this obligation to them, he handed over the tax revenues to him.

---

4. Adviser and vizier to al-Ma'mūn till his assassination in 202 (818) (see below, 80); see Sourdel, *Vizirat*, I, 196–213; id., *EI²* s.v.

5. Al-Ma'mūn's general in the civil war with his brother al-Amīn, and member of an Iranian family long in the service of the ʿAbbāsids; see C.E. Bosworth, in *Cambridge history of Iran*, IV, 90–5; *EI¹* s.v. (W. Barthold).

6. Yaʿqūbī, *Ta'rīkh*, II, 539; anon., *Kitāb ʿUyūn al-ḥadā'iq*, 344; Ibn al-Athīr, *al-Kāmil, VI*, 297–8.

7. Al-Ma'mūn himself was at this time in his eastern Khurasanian capital of Marw.

8. The main town of Diyār Muḍar, on the upper Euphrates, in what is now northern Syria; see Yāqūt, *Muʿjam al-buldān*, III, 58–60; Le Strange, *Lands*, 101–3; M. Canard, *Histoire de la dynastie des H'amdânides*, I, 90–1; *EI¹* s.v. al-Raḳḳa (E. Honigmann).

9. Arab leader from the ʿUqayl tribe who took advantage of the confused situation in the Jazīrah during the civil war period to head bands of Zawāqīl or Qaysī Arabs against the central government till his submission in 209 (824/5) (see below, 138–44); see H. Kennedy, *The early Abbasid caliphate*, 168–9.

10. *ʿUyūn*, 344; Ibn al-Athīr, *al-Kāmil*, VI, 298.

11. Khurasanian and cousin of al-Ḥasan b. Sahl, bearer of the honorific of Dhū al-Qalamayn and administrator of Iraq for al-Ḥasan after the death of al-Amīn; see Sourdel, *Vizirat*, I, 202, 205, 216.

In this year, al-Maʾmūn wrote to Harthamah (b. Aʿyan) ordering him to proceed to Khurasan.[12] [976]

In this year, al-ʿAbbās b. Mūsā b. ʿĪsā b. Mūsā b. Muḥammad b. ʿAlī led the pilgrimage.[13]

---

12. *ʿUyūn,* loc. cit.; Ibn al-Athīr, *al-Kāmil,* loc. cit. Harthamah was a Khurasanian commander long in the service of the ʿAbbāsids until he was killed on al-Faḍl b. Sahl's orders in 200 (816) (see below, 39–41); see Patricia Crone, *Slaves on horses,* 177; *EI*[2] s.v. (Ch. Pellat).

13. Azdī, *Taʾrīkh al-Mawṣil,* 333; Ibn al-Athīr, *al-Kāmil,* loc. cit.

The Events of the Year

199

(August 22, 814–August 10, 815)

The notable events taking place during this year included the arrival in Baghdad of al-Ḥasan b. Sahl, as al-Ma'mūn's appointee with responsibility for both military and financial matters. When he reached the city, he divided up his tax collectors (*ʿummāl*) amongst the various districts and provinces.[14]

In this year, in Jumādā I (December 814–January 815), Ṭāhir, together with ʿĪsā b. Muḥammad b. Abī Khālid,[15] set out for Raqqah.

In this year, Harthamah also set out for Khurasan.

In this year, Azhar b. Zuhayr b. al-Musayyab marched out against al-Hirsh and then killed him in Muḥarram (August–September 814).

In this year, on Thursday, the tenth of Jumādā II (January 26, 815), Muḥammad b. Ibrāhīm b. Ismāʿīl b. Ibrāhīm b. al-Ḥasan b. al-Ḥasan b. ʿAlī b. Abī Ṭālib rebelled at Kufāh, proclaiming the cause of "the one well-pleasing [to God] from the house of Muḥammad" and of acting in conformity with the Book (the Qu-

14. Azdī, 334; ʿ*Uyūn*, loc. cit.

15. Son of the Abnā' leader in Baghdad Muḥammad b. Abī Khālid (on whom see below, 42, n.117) and brother of ʿAbdūs (see below, 15–16).

r'ān) and *sunnah*. This is the person known as Ibn Ṭabāṭabā.[16] The one who took charge of affairs for him in the conduct of war and who acted as commander of his forces was Abū al-Sarāyā, whose given name was al-Sarī b. Manṣūr; he used to mention that he was from the progeny of Hāni' b. Qabīṣah b. Hāni' b. Mas'ūd b. 'Āmir b. 'Amr b. Abī Rabī'ah b. Dhuhl b. Shaybān.[17]

The Reasons behind the Revolt of Muḥammad b. Ibrāhīm, called Ibn Ṭabāṭabā

There are differing accounts about that. Some people say that the reason for his rebellion was al-Ma'mūn's dismissal of [977] Ṭāhir b. al-Ḥusayn from the responsibility of collecting the taxes from the provinces which he had conquered and the Caliph's dispatch of al-Ḥasan b. Sahl for this duty. When he did this, people in Iraq talked (about it) among themselves, saying that al-Faḍl b. Sahl had secured an ascendancy over al-Ma'mūn; (they said) that he had installed al-Ma'mūn in a palace, where he had forbidden the members of his own family (the 'Abbāsids) and his chief military commanders, whether from his intimate circle or from the population at large, access to the Caliph. It was alleged, moreover, that al-Faḍl was managing affairs of state according to his own desires and was assuming sole judgment over public affairs without reference to the Caliph. Hence those members of the Hāshimite family and the leading men of the community who were in Iraq grew angry at this. They reacted strongly against al-Faḍl b. Sahl's ascendancy

16. Ya'qūbī, *Ta'rīkh*, II, 539–40; Mas'ūdī, *Murūj al-dhahab*, VII, 55 = ed. Pellat, § 2740; a detailed account of Ibn Ṭabāṭabā's revolt in Iṣfahānī, *Maqātil al-Ṭalibiyyīn*, 518–36, with the story of Abū al-Sarāyā's revolt continued at 542–59; Azdī, loc. cit.; A. Arioli, "La rivolta di Abū Sarāyā: appunti per una tipologia del leader islamico," *Annali di Ca' Foscari*, V (1974), 189–97; Kennedy, 207–11. It seems that there is nothing to indicate that Abū al-Sarāyā had any ideological commitment to Shī'ism, but that he saw the 'Alids as convenient tools to further his own military ambitions.

17. See on Abū al-Sarāyā, *EI*[2] s.v. (H.A.R. Gibb). His alleged ancestor Hāni' b. Qabīṣah had been one of the Arab chiefs of central Iraq connected with the last Lakhmid rulers of Ḥīrah; see Th. Nöldeke, *Geschichte der Perser und Araber zur Zeit der Sasaniden*, 332 ff.

over al-Ma'mūn and assumed a provocative attitude towards al-Ḥasan b. Sahl because of it. Civil strife broke out in the garrison cities, and the first to come out in rebellion at Kūfah was Ibn Ṭabāṭabā, whom I have mentioned.

An alternative account about why he rebelled says that Abū al-Sarāyā was one of Harthamah's commanders, but that Harthamah held back his pay allowances and kept putting off payment to him. Abū al-Sarāyā accordingly grew angry at this procrastination, and went off to Kūfah and proclaimed his allegiance to Muḥammad b. Ibrāhīm. He seized control of Kūfah, and the people there came together and gave him their obedience. He set up Muḥammad b. Ibrāhīm in the city, and the people of the surrounding rural districts, the tribesmen and others flocked to his standard.[18]

In this year, al-Ḥasan b. Sahl sent Zuhayr b. al-Musayyab (al-Ḍabbī)[19] with his personal forces to Kūfah. The official in charge of the taxes of Kūfah when Ibn Ṭabāṭabā entered the city was Sulaymān b. Abī Ja'far al-Manṣūr,[20] an appointee of al-Ḥasan b. Sahl's; Sulaymān's deputy there was Khālid b. Muḥajjal al-Ḍabbī. When the news (of Ibn Ṭabāṭabā's arrival in Kūfah) reached al-Ḥasan b. Sahl, he upbraided Sulaymān harshly and denounced him for his weakness. He dispatched Zuhayr b. al-Musayyab with an army of ten thousand calvary and infantry, and Zuhayr advanced towards them. When they heard reports of Zuhayr's approach, the rebels in Kūfah prepared to march out against him, but they did not have sufficient strength for such a counteradvance. So they stood fast until Zuhayr reached Qaryat Shāhī;[21] then they made a sortie, and stood fast (at the bridge) until Zuhayr encountered them there.
[978] He pitched camp on the Tuesday evening at Ṣa'nabā,[22] and then fell upon them the next morning. But the Kūfans put him

18. Iṣfahānī, *Maqātil*, 521, 523–4, with the date of Ibn Ṭabāṭabā's receiving the homage of the people of Kūfah given as the tenth of Jumādā I, 199 (December 27, 814); C.L. Geddes, "Al-Ma'mūn's Šī'ite policy in Yemen." *WZKM*, LIX–LX (1963–4), 99.

19. Veteran Khurasanian commander of the 'Abbāsids; see Crone, 186–7.

20. Great-uncle of al-Ma'mūn and governor of Baṣrah under Hārūn al-Rashīd.

21. "The royal village," presumably the one near Qādisiyyah of Kūfah given in Yāqūt, *Mu'jam*, III, 316.

22. Presumably the village of the Sawād mentioned in ibid., III, 408.

to flight, treated his army camp as legitimate plunder (*istabāḥū ʿaskarahu*), and seized all the money, weapons, beasts, etc., which he had with him. This was on Wednesday.[23]

On the day after this battle between the people of Kūfah and Zuhayr b. al-Musayyab, i.e., Thursday, the first of Rajab, 199 (February 15, 815), Muḥammad b. Ibrāhīm, (called) Ibn Ṭabāṭabā, suddenly died.[24] People said that Abū al-Sarāyā had poisoned him because, it was alleged, when Ibn Ṭabāṭabā had placed a secure guard on all the money, weapons, beasts, etc., captured from Zuhayr's army encampment, he had refused to give Abū al-Sarāyā any of it and had prevented his access to it; moreover, he had the obedience of all the people. Abū al-Sarāyā realized that he had no control over Ibn Ṭabāṭabā, so he poisoned him. On the latter's death, Abū al-Sarāyā set up in his place a young, beardless lad called Muḥammad b. Muḥammad b. Zayd b. ʿAlī b. al-Ḥusayn b. ʿAlī b. Abī Ṭālib;[25] but Abū al-Sarāyā was really the one who executed all affairs, appointing whomsoever he saw fit to official positions and dismissing whomsoever he pleased, and all affairs were in his hands.[26]

Abū al-Sarāyā kills ʿAbdūs

Zuhayr withdrew on the same day of his defeat to Qaṣr Ibn Hubayrah[27] and took up his position there. Now al-Ḥasan b. Sahl had dispatched ʿAbdūs b. Muḥammad b. Abī Khālid al-Marwarrūdhī[28] to Nīl at the same time as Zuhayr was sent to Kūfah. After Zuhayr's defeat, ʿAbdūs set out for Kūfah, according to al-Ḥasan b. Sahl's instructions, and he and his forces

---

23. Yaʿqūbī, *Taʾrīkh*, II, 542–3.

24. Ibid., II, 540; Iṣfahānī, *Maqātil*, 525–32; Azdī, 335.

25. I.e., of the Zaydī branch of the Ḥusaynids; as Kennedy, 208–9, points out, he was doubtless acceptable in Kūfah because his grandfather, Zayd b. ʿAlī Zayn al-ʿĀbidīn, had led an ʿAlid rising there against the Umayyad Caliph Hishām in 122 (740); see *EI*[1] s.v. Zaid b. ʿAlī (R. Strothmann).

26. Yaʿqūbī, *Taʾrīkh*, loc. cit.; Masʿūdī, *Murūj*, VII, 55–6 = ed. Pellat, § 2740; Iṣfahānī, *Maqātil*, 532–4, 545–50.

27. A town to the north of Ḥillah and named after its founder, the Umayyad governor Yazīd b. ʿUmar b. Hubayrah; see Yāqūt *Muʿjam*, IV, 365; Le Strange, *Lands*, 70–1; *EI*[2] s.v. Ḳaṣr Ibn Hubayra (J. Lassner).

28. Brother of ʿĪsā and son of the Abnāʾ leader in Baghdad (see below, 42, n.117).

reached Jāmiʿ;[29] Zuhayr in the meantime had taken up his position at Qaṣr (Qaṣr Ibn Hubayrah). Abū al-Sarāyā marched out against ʿAbdūs and fell upon him at Jāmiʿ on Sunday, the seventeenth of Rajab[30] (March 3, 815). In this (confrontation) Abū al-Sarāyā killed ʿAbdūs, captured Hārūn b. Muḥammad b. Abī Khālid and proclaimed ʿAbdūs's army camp to be lawful plunder.[31] It is reported that ʿAbdūs had four thousand cavalrymen, of whom every one was either killed or taken prisoner. The Ṭālibids were able to spread themselves through the land, and
[979] Abū al-Sarāyā now coined dirhams at Kūfah with the inscription, "God loves those who fight in His way in ranks, as though they were a building well-compacted."[32]

When the news reached Zuhayr that Abū al-Sarāyā had killed ʿAbdūs—at that time (Zuhayr was) still at Qaṣr—he and his forces retired to Nahr al-Malik.[33] Abū al-Sarāyā now advanced and encamped with his troops at Qaṣr Ibn Hubayrah, with his advance scouts penetrating as far as Kūthā[34] and Nahr al-Malik. He then sent out armies to Baṣrah and Wāsiṭ, which occupied those two cities. ʿAbdallāh b. Saʿīd al-Ḥarashī[35] was the governor of Wāsiṭ and its environs on al-Ḥasan b. Sahl's behalf. Abū al-Sarāyā's army engaged ʿAbdallāh's army near Wāsiṭ and put ʿAbdallāh to flight; accordingly, he had to fall back on Baghdad, having lost a considerable number of his forces either killed or taken captive. When al-Ḥasan b. Sahl realized that any army which he might send against Abū al-Sarāyā and

---

29. More usually in the dual form Jāmiʿān, the settlement on the Sūrā branch of the Euphrates which later developed into the town of Ḥillah; see Yāqūt, *Muʿjam*, II, 96; Le Strange, *Lands*, 71–2; G. Makdisi, "Notes on Ḥilla and the Mazyadids in mediaeval Islam," *JAOS*, LXXIV (1954), 249–62.

30. Actually a Saturday.

31. Yaʿqūbī, *Ta'rīkh*, II, 543, with the same date for the battle.

32. Qur'ān, LXI, 4. At least one dirham of this type is extant; see C.J. Tornberg, "Ueber muhammedanische Revolutions-Münzen," *ZDMG*, XXII (1868), 706–7.

33. Town on the canal of the same name, to the south of Baghdad and connecting the Euphrates and Tigris; see Yāqūt, *Muʿjam*, V, 324; Le Strange, *Lands*, 70–1.

34. Town on the canal of the same name, to the south of Nahr al-Malik; see Yāqūt, *Muʿjam*, IV, 487–8; Le Strange, *Lands*, 68–9.

35. Commander of al-Rashīd who fought for al-Amīn but who obviously recovered favor under the new régime; see Crone, 145.

his partisans would inevitably be put to flight; that whatever province they marched against, they occupied; and that, moreover, he had no commander in his own entourage who could successfully undertake a counter-campaign against Abū al-Sarāyā, he was compelled to have recourse to Harthamah. Now when Al-Ḥasan b. Sahl had come to Harthamah in Iraq as the governor appointed over it by al-Ma'mūn, Harthamah had handed over to him what tax revenues he then had in his possession and had set off for Khurasan, bitterly angry at al-Ḥasan. He journeyed onwards as far as Ḥulwān.[36] At that point, al-Ḥasan sent al-Sindī[37] and the *ṣāḥib al-muṣallā* Ṣāliḥ,[38] begging Harthamah to return to Baghdad and take charge of the warfare against Abū al-Sarāyā. However, he rejected the approach and refused. The envoy returned to al-Ḥasan bearing his refusal, so he sent al-Sindī back to him once more with conciliatory and flattering letters. Harthamah then agreed and turned back towards Baghdad; he entered Baghdad in Sha'bān (March–April 815). As he got ready to march on Kūfah, al-Ḥasan b. Sahl ordered 'Alī b. Abī Sa'īd to move out to the neighborhood of Madā'in, Wāsiṭ and Baṣrah; this he and his forces prepared to [980]
do.

Harthamah Marches Against Abū al-Sarāyā

News of all this reached Abū al-Sarāyā, all this time still at Qaṣr Ibn Hubayrah. He sent a force against Madā'in, and his troops entered it in Ramaḍān (April–May 815). In this same month of Ramaḍān, he himself and his forces moved forwards

36. Town of western Persia on the high road to Khurasan, and the first one in the mountain zone after leaving the plains of Iraq; see Yāqūt, *Mu'jam*, II, 293–4; Le Strange, *Lands*, 191; P. Schwarz, *Iran im Mittelalter*, 673 ff.; *EI*² s.v. (L. Lockhart).

37. Presumably al-Sindī b. Yaḥyā b. Sa'īd al-Ḥarashī, of the old Qaysī family, hence a nephew of the 'Abdallāh b. Sa'īd mentioned above, and again a former supporter of al-Amīn; see Crone, 145.

38. Court official of al-Rashīd, who had charge of the prayer carpet (*muṣallā*) which was spread over the Caliph's *sarīr* (the divan which served as a throne) and which was regarded as one of the insignia of royalty; this might also be allotted for the use of distinguished visitors. See Sourdel, *Vizirat*, I, 172; id., "Questions de cérémonial 'abbaside," *REI*, XXVIII (1960), 131–2.

and encamped at the Nahr Ṣarṣar,[39] in the district which lies along the road to Kūfah. While Harthamah was still holding back from returning to al-Ḥasan at Baghdad, he had ordered al-Manṣūr b. al-Mahdī[40] to move forward and encamp at Yāsiriyyah[41] until Harthamah himself should join up with him. This al-Manṣūr did. When Harthamah arrived, he went forward and encamped at al-Safīniyyīn[42] in front of (al-) Manṣūr. Then he pushed on until he made camp at the Nahr Ṣarṣar, facing Abū al-Sarāyā and with the canal between them. Meanwhile, ʿAlī b. Abī Saʿīd was encamped at Kalwādhā.[43] He set off on Tuesday, one day after the ʿĪd al-Fiṭr, and sent his vanguard on to Madā'in. There he engaged Abū al-Sarāyā's force in fierce fighting from the morning of Thursday till nightfall on that day. The next morning, he and his troops renewed the battle. Abū al-Sarāyā's soldiers were defeated, and Ibn Abī Saʿīd occupied Madā'in. The news (of the defeat) and Ibn Abī Saʿīd's capture of Madā'in reached Abū al-Sarāyā, and during the night of (Friday) Saturday the (twenty-fourth twenty-) fifth of Shawwāl (June 7–8, 814) he fell back from the Nahr Ṣarṣar to Qaṣr Ibn Hubayrah and encamped there. Harthamah moved forward the next morning and hurried in pursuit of him. He came upon a substantial detachment of Abū al-Sarāyā's troops and slaugh-
[981] tered them, sending their heads to al-Ḥasan b. Sahl. Harthamah then proceeded to Qaṣr Ibn Hubayrah, and there took place a battle between him and Abū al-Sarāyā in which a large number of the latter's soldiers were killed; therefore Abū al-

39. The transverse canal connecting the Euphrates and Tigris immediately to the south of Baghdad, on which lay the town of Ṣarṣar; see Yāqūt, *Muʿjam*, III, 401; Le Strange, *Lands*, 67–8.

40. Leading member of the ʿAbbāsid family in Iraq during al-Ma'mūn's absence, whom the opponents of al-Ḥasan b. Sahl later tried to set up as Caliph there; see below, fol. 23, and Kennedy, index s.v.

41. Township on the Nahr ʿĪsā Canal, to the west of Baghdad, where there was a bridge over the canal; see Yāqūt, *Muʿjam*, V, 425; Le Strange, *Baghdad under the Abbasid Caliphate*, 151–2; Lassner, *The topography of Baghdad*, 100, 259.

42. Reading uncertain; this is the one adopted by the editor here and at III, 865, of the text, but in M.J. de Goeje's *Addenda et emendanda*, p. DCCLXVIII, and in *ʿUyūn*, 422, we have al-Safīnatayn.

43. District and town on the left bank of the Tigris just below Baghdad; see Yāqūt, *Muʿjam*, IV, 477–8; Le Strange, *Lands*, 32; *EI*[2] s.v. (ed.).

Sarāyā had to retreat towards Kūfah. Muḥammad b. Muḥammad and the group of Ṭālibids accompanying him now swept down on the houses of the ʿAbbāsid family in Kūfah and on the houses of their clients and retainers (*mawālīhim wa-atbāʿihim*), ransacking and destroying these houses, expelling the ʿAbbāsids and their followers from the city, and searching out their goods and possessions which had been deposited with other people and appropriating them.[44] They behaved in an abominable fashion.

Meanwhile, Harthamah was telling the people, so it is said, that his intention was to lead the pilgrimage. During this period, he had held back pilgrims from Khurasan, Jibāl and the Jazīrah, and the pilgrims of Baghdad and others, and had not allowed anyone to set off on the pilgrimage, hoping that he himself would take Kūfah. Abū al-Sarāyā sent representatives to Mecca and Madīnah who would take control there and take charge of the pilgrimage. The governor of Mecca and Madīnah at that time was Dāwūd b. ʿĪsā b. Mūsā b. Muḥammad b. ʿAlī b. ʿAbdallāh b. al-ʿAbbās.[45] The person whom Abū al-Sarāyā sent to Mecca was Ḥusayn b. Ḥasan al-Afṭas b. ʿAlī b. al-Ḥusayn b. ʿAlī b. Abī Ṭālib[46] and the one whom he sent to Madīnah was Muḥammad b. Sulaymān b. Dāwūd b. al-Ḥasan b. al-Ḥasan b. ʿAlī b. Abī Ṭālib.[47] The latter entered Madīnah without encountering any resistance at all. Ḥusayn b. Ḥasan travelled towards Mecca, and when he drew near to it he halted for a brief while because of the garrison within the city.

Events at Mecca

When Dāwūd b. ʿĪsā heard the news that Abū al-Sarāyā had sent Ḥusayn b. Ḥasan to Mecca in order to take charge of the [982] rites of the pilgrimage, he gathered together the clients of the ʿAbbāsid family and the slaves who worked on their agricul-

44. Khalīfah b. Khayyāṭ, *Taʾrīkh*, II, 760–1; Iṣfahānī, *Maqātil*, 542–4; Azdī, 335; *ʿUyūn*, 345–7; Ibn al-Athīr, *al-Kāmil*, VI, 302–6.

45. Great-nephew of al-Saffāḥ and first cousin once removed of al-Maʾmūn.

46. I.e., grandson of the fourth Imām ʿAlī Zayn al-ʿĀbidīn.

47. Khalīfah, *Taʾrīkh*, II, 760; Masʿūdī, *Murūj*, VII, 55, 58 = ed. Pellat, §§ 2740, 2743; Iṣfahānī, *Maqātil*, 540.

tural properties (*ʿabīd ḥawā'iṭihim*).[48] The eunuch Masrūr al-Kabīr[49] had made the pilgrimage that year with a force of two hundred cavalrymen from amongst his own troops. He now got ready to oppose the Ṭālibid forces attempting to enter and take over Mecca. He said to Dāwūd b. ʿĪsā, "Set yourself up, or one of your sons, as my chief, and I will take upon myself the responsibility for fighting them."[50] Dāwūd replied, "I cannot declare lawful the idea of fighting in the sacred enclosure [*al-ḥaram*]. By God, if they enter by this way down through the mountains, I myself shall leave by another defile." Masrūr said to him, "You would hand over your ruling power and authority to your enemy! Who is there who will not criticize you for this, reproaching you for an act against your religion, the honor of your family and your own material interests?" Dāwūd responded to him, "What ruling power do I really have? By God, I have dwelled in their midst till I have grown aged, and they never appointed me to any administrative office till I had become an old man and my life had almost run. Then they made me governor of a part of the Hijaz which does not provide me with any sustenance. You and your likes can have this ruling power, so put up a fight or abandon the struggle, just as you wish!" Thereupon, Dāwūd left Mecca and retired to the vicinity of Mushāsh.[51] He had already loaded his bulkier possessions on camels, and he now sent them off on the road to Iraq and on his own initiative forged a diploma from al-Ma'mūn appointing his own son Muḥammad b. Dāwūd as leader of the worship during the pilgrimage period. He told him, "Go forth and lead the people in the midday and afternoon worship at Minā and then the sunset and evening worship. Stay overnight at Minā

48. The *ḥawā'iṭ* (sing. *ḥā'iṭ*) of Mecca are listed by Azraqī, *Akhbār Makkah*, II, 227–30, cf. 301, and described as embanked pieces of agricultural land irrigated by water brought in through conduits leading ultimately to the Ḥaram.

49. Abū Hāshim Masrūr, official in the service of al-Rashīd, and then apparently of al-Amīn and al-Ma'mūn; see Crone, 192–3.

50. I.e., the ʿAbbāsid Dāwūd would be nominal leader of the forces, while the slave or freedman Masrūr would be the real commander.

51. A well-irrigated district between the hill of ʿArafāt and Ṭā'if, according to Yāqūt, *Mu'jam*, V, 131; or a place half-a-stage from Mecca between there and the territory of the Banū Sulaym, according to Bakrī, *Mu'jam mā 'staʿjam*, IV, 1230.

and lead the dawn worship, then mount your steeds and go down via the ʿArafah Road and take the route on your left to the ravine of ʿAmr until you get on to the Mushāsh Road, and then join up with me at Ibn ʿĀmir's garden."[52] Muḥammad b. Dāwūd did that, and the body of men who had been with Dāwūd b. ʿĪsā in Mecca, comprising the clients of the ʿAbbāsid family and the slaves who worked on their agricultural properties, split up. This weakened the eunuch Masrūr's military strength, and he grew apprehensive that if he resisted the Ṭālibid forces, the majority of the people (i.e., the pilgrims) would [983] join their side. Hence he set off on Dāwūd's tracks, returning to Iraq, and the pilgrims remained at ʿArafah.

When the sun began to decline and it was time for the worship, a group (of religious leaders) from the people of Mecca successively refused to undertake the task of leading it. When they found that none of the rulers were present, Aḥmad b. Muḥammad b. al-Walīd al-Radmī,[53] who was the muezzin, judge of the community of pilgrims (*qāḍī al-jamāʿah*) and imām for the congregation of the Sacred Mosque of Mecca, then said to the judge of Mecca, Muḥammad b. ʿAbd al-Raḥmān al-Makhzūmī, "Step forward, deliver the sermon [*khuṭbah*] for the people and lead them in the two worships [midday and afternoon], for you are indeed the judge of the city." He replied, "In whose name shall I deliver the sermon, when the governor has fled, and these fellows [the Ṭālibids and their followers] are on the point of entering [the city]?" Aḥmad replied, "Don't make the prayers for anyone specifically." Muḥammad retorted, "No, you do it. Step forward, deliver the sermon and lead the people in the worship." Nevertheless he refused. Then they pushed forward a man from the lower classes of Mecca, and he led the

52. According to Yāqūt, *Muʿjam*, I, 414, this was the vulgar name for Bustān Ibn Maʿmar, described as two wadis filled with date palms, and identified by Bakrī, *Muʿjam mā ʾstaʿjam*, IV, 1304, with the date grove called Nakhlat al-Yamāniyyah.

53. Vocalization of this *nisbah* or gentilic uncertain, unless from *radm*, "barrier." Several *rudūm* in Mecca are mentioned by Azraqī, e.g., *Akhbār Makkah*, II, 33, 167, as being barriers or embankments constructed to keep water in the wadis in check and to prevent flooding of the courtyard of the Kaʿbah; cf. also the Radm Banī Jumaḥ of Yāqūt, *Muʿjam* III, 40.

people in the midday and afternoon worship without delivering any sermon. They proceeded and halted, in a body, at the standing-place of ʿArafah until the sun went down. Then the people began to go down from ʿArafah by themselves without any imām until they came to Muzdalifah. Another man from the lower classes of Mecca led them in the sunset and evening worships.

Meanwhile, Ḥusayn b. Ḥasan was pausing at Sarif,[54] reluctant to enter Mecca for fear of being repulsed from it and of being forcibly opposed by its defenders, until a deputation of the citizens of Mecca who were favorably disposed towards the Ṭālibids and fearful of the ʿAbbāsids went out to meet him. They told him that Mecca, Minā and ʿArafah had now become empty of any representatives of the (ʿAbbāsid) ruling power, and that these leaders had departed in the direction of Iraq. Hence Ḥusayn b. Ḥasan was able to enter Mecca before the time of the sunset worship on the Day of ʿArafah, together with all his retinue, numbering less than ten persons. They made the circumambulation (*ṭawāf*) round the Holy House, the running (*saʿy*) between Ṣafā' and Marwah, and proceeded to ʿArafah during the night. They then remained there during a period of time of that night for the standing (*wuqūf*), and then returned to Muzdalifah. Ḥusayn led the people in the dawn worship and
[984] performed the standing at the place of Quzaḥ, and kept the press of people away from himself. He halted at Minā for the remaining days of the pilgrimage, staying there until the year 199 came to its end (August 10, 815). The Ṭālibid Muḥammad b. Sulaymān b. Dāwūd remained at Madīnah for the rest of the year also. Then the pilgrims, and all of those who had been in Mecca and had taken part in the ceremonies of the pilgrimage, returned homewards—the pilgrims having had to make the running down (*ifāḍah*) from ʿArafah without any leader, however.[55]

---

54. A hollow or wadi, according to Azraqī, *Akhbār Makkah*, II, 208, 213.

55. Khalīfah, *Ta'rīkh*, II, 761; Masʿūdī, *Murūj*, IX, 69 = ed. Pellat, § 3648; Azdī, 335, 338; Ibn al-Athīr, *al-Kāmil*, VI, 306–7; Geddes, 99–100. For the various features of the pilgrimage ceremonies mentioned here, see *EI*[2] Ḥadjdj (A.J. Wensinck—J. Jomier).

Meanwhile, when Harthamah had grown afraid that he would not be able to make the pilgrimage (i.e., that he would lose too much time over the military operations in Iraq to be able to lead the pilgrims on their way across Arabia) and had encamped at Qaryat Shāhī, he attacked Abū al-Sarāyā and his partisans at the very same spot that Zuhayr had attacked him (previously). In the first part of the daylight hours, Harthamah was pushed back, but in the latter part, Abū al-Sarāyā's forces were defeated. When Harthamah realized that he had not managed to attain his aim (of taking charge personally of the pilgrims of Persia and Iraq), he remained at Qaryat Shāhī, made the pilgrims and others retrace their steps, and sent for al-Manṣūr b. al-Mahdī, who joined up with him at Qaryat Shāhī. Harthamah kept sending letters to the leading men in Kūfah. After ʿAlī b. Abī Saʿīd had occupied Madāʾin, he had gone on to Wāsiṭ and seized that city; then he had marched to Baṣrah, but did not manage to capture it till the end of this year.[56]

56. Yaʿqūbī, *Taʾrīkh*, II, 543–4; Ibn al-Athīr, *al-Kāmil*, VI, 307.

The Events of the Year 200
(August 11, 815–July 29, 816)

One of the events taking place during this year was the flight of Abū al-Sarāyā from Kūfah and Harthamah's entering the city. It is mentioned that Abū al-Sarāyā and his supporters from amongst the Ṭālibids fled from Kūfah during the night of (Saturday-) Sunday, the (fifteenth-) sixteenth of Muḥarram, 200 (August 26–7, 815) until they reached Qādisiyyah.[57] Manṣūr b. al-Mahdī and Harthamah entered Kūfah the morning after that night and gave the people a guarantee of safety; they did not, indeed, lay a hand on a single one of the townspeople. Manṣūr and Harthamah and their forces remained there during that day until the time of the afternoon worship, and then they went back to their encampment, leaving behind as their representa-
[985] tive in Kūfah one of their men called Abū Ibrāhīm Ghassān b. Abī al-Faraj b. Ghassān,[58] who held the office of commander of

---

57. I.e., that of Kūfah, lying to the west of the latter on the road to Mecca, and the site of the great battle between the Arabs and Persians in the conquest period; see Yāqūt, *Muʿjam*, IV, 291–3; Le Strange, *Lands*, 76.

58. The person mentioned below, 53, as Abū Ibrāhīm b. Ghassān; the text seems disturbed in both places, and confusion seems to have occurred in the latter place with the governor of Khurasan Ghassān b. ʿAbbād.

the guard for the governor of Khurasan. He set up his residence in the house which had been formerly occupied by Muḥammad b. Muḥammad and Abū al-Sarāyā.[59]

Abū al-Sarāyā Is Captured and Executed

Abū al-Sarāyā, together with his retainers, left Qādisiyya and went to the neighborhood of Wāsiṭ, ʿAlī b. Abī Saʿīd being at Wāsiṭ itself. At this point Baṣrah was still in the hands of the ʿAlids, so Abū al-Sarāyā travelled onwards till he crossed the Tigris below Wāsiṭ and came to ʿAbdasī.[60] There he found a sum of money which had been brought thither from Ahwāz, so he appropriated it. Then he proceeded further until he reached Sūs.[61] He encamped there with his forces, remaining there for four days, and he started to allot one thousand (dirhams) each to the cavalrymen and five hundred (dirhams) each to the foot-soldiers. On the fourth day of their stay, al-Ḥasan b. ʿAlī al-Bādhghīsī, known also as al-Ma'mūnī,[62] advanced towards them and sent a message, "Depart to wherever you like, for I see no point in engaging in fighting with you; and if you leave my province, I shall make no attempt to pursue you." But Abū al-Sarāyā was determined to provoke an engagement, and he attacked al-Ḥasan b. ʿAlī's troops. The latter, however, defeated Abū al-Sarāyā's forces and plundered their encampment; Abū al-Sarāyā himself was severely wounded.[63] He now took to flight. He and Muḥammad b. Muḥammad and Abū al-Shawk joined together, after their troops had split up and dispersed. They made for the region of the road to the Jazīrah, intending to go to Abū al-Sarāyā's residence at Ra's al-ʿAyn.[64] But when

59. Yaʿqūbī, *Ta'rīkh*, II, 543; Iṣfahānī, *Maqātil*, 545–7.
60. Settlement of the district of Kaskar, on the course of the modern Tigris channel just north of Qurnah; see Yāqūt, *Muʿjam*, III, 77; Le Strange, *Lands*, 42–3.
61. Town in Ahwāz, the ancient Susa; see Yāqūt, *Muʿjam*, III, 280–1; Le Strange, *Lands*, 240; Schwarz, 358–64.
62. Khurasanian mawlā of al-Ma'mūn, appointed governor of Armenia in 214 (829); see Yaʿqūbī, *Ta'rīkh*, II, 566; Crone, 257.
63. According to Yaʿqūbī, op. cit., II, 543, in the abdomen.
64. Town of the Jazīrah, on the headwaters of the Great Khābūr River and famed for its springs; see Yāqūt, *Muʿjam*, III, 13–14; Le Strange, *Lands*, 95; Canard, 97–8; EI^1 s.v. (Honigmann).

they reached Jalūlā,[65] they were intercepted. Ḥammād al-Kundughūsh came upon them and seized them, and then brought them to al-Ḥasan b. Sahl, who stationed himself at Nahrawān when the Ḥarbiyyah troops drove him out (of Baghdad). Abū al-Sarāyā was brought forward and decapitated on Thursday, the tenth of Rabīʿ I (October 18, 815). It is mentioned that the man who took charge of his execution was Hārūn b. Muḥammad b. Abī Khālid, who had been a captive in Abū al-Sarāyā's hands. They mention that they never saw anyone, at the time of his [986] execution, more terror-stricken than Abū al-Sarāyā; his arms and legs were violently agitated, and he was shrieking at the top of his voice. Finally, they put a halter round his neck; he was in a state of violent agitation, writhing and shrieking, until his head was actually cut off. Then his head was sent to al-Ḥasan b. Sahl's army camp and publicly paraded round it, while his corpse was sent to Baghdad, where it was gibbeted in two halves on the bridge (over the Tigris), one half at each end of it. Ten months had elapsed between his rebellion at Kūfah and his execution.[66]

At the time of Abū al-Sarāyā's crossing of the river, ʿAlī b. Abī Saʿīd had moved towards him, but when he had missed him, he had pressed on to Baṣrah and recovered it. The member of the Ṭālibids who was at Baṣrah, together with a group of other members of the Ahl al-Bayt,[67] was Zayd b. Mūsā b. Jaʿfar b. Muḥammad b. ʿAlī b. Ḥusayn b. ʿAlī b. Abī Ṭālib.[68] It was he who acquired the nickname of Zayd al-Nār ("Zayd of the Fire"), simply because of the large number of houses belonging to the ʿAbbāsid family and their retainers at Baṣrah which he

65. Town of Iraq on the road from Baghdad to Ḥulwān and Khurasan; see Yāqūt, *Muʿjam*, II, 156–7; Le Strange, *Lands*, 62–3. According to Yaʿqūbī, loc. cit., the interception took place at Rustaqābādh (conjectural reading of the text), but since this was in Ahwāz (the later ʿAskar Mukram, Le Strange, *Lands*, 237), this can hardly be correct.

66. Khalīfah, *Ta'rīkh*, II, 765; Yaʿqūbī, loc. cit.; Masʿūdī, *Murūj*, VII, 59 = ed. Pellat, § 2744; Iṣfahānī, *Maqātil*, 547–9; Azdī, 338–9; *ʿUyūn*, 347; Ibn al-Athīr, *al-Kāmil*, VI, 309–10; F. Gabrieli, *Al-Ma'mun e gli Alidi*, 10–23.

67. Here used apparently in the strict sense of the ʿAlids, but the term had varying degrees of wideness; see EI^2 s.v. (I. Goldziher—Wensinck—A.S. Tritton).

68. I.e., the son of the sixth Imām Mūsā al-Kāẓim.

burnt down.[69] Whenever a member of the Musawwidah[70] was brought before him, he used to decree that his punishment was to be burnt alive. Zayd's supporters also plundered wealth and possessions at Baṣrah. ʿAlī b. Abī Saʿid now took Zayd prisoner; it is said that the latter sought a guarantee of safety, and ʿAlī granted this to him. From amongst the commanders who were with him, ʿAlī b. Saʿīd then sent ʿĪsā b. Yazīd al-Julūdī,[71] Warqāʾ b. Jamīl, Ḥamdawayh b. ʿAlī b. ʿĪsā b. Māhān[72] and Hārūn b. al-Musayyab[73] to Mecca, Madīnah and the Yemen, ordering them to make war on any of the Ṭālibids in those places.[74] Al-Taymī[75] composed the following verses about al-Ḥasan b. Sahl's killing of Abū al-Sarāyā:

Have you not considered al-Ḥasan b. Sahl's blow,
dealt with your sword, O Commander of the Faithful?

It sent Abū al-Sarāyā's head spinning as far as Marw,
but preserved a warning [the corpse] to those crossing over [the bridge]. [987]

When Abū al-Sarāyā was killed, al-Ḥasan b. Sahl sent Muḥammad b. Muḥammad to al-Maʾmūn in Khurasan.

---

69. Yaʿqūbī, *Taʾrīkh*, II, 546; Iṣfahānī, *Maqātil*, 534. On the significance of Zayd's insurrection, see Pellat, *Le milieu baṣrien et la formation de Ǧāḥiẓ*, 198–9.

70. "Those who wear black garments," the supporters of the ʿAbbāsids.

71. Subsequently governor of Egypt in 212 (827) after ʿAbdallāh b. Ṭāhir's pacification of the country (see below, 159 ff.); see Kindī, *Kitāb al-Wulāt wa-Kitāb al-Quḍāt*, 184 ff.

72. Member of an Abnāʾ family and son of the ʿAlī b. ʿĪsā b. Māhān whose governorship in Khurasan under al-Rashīd had been so oppressive; Ḥamdawayh himself subsequently became governor of the Yemen (see below, 38). See E. Daniel, *The political and social history of Khurasan under Abbasid rule 747–820*, 170–4; Crone, 187.

73. Scion of a family of prominent ʿAbbāsid supporters in Khurasan; see Crone, 187.

74. Yaʿqūbī, loc. cit.; Ibn al-Athīr, *al-Kāmil*, VI, 310.

75. Text, al-Tamīmī. The correct reading appears in Azdī, 339, the poet in question being the *mājin* or libertine poet and colleague of Ibrāhīm al-Mawṣilī, ʿAbdallāh b. Ayyūb, a mawlā of the Meccan clan of Taym; see Iṣfahānī, *Aghānī*, XVIII, 114–25.

In this year, Ibrāhīm b. Mūsā b. Ja'far b. Muḥammad b. 'Alī b. Ḥusayn b. 'Alī b. Abī Ṭālib rebelled in the Yemen.[76]

Ibrāhīm b. Mūsā Rebels in the Yemen

According to what has been mentioned, Ibrāhīm b. Mūsā and a group of members of his family were at Mecca when Abū al-Sarāyā rebelled and the fate of the latter and that of the Ṭālibids in Iraq were as described. News of them reached Ibrāhīm b. Mūsā. He therefore set out from Mecca, together with those of his family who were with him, making for the Yemen; the governor of the Yemen at that time was Isḥāq b. Mūsā b. 'Īsā b. Mūsā b. Muḥammad b. 'Alī b. 'Abdallāh b. 'Abbās, who resided there and held power on al-Ma'mūn's behalf.[77] When Isḥāq heard about the 'Alid Ibrāhīm b. Mūsā's approach and how near he was to Ṣan'ā', he set off from the Yemen along the Najd Road with all his troops, comprising cavalry and footsoldiers, and abandoned the Yemen to Ibrāhīm b. Mūsā b. Ja'far, recoiling from the prospect of fighting him. He had heard news of how his paternal uncle Dāwūd b. 'Īsā had acted at Mecca and Madīnah, so he did the same thing, (abandoning his charge without striking a blow). He journeyed onwards in the direction of Mecca until he descended to Mushāsh and then encamped there. He planned to enter Mecca, but the body of 'Alids within the city prevented him. Isḥāq b. Mūsā b. 'Īsā's mother was at this time in Mecca, in concealment from the 'Alids; they were searching for her, but she remained in hiding from them. Meanwhile, Isḥāq b. Mūsā remained encamped at Mushāsh. Those persons who had gone underground in Mecca
[988] now began to slip away along the mountaintops, and they brought 'Īsā's mother to him at his camp. Ibrāhīm b. Mūsā used to be called al-Jazzār ("The Butcher") because of the large num-

76. Khalīfah, *Ta'rīkh*, II, 760; Ya'qūbī, *Ta'rīkh*, II, 540, Mas'ūdī, *Murūj*, VII, 56 = ed. Pellat, § 2740; Iṣfahānī, *Maqātil*, 533–4; Geddes, 100–1. Ibrāhīm was the brother of Zayd al-Nār (see above, 26–7), hence also a son of the Imām Mūsā al-Kāẓim.

77. Great-grandson of al-Saffāḥ's brother Mūsā and third cousin of al-Ma'mūn.

ber of people whom he killed in the Yemen; he also took people as slaves and confiscated people's wealth.[78]

In this year, on the first day of Muḥarram (August 11, 815), after the pilgrims had dispersed on their various ways from Mecca, Ḥusayn b. Ḥasan al-Afṭas took up his position behind the *maqām* (*Ibrāhīm*),[79] on a doubled-over saddle cushion, and then gave orders regarding the covering of the Kaʿbah.[80] As a result, the covering was stripped off until he left nothing at all of it, and the Kaʿbah was left as a bare piece of stonework.[81] Then he had it covered with two pieces of fine silk which Abū al-Sarāyā had sent with him and which had written on them the following: "Al-Aṣfar b. al-Aṣfar[82] Abū al-Sarāyā, the propagandist for the house of Muḥammad, ordered this to be made as the covering of God's Holy House, and [he also ordered] that the covering of the tyrants from the progeny of al-ʿAbbās should be flung away so that the Holy House might be purified from [the profanation of] their covering. He wrote [this] in the year 199 [814/15]."[83]

Then Ḥusayn b. Ḥasan issued a command about the original covering of the Kaʿbah, and as a result, it was divided up amongst his ʿAlid supporters and their followers according to what he considered to be their respective statuses.[84] He directed his attention to the wealth in the treasury of the Kaʿbah-

78. Yaʿqūbī, *Taʾrīkh*, II, 544; *ʿUyūn*, 347–8; Ibn al-Athīr, *al-Kāmil*, VI, 310–11.

79. "The standing-place of Abraham," the stone, now kept in a small building in front of the façade of the Kaʿbah, on which Abraham, re-founder of the Kaʿbah after the Flood, is said to have stood; see *EI*² s.v. Kaʿba (Wensinck—Jomier).

80. I.e., the *kiswah*, the ornate, embroidered brocade covering, see ibid.

81. Masʿūdī, *Murūj*, VII, 58 = ed. Pellat, § 2743.

82. *Aṣfar*, literally, "the light-coloured one;" the term Banū al-Aṣfar was often applied to the Byzantines and other Europeans (see *EI*² s.v. "Aṣfar" [Goldziher]), but is perhaps here used as a contrast to the use of black as the color par excellence of the ʿAbbāsids (cf. the Musawwidah, above, 27). Abū al-Sarāyā's name al-Aṣfar was apparently used on the coins minted by him at Kūfah in the year 199 (814/5), see above, 16.

83. Cf. Azraqī, *Akhbār Makkah*, I, 264.

84. Or: "according to how he viewed their importance to his cause," *ʿalā qadri manāzilihim ʿindahu.*

and seized it.[85] He swept down on the house of every person who, so he heard, had deposited with him valuables entrusted to him by a member of the ʿAbbāsid family or their followers. If he found there anything of these valuables, he seized them and inflicted punishment on the house owner; and if he found nothing there, he jailed and tortured the owner so that he
[989] should have to procure his release by handing over the whole of his personal fortune and should have to make an attestation before the legal witnesses that the money in question belonged to the Musawwidah from the progeny of al-ʿAbbās and their followers. This procedure came to affect a large number of people. The man charged with torturing the victims was a man from Kūfah called Muḥammad b. Maslamah, who was living in a special house[86] near the (quarter of) the wheat dealers, which became known as the "House of Torture." The ʿAlids so terrified the populace that a considerable number of the better-off citizens fled; the ʿAlids thereupon punished these fugitives by pulling down their houses. They went so far as to interfere with people's womenfolk and to seize people's children, causing great scandal. They started scraping off the thin gilded covering on the capitals of the columns of the (Sacred) Mosque, and obtained from a single column, after much tedious labor, one *mithqāl* (4.25 gr.) or so of gold; this process was consequently applied to the majority of the columns of the Sacred Mosque. They wrenched out the iron which formed the gratings around Zamzam[87] and also beams of teak, and these were sold off for a negligible price.

Anti-Caliph in Mecca

When Ḥusayn b. Ḥasan and the members of his family accompanying him saw how the people's attitude towards them had

85. According to Azraqī, *Akhbār Makkah*, I, 248, five thousand dirhams were appropriated as a forced loan; the custodians of the Kaʿbah pursued their claim before al-Ma'mūn after Muḥammad b. Jaʿfar (see below) lost power in Mecca and managed to recover the money.

86. *Dār khāliṣah*, which might be alternatively rendered as "a white house;" the expression echoes Qur'ān, XXXVIII, 46.

87. The well in the courtyard of the Kaʿbah; see EI^1 s.v. (Carra de Vaux).

changed on account of their behavior, and when they received news of Abū al-Sarāyā's execution, of the expulsion of the Ṭālibids resident there in Kūfah, Baṣrah and the regions of Iraq, and of the re-imposition of control there by the ʿAbbāsids, they went together in a body to Muḥammad b. Jaʿfar b. Muḥammad b. ʿAlī b. Ḥusayn b. ʿAlī b. Abī Ṭālib.[88] The latter was a venerable figure, of a very pacific nature, well-loved by the people at large and in no way associated with the evil activities of which many of the members of his house were guilty. He used to relate traditions concerning the religious sciences (*ʿilm*) from his father Jaʿfar (al-Ṣādiq) b. Muḥammad; people used to write down this knowledge from his transmission, and he used to [990] show forth seemly behavior and asceticism.[89] They now said to him, "You are probably aware of your high status in the eyes of the people; so show yourself publicly, and we will give allegiance to you as Caliph, for if you do that, no two persons would dispute your status." Nevertheless he refused to accede to their request. But his son, ʿAlī b. Muḥammad b. Jaʿfar, and Ḥusayn b. Ḥasan al-Afṭas kept on at him until they persuaded the old man, against his better judgement, and he agreed to their plan. Thus they set him up on Friday, after the worship, the sixth of Rabīʿ II (November 13, 815). Then they did homage to him as Caliph, and all the people, including the permanent residents of Mecca and the temporary foreign immigrants (*mujāwirūn*), gathered round him in a body and pledged their allegiance, whether willingly or unwillingly, and addressed him by the title of "Commander of the Faithful."

He remained in this position and dignity for a few months, but held only the title and not the substance of power, while his son ʿAlī, Ḥusayn b. Ḥasan and a group of their partisans behaved in the most outrageous possible way and committed the most reprehensible deeds. Thus Ḥusayn b. Ḥasan assaulted a woman of Quraysh from the Banū Fihr, whose husband belonged to the Banū Makhzūm and who was outstandingly

88. Yaʿqūbī, *Taʾrīkh*, II, 540; Iṣfahānī, *Maqātil*, 537–41.

89. Masʿūdī, *Murūj*, VII, 56–7 = ed. Pellat, §§ 2741–2. His honorific title was al-Dībājah, "embellishment, handsome [face]," from his handsomeness and accomplishments.

beautiful. He sent a message to her[90] that she should come to him, but she refused his demand. He frightened her husband (with threats) and gave orders for him to be sought out, with the result that the husband went into hiding from him. Then, during the night, Ḥusayn sent a gang of his associates who broke down the house door, seized the woman's person and carried her off to Ḥusayn. She remained in his clutches almost till his departure from Mecca, but managed at that point to escape from him and return to her own family, who were at that moment involved in the fighting at Mecca. ʿAlī b. Muḥammad b. Jaʿfar assaulted a youth of Quraysh, the son of a judge in Mecca, called Isḥāq b. Muḥammad, who was extremely handsome. He rushed in and seized him, openly and by the full light of day, in his house on al-Ṣafā', overlooking the route of the pilgrims' *saʿy*; he hoisted him up on the saddle of his horse and himself rode behind him on the beast's hindquarters. ʿAlī b. Muḥammad rode off with him and went right through the market until he came to Bi'r Maymūn[91] (he used to reside in the
[991] house belonging to Dāwūd b. ʿĪsā on the road to Minā). When the indigenous people of Mecca and the temporary foreign immigrants saw that, they all sallied forth and gathered together in the Sacred Mosque. The shops were closed and locked up, and the pilgrims who were circumambulating the Kaʿbah (on the ʿUmrah) joined up with them. They then went along to Muḥammad b. Jaʿfar b. Muḥammad, who was residing in Dāwūd's house and said, "By God, we shall certainly renounce our allegiance to you and kill you, unless you restore to us this youth whom your son has seized openly!" Muḥammad barred the door of the house and spoke to them from behind the grill of the window which opened on to the mosque and replied, "By God, I knew nothing [of this]!" He sent a message to Ḥusayn b. Ḥasan asking him to ride off to his son ʿAlī and rescue the youth from him. But Ḥusayn refused to undertake this, protesting, "By God, you know perfectly well that I have no power over your son. If I were to go to him, he would attack me

90. Reading, with the editor, n. *b*, *ilayhā* for the text's *ilayhi*.
91. See concerning this, Azraqī, *Akhbār Makkah*, II, 222; Yāqūt, *Muʿjam*, I, 302.

and set upon me with his band of partisans." When Muḥammad realized the position, he said to the people of Mecca, "Give me a guarantee of safety, so that I may ride along to ʿAlī and take the youth away from him." They provided him with the required guarantee and allowed him to ride off. He rode along unescorted till he reached his son. Then he took back the youth from him and restored him to his family.

The narrator continues: Only a short while elapsed before the ʿAbbāsid, Isḥāq b. Mūsā b. ʿĪsā, approached from the Yemen and halted at Mushāsh. The ʿAlids gathered round Muḥammad b. Jaʿfar b. Muḥammad and said to him, "O Commander of the Faithful, this is Isḥāq b. Mūsā approaching us with a force of both cavalry and infantry. We have come to the opinion that we should excavate a protective ditch and rampart around the higher parts of Mecca, and that you should show yourself publicly [in Mecca] so that the populace will see you and will take up arms at your side." They also sent messages to secure the support of the tribesmen of the surrounding districts and allotted subsidies to them, and they constructed the ditch and rampart around Mecca so that they might combat Isḥāq b. Mūsā from behind it. Isḥāq engaged them in battle over a period of several days, but then became disinclined to continue the fighting and the battle, and withdrew in the direction of Iraq. En route, Warqāʾ b. Jamīl and his personal force, and also those who were with him of al-Julūdī's force, met Isḥāq and said to [992]
him, "Go back to Mecca with us, and we will bring this fighting to a satisfactory conclusion for you." So he turned back in company with them till they drew near to Mecca and halted at Mushāsh. Those members of the Meccan mob who supported Muḥammad b. Jaʿfar, the blacks employed as water-carriers (*sūdān ahl al-miyāh*)[92] and the tribesmen who had received subsidies, rallied round Muḥammad b. Jaʿfar, and he then got them ready for battle at Biʾr Maymūn. Isḥāq b. Mūsā and Warqāʾ b. Jamīl, together with the latter's commanders and

92. Presumably slaves or ex-slaves. This interpretation of the phrase is that of Kennedy, 211, and fits well in the context; he notes the ʿAlid attempts, here as in Kūfah, to enlist support amongst the lowest strata of society, the slaves and laborers.

troops, approached and engaged them in combat at Bi'r Maymūn, and a considerable number on both sides were killed or wounded. Isḥāq and Warqā' then returned to their encampment, but returned to the fray a day later and resumed fighting the enemy.

Muḥammad b. Ja'far and his forces were now put to flight. When Muḥammad perceived this, he sent a group of envoys from Quraysh, including the judge of Mecca, asking them (Isḥāq and Warqā') for a guarantee of protection so that they might evacuate Mecca and go off to wherever they liked. Isḥāq and Warqā' b. Jamīl agreed to this request and guaranteed them a period of safety lasting for three days. When Tuesday arrived, Isḥāq and Warqā' entered Mecca, this being in the month of Jumādā II (January–February 816), with Warqā' acting as governor over Mecca on behalf of al-Julūdī. The Ṭālibids dispersed from the city, with groups of them making for various destinations. As for Muḥammad b. Ja'far, he started out in the direction of Juddah[93] and then went off towards Juḥfah.[94] However, he was intercepted by one of the clients of the 'Abbāsids called Muḥammad b. Ḥakīm b. Marwān. The Ṭālibids had despoiled Muḥammad b. Ḥakīm's house in Mecca and had violently ill-treated him; he used to act as the agent and steward (*yatawakkalu*) for one of the 'Abbāsids in Mecca from the family of Ja'far b. Sulaymān. He had now gathered together a force of the 'Abbāsids' slaves, those who worked in the gardens and orchards, and he eventually overtook Muḥammad b. Ja'far between Juddah and 'Usfān.[95] He then plundered and stripped him of everything which Muḥammad had brought with him from Mecca, to the point that he left him with nothing but his drawers, and fully intended to kill him; but in the end he threw him

93. The modern port of Jeddah; see *EI*[2] s.v. Djudda (R. Hartmann—P.A. Marr).

94. A settlement in the Tihāmah or Red Sea coastland of Arabia, on the pilgrimage route from Syria, between Madīnah and Mecca; see Yāqūt, *Mu'jam*, II, 111; Abdullah al-Wohaibi, *The Northern Hijaz in the writings of the Arab geographers 800–1150*, 102–12.

95. A settlement on the Madinah-Mecca pilgrimage route some forty miles northwest of the latter; see Yāqūt, *Mu'jam*, IV, 121–2; Al-Wohaibi, 284–9.

a shirt, a turban, a cloak and a few dirhams (or: a very few dirhams, *durayhimāt*) on which he could eke out an existence. [993]

Muḥammad b. Jaʿfar set out and came to the territory of the Juhaynah on the (Red Sea) coast.[96] He remained there until the pilgrimage season came to an end, gathering together followers during this period, and on several occasions he clashed at Shajarah.[97] and elsewhere with Hārūn b. al-Musayyab, governor of Madīnah. The explanation of these clashes was that Hārūn sent men to seize Muḥammad b. Jaʿfar, and when the latter realized this intention, he marched out against Hārūn with the force which he had collected round himself until he reached Shajarah. Hārūn moved forward to confront him and gave battle. Muḥammad b. Jaʿfar's forces were defeated; he himself lost an eye through an arrow-shot, and a large part of his force was killed. Hence he withdrew and established himself at his original encampment, awaiting the outcome of the pilgrimage (in the hope that some of the pilgrims would join his cause). But none of those who had given promises to him ever showed up. So when he realized this, and when the pilgrimage season was over, he sought a guarantee of personal security from al-Julūdī and from Rajā' (b. Abī al-Ḍaḥḥāk)[98] al-Faḍl b. Sahl's cousin on his father's side.[99] Rajā' gave him guarantees in regard to al-Ma'mūn and al-Faḍl b. Sahl, that he should not be personally harassed and that the promise of security should be fully honored. He willingly accepted these conditions, and Rajā' brought him to Mecca eight days after the final dispersion of the pilgrims back to Mecca from Minā, on Sunday, the nineteenth of Dhu al-Ḥijjah (July 19, 816). ʿĪsā b. Yazīd al-Julūdī and Rajā' b. Abī al-Ḍaḥḥāk, al-Faḍl b. Sahl's cousin on his father's side, ordered the pulpit (*minbar*) to be brought forward and set up be-

96. The Banū Juhaynah, part of the Quḍāʿah group, occupied a large tract of the northern Hijaz, lying to the north of Madinah; see *EI*[2] s.v. s.v. Ḳuḍāʿa (M.J. Kister).

97. A place just to the west of Madīnah; see Yāqūt, *Muʿjam*, III, 325; Al-Wohaibi, 337.

98. Official under al-Ma'mūn and al-Muʿtaṣim, and subsequently head of the *Dīwān al-kharāj* or financial department for the former; see Sourdel, *Vizirat*, I, 240 n. 1.

99. *ʿUyūn*, 347–9.

tween the corner of the Kaʿbah[100] and the *maqām* (*Ibrāhīm*), in the very same spot where homage had been given to Muḥammad b. Jaʿfar. The populace, Quraysh and the rest, had been assembled, and al-Julūdī then went up to the top of the pulpit, with Muḥammad b. Jaʿfar standing one step below him, wearing a short black coat and a pointed black cap, but without a sword, so that he might formally divest himself of power.

Then Muḥammad arose and delivered a speech, thus:

[994] O people, those of you who recognize me now knew me formerly, and those of you who do not recognize me, well, I am Muḥammad b. Jaʿfar b. Muḥammad b. ʿAlī b. Ḥusayn b. ʿAlī b. Abī Ṭālib. Originally I pledged my allegiance to the servant of God, the Commander of the Faithful, ʿAbdallāh, an allegiance by hearing and obedience, one freely entered into and not extracted by compulsion, and I was one of the legal witnesses who attested in the Ka'bah the two succession documents of Hārūn al-Rashīd regarding his two sons, the deposed one Muḥammad [al-Amīn] and the Commander of the Faithful, ʿAbdallāh al-Ma'mūn.[101] Then, indeed, there arose civil strife which enveloped[102] the whole earth, involving ourselves and others, and a report reached me that the servant of God, ʿAbdallāh al-Ma'mūn, had died. This information led me to the position where they did homage to me as Commander of the Faithful, and I deemed the acceptance of that honor as lawful because of my earlier promises and convenants regarding my allegiance to the servant of God, ʿAbdallāh; the Imām, al-Ma'mūn.[103] So you gave homage to me, [O people], or at least, those of you who did give homage [gave it]. But verily, the news has now reached me, and I attach full cre-

100. I.e., the northern ʿIrāqī one, or, more probably, the eastern, Black Stone one.

101. The famous "Meccan documents" of 186 (802) in which al-Rashīd endeavored to arrange the succession and reconcile the conflicting claims of his sons; see Gabrieli, "La successione di Hārūn al-Rašīd et la guerra tra al-Amīn e al-Ma'mūn," *RSO*, XI (1926–8), 341–97; Kennedy, 124–5.

102. Reading *ghashiyat* for the text's *ghushiyat*.

103. I.e., he regarded himself as released from his earlier pledge of allegiance because of his belief that al-Ma'mūn was dead.

dence to it, that he is alive and sound in body. Indeed, I now ask pardon of God for having drawn you into giving allegiance to me, and I have cast off the allegiance which you pledged to me in exactly the same way as I have taken off this ring of mine from my finger. I have reverted to the status of being an ordinary Muslim, so that the Muslims have no obligation of allegiance to me, and I have extricated myself from all that affair. God has restored the rightful authority to the trusty Caliph, the servant of God, ʿAbdallāh al-Maʾmūn, Commander of the Faithful. Praise to be God, the lord of the worlds, and blessings be upon Muḥammad, the seal of the prophets. Farewell, O Muslims!

Then he descended from the pulpit, and ʿĪsā b. Yazīd al-Julūdī set off with him towards Iraq. He left behind as governor over Mecca his son, Muḥammad b. ʿĪsā, in the year 201 (816/17). ʿĪsā and Muḥammad b. Jaʿfar travelled onwards until ʿĪsā handed the latter over to al-Ḥasan b. Sahl, who then sent [995]
him onwards, in the custodianship of Rajāʾ b. Abī al-Ḍaḥḥāk, to al-Maʾmūn at Marw.[104]

In this year, the Ṭālibid Ibrāhīm b. Mūsā b. Jaʿfar b. Muḥammad sent one of the progeny of ʿAqīl b. Abī Ṭālib[105] from the Yemen to Mecca with a numerous military force in order that he might lead the pilgrimage. But the ʿAqīlī was met by armed resistance and put to flight, and was unable to enter Mecca.

The affair of Ibrāhīm and the ʿAqīlī

It is mentioned that Abū Isḥāq b. Hārūn al-Rashīd[106] led the pilgrimage in the year 200 (816). He travelled onwards until he en-

104. Khalīfah, *Taʾrīkh,* II, 761, 763; Yaʿqūbī, *Taʾrīkh,* II, 544; Iṣfahānī, *Maqātil,* 540; Ibn al-Athīr, *al-Kāmil,* VI, 311–13. Muḥammad b. Jaʿfar died in Gurgān en route for Marw; Yaʿqūbī, loc. cit.

105. I.e., a descendant of the Caliph ʿAlī's half-brother; although ʿAqīl had supported Muʿāwiyah, his descendants adopted pro-ʿAlid views and are often reckoned among the Ahl al-Bayt (see above, 26). It now seems possible that the later Fāṭimid caliphs of Egypt and Syria arose from the ʿAqīlī branch of the Ṭālibids; Professor Heinz Halm of Tübingen University hopes to document this in a future publication.

106. I.e., the later Caliph al-Muʿtaṣim.

tered Mecca, being accompanied by a large number of his commanders, including Ḥamdawayh b. ʿAlī b. ʿĪsā b. Māhān, whom al-Ḥasan b. Sahl had appointed governor over the Yemen. They went into Mecca, where al-Julūdī and his troops and commanders were in control. The ʿAlid Ibrāhīm b. Mūsā b. Jaʿfar b. Muḥammad dispatched from the Yemen one of the progeny of ʿAqīl b. Abī Ṭālib, ordering him to lead the pilgrimage. When the ʿAqīlī got as far as the garden of Ibn ʿĀmir, he heard the news that Abū Isḥāq b. Hārūn al-Rashīd had taken charge of the pilgrimage and that he had with him commanders and troops (so numerous) that no one had power to withstand him. The ʿAqīlī halted at the garden of Ibn ʿĀmir, and then there passed by him a caravan of pilgrims and merchants which also had with it the covering (*kiswah*) for the Kaʿbah and fragrant perfumes for it. He seized the merchants' goods and the covering and perfumes for the Kaʿbah, and the pilgrims and traders reached Mecca naked and stripped of their possessions.

News of this reached Abū Isḥāq b. al-Rashīd, who was at that moment residing in the house (or: factory, storehouse) of the glass vessels (*dār al-qawārīr*)[107] in Mecca. He gathered together
[996] his commanders and sought their advice. Al-Julūdī told him—this being two or three days before the Day of Refreshment ([Yawm] al-Tarwiyah)[108]—"May God keep the Amīr in the upright way! I will deal with these rebels for you. I will sally forth against them with fifty of the élite of my companions and another fifty whom I shall select from the rest of the commanders." They all agreed with him about this plan. Hence al-Julūdī marched out with his hundred men, until he fell upon the ʿAqīlī and his companions in the morning at the garden of Ibn ʿĀmir. He surrounded them and took the greater part of them prisoner. Some of them took to flight, running away on foot. He got back the covering of the Kaʿbah, except for part of it which the deserters from the ʿAqīlī's force had fled with a day previously, and also the perfumes and the goods of

107. Mentioned several times in Azraqī, *Akhbār Makkah*, e.g., II, 75, 87, 250, as marking an open space and also a gate adjoining the Sacred Mosque.

108. The eighth day of Dhū al-Ḥijjah, when the pilgrims shift from the rites performed within Mecca to those performed on the hills outside.

the merchants and pilgrims. He sent the ʿAqīlī captive to Mecca, and he had all the ʿAqīlī's captured companions brought before him. He ordered each of them to be beaten round the head with ten strokes, and then said to them, "O dogs destined for hell fire, get you hence, for by God, there would be no difficulty in slaughtering you and no advantage in keeping you captive." Accordingly, he released them, and they went back to the Yemen, begging for food along the road until the majority of them perished from hunger and from exposure.[109]

Ibn Abī Saʿīd adopted an attitude of opposition towards al-Ḥasan b. Sahl. Al-Ma'mūn sent the eunuch Sirāj and gave him instructions, "If ʿAlī places his hands in al-Ḥasan's hand [in submission], or makes his way towards me at Marw, [then well and good]; but if not, cut off his head!" So Ibn Abī Saʿīd went to al-Ma'mūn in the company of Harthamah b. Aʿyan.

In this year, in the month of Rabīʿ I (October–November 815), Harthamah travelled from his army camp to al-Ma'mūn at Marw.

Harthamah's Journey to al-Ma'mūn and what befell him

It is mentioned that Harthamah, having dealt with the revolt of Abū al-Sarāyā and the ʿAlid, Muḥammad b. Muḥammad, and having entered Kūfah, remained in his encampment till Rabīʿ I. Then, as soon as the new month began, he set off towards the [997]
Nahr Ṣarṣar. People thought that he was going to al-Ḥasan b. Sahl at Madā'in, but when he reached the Nahr Ṣarṣar he continued in the direction of ʿAqarqūf,[110] then to Baradān,[111] then to

109. Ibn al-Athīr, *al-Kāmil*, VI, 313–14; Geddes, 101–2. According to Yaʿqūbī, *Ta'rīkh*, II, 544–6, the ʿAlid Ibrāhīm b. Mūsā himself successfully occupied Mecca after driving out its governor Yazīd b. Muḥammad b. Ḥanẓalah al-Makhzūmī, and remained there to enforce the *bayʿah* or oath of allegiance to the Imām ʿAlī b. Muḥammad al-Riḍā in 201 (817); cf. also Geddes, 102–3.

110. Settlement on the West Side of Baghdad, famed as the site of a large tell; see Yāqūt, *Muʿjam*, III, 137–8; Le Strange, *Lands*, 67; *EI*² s.v. (S.M. Stern).

111. Village on the left bank of the Tigris above Baghdad; see Yāqūt, I, 375–6; Le Strange, *Lands*, 50.

Nahrawān,[112] and he proceeded until he reached Khurasan. Before this, letters had come to him from al-Ma'mūn, reaching him at various stages of his journey, to the effect that he should turn back and take up the governorship of Syria or the Hijaz. Harthamah refused, however, saying that he would not retrace his steps until he had had a personal meeting with the Commander of the Faithful in order to give proof on his part against al-Faḍl because of his acknowledged wise counsels in the past to al-Ma'mūn and his forefathers. He wished to inform the Caliph about how al-Faḍl b. Sahl was conducting affairs to the detriment of al-Ma'mūn's interests and how al-Fadl was concealing items of information from him, and that he, Harthamah, would not leave him until he had brought him, al-Ma'mūn, back to Baghdad, the seat of the caliphate of his ancestors and their royal power, in order that he might assume direct control of his own sphere of authority and watch over its outlying parts. Al-Faḍl realized what Harthamah was aiming at, and he said to al-Ma'mūn, "Harthamah has stirred up unrest in your territories and amongst your subjects; he has given support against you to your enemies and has shown hostility to your supporters. He secretly used Abū al-Sarāyā for his own nefarious designs, Abū al-Sarāyā being one of the soldiers in his army, until Abū al-Sarāyā came to act as he did; if Harthamah had really wanted Abū al-Sarāyā not to behave in that way, Abū al-Sarāyā would not have done so. The Commander of the Faithful has written numerous letters to him instructing him to go back and take up the governorship of Syria or the Hijaz, but he has refused; he has come back to the Commander of the Faithful's door in a state of rebelliousness and dissension, openly using harsh words and uttering threats with the intention of making a great issue of it. If, despite all these crimes, he is allowed to go free, this will be a cause of corruption for others." In this way, he filled the Commander of the Faithful's heart (with anger) against him.

---

112. Town to the northeast of Baghdad where there was a bridge, carrying the road to Khurasan, over the Nahrawān Canal; see Yāqūt, *Muʿjam*, V, 324–7; Le Strange, *Lands*, 59–61; R. McC. Adams, *Land behind Baghdad*, 91–2.

Harthamah's journey was a protracted one, and he did not reach Khurasan till Dhū al-Qa'dah (June 816). When he arrived in Marw he was afraid lest his coming be kept from al-Ma'mūn, hence he had drums beaten so that al-Ma'mūn should hear the noise. The latter did in fact hear them, and exclaimed, "What is this?" They told him, "Harthamah has begun to thunder and lighten!" Harthamah himself imagined that he was in full fa- [998]
vor. Al-Ma'mūn then ordered him to be brought in. When he was brought in—the Caliph's heart having been changed against him, as described above—al-Ma'mūn upbraided him, "You have conspired with the people of Kūfah and the 'Alids, and you have intrigued and plotted with Abū al-Sarāyā until he came out in revolt and perpetrated his various misdeeds. He was one of your retainers, and if you had really wanted to arrest the whole lot of them, you could have done so; but you let the rope around their throats be slack and you let the halter on their necks hang loosely." Harthamah was impelled to speak out, to make excuses and to defend himself against the charges levelled at him; but al-Ma'mūn would not listen to any of this. He gave orders; Harthamah's nose was violently struck, his belly was trampled on and he was dragged out of the Caliph's presence. Al-Faḍl b. Sahl had previously instructed his minions to treat Harthamah with harshness and violence, and he was then jailed. He remained in prison for a few days, and then they secretly conspired to kill him, reporting to the Caliph that he had died.[113]

In this year, an émeute was stirred up in Baghdad between the troops of the Ḥarbiyyah quarter[114] and al-Ḥasan b. Sahl.[115]

113. Ya'qūbī, *Ta'rīkh*, II, 546; Jahshiyārī, *Kitāb al-Wuzarā' wa-al-kuttāb*, 259–61; Azdī, 341; *'Uyūn*, 349–50.

114. The suburb to the north and northwest of the Round City, originally occupied by various groups of the 'Abbāsids' Khurasanian troops and named after al-Manṣūr's commander Ḥarb b. 'Abdallāh; see Le Strange, *Baghdad*, 107–35; Lassner, *Topography*, 68, 112, 152, 254 n. 26.

115. *'Uyūn*, 351.

Trouble in Baghdad between the Troops of Ḥarbiyyah and al-Ḥasan b. Sahl

It is mentioned that al-Ḥasan b. Sahl was at Madā'in when Harthamah set off for Khurasan, and he remained there until the news of what had been done to Harthamah reached the people of Baghdad and Ḥarbiyyah. Al-Ḥasan b. Sahl now sent a message to ʿAlī b. Hishām,[116] the governor of Baghdad appointed by himself, as follows: "Delay payment of their stipends to the army, both the Ḥarbiyyah and Baghdad troops; inspire them with promises of payment, but do not actually give it to them." Previously, al-Ḥasan had given promises to them that he would pay their stipends. Also, the Ḥarbiyyah troops had erupted when Harthamah had departed for Khurasan, and had proclaimed, "We shall not be content until we have driven al-Ḥasan b. Sahl out of Baghdad." Al-Ḥasan's financial officials in Baghdad included Muḥammad b. Abī Khālid (al-Marwarrūdhī)[117] and Asad b. Abī al-Asad. The Ḥarbiyyah troops now
[999] rose up against them, expelled them and appointed Isḥāq b. Mūsā b. al-Mahdī[118] as al-Ma'mūn's representative in Baghdad. The citizens of Baghdad from both sides of the river concurred in this and approved of Isḥāq as governor. But al-Ḥasan used trickery towards them and was in correspondence with their commanders, until they rose up on the side of the ʿAskar al-Mahdī.[119] He also began to pay out their stipends due for the previous six months, but only actually paid out exiguous amounts. The Ḥarbiyyah troops then transferred Isḥāq to their

116. Prominent Khurasanian, apparently brought westwards by al-Ḥasan b. Sahl to govern Baghdad, and subsequently executed, with his brother Ḥusayn, by al-Ma'mūn in 217 (832), see below, 192–4, and Kennedy, 152, 154–5. He was also a littérateur; see Sezgin, *GAS*, II, 617; J. Sadan, "Kings and craftsmen—a pattern of contrasts. On the history of a medieval Arabic humoristic form," *SI*, LVI (1982), 21–2.

117. Son of an Abnā' leader with a power base in the Ḥarbiyyah quarter, and ally of Ṭāhir b. al-Ḥusayn during the civil war between al-Amīn and al-Ma'mūn; see Kennedy, 105, 144–5, 151, 154–6.

118. I.e., the son of the former Caliph al-Hādī.

119. The territories in the Ruṣāfah district of eastern Baghdad allotted by the Caliph al-Mahdī after his father al-Manṣūr had laid out Ruṣāfah, hence named after the former; see Le Strange, *Baghdad*, 42, 189; Lassner, *Topography*, 64, 251.

own camp and they installed him at Dujayl.[120] Zuhayr b. al-Musayyab arrived and then encamped at ʿAskar al-Mahdī. Al-Ḥasan b. Sahl sent ʿAlī b. Hishām, and ʿAlī made his way round the other flank and encamped at the Nahr Ṣarṣar. Then he, Muḥammad b. Abī Khālid and their commanders came by night and entered Baghdad. ʿAlī b. Hishām lodged in the house of al-ʿAbbās b. Jaʿfar b. Muḥammad b. al-Ashʿath al-Khuzāʿī[121] near the Bāb al-Muḥawwal[122] on the eighth of Shaʿbān (March 12, 816).

A little before that, the Ḥarbiyyah troops, hearing reports that the people of Karkh were intending to admit Zuhayr and ʿAlī b. Hishām, had attacked the Bāb al-Karkh[123] and had gone on to burn it down and to plunder everywhere from the limits of the Qaṣr al-Waḍḍāḥ[124] to the area within the Bāb al-Karkh and to (the quarter of) the booksellers and paper vendors[125] during the night of (Monday-) Tuesday. On the Tuesday morning, ʿAlī b. Hishām entered and engaged in battle with the Ḥarbiyyah troops over a period of three days at the old bridge and the new bridge of Ṣarāt[126] and at the water mills.[127] Then he promised the Ḥarbiyyah troops that he would pay their six months' stipend as soon as the tax revenues were gathered in. They, in turn, asked him for an immediate advance of fifty

120. The district of the Old Dujayl Canal which ran northwestwards from Baghdad to the Euphrates at Rabb; see Le Strange, *Baghdad*, 53; id., *Lands*, 51.

121. Former governor of Khurasan under al-Rashīd; see Crone, 185.

122. The gate leading out of the suburb to the southwest of the Round City, through which the nearby town of Muḥawwal ("the place of transfer," i.e., landing-stage) on the Nahr ʿĪsā was reached; see Le Strange, *Baghdad*, 136–52; id., *Lands*, 67.

123. The gate of the suburb of Karkh to the south of the Round City, reached through the Bāb al-Kūfah of the Round City; see Le Strange, *Baghdad*, 63; *EI*[2] s.v. al-Karkh (M. Streck—Lassner).

124. Palace said to be formerly that of al-Mahdī, which marked the northern limits of Karkh; see Le Strange, *Baghdad*, 58, 92; Lassner, *Topography*, 61, 73, 248.

125. The Qaṣr al-Waḍḍāḥ quarter was famed for its booksellers and paper vendors.

126. The Ṣarāt Canal passed to the south of the Round City to join the Tigris; see Lassner, *Topography*, 101, 277.

127. The so-called "Mills of the Patricius" at the junction of the Greater and Lesser channels of the Ṣarāt Canal; see Le Strange, *Baghdad*, 148; Lassner, *Topography*, 75–6, 260.

dirhams to each soldier for their living expenses during the month of Ramaḍān. He agreed to this, and began to pay out the promised money, but had not paid over to them the whole of their stipends by the time that Zayd b. Mūsā b. Jaʿfar b. Muḥammad b. ʿAlī b. Ḥusayn b. ʿAlī b. Abī Ṭālib, the person known as Zayd al-Nār, had rebelled at Baṣrah.[128] He had escaped
[1000] from his imprisonment at the hands of ʿAlī b. Abī Saʿīd, and then had rebelled in the district of Anbār,[129] together with the brother of Abū al-Sarāyā, in Dhū al-Qaʿdah 200 (June 816). They sent forces against him, and he was captured and brought before ʿAlī b. Hishām.

However, only Friday elapsed before ʿAlī b. Hishām fled from the Ḥarbiyyah troops and set up his camp by the Nahr Ṣarṣar. The reason for this was that he had tricked the Ḥarbiyyah troops and had not fulfilled his promise to them to pay fifty (dirhams) by the time the ʿĪd al-Aḍḥā (the tenth of Dhū al-Ḥijjah [July 10, 816]) came round. Furthermore they heard the news about Harthamah and his fate, so they fell upon ʿAlī and drove him out, the guiding spirit behind this action and their leader in war being Muḥammad b. Abī Khālid. This arose from the fact that when ʿAlī b. Hishām had entered Baghdad, he had treated Muḥammad with contempt. Furthermore, relations between Muḥammad b. Abī Khālid and Zuhayr b. al-Musayyab had deteriorated to such a point that Zuhayr caused Muḥammad to be flogged. Accordingly, the latter reacted angrily to this treatment, and in Dhū al-Qaʿdah (June 816) went over to the side of the Ḥarbiyyah troops. He took the lead in proclaiming war against ʿAlī b. Hishām and his forces, and people flocked to his standard. ʿAlī b. Hishām lacked the strength to stand up to him, so they were able to expel him from Baghdad. Then they went after him in pursuit, until they defeated and
[1001] dislodged him from the Nahr Ṣarṣar.[130]

In this year, al-Ma'mūn sent Rajā' b. Abī al-Ḍaḥḥāk and the

128. See above, 26–7.

129. Town on the Euphrates to the west of Baghdad; see Yāqūt, *Muʿjam*, I, 257–8; Le Strange, *Lands*, 65–6; EI^2 s.v. (Streck—A.A. Dixon).

130. Yaʿqūbī, *Ta'rīkh*, II, 547; Ibn al-Athīr, *al-Kāmil*, VI, 315–16.

eunuch Firnās to bring back ʿAlī (al-Riḍā) b. Mūsā b. Jaʿfar b. Muḥammad[131] and Muḥammad (al-Dībājah) b. Jaʿfar.[132]

In this year, the progeny of al-ʿAbbās were counted, and their number amounted to thirty-three thousand, including males and females.[133]

In this year, the Byzantines murdered their king Leo, who had ruled over them for seven years and six months, and they set up as ruler for his second reign Michael, son of George.[134]

In this year, al-Ma'mūn executed Yaḥyā b. ʿĀmir b. Ismāʿīl (al-Ḥārithī), because Yaḥyā had upbraided him in an unseemly fashion and had stigmatized him as "Commander of the Unbelievers" (Amīr al-Kāfirīn). Hence he was killed in his presnece.[135]

In this year, Abū Isḥāq (al-Muʿtaṣim) b. al-Rashīd led the pilgrimage.[136]

---

131. I.e., the eighth Imām of the Shīʿa, whom al-Ma'mūn was planning to nominate as his heir; see below, 61–2.

132. Yaʿqūbī, *Ta'rīkh*, II, 544–5; Masʿūdī, *Murūj*, VII, 59 = ed. Pellat, § 2745; Ibn al-Athīr, *al-Kāmil*, VI, 319.

133. Masʿūdī, *Murūj*, loc. cit.; Azdī, 339; *ʿUyūn*, 351; Ibn al-Athīr, loc. cit.

134. Ibid. Leo V the Armenian (813–30) was murdered in 820 by the partisans of Michael II the Stammerer (820–9), founder of the Amorian dynasty; see M.V. Anastos, in *Cambridge medieval history. IV. The Byzantine empire. 1. Byzantium and its neighbours*, 99–100; A.A. Vasiliev, *Byzance et les Arabes. I. La dynastie d'Amorium* (820–867), 280, noting that Arab authors confused Michael I Rhangabé and Michael II; id., *History of the Byzantine empire*, I, 272. Ṭabarī's date for the Emperor's death is therefore four years too early.

135. According to Yaʿqūbī, *Ta'rīkh*, II, 546, Yaḥyā was a confrère of Harthamah; see also Ibn al-Athīr, *al-Kāmil*, VI, 320; Crone, 257 n. 604, citing this incident as an instance of the opposition of the old Abnā' to al-Ma'mūn's Persianizing policies and reliance on Persian advisers.

136. Khalīfah, *Ta'rīkh*, II, 764; Azdī, 341; Ibn al-Athīr, loc. cit.

The Events of the Year

201

(July 30, 816–July 19, 817)

The events taking place during this year included the populace of Baghdad's attempt to persuade Manṣūr b. al-Mahdī to accept the caliphate; but he refused to accept it. On his affirming this refusal, they then dangled before him the prospect of assuming the military command (*imrah*) over them, with the proviso that they would recognise al-Ma'mūn in the Friday worship as Caliph, and he agreed to this.[137]

Manṣūr b. al-Mahdī Accepts the Military Command over Baghdad

We have already mentioned previously the reason why the people of Baghdad expelled thence ʿAlī b. Hishām. It is recorded concerning al-Ḥasan b. Sahl that, when the news of the Baghdādīs' expulsion of ʿAlī b. Hishām from the city reached him at Madā'in, he took to flight and retreated to Wāsiṭ. This took place at the opening of the year 201 (end of July 816). It has already been stated how the cause of ʿAlī b. Hishām's ejection

137. *ʿUyūn*, 352.

from the city by the Baghdādīs was al-Ḥasan b. Sahl's sending Muḥammad b. Abī Khālid al-Marwarrūdhī after Abū al-Sarāyā's execution and his rebellion[138] and his appointing ʿAlī b. Hishām as governor of the West Side of Baghdad, whilst Zuhayr b. al-Musayyab was to become governor over the East Side. Al-Ḥasan himself had remained at Khayzurāniyyah.[139] He had had ʿAbdallāh b. ʿAlī b. ʿĪsā b. Māhān[140] flogged for an infringement of the *sharīʿah*, so that the anger of the Abnāʾ was aroused; the populace rose up, and al-Ḥasan was forced to flee to Jarjarāyā[141] and then to Bāsalāmā.[142] He had ordered the [1002] troops of ʿAskar al-Mahdī to be paid their stipends but had refused to pay the troops of the West Side, and fighting had broken out between the soldiers of the two sides of the city. Muḥammad b. Abī Khālid had distributed money to the Ḥarbiyyah troops and had put to flight ʿAlī b. Hishām. Al-Ḥasan b. Sahl had then been forced to flee because of ʿAlī's flight.

Al-Ḥasan fell back to Wāsiṭ, and Muḥammad b. Abī Khālid b. al-Hinduwān pursued him, in open revolt against him, Muḥammad had himself assumed leadership over the people in Baghdad; he appointed Saʿīd b. al-Ḥasan b. Qaḥṭabah (al-Ṭāʾī)[143] as governor of the West Side and Naṣr b. Ḥamzah b. Mālik (al-Khuzāʿī[144] over the East Side. Manṣūr b. al-Mahdī, Khuzaymah

---

138. Reading here *wa-fasādihi*. One might also read *baʿd qatli Abī al-Sarāyā wa-fasādihi/ifsādihi*; the editor's n. *c* queries the manuscript's reading.

139. The quarter of Baghdad where Khayzurān, wife of al-Mahdī and grandmother of al-Maʾmūn, had had much property; see Nabia Abbott, *Two queens of Baghdad*, 120–1.

140. Brother of Ḥamdawayh, on whom see above, n. 72, and Crone, 179.

141. Clearly the emendation required of the text's Barbakhā, in the light of 50 below. Jarjarāyā was a town on the Tigris below Baghdad in the direction of Wāsiṭ; see Yāqūt, *Muʿjam*, II, 123; Le Strange, *Lands*, 37.

142. According to Yāqūt, *Muʿjam*, I, 322 (spelling Bāsalāmah), a village of the Baghdad district.

143. Member of an old Abnāʾ family, whose father and grandfather had been prominent in the ʿAbbāsid revolution; the family had fought strongly for al-Amīn in the civil war; see Crone, 188–9; Kennedy, 79–81.

144. From a similar background to Saʿīd's; his father had been governor of Khurasan for al-Rashīd; Naṣr's cousin Muṭṭalib b. ʿAbdallāh was a supporter of Ibrāhīm b. al-Mahdī's anti-caliphate in Baghdad, see below, 66; and another cousin, Aḥmad b. Naṣr, suffered death under the *miḥnah* of al-Wāthiq. See Crone, 180–1; Kennedy, 80–1.

b. Khāzim (al-Tamīmī)[145] and al-Faḍl b. al-Rabī[146] gave him their support in Baghdad. It has been stated that ʿĪsā b. Muḥammad b. Abī Khālid arrived during the course of this year from Raqqah, where he had been in the entourage of Ṭāhir b. al-Ḥusayn, and he and his father agreed to attack al-Ḥasan. The two of them, together with those of the Ḥarbiyyah troops and the members of the Baghdad forces who were with them, proceeded until they reached the village of Abū Quraysh[147] near Wāsiṭ. Whenever they came upon a detachment of al-Ḥasan's forces in some place and a clash occurred there, al-Ḥasan's troops were on every occasion put to flight. When Muḥammad b. Abī Khālid came to Dayr al-ʿĀqūl,[148] he remained there for three (nights). At that moment, Zuhayr b. al-Musayyab was at Iskāf Banī al-Junayd,[149] acting as al-Ḥasan's financial agent (*ʿāmil*) over Jūkhā,[150] hence resident within his administrative charge. He kept sending messages to the commanders of the troops in Baghdad, and then sent his son al-Azhar. He himself proceeded as far as the Nahr al-Nahrawān, but came up against Muḥammad b. Abī Khālid. The latter rode forward against him and encountered him at Iskāf (Banī al-Junayd). He surrounded Zuhayr's force, but gave him a guarantee of personal security and took him captive. He brought Zuhayr into his camp at Dayr al-ʿĀqūl and stripped him of all the wealth and possessions, every single item, small or great, which he had with him. Then Muḥammad b. Abī Khālid advanced, and when he

---

145. From a similar background to that of Saʿīd and Naṣr, and now a leader in the anti-Sahlid movement in Baghdad; see Crone, 180–1; Kennedy, 81–2.

146. Formerly vizier to al-Rashīd and al-Amīn, subsequently a supporter of Ibrāhīm b. al-Mahdī; see Sourdel, *Vizirat*, I, 183–94; A.J. Chejne, "Al-Faḍl b. al-Rabīʿ—a politician of the early ʿAbbāsid period," *IC*, XXXVI (1962), 167–81; *EI²* s.v. (Sourdel).

147. A village between Wāsiṭ and Quraysh, the latter on the canal of the same name flowing into the Tigris below Wāsiṭ; see Yāqūt, *Muʿjam*, IV, 337; Le Strange, *Lands*, 35.

148. Town on the Tigris below Madā'in; see Yāqūt, *Muʿjam*, II, 520–1; Le Strange, *Lands*, 35–6; Adams, *Land behind Baghdad*, 91; *EI²* s.v. (S.A. El-Ali).

149. Town on the Nahrawān Canal to the east of Baghdad; see Yāqūt, *Muʿjam*, I, 181; Le Strange, *Lands*, 59–60; Adams, 95–6.

150. District to the east of the present course of the Tigris, to the north of Maysān; see Yāqūt, *Muʿjam*, II, 179; Le Strange, *Lands*, 42.

reached Wāsiṭ, he sent Zuhayr back to Baghdad for imprisonment at the hands of a blind son of his named Jaʿfar.

Meanwhile al-Ḥasan remained at Jarjarāyā, but when he [1003] heard the news that Zuhayr had fallen into the hands of Muḥammad b. Abī Khālid, he travelled onwards till he entered Wāsiṭ and then encamped at Fam al-Ṣilḥ.[151] From Dayr al-ʿĀqūl, Muḥammad sent his son Hārūn to Nīl, which was being held by Saʿīd b. al-Sājūr al-Kūfī.[152] Hārūn defeated him and then pursued him until he (Hārūn) entered Kūfah, which he occupied, appointing a governor over it. ʿĪsā b. Yazīd al-Julūdī arrived from Mecca, accompanied by Muḥammad b. Jaʿfar. They set off together until they came to Wāsiṭ, via the land route. Then Hārūn retraced his steps towards his father, and they all met up together at the village of Abū Quraysh in order to enter Wāsiṭ, where al-Ḥasan b. Sahl was. Al-Ḥasan b. Sahl then moved forward and encamped behind Wāsiṭ on its outer fringes. Al-Faḍl b. al-Rabīʿ had been in concealment since the killing of the deposed one (al-Amīn), but when he saw that Muḥammad b. Abī Khālid had reached Wāsiṭ, he sent a message to him seeking a guarantee of personal safety; Muḥammad granted him this, and he emerged into the open.

Muḥammad b. Abī Khālid now prepared for battle. He and [1004] his son ʿĪsā and their forces advanced to a position two miles from Wāsiṭ. Al-Ḥasan sent against them his troops and his commanders, and a fierce struggle took place by the residential area (*abyāt*) of Wāsiṭ. At a point after the time of the afternoon worship, a violent wind and dust storm blew up, until the combatants were completely mixed up with each other and confused together. Muḥammad b. Abī Khālid's forces were defeated; he himself stood firm against the enemy, but received

---

151. Town on the Tigris at its confluence with the Ṣilḥ Canal, to the south of modern Kut el-Amara, shortly to be famed as the venue for the opulent celebrations of the consummation of al-Maʾmūn's marriage to al-Ḥasan b. Sahl's daughter Būrān (see below, 153ff.); see Yāqūt, *Muʿjam*, IV, 276; Le Strange, *Lands*, 38.

152. Former supporter of al-Amīn, who soon after this deserted al-Ḥasan's side for that of the Baghdad insurrectionists (see below, 69–75); see Kennedy, 156, 159–60.

several severe wounds on his body.[153] He and his soldiers fled in total disarray, and al-Ḥasan's forces routed them.[154] This battle took place on Sunday the twenty-third of Rabīʿ I, 201 (October 19, 816).

When Muḥammad (and his forces) reached Fam al-Ṣilḥ, al-Ḥasan's forces marched out against them and drew up their ranks ready to give battle to Muḥammad's army. But when nightfall came, Muḥammad and his forces travelled onwards until they halted at Mubārak[155] and then encamped there. The next morning, al-Ḥasan's forces moved up towards them. They drew up their ranks against them for battle and the two sides clashed. When night enveloped them, they marched off till they reached Jabbul[156] and encamped there. Muḥammad sent his son Hārūn to Nīl, where he then took up his position, while Muḥammad remained at Jarjarāyā. His wounds became worse; he left his commanders behind with the rest of his army, and his son Abū Zanbīl had him carried till he brought him to Baghdad on the night of Saturday (Friday–Saturday),[157] the sixth of Rabīʿ II (October 31,–November 1, 816). Abū Zanbīl entered the city on the night of Monday (Sunday–Monday),[158] and Muḥammad b. Abī Khālid died of his wounds that very night. He was buried secretly in his house during that same night. Meanwhile, Zuhayr b. al-Musayyab was kept in prison at the hands of Jaʿfar b. Muḥammad b. Abī Khālid. When Abū Zanbīl arrived, he went to Khuzaymah b. Khāzim on Monday, the eighth of Rabīʿ II (November 3, 816) and told him the news about his father. Khuzaymah sent to the Hāshimites and the commanders and

153. According to Yaʿqūbī, *Ta'rīkh*, II, 547, from an arrow.

154. As the editor notes, this phrase seems superfluous and adds nothing to the sense; if it is retained, one would have to emend *hazama* to *hazamahum*.

155. Village and canal on the Tigris to the north of Wāsiṭ; see Yāqūt, *Muʿjam*, V, 50–1; Le Strange, *Lands*, 38.

156. Small town on the eastern bank of the Tigris below Jarjarāyā; see Yāqūt, *Muʿjam*, II, 103–4; Le Strange, *Lands*, 36.

157. Reading, after the editor's suggestion in n. *e*, *laylat al-sabt* for *laylat al-ithnayn*, which gives the correct correspondence of date and day of the week and is congruent with the date of Monday, the eighth of Rabīʿ II below.

158. As the editor despairingly points out, this does not seem to accord with the reading *laylat al-sabt* possibly to be adopted, following also Ibn al-Athīr, for the preceding line (see n. 157 above); perhaps we should accordingly emend this also to *laylat al-sabt*.

gave them this information. He read out to them ʿĪsā b. Muḥammad b. Abī Khālid's message, to the effect that he would assume the burden of the leadership in the war on their behalf, and they assented to this. ʿĪsā accordingly assumed the military leadership in succession to his father. Abū Zanbīl left Khuzaymah and went to Zuhayr b. al-Musayyab, dragged him out of his cell and cut off his head; it is said that he slaughtered him like a sacrificial victim. He took Zuhayr's head and sent it [1005]
to ʿĪsā in his camp, and ʿĪsā stuck it up on a spearpoint. As for the body, they took it, tied a rope round the feet and then paraded it through Baghdad, carrying it past his own houses and those of his family in the quarter near the Bāb al-Kūfah.[159] Then they bore it publicly round Karkh, and brought it back to the Bāb al-Shām[160] in the evening; finally, when night came down, they threw it into the Tigris. This was on Monday, the eighth of Rabīʿ II (November 3, 816). Abū Zanbīl now made his way back to ʿĪsā, who dispatched him to Fam al-Ṣarāt.[161]

News of Muḥammad b. Abī Khālid's death reached al-Ḥasan b. Sahl, so he set off from Wāsiṭ and travelled as far as Mubārak. He halted there, and when it was Jumādā II (December 816–January 817), he sent Ḥumayd b. ʿAbd al-Ḥamīd al-Ṭūsī,[162] in company with ʿ.r.kū[163] al-Aʿrābī, Saʿīd b. al-Sājūr, Abū al-Baṭṭ, Muḥammad b. Ibrāhīm al-Ifrīqī and a number of other commanders. They encountered Abū Zanbīl at Fam al-Ṣarāt and defeated him. He fled to his brother Hārūn at Nīl, and the forces of the two of them engaged in battle with al-Ḥasan's army by the residential area (*buyūt*) of Nīl. They fought together for a while, and then Hārūn's and Abū Zanbīl's forces were defeated, and they fled as far as Madā'in. This was on Monday, the twenty-fourth of Jumādā II[164] (January 17, 817). Ḥumayd and

159. The southwestern gate of the Round City; see Le Strange, *Baghdad*, 17.
160. The northwestern gate of the Round City; see ibid.
161. The mouth of the Ṣarāt Canal which ran along the southwestern fringes of Baghdad.
162. Kinsman of Qaḥṭabah b. Shabīb, and newly-arrived at this time from Khurasan to take command of al-Ḥasan's army; see Kennedy, 156, 159–60; *EI*² s.v. (ed.).
163. A conceivable reading for this same might be ʿUrwah.
164. Actually a Saturday.

his forces entered Nīl and sacked it for three days; they plundered the wealth and goods of the local people and further plundered the surrounding villages. Meanwhile, when Muḥammad b. Abī Khālid died, the Hāshimites and the commanders discussed the new situation together and said, "We will appoint one of ourselves as Caliph and throw off allegiance to al-Ma'mūn." They were urging each other on to these alluring courses when they received the news of the defeat of Hārūn and Abū Zanbīl. This only made them hurry even more in their plans, and they importuned Manṣūr b. al-Mahdī to accept the
[1006] caliphate. He refused to accept the office, but they kept on at him until they made him amīr and representative (*khalīfah*) of al-Ma'mūn in Baghdad and Iraq, saying, "We won't accept the Zoroastrian, son of the Zoroastrian (*al-majūsī ibn al-majūsī*) al-Ḥasan b. Sahl, and we'll drive him out until he returns to Khurasan."[165]

It has been stated that, when the people of Baghdad rallied round ʿĪsā b. Muḥammad b. Abī Khālid and gave him support in the struggle against al-Ḥasan b. Sahl, al-Ḥasan realized that he had insufficient military power to overcome ʿĪsā. So he sent, as an envoy to him, Wahb b. Saʿīd al-Kātib,[166] promising ʿĪsā a marriage alliance with one of his daughters; a sum of a hundred thousand dīnārs; a guarantee of personal security for himself, his family and the people of Baghdad in general; and the governorship of any region he might choose for himself. ʿĪsā sought from al-Ma'mūn a document in the Caliph's own hand setting forth these conditions. Al-Ḥasan b. Sahl sent Wahb back with a favorable answer, but Wahb was drowned between Mubārak and Jabbul.[167] ʿĪsā now wrote to the Baghdad troops

165. *ʿUyūn*, 352. In a letter couched in violent and denunciatory language these rebellious partisans of the ʿAbbāsid family in Baghdad were later to castigate al-Ma'mūn for setting over them Magian governors; see below, 85, and W. Madelung, "New documents concerning al-Ma'mūn, al-Faḍl b. Sahl and ʿAlī al-Riḍā," in *Studia arabica et islamica, Festschrift for Iḥsān ʿAbbās*, 344.

166. Presumably the son of the Nestorian Christian secretary of the Barmakids, Saʿīd b. Wahb, from whom there later descended a line of viziers to the caliphs; see Sourdel, *Vizirat*, I, 143, 312.

167. See for these two places, above, 50 nn. 155–6.

that he was too preoccupied with the conduct of the warfare to concern himself with the collection of the land tax, and that they should appoint for this function one of the Hāshimites. So they nominated Manṣūr b. al-Mahdī. The latter encamped with his forces at Kalwādhā. They urged him to accept the caliphate, but he refused and said, "I am only the representative (*khalīfah*) of the Commander of the Faithful until he comes personally or until he appoints his own nominee as governor." The Hāshimites, the commanders and the army at large accepted this arrangement. The moving spirit behind this was Khuzaymah b. Khāzim. He now sent out commanders into every district.

Ḥumayd al-Ṭūsī came immediately in pursuit of the sons of Muḥammad (b. Abī Khālid) until he reached Madā'in. He stayed there for just one day and then left for Nīl. When the news about these movements of Ḥumayd reached Manṣūr, he marched out and encamped at Kalwādhā. Yaḥyā b. ʿAlī b. ʿĪsā b. Māhān[168] came to Madā'in and then Manṣūr dispatched Isḥāq b. al-ʿAbbās b. Muḥammad al-Hāshimī[169] from the other side, and he himself encamped at the Nahr Ṣarṣar. Ghassān b. ʿAbbād b. Abī al-Faraj[170] sent Abū Ibrāhīm b. Ghassān,[171] the governor of Khurasan's commander of the guard, to the region of Kūfah. [1007] Ghassān proceeded until he reached Qaṣr Ibn Hubayra and then halted there. When the news of this reached Ḥumayd —Ghassān being unaware of the fact that Ḥumayd had surrounded Qaṣr Ibn Hubayrah—he took Ghassān captive, despoiled his retainers and killed some of them. This happened on Monday, the fourth of Rajab (January 26, 817). All the forces involved then remained in their respective encampments, ex-

168. Brother of the Ḥamdawayh and ʿAbdallāh mentioned above, 27, 47, and deputy of his father ʿAlī b. ʿĪsā in the decisive battle of 195 (811) between al-Amīn's forces in Persia and Ṭāhir b. al-Ḥusayn; see Kennedy, 140.

169. Grandson of Abū ʿAbdallah Muḥammad, hence nephew of al-Saffāḥ and al-Manṣūr.

170. Cousin of the Sahl brothers, and subsequently governor of Khurasan before Ṭāhir's nomination and then governor in Sind; see below, 104, 179–80, 189.

171. On the apparent confusion between these two personages, see above, 24–5 and n. 58.

cept that Muḥammad b. Yaqṭīn b. Mūsā,[172] who was with al-Ḥasan b. Sahl, now fled from al-Ḥasan to ʿĪsā's side. ʿĪsā sent him to Manṣūr, who in turn sent him to the vicinity of Ḥumayd (and his forces). Ḥumayd was encamped at Nīl, except for a cavalry detachment at Qaṣr (Ibn Hubayrah). Ibn Yaqṭīn set off from Baghdad on Saturday, the second of Shaʿbān[173] (February 23, 817), until he arrived at Kūthā.[174] Ḥumayd received news of this movement, but Ibn Yaqṭīn knew nothing of this last fact until Ḥumayd and his troops confronted him at Kūthā. They attacked Ibn Yaqṭīn and defeated him, killing some of his force and capturing others; a large number were drowned, too. Ḥumayd and his troops plundered the villages in the environs of Kūthā and seized cattle, sheep and goats, asses, and every piece of jewelry and finery, possessions, etc., which they could lay their hands on. Then Ḥumayd went back as far as Nīl, while Ibn Yaqṭīn withdrew and encamped at the Nahr Ṣarṣar.

Abū al-Shaddākh[175] has recited concerning Muḥammad b. Abī Khālid,

The lofty pride of the Abnā' has crashed to the ground after Muḥammad,
and the great man of them who enjoyed power and respect has been brought low.

Yet do not rejoice at his death, O house of Sahl,
for at some day in the future, the field of slaughter will be your lot too.

ʿĪsā b. Muḥammad b. Abī Khālid counted the number of men
[1008] in his army, and they came to one hundred twenty-five thousand, comprising both cavalrymen and foot soldiers; he then

172. Presumably the brother of the secretary and official for previous caliphs like al-Mahdī and al-Hādī, ʿAlī b. Yaqṭīn, several times mentioned in Ṭabarī; see Sourdel, *Vizirat*, I, 112–14.

173. Actually a Monday.

174. The town of Kūthā Rabba, where there was a bridge of boats across the Kūthā Canal, running to the south of Baghdad; see Yāqūt, *Muʿjam*, IV, 487–8; Le Strange, *Lands*, 68–9; *EI*² s.v. (M. Plessner).

175. I have not been able to identify this poet.

gave each cavalryman a pay allowance of forty dirhams and each foot soldier an allowance of twenty dirhams.[176]

In this year, the volunteer fighters (*al-muṭṭawwaiʿah*) enthusiastically set about suppressing evildoers in Baghdad, under the leadership of Khālid al-Daryūsh and the Khurasanian Abū Ḥātim Sahl b. Salāmah al-Anṣārī.[177]

The Volunteer Fighters Suppress Crime in Baghdad

The reason for this was that the evildoers (*fussāq*) from amongst the Ḥarbiyyah troops and the mobsters (*shuṭṭār*) who were in Baghdad and Karkh inflicted great harm on the populace and indulged in evil behavior, brigandage and the seizing of youths and women openly from the streets.[178] They used to band together, go up to a man, seize his son and carry him off, and nothing could be done to stop them. They used to demand that people lend them money or give it to them as a gift, and nothing could be done to stop them. They used to band together, and then go out to the villages and overpower the local people, seizing all the goods, money, etc., which they could lay

---

176. Ibn al-Athīr, *al-Kāmil*, VI, 321–4.

177. Masʿūdī, *Murūj*, VII, 62 = ed. Pellat, § 2748, stigmatizing the volunteers as *ruwaybiḍah* "dregs of the population." Ṭabarī's qualification here *min ahl Khurāsān* most naturally refers to Sahl only, but in view of Khālid's Iranian other name, it was probably applicable to them both. For this most interesting episode, in which Khālid and Sahl, with slightly differing aims and attitudes, endeavored to halt the social and moral disintegration within Baghdad caused by the lack of discipline of the anti-Sahlid forces there and, doubtless, by the previous anarchy in the latter days of al-Amīn, see R. Levy, *A Baghdad chronicle*, 82–5; I.M. Lapidus, "The separation of state and religion in the development of early Islamic society," *IJMES*, VI (1975), 372–8; M.A. Shaban, *Islamic history, a new interpretation. 2. A.D. 750–1055* (A.H. *132–448*), 46; Kennedy, 156–7.

178. Ṭabarī does not use here the term *ʿayyārūn* (although it is used in the corresponding context in *ʿUyūn*, 353), but it is clearly these anti-social, semi-criminal elements who are meant. On them and the *shuṭṭār*, elements of society much discussed recently by historians, see Cl. Cahen, *Mouvements populaires et autonomisme urbain dans l'Asie musulmane du Moyen Âge*, [40] ff.; Shaban, 45; R.P. Mottahedeh, *Loyalty and leadership in an early Islamic society*, 157 ff.; S. Sabari, *Mouvements populaires à Baghdad à l'époque ʿabbaside*, 77 ff.; *EI*² s.v. Ayyār (F. Taeschner).

their hands on. There was no government authority (*sulṭān*) which could restrain them, and none of its representatives had any control over them because the government authority itself depended on them for its power and they were, indeed, the government's own trusted guards. Hence it was impossible for the government to hold them back from any evil deed which they were perpetrating. They used to exact money from passersby on the roads, from passengers in the boats and from those riding on mounts. They used to demand protection money for watching over gardens, and they openly used to commit robberies on the roads. No one was able to stand up against them, and the people were in extreme misery because of them.

The culmination of their activities was that they sallied forth to Qaṭrabbul[179] and openly plundered the town, seizing
[1009] goods, gold, silver, sheep and goats, cattle, asses, etc. They brought all these back to Baghdad and started publicly to offer them for sale. The rightful owners came along and appealed for the government authority's protection against them, but it was totally unable to punish them, nor was it able to get back for them, the rightful owners, anything at all of what had been seized. This was at the end of Sha'bān (ca. March 22, 817).

When the people perceived all that—what had been seized from them, the sale of their own possessions in their very own markets, and all the evil in the land, the oppression, iniquity and brigandage which the evildoers and mobsters had unleashed—and when they saw that the government authority was not reproving them in any way,[180] the God-fearing men from each suburban district and street (of the city) (*ṣulaḥā' kull rabaḍ wa-kull darb*)[181] rose up and went to each other, saying, "In each street there is just one evildoer, or a couple, or up to

179. Small town and district to the northwest of Baghdad, on the 'Isā Canal; see Yāqūt, *Mu'jam*, IV, 371–2; Le Strange, *Lands*, 65–6; *EI*² s.v. (Lassner).

180. Reading here, and in two places below, with the *Addenda et emendanda*, p. DCCLXVIII, the verb *'ayyara* instead of the text's use of *ghayyara*.

181. The movement accordingly took advantage of local religious leadership. As appears from below, Khālid's center of power was in the western, Anbār Road area of the city, and Sahl's in the northern Ḥarbiyyah one; see Lapidus, 376. It is hard to see here, as does Shaban, 46, a movement deliberately manipulated by reactionary, wealthy, proto-Ḥanbalī merchants.

ten of them,yet they have managed to get the upper hand over you, despite your superior numbers. If only you would join together and agree on a concerted policy, you would put down these evildoers and they would not be able to commit all this iniquity in your midst." A certain man from the Anbār Road district, called Khālid al-Daryūsh, then came forward and summoned his neighbors, the members of his family and the inhabitants of his quarter to assist him in the enjoining of praiseworthy measures and the forbidding of reprehensible actions (*al-amr bi-al-maʿrūf wa-al-nahy ʿan al-munkar*).[182] They responded to his call, and he launched an attack on the local evildoers and mobsters and prevented them from carrying out their former depredations. They in turn put up resistance to him and intended to oppose him forcibly; so he fought them and defeated them, seizing some of them, beating them, imprisoning them and hauling them up before the government authority—not that he intended to criticize or blame that authority in any way.

Then after him, there arose a man from the Ḥarbiyyah populace called Sahl b. Salāmah al-Anṣārī, one of the Khurasanians, who had the patronymic of Abū Ḥātim. He summoned the people to enjoin praiseworthy measures and to forbid reprehensible actions and to behave in conformity with the Book of God and the *sunnah* of His Prophet. He tied leaves of the Qur'ān round his neck and then began with his neighbors and the inhabitants of his quarter, giving them both positive injunctions and prohibitions; and they accepted these instructions from [1010]
him. Then he summoned the populace en masse along these same lines, from the noble to the humble, from the Hāshimites to those socially inferior to them. He set up a register (*dīwān*) for this purpose in which were written the names of all who came and pledged loyalty to him (*bāyaʿahu*) in pursuance of these aims and in combatting all who opposed him and the

182. Qur'ān, III, 100, the classic expression of the ruler's (or his deputy's, such as the *muḥtasib* or market inspector) duty to point the subjects in the direction of conformity with the *sharīʿah*; see e.g., Māwardī, *al-Aḥkām al-sulṭāniyyah*, tr. E. Fagnan, *Les statuts gouvernementaux*, ch. xx, 513–53; Lapidus, 376.

measures which he advocated, whoever they might be. A great number of people came to him and pledged loyalty to him. Next, he went all round Baghdad, its markets, its suburban districts and its thoroughfares, and he prevented all those who were levying protection money and exacting payments from (making their demands on) passing travellers and on those visiting (the capital), announcing that "There is no protection-money [*khifārah*] in Islam." *Al-khifārah* meant that a man used to go along to the owner of a garden or an orchard and tell him, "Your garden is under my protection; I will ward off anyone intending damage to it, and you will have to pay me such-and-such amount of dirhams each month."[183] He had to hand over this money willy-nilly. The extortioner would have grown powerful through this if al-Daryūsh had not opposed him and said, "I do not mean to brand the government authority as being corrupt, nor to blame it, nor to combat it, nor to issue orders and prohibitions to it about anything." And Sahl b. Salāmah added, "But I shall attack anyone who opposes the Book and the *sunnah* whoever it may be, the government authority itself or anyone else; what is just and right [*al-ḥaqq*] is now established in the community as a whole, and whoever has pledged loyalty to me in this I shall accept, and whoever opposes me, I shall attack."[184] Sahl's proclamation of this took place on Thusday, the fourth of Ramaḍān, 201 (March 26, 817) in the mosque of Ṭāhir b. al-Ḥusayn which the latter had built in the Ḥarbiyyah quarter; Khālid al-Daryūsh had made his call two or three days previously.

At this time Manṣūr b. al-Mahdī remained in his encampment at Jabbul. When these events involving the rise of Sahl b. Salāmah and his companions took place, and the news reached Manṣūr and ʿĪsā, it shattered them, for the greater part of their

183. *Khifārah, khafārah,* "protection money" is in fact a term of ancient tribal life, the sum paid over to a *khafīr* or leader of tribal escorts for a caravan journeying through tribal territories; see H. Lammens, *La Mecque à la veille de l'Hégire,* 178–84. For a modern form of this due, *khâwah* (< *khuwwah,* "fraternity"), see H.R.P. Dickson, *The Arab of the desert,* 442–3.

184. I.e., Sahl is emphasizing the responsibility of the godly community as a whole, and not just the Caliph and his representatives, for bringing about the just society, one conformable to the *sharīʿah*; see Lapidus, 376.

forces was composed of mobsters and evildoers. Manṣūr now entered Baghdad. Meanwhile, ʿĪsā had been corresponding with [1011] al-Ḥasan b. Sahl, so when ʿĪsā heard the news about events in Baghdad, he asked al-Ḥasan b. Sahl to grant himself, his family and his retainers a guarantee of safety, with the further proviso that al-Ḥasan would issue six months' pay allotment to his retainers, his troops and the remainder of the Baghdad troops when he had received the revenues from the tax collection. Al-Ḥasan agreed to this, and ʿĪsā left his encampment and entered Baghdad on Monday, the thirteenth of Shawwāl (May 4, 817). The whole of their forces was thrown into disarray, and then they entered Baghdad. ʿĪsā informed them of the peace agreement which he had made with al-Ḥasan b. Sahl on their behalf, and they assented to this.[185]

ʿĪsā then retraced his steps to Madāʾin. Yaḥyā b. ʿAbdallāh, al-Ḥasan b. Sahl's cousin on his father's side, came to him, until he halted at Dayr al-ʿAqūl. They appointed Yaḥyā governor of the Sawād, associating him and ʿĪsā together in the exercising of the power of governorship. Each one was given a number of the sub-districts (*ṭasāsīj*) and tax divisions (*aʿmāl*) of Baghdad. When ʿĪsā took up the appointments which had been granted to him, this being at a time when the troops of ʿAskar al-Mahdī were hostile to him, there suddenly rose up al-Muṭṭalib b. ʿAbdallāh b. Mālik al-Khuzāʿī[186] proclaiming al-Maʾmūn's name and those of the two sons of Sahl, al-Faḍl and al-Ḥasan. Sahl b. Salāmah, however, displayed an attitude of aversion from him, saying, "You did not pledge your loyalty to me for this!"

Manṣūr b. al-Mahdī, Khuzaymah b. Khāzim and al-Faḍl b. Rabīʿ now removed themselves, having on the very day of their departure pledged their loyalty to Sahl b. Salāmah on the basis of behavior in conformity with the Book and the *sunnah*, to which Sahl had been summoning people. They encamped in the Ḥarbiyyah quarter, in flight from al-Muṭṭalib. Sahl b. Sa-

185. Ibn al-Athīr, *al-Kāmil*, VI, 324–6.

186. Member of the family of the ʿAbbāsid *naqīb* or agent Mālik b. al-Haytham (see above, 47 n. 144) and former governor of Egypt, whose conduct was was characterized by such tergiversations as these; see Lapidus, 373–4; Crone, 182.

lāma came to the bridge[187] and sent a message to al-Muṭṭalib asking him to come to him; he also reiterated, "You did not pledge loyalty to me for this!" Al-Muṭṭalib, however, refused to come to him, so Sahl engaged in violent fighting with him extending over two or three days until ʿĪsā and al-Muṭṭalib
[1012] made peace together. ʿĪsā now contrived secretly to send someone to assassinate Sahl. The assassin struck Sahl with his sword, but the blow did not have any serious effect on him. After this attempt on his life, Sahl retired to his house. ʿĪsā thus became the people's leader, and they then all ceased from fighting.

Ḥumayd b. ʿAbd al-Ḥamīd had remained at Nīl, but when he heard the news of this, he entered Kūfah and remained there for some days, before departing for Qaṣr Ibn Hubayrah, where he took up his position, obtaining a house and fortifying it with a wall and a trench; this was at the end of Dhū al-Qaʿdah (mid-June 817). ʿĪsā remained in Baghdad, inspecting and reviewing the troops and approving their fitness for service (*yaʿriḍu al-junda wa-yusaḥḥiḥuhum*)[188] until the tax revenues were gathered in. He sent a message to Sahl b. Salāmah and apologized to him for what he had done (that is, for attempting his assassination), pledging his loyalty to Sahl and adjuring him to go back to his previous mission in direction people to praisworthy measures and restraining them from reprehensible actions, and promising that he would be Sahl's helper in all that. Sahl accordingly resumed his original rôle of summoning people to behavior in conformity with the Book and the *sunnah*.[189]

In this year, al-Ma'mūn designated ʿAlī b. Mūsā b. Jaʿfar b. Muḥammad b. ʿAlī b. Abī Ṭālib as heir to the throne for the Muslims and as Caliph after himself, and gave him the name of The One Well-pleasing [to God] from the House of Muḥammad (*al-Riḍā* min āl Muḥammad); he further ordered his troops to

187. Reading, with n. *d* of the editor, *al-jisr* for *al-Ḥasan.*
188. On the institution of army reviews and musters, see *EI*² "Istiʿrāḍ" (Bosworth), and id., "Recruitment, muster and review in medieval Islamic armies," in *War, technology and society in the Middle East*, 59–77.
189. *ʿUyūn*, 352–3; Ibn al-Athīr, *al-Kāmil*, VI, 326.

discard their black robes and start wearing green ones, and he wrote letters announcing that to the farthest corners of the realm.[190]

Al-Ma'mūn Designates ʿAlī b. Mūsā as Heir to the Throne

It is mentioned that, while ʿĪsā b. Muḥammad b. Abī Khālid was busy reviewing and inspecting his troops after his return from his encampment to Baghdad, he received unexpectedly a [1013] message from al-Ḥasan b. Sahl informing him that the Commander of the Faithful al-Ma'mūn had made ʿAlī b. Mūsā b. Jaʿfar b. Muḥammad heir to the throne after himself. The reason for this, it said, was that al-Ma'mūn had given consideration to the members of the two houses of al-ʿAbbās and ʿAlī but had not found anyone more excellent,[191] more pious or more learned than ʿAlī. The message went on to say that al-Ma'mūn had given him the title of The One Well-pleasing [to God] from the House of Muḥammad, and it ordered him to throw off his black robes and put on green ones. This was on Tuesday, the second of Ramaḍān, 201 (March 24, 817). In the text of the message, al-Ḥasan b. Sahl further ordered ʿĪsā to convey the command to all his subordinates and appointees—personal retainers, soldiers and commanders—and to the Hāshimites, that they should take an oath of allegiance to ʿAlī (as heir to the throne); to require them to wear green-sleeved coats (*aq-*

---

190. Khalīfah, *Ta'rīkh*, II, 764; Yaʿqūbī, *Ta'rīkh*, II, 545; Jahshiyārī, *Kitāb al-Wuzarā'*, 255–6; Iṣfahānī, *Maqātil*, 562 ff.; *ʿUyūn*, 350, 353; Ibn al-Athīr, *al-Kāmil*, VI, 326–7. On this episode in general, see Levy, *A Baghdad chronicle*, 80–1; Gabrieli, *Al-Ma'mūn e gli Alidi*, 35 ff.; D.M. Donaldson, *The Shī'ite religion*, 161–7; Abbott, 224; Sourdel, "La politique religieuse du calife ʿabbāside al-Ma'mūn," *REI*, XXX (1962), 33–7; Y. Marquet, "Le Šīʿisme au IXe siècle à travers l'histoire de Yaʿqūbī," *Arabica*, XIX (1972), 111; W.M. Watt, *The formative period of Islamic thought*, 176–8; Lapidus, 378–9; Kennedy, 157 ff.; Madelung, "New documents concerning al-Ma'mūn, al-Faḍl b. Sahl and ʿAlī al-Riḍā," 333–46; *EI*^{2} s.v. ʿAlī al-Riḍā (B. Lewis).

191. *Afḍal*. This adjective had emotive connotations for the Shīʿah when applied to ʿAlī and his line, for the Shīʿah regarded each of these last as *al-imām al-afḍal*, "the most excellent leader of the community;" on this topic of *faḍl* as a characteristic of the imamate, see Watt, 226–8.

biyah),[192] tall pointed caps (*qalānis*) and other distinguishing features (*aʿlām*);[193] and to compel the people of Bahgdad in general to adopt these measures. When ʿĪsā received these instructions, he proclaimed to the Baghdad troops that they should put them into practice, stipulating however to al-Ḥasan that he should expedite payment to them of a month's pay allotment and then the remainder when the tax revenues came in. Some of them replied, "We agree to take the oath of allegiance and to wear green;" but others answered, "We will not take the oath of allegiance, we will not wear green and we will not let this question of the succession pass out of the line of al-ʿAbbās; all this is nothing but machinations on the part of al-Faḍl b. Sahl." They persisted in this attitude for several days. The members of the ʿAbbāsid family were angered by this; they banded together and discussed the question, and finally announced, "We will appoint as ruler one of ourselves and throw off our allegiance to al-Ma'mūn." The spokesmen here, the ones who were ceaselessly occupied in the negotiations involved in this matter and the ones who assumed the responsibility for it, were Ibrāhīm and Manṣūr, the two sons of al-Mahdī.[194]

In this year, the people of Baghdad gave their allegiance to Ibrāhīm b. al-Mahdī as Caliph and declared al-Ma'mūn deposed.[195]

The People of Baghdad give allegiance to Ibrāhīm b. al-Mahdī

We have already mentioned the reason for the members of the ʿAbbāsid family in Baghdad rejecting al-Ma'mūn's provisions as

---

192. The *qabā'*, a short coat of Persian origin, was becoming the general garment for ceremonial and court wear during this period; see Sourdel, "Questions de cérémoniale ʿabbaside," 135.

193. This seems here a better translation than "flags" after the verbal noun *libs* on which these three nouns depend.

194. Yaʿqūbī, *Ta'rīkh*, II, 545; Masʿūdī, *Murūj*, VII, 60–1 = ed. Pellat, § 2746; Azdī, 341–2; *ʿUyūn*, 353–4; Ibn al-Athīr, *al-Kāmil*, VI, 326–7.

195. Khalīfah, *Ta'rīkh*, II, 764; Yaʿqūbī, *Ta'rīkh*, II, 547–8; Masʿūdī, *Murūj*, loc. cit.; *ʿUyūn*, 350, 353. On this episode in general, see C. Barbier de Meynard, "Ibrahim, fils de Mehdi, fragments historiques . . . ," *JA*, ser. 6. vol. XIII (1869), 225 ff.; Levy, *A Baghdad chronicle*, 80–5; Shaban, 45 ff.; Kennedy, 158–62; *EI*[2] s.v. Ibrāhīm b. al-Mahdī (Sourdel).

they did, and the banding together of members of their group with the aim of combatting al-al-Ḥasan b. al-Sahl militarily, until he departed from Baghdad. When al-Ma'mūn proclaimed [1014] ʿAlī b. Mūsā b. Jaʿfar as his heir and commanded the people to wear green, and when al-Ḥasan's letter reached ʿĪsā b. Muḥammad b. Abī Khālid ordering him to put the measures into practice, and when he required the people in Baghdad to set about adopting them—this being on Tuesday, the twenty-fifth of Dhū al-Ḥijjah (July 14, 817)—the members of the ʿAbbāsid family in Baghdad proclaimed that they had given their allegiance to Ibrāhīm b. al-Mahdī as Caliph and, after him, to his nephew Isḥāq b. Mūsā b. al-Mahdī. They declared al-Ma'mūn deposed and that they would issue a pay allotment of ten dīnārs to each man on the first day of Muḥarram, that is, on the first day of the coming year. Some people (among the Baghdad troops) agreed to this, but some would not agree to it until they actually got the payment. When Friday came round and they wished to perform the worship, they wished to set up Ibrāhīm as al-Ma'mūn's representative (in Baghdad) in place of Manṣūr. Therefore they gave instructions to a certain man who was to say, when the muezzin gave the call to worship, "We desire to pray for al-Ma'mūn and then, after him, for Ibrāhīm, who is to act as a representative." They had also secretly suborned a group of people and had told them, "When he gets up, saying, 'We will pray for al-Ma'mūn,' then you yourselves are to get up and say, 'We will only be satisfied by your giving allegiance to Ibrāhīm and to Isḥāq after him and by your declaring al-Ma'mūn irrevocably deposed; we do not wish you to seize our wealth and possessions, as Manṣūr did.' Then remain in your houses." Thus when the man got up to speak, this group of people answered him. Hence he did not lead them in the Friday worship on that particular Friday nor did anyone deliver the sermon. The people merely performed four cycles of inclinations (*rakʿahs*) and then went home. That took place on Friday, the twenty-eighth of Dhū al-Ḥijjah, 201 (July 17, 817).[196]

196. Ibn al-Athīr, *al-Kāmil*, VI, 327.

In this year, ʿAbdallāh b. Khurradādhbih,[197] governor of
[1015] Ṭabaristān, conquered Lāriz[198] and Shirrīz[199] in Daylam and added them to the lands of Islam; he conquered the mountainous parts of Ṭabaristān; and he dislodged Shahriyār b. Sharwīn from them.[200] Salm[201] al-Khāsir has said (concerning these events):

Indeed, we expect the conquest of Byzantium and of China
at the hands of one who has made us to prevail over[202] the royal power of Sharwīn!

So strengthen your hands by means of ʿAbdallāh!
Indeed, he possesses an untiring faculty of judgment as well as faithfulness.

In this year, he sent Māzyār b. Qārin to al-Ma'mūn and took prisoner Abū Laylā, king of Daylam, without making any peace agreement with him.[203]

In this year, Abū al-Sarāyā's protégé Muḥammad b. Muḥammad died.[204]

---

197. Khurasanian commander and father of the geographer Abū al-Qāsim ʿUbaydallāh, called Ibn Khurradādhbih; for his governorship, see H.L. Rabino di Borgomale, "Les préfets du Califat au Ṭabaristān, de 18 à 328/639 à 939–40," *JA*, CCXXXI (1939), 262 (not recorded in E. von Zambaur's *Manuel de généalogie et de chronologie*).

198. Perhaps identical with Lārijān, also in this region near Āmul, *pace* Yāqūt, *Muʿjam*, V, 7; see Schwarz, 786; *EI*² s.v. Lār and Läridjān (J. Calmard).

199. Yāqūt, *Muʿjam*, III, 334; Schwarz, loc. cit.; according to Rabino di Borgomale, *Mázandarán and Astarábád*, 132, probably the present-day Shīr-rūd.

200. J. Marquart, *Ērānšahr nach der Geographie des Ps. Moses Xorenacʿi*, 127–9. Shahriyār was a local ruler of the Bāwandid dynasty; see Zambaur, 187; *EI*² s.v. Bāwand (R.N. Frye).

201. Text, Sallām. Salm was a eulogist of the early ʿAbbāsids, see Sezgin, *GAS*, II, 511–12. However, these verses must be attributed to him erroneously since, as G.E. von Grunebaum has pointed out, Salm died fifteen years before these events, in 186 (802); see his "Three Arabic poets of the early Abbasid age," *Orientalia*, XIX (1950), 56, 79.

202. Following here the correction of the *Addenda et emendenda*, p. DCCLXVIII.

203. Ibn al-Athīr, *al-Kāmil*, VI, 328. On Māzyār and his family, the Qārinids of Ṭabaristān, see *EI*¹ s.v. Māzyār (V. Minorsky) and *EI*² s.v. Ḳārinids (M. Rekaya); Madelung, in *Cambridge history of Iran*, IV, 204–5.

204. Ibn al-Athīr, *al-Kāmil*, VI, 340. The Zaydī youth mentioned above, is meant.

In this year, Bābak al-Khurramī became active with the Jāwīdhāniyyah, the partisans of Jāwīdhān b. Sahl, ruler of Badhdh;[205] he claimed that Jāwīdhān's spirit had entered into him, and embarked on mischief-making and evildoing.[206]

In this year, the people of Khurasan, Rayy and Iṣfahān were afflicted by famine; the price of food rose high and deaths resulted.[207]

In this year, Isḥāq b. Mūsā b. ʿĪsā b. Mūsā b. Mūsā b. Muḥammad b. ʿAlī led the pilgrimage.[208]

---

205. Jāwīdhān was a leader of the Khurramiyyah before the rise of Bābak; see B. Scarcia Amoretti, in *Cambridge history of Iran*, IV, 505–6, 517. For al-Badhdh, the capital and bastion of these sectarians, see *EI*[2] Suppl. s.v. (Bosworth).

206. *ʿUyūn*, 354; Ibn al-Athīr, *al-Kāmil*, VI, 328. Of the extensive literature on Bābak and the Khurramiyyah movement, see G.-H. Sadighi, *Les mouvements religieux iraniens*, 229–80; E.M. Wright, "Bābak of Badhdh and al-Afshīn during the years 816–41 A.D.," *MW*, XXXVIII (1948), 43–59, 124–31; Amoretti, op. cit., 503–9; *EI*[2] s.v. Bābak (Sourdel), s.v. Khurramiyya (Madelung).

207. Ibn al-Athīr, *al-Kāmil*, VI, 340.

208. Ibid.; but in Khalīfah, *Taʾrīkh*, II, 764, Dāwūd b. Mūsā b. ʿĪsā is named, and in Azdī, 342, Dāwūd b. ʿĪsā b. Mūsā.

The Events of the Year

202

(July 20, 817–July 8, 818)

The events taking place during this year included the people of Baghdad's giving their allegiance to Ibrāhīm b. al-Mahdī as Caliph and their addressing him by the (regnal) name of al-Mubārak—it is said that they hailed him as Caliph on the first day
[1016] of Muḥarram (July 20, 817) and declared al-Ma'mūn deposed.[209] When Friday came round, Ibrāhīm ascended the pulpit, and the first person to do homage to him was the Hāshimite ʿUbaydallāh b. al-ʿAbbās b. Muḥammad,[210] then Manṣūr b. al-Mahdī, then the rest of the Hāshimites and then the commanders. The person who organized the ceremony of taking the oath of allegiance was al-Muṭṭalib b. ʿAbdallāh b. Mālik, and the ones who busied themselves and took charge of the whole affair were al-Sindī, the *ṣāḥib al-muṣallā* Ṣāliḥ, Minjab, Nuṣayr the slave retainer (*al-waṣīf*) and the rest of the clients and freedmen; these

---

209. Yaʿqūbī, *Ta'rīkh*, II, 547, gives Ibrāhīm the regnal name of al-Marḍī and gives the date of the *bayʿah* to him as the fifth of Muḥarram, the same as in Masʿūdī, *al-Tanbīh wa-al-ishrāf*, 349–50, tr. Carra de Vaux, *Le livre de l'avertissement*, 449.

210. Grandson of Abū ʿAbdallāh Muḥammad and nephew of al-Saffāḥ and al-Manṣūr.

persons were indeed the leaders and foremost persons, (and did this) because of their anger against al-Ma'mūn when he wished to transfer the caliphate from the descendants of al-ʿAbbās to those of ʿAlī and because he had abandoned the black garments of his forefathers in favor of green ones. When he had finished with the ceremony of pledging allegiance, he promised the army that he would give them pay allotments for six (months), but in fact he kept this back from them. When they realized this, they rose up in a clamor against him, so he gave each man two hundred dirhams. He also wrote to the Sawād on behalf of certain amongst them for the equivalent of the amount of pay owing to them in the form of wheat and barley. Hence they sallied forth to take possession of that, and everything in their path they carried off as plunder. In this way, they appropriated two shares in one operation, that of the local people and that of the ruling authority. With the aid of the Baghdad troops, Ibrāhīm secured power over the people of Kūfah and the whole of the Sawād. He established his encampment at Madā'in, and appointed as governor of the East Side of Baghdad al-ʿAbbās b. Mūsā al-Hādī and over the West Side Isḥāq b. Mūsā al-Hādī.[211] Ibrāhīm b. al-Mahdī recited the following:

O house of Fihr,[212] have you not realized that
I have devoted myself to your defence in the perilous places?

In this year, Mahdī b. ʿAlwān al-Ḥarūrī proclaimed a Khārijite rising (*ḥakkama*).[213] He raised the standard of rebellion at [1017]
Buzurjshābūr and secured control of the sub-districts there and of the Nahr Būq and Rādhānayn.[214] Some people have asserted

211. Azdī, 342, 343; Ibn al-Athīr, *al-Kāmil*, VI, 341.

212. I.e., Quraysh, Fihr usually being identified with the eponymous ancestor Quraysh.

213. The Khārijites were often called the Muḥakkimah because of their original call to ʿAlī to submit to the judgment (*taḥkīm*) of God, and Ḥarūriyyah because their original secession from ʿAlī's army took them to Ḥarūrā'.

214. Buzurjshābūr was a district to the east of the Tigris between Baghdad and Ḥarbā'; the Būq Canal connected Baghdad and Nahrawān; and the "two Rādhāns," Upper and Lower, comprised the district north of Madā'in to Nahrawān; see Yāqūt, *Muʿjam*, I, 410, 510, III, 12–13, V, 318; Le Strange, *Lands*, 31, 35.

that Mahdī's rebellion took place in the year 203, in the month of Shawwāl (April 819). Ibrāhīm b. al-Mahdī sent against him Abū Isḥāq b. al-Rashīd (the future Caliph al-Muʿtaṣim), together with a group of commanders, including Abū al-Baṭṭ and Saʿīd b. al-Sājūr. In addition Abū Isḥāq had with him some Turkish military slaves (*ghilmān*). It is mentioned from Shubayl, the *ṣāḥib al-s.l.bah,*[215] that he accompanied Abū Isḥāq when he was himself a military slave, and they encountered the Khārijites (al-Shurāt)[216] in battle. One of the tribesmen aimed a lance-thrust at Abū Isḥāq, but one of his Turkish military slaves interposed himself to protect Abu Isḥāq, saying to the tribesman, "*ashinās mā-rā* [recognise me]!"[217] Abū Isḥāq gave him the name of Ashinās on that very day; he was Abū Jaʿfar Ashinās. Mahdī was defeated and driven back to Ḥawlāyā.[218]

A certain person (of those relating historical traditions) has said that Ibrāhīm sent only al-Muṭṭalib against Mahdī b. ʿAlwān al-Dihqān al-Ḥarūrī. He marched against Mahdī, and when he drew near to the latter, he captured one of the nonactivist Khārijites (*qaʿad al-Ḥarūriyyah*) called Aqdhā and killed him. The tribesmen banded together and attacked him, and routed him, compelling him to retreat into Baghdad.

In this year, the brother of Abū al-Sarāyā[219] rose in rebellion at Kūfah and adopted the wearing of white garments.[220] A group

---

215. Unexplained. Possibly a reference to an estate owned by this man, although Yāqūt, *Muʿjam*, III, 235, knows only vaguely of a Salabah mentioned in the historical traditions; perhaps more probably, given the military context of the passage, Shubayl was the official charged with the division of plunder, *salab(ah)*, after a battle.

216. Again, the Khārijites were also known as "sellers" because they allegedly bartered (*sharaw*) their present life for a martyr's heavenly crown, echoing Qur'ān, II, 203.

217. In Persian.

218. Yaʿqūbī, *Ta'rīkh*, II, 548; Azdī, 343, 345, 350–2; *ʿUyūn*, 354; Ibn al-Athīr, *al-Kāmil*, VI, 342. Ḥawlāyā was a village in the district of Nahrawān; see Yāqūt, *Muʿjam*, II, 322.

219. Named as Abū ʿAbdallāh, below, 72.

220. I.e., an anti-ʿAbbāsid, in this case almost certainly pro-ʿAlid, symbolic gesture; the wearing of green garments was an innovation of al-Ma'mūn, symbol of his hope of reconciling the two wings of Islam; see Sourdel, "La politique religieuse du calife ʿabbāside al-Ma'mūn," 35. In Jahshiyārī, *Kitāb*

of adherents gathered round him. Ghassān b. Abī al-Faraj then confronted him in battle in Rajab (January–February 818), killed him and sent his head to Ibrāhīm b. al-Mahdī.[221]

Abū al-Sarāyā's Brother Adopts White Garments (tabyīḍ) *and Appears at Kūfah*

It is mentioned that al-Ma'mūn's message ordering him to adopt green clothing and to take the oath of allegiance to ʿAlī b. Mūsā b. Jaʿfar b. Muḥammad as heir to the throne after his own death reached al-Ḥasan b. Sahl when he was at Mubārak in his military encampment. The message further ordered him to move forward against Baghdad and besiege the people in it. Al-Ḥasan therefore struck camp and arrived at Simmar.[222] He wrote to Ḥumayd b. ʿAbd al-Ḥamīd instructing him to move forward against Baghdad in order to besiege the people there from another side, and ordering him to adopt green clothing; this Ḥumayd duly did. Saʿīd b. al-Sājūr, Abū al-Baṭṭ, Ghassān b. Abī al-Faraj, Muḥammad b. Ibrāhīm al-Ifrīqī and a number of Ḥumayd's other commanders had written to Ibrāhīm b. al-Mahdī undertaking to seize Qaṣr Ibn Hubayrah on his behalf. There happened to have arisen a considerable distance between them and Ḥumayd himself, and at the same time, they were in correspondence with al-Ḥasan b. Sahl, telling him that Ḥumayd was in communication with Ibrāhīm, whilst Ḥumayd was writing similar information about them. Al-Ḥasan himself was writing to Ḥumayd summoning the latter to him; but Ḥumayd did not comply with this, fearing that if he set off to- [1018]

al-Wuzarā', 256, Nuʿaym b. Khāzim protests to al-Faḍl b. Sahl that white is the traditional color of the ʿAlids, and green that of Kisrā and the Magians. In fact, as Farouk Omar rightly observes, there is much confusion and contradiction in the sources on this question of colors; what seems clear is that the wearing of white expressed opposition to the official ʿAbbāsid authority, whether these opponents were pro-Umayyad, pro-ʿAlid or adherents of heterodox Iranian sects like the partisans of al-Muqannaʿ and the Khurramiyyah. See F. Omar, "The significance of the colours of banners in the early ʿAbbasid period," in *ʿAbbāsiyyāt. Studies in the history of the early ʿAbbāsids*, 148–54.

221. Azdī, 343.

222. A village in the district of Kaskar, i.e., the region to the north and east of Wāsiṭ, according to Yāqūt, *Muʿjam*, III, 246.

wards al-Ḥasan, the others would swoop down on his army. They, for their part, were writing to al-Ḥasan to the effect that there was nothing preventing Ḥumayd from going to al-Ḥasan except the fact that he was showing opposition to him and that he had purchased landed properties in the districts bounded by Ṣarāt, Sūrā[223] and the Sawād.[224]

When al-Ḥasan wrote messages to Ḥumayd insisting that he should come, Ḥumayd set out to go to him on Thursday, the fifth of Rabīʿ II[225] (October 21, 817). At that point, Saʿīd and his confederates wrote to Ibrāhīm passing on this information and asking him to dispatch to them ʿĪsā b. Muḥammad b. Abī Khālid, so that they could transfer to his control Qaṣr Ibn Hubayrah and Ḥumayd's army. Ibrāhīm had left Baghdad on the Tuesday and had encamped at Kalwādhā en route for Madā'in. When the message reached him, he sent ʿĪsā to them. When the troops in Ḥumayd's army camp heard about ʿĪsā's advance and
[1019] his encamping at Qaryat al-Aʿrāb,[226] only one *farsakh* (six km) from Qaṣr Ibn Hubayrah, they prepared for flight; this was on the night of (Monday–) Tuesday. The troops of Saʿīd, Abū al-Baṭṭ and al-Faḍl b. Muḥammad b. al-Ṣabbāḥ al-Kindī al-Kūfī[227] fell upon Ḥumayd's encampment and plundered everything in it. It is reported that they seized a hundred bags of wealth and goods belonging to Ḥumayd. One of Ḥumayd's sons and Muʿādh b. ʿAbdallāh fled; some of the fleeing troops proceeded in the direction of Kūfah and some in that of Nīl. Regarding Ḥumayd's son, he fled with his father's slavegirls to Kūfah, where he hired mules, and then set off along the highway till he caught up with his father at al-Ḥasan's camp. Meanwhile ʿĪsā entered Qaṣr Ibn Hubayrah; Saʿīd and his confederates handed it over to him, and ʿĪsā took formal possession of it

223. Presumably the district of the Sūrā channel of the Euphrates (the main one at the present day), or the channel itself, which flowed by Ḥillah; see ibid., V, 321; Le Strange, *Lands*, 26, 70–2.

224. Presumably meant here in the restricted sense of the Sawād, i.e., the surrounding agricultural region, of Kūfah.

225. Actually a Wednesday.

226. "The village of the tribesmen, Bedouins."

227. Descendant of the great Kūfan family of al-Ashʿath b. Qays al-Kindī; shortly after this he was appointed governor of the city by Ibrāhīm b. al-Mahdī's supporters (below, 74); see Crone, 111.

from them. This was on Tuesday, the tenth of Rabīʿ II[228] (October 26, 817).

(This news) reached al-Ḥasan b. Sahl when Ḥumayd was with him, and the latter said to al-Hasan, "Didn't I tell you that this would happen? But you let yourself be deceived!" He then left al-Ḥasan and set off and came to Kūfah, where he collected some money and possessions of his which were deposited there. He also appointed as governor of Kūfah the ʿAlid al-ʿAbbās b. Mūsā b. Jaʿfar[229] and ordered him to wear green garments and to put in the sermon al-Maʾmūn's name and then after it that of his own brother ʿAlī b. Mūsā. He provided him with a subvention of a hundred thousand dirhams and told him, "Fight on your brother's behalf, for the people of Kūfah will respond to your call for this cause and I shall, moreover, be at your side." After nightfall, Ḥumayd set out from Kūfah and left him there. Meanwhile, when al-Ḥasan had received the news, he had sent Ḥakīm al-Ḥārithī to Nīl. When all this came to ʿĪsā's notice—he being at Qaṣr Ibn Hubayrah—he and his forces got ready and then set out for Nīl. During the night of Saturday (Friday–Saturday), the fourteenth of Rabī II[230] (October 29–30, 817), a red glow appeared in the sky and then faded, leaving two red pillars in the sky which lasted till the end of the night.

On the Saturday morning, ʿĪsā and his troops marched out of [1020]
Qaṣr Ibn Hubayrah to Nīl. Ḥakīm fell on them in battle. ʿĪsā and Saʿīd actually arrived when the battle was already on. Ḥakīm was defeated, and the victors entered Nīl. While there, they received the news about the ʿAlid al-ʿAbbās b. Mūsā b. Jaʿfar, how he had summoned the people of Kūfah (to acknowledge al-Maʾmūn and then his own brother ʿAlī b. Mūsā) and how a large number of the citizens of Kūfah had joined him. Another group of the people had, however, told him, "If you are going to place al-Maʾmūn's name in the sermon, and only after him your brother's name, then your appeal is of no concern to us; but if you will invoke your brother's name [first], or

228. Actually a Wednesday.
229. I.e., the brother of the Imām ʿAlī al-Riḍā and Zayd al-Nār.
230. Actually a Friday.

some other member of the ʿAlid family or yourself, then we will join you." Al-ʿAbbās replied, "I am invoking al-Ma'mūn's name [first], and after his name, my brother's." Accordingly, the extremist faction (*al-Ghāliyah*) of the Rāfiḍah[231] and most of the Shīʿah[232] refused to support him. Al-ʿAbbās was also proclaiming publicly that Ḥumayd was going to come back with aid and military support for him and that al-Ḥasan was sending a detachment of his own troops as reinforcements; but not a single person of these ever reached him.

Saʿīd and Abū al-Baṭṭ set out from Nīl against Kūfah. When they reached Dayr al-Aʿwar,[233] they took a road which brought them to Harthamah's encampment at Qaryat Shāhī. When Saʿīd's forces had gathered round him, they set out on Monday, the second of Jumādā I (November 16, 817). When they reached the vicinity of Qanṭarah[234] there marched out to engage them in battle the ʿAlid ʿAlī b. Muḥammad b. Jaʿfar, the son of the man who had been hailed as Caliph at Mecca, and Abū ʿAbdallāh, the brother of Abū al-Sarāyā, accompanied by a numerous host which his cousin the governor of Kūfah, al-ʿAbbās b. Mūsā b. Jaʿfar, had sent with ʿAlī b. Muḥammad. They fought with their opponents for a period of time and then ʿAlī and his followers fled in defeat back into Kūfah.

Saʿīd and his accompanying forces advanced until they made camp at Ḥīrah.[235] On the Tuesday morning, they set out and gave battle to ʿAlī's forces in the neighborhood of ʿĪsā b. Mūsā's house.[236] The members of the ʿAbbāsid family and their clients

231. Originally, those who rejected (*rafaḍa*) the first three Caliphs. See Nöldeke, "Zur Ausbreitung des Schiitismus," *Isl.*, XIII (1923), 73–4; Watt, index, and esp. 158–60, where the term's different denotations are given; *EI*² s.v. Ghulāt (M.G.S. Hodgson).

232. I.e., the more moderate Shīʿīs, contrasted to the extremists.

233. According to Yāqūt, *Muʿjam*, II, 499, a monastery in the environs of Kūfah, but not apparently mentioned in Shābushtī's *Kitāb al-Diyārāt.*

234. Often rendered as Qanṭarat al-Kūfah or al-Qanāṭir, bridge point and settlement on the Badāt Canal leading off the Euphrates to the north of Kūfah; see Le Strange, *Lands*, 74.

235. The ancient capital of the pre-Islamic Lakhmid kings, by now eclipsed by Kūfah, and lying just to the south of that city; see Yāqūt, *Muʿjam*, II, 328–31; Le Strange, *Lands*, 75–6; *EI*² s.v. (A.F.L. Beeston—I. Shahid).

236. I.e., that of the ʿAbbāsid prince ʿĪsā b. Mūsā b. Muḥammad, nephew of al-Saffāḥ and al-Manṣūr and one-time heir apparent to the throne, for fifteen

and freedmen acceded to Saʿīd and came out from Kūfah (to join him). A battle then took place lasting all through the day till nightfall. Saʿīd's troops' battle-cry was, "For Ibrāhīm and [1021] Manṣūr, and no obedience to al-Ma'mūn;" they wore black, whereas al-ʿAbbās and his forces drawn from the people of Kūfah wore green. When Wednesday came, they fought again in the same spot, and every detachment of the troops was involved; whenever they secured control of something, they set fire to it. When the leading men of Kūfah perceived this, they went to Saʿīd and his confederates and asked for a guarantee of safety for al-ʿAbbās b. Mūsā b. Jaʿfar and his companions on condition that they evacuate Kūfah. Saʿīd and his confederates agreed to this. The Kūfan leaders then went back to al-ʿAbbās and informed him of this arrangement. They said, "The greater part of your forces is composed of the rabble [*ghawghā'*].[237] You must have seen what the local citizens have had to suffer—burning, plundering and slaughter—so depart from our midst, for we no longer want to be burdened with you." Al-ʿAbbās accepted their instructions, fearing that they were going to hand him over. He moved out of the house which he had been occupying by the open space of al-Kunāsah;[238] his followers, however, remained unaware of this arrangement. When Saʿīd and his forces fell back on Ḥīrah, al-ʿAbbās b. Mūsā's followers suddenly attacked those of Saʿīd's forces and the clients and freedmen of the ʿAbbāsid ʿĪsā b. Mūsā who had remained behind in Kūfah. Al-ʿAbbās's followers put them to flight, driving them back to the protective rampart and ditch (*khandaq*) (round the city)[239] and plundering the suburb (*rabaḍ*) of ʿĪsā b. Mūsā; then

---

years governor of Kūfah, died in 167 (783/4); see Lassner, *The shaping of ʿAbbāsid rule*, index; Kennedy, 91–3; *EI*² s.v. (Sourdel).

237. An indication that, as in Mecca (see above, 33), the ʿAlids' appeal was especially to the lower classes and mob; cf. Kennedy, 160.

238. Originally, as its name implies, a rubbish dump on the west side of the city, then an open space used for unloading caravans, for fairs, etc., but clearly by now containing buildings; see Le Strange, *Lands*, 75; *EI*² s.v. al-Kūfa (H. Djaït).

239. Presumably the rampart and ditch constructed in al-Manṣūr's time, but not enclosing, in Djaït's surmise, the Kunāsah and some of the suburbs; see ibid.

they set fire to the houses and killed everyone they could get hold of.

The members of the ʿAbbāsid family and their clients and freedmen sent to Saʿīd informing him of these events and telling him that al-ʿAbbās had failed to keep his side of the guarantee of security which he had sought. Saʿīd and Abū al-Baṭṭ rode forth with their troops and reached Kūfah by the early part of the night. Every person who had been involved in the plundering whom they caught, they killed, and every possession belonging to al-ʿAbbās's partisans which they got hold of, they burned. Finally, they came to the open space of al-Kunāsah, and remained there for the greater part of the night, until the leading men of Kūfah came to them and informed them that the breaches of the guarantee had been the responsibility of the rabble and that al-ʿAbbās himself was blameless here; then they returned (to their homes). When morning came—this being Thursday, the fifth of Jumādā I (November 19, 817)—Saʿīd
[1022] and Abū al-Baṭṭ entered Kūfah (proper).[240] A herald of theirs proclaimed that there was a guarantee of safety for everyone (literally, "for the white and the black"); the only measures which they took affecting people were beneficial ones. They appointed as governor of Kūfah a local citizen, al-Faḍl b. Muhammad b. al-Ṣabbāḥ al-Kindī.

At this point, Ibrāhīm b. al-Mahdī wrote instructing them to move to the neighborhood of Wāsiṭ, and he wrote specifically to Saʿīd instructing him to appoint someone other than al-Kindī as governor of Kūfah because of his bias in favor of his fellow-townsmen. So he appointed over it Ghassān b. Abī al-Faraj but then removed him after he had killed Abū ʿAbdallāh, Abū al-Sarāyā's brother. Next, Saʿīd appointed over Kūfah his nephew al-Hawl. The latter remained governor until Ḥumayd b. ʿAbd Ḥamīd marched on Kūfah and al-Hawl had to flee. Ibrāhīm b. al-Mahdī also ordered ʿĪsā b. Muḥammad b. Abī Khālid to make his way to the neighborhood of Wāsiṭ via the

---

240. Presumably the *madīnah*, that part of the city enclosed by the rampart and ditch.

Nīl Road, and Ibn ʿĀʾishah al-Hāshimī[241] and Nuʿaym b. Khāzim[242] to travel together; these last two set out from the region of Jūkhā, as Ibrāhīm had ordered them. This was in Jumādā I (November–December 817). Saʿīd, Abū al-Baṭṭ and al-Ifrīqī caught up with Ibn ʿĀʾishah and Nuʿaym, and they encamped at Ṣiyādah[243] near Wāsiṭ. They assembled all the forces in one place, under the leadership of ʿĪsā b. Muḥammad b. Abī Khālid. They kept on making cavalry sorties each day as far as the encampment of al-Ḥasan and his troops at Wāsiṭ; but none of al-Ḥasan's forces would ever come out and engage them, remaining fortified within the town of Wāsiṭ. Then al-Ḥasan gave his troops the order to prepare to march out for battle, and they did this on Saturday, the twenty-sixth of Rajab[244] (February 7, 818). Fierce fighting raged till almost noon, but then ʿĪsā and his army were put to flight. They retreated till they came to Ṭarnāyā and Nīl, and al-Ḥasan's troops seized everything there [1023]
was—weapons, beasts, etc.—in ʿĪsā's camp.[245]

In this year, Ibrāhīm b. al-Mahdī arrested the vigilante leader Sahl b. Salāmah and then jailed and ill-treated him.

Ibrāhīm Arrests and Imprisons Sahl b. Salāmah

It is mentioned that Sahl b. Salāmah remained resident in Baghdad, adjuring people to act in accordance with the Book of God and the *sunnah* of His Prophet; he kept on urging people thus until the majority of the population of Baghdad had rallied to him and had taken up their abode around him, with the exception of those who remained within their own houses but who nevertheless agreed with and supported his views.

241. The ʿAbbāsid prince Ibrāhīm b. Muḥammad b. ʿAbd al-Wahhāb b. Ibrāhīm al-Imām, great-great-nephew of al-Saffāḥ, active in support of Ibrāhīm b. al-Mahdī and in 210 (825) executed by al-Maʾmūn, see below, 145–6, 147–8.

242. Presumably a brother of the Khuzaymah b. Khāzim who was also a supporter of Manṣūr b. al-Mahdī, see above, 47–8.

243. Or perhaps Ṣayyādah; unidentified, but presumably meaning, "place where traps, snares, etc., are set for game or fish."

244. Actually a Sunday.

245. Ibn al-Athīr, *al-Kāmil*, VI, 342–4.

Ibrāhīm had intended to attack Sahl before the battle (in which ʿĪsā was defeated at Wāsiṭ), but he had held back. When the battle actually took place, and ʿĪsā's confederates and the troops with him were beaten, Ibrāhīm turned his attention to Sahl b. Salāmah. He now began to intrigue against Sahl and those supporters of his who had pledged their allegiance to Sahl on the basis of behavior in conformity with the Book and the *sunnah* and of denying obedience to anyone of God's creation who was in rebellion against his Creator.[246] Every person who had pledged himself to Sahl had constructed by the door of his house a tower of plaster and fired brick, with weapons and copies of the Qur'ān on it. These adherents of his reached as far as the Bāb al-Shām, in addition to his adherents among the people of Karkh and others.

When ʿĪsā got back to Baghdad after his defeat, he, his brothers and his body of retainers proceeded against Sahl b. Salāmah, because he had been denouncing them for the most vicious of their works and activities and had been stigmatizing them as "evildoers" (*fussāq*);[247] he never used any other word in reference to them but this. So they fought with him over a period of several days, the leader in this struggle being ʿĪsā b. Muḥam-
[1024] mad b. Abī Khālid. When ʿĪsā came to the streets and alleys which were near Sahl, he gave the people living along these ways a thousand or two thousand dirhams on condition that they would stand aside from the streets and alleys for him (and admit ʿĪsā's troops). Thereupon they agreed to this, and each man received as his share one or two dirhams or suchlike. On Saturday, the twenty-fourth of Shaʿbān[248] (March 7, 818), they prepared an onslaught from every direction. The inhabitants of

246. Lapidus, 376–8, notes that these two slogans had been used by previous revolutionary movements, the first originally by the Khārijites, the second by the ʿAbbāsids themselves in their *daʿwah* or campaign to achieve power; by adopting these, Sahl was setting himself up as the embodiment of the righteous community, if necessary against the caliphate itself, no longer regarded as the sole mouthpiece for the community or its sole representative.

247. Much theological discussion in early Islam revolved around the salvational status of the *fāsiq*, the man guilty of grave sins (*kabā'ir*); the Khārijites held that he was doomed to perpetual hell fire, and both they and the Muʿtazilah taught that a *fāsiq* imām or caliph should be deposed.

248. Actually a Sunday.

the streets and alleys deserted Sahl, until the attackers penetrated to the mosque of Ṭāhir b. al-Ḥusayn and to Sahl's own house, while he himself was in the neighborhood of the mosque.

When they drew near to him, he concealed himself, threw away his arms and mingled with the crowd of onlookers and slipped in amongst the womenfolk. The attackers entered his house, and when they were unable to find him, set agents and informers to watch out for him. During the night, they arrested him in one of the streets near his house and brought him to Isḥāq b. Mūsā al-Hādī, the next in succession after his paternal uncle Ibrāhīm b. al-Mahdī, who was in the City of Peace. Isḥāq questioned him and argued with him; he brought him into the presence of his companions and accused him, "You have incited the people against us, and have impugned the validity of our rule." Sahl replied, "My movement was in the name of the ʿAbbāsids, and I was only adjuring people to act in accordance with the Book and *sunnah*; and at this present moment, I summon you to adhere to the program which I have laid down." However, they rejected his justification and then told him, "Go forth to the people and confess to them that the program to which you summoned them is invalid." He was brought out before the people, but told them, "You have been fully cognizant of what I summoned you to—to act in conformity with the Book and the *sunnah*—and I still summon you to it at this present moment." When he uttered these words to the people, ʿĪsā's men slashed his neck and beat him in the face. When [1025] they did that to him, he cried out, "The one who has been deceived is the one whom you have deceived, O men of Ḥarbiyyah!" He was seized and taken in to Isḥāq, who put him in fetters. This was on the Sunday.

During the night of Monday (Sunday–Monday), they took him along to Ibrāhīm at Madā'in. When he came into Ibrāhīm's presence, Ibrāhīm spoke to him in the same terms as Isḥāq had done, but he still returned the same answer as before. They had captured one of Sahl's adherents called Muḥammad al-Rawwāʿī. Ibrāhīm struck him, pulled out the hairs of his beard, put him in irons and jailed him. When Sahl b. Salāmah was arrested, they jailed him also and gave out the supposed information that Sahl had been handed back to ʿĪsā and that the latter had killed him. They only spread this story out of fear that the people would get to know where Sahl was and rescue him. The period between his first public appeal and his arrest and imprisonment was twelve months.[249]

In this year, al-Ma'mūn set out from Marw intending to go to Iraq.

Al-Ma'mūn's Departure from Marw

It is mentioned that the ʿAlid ʿAlī b. Mūsā b. Jaʿfar b. Muḥammad told al-Ma'mūn about the conditions of civil tumult and fighting into which the people had been plunged since his brother had been killed; about how al-Faḍl b. Sahl had been concealing reports from him; that his own family and the people in general had condemned him for various things, saying that he was bewitched and mentally deranged; and that, when they had perceived all that, they had pledged their allegiance to his paternal uncle Ibrāhīm b. al-Mahdī as Caliph. Al-Ma'mūn replied that, according to what al-Faḍl had informed him, they had not pledged allegiance to Ibrāhīm as Caliph but had merely set him up as amīr to rule over and look after their interests.

ʿAlī then told al-Ma'mūn that al-Faḍl had misinformed and hoodwinked him, that a state of war existed between Ibrāhīm and al-Ḥasan b. Sahl and that people were condemning al-Ma'mūn for al-Faḍl's position and influence and that of his brother (al-Ḥasan), and for ʿAlī's own rôle and al-Ma'mūn's requirement of homage to him as successor to the throne after al-Ma'mūn. Al-Ma'mūn asked, "Who of my military commanders knows
[1026] all this?" ʿAlī told him, "Yaḥyā b. Muʿādh[250] and ʿAbd al-ʿAzīz b. ʿImrān and a number of other leading commanders." The Caliph told ʿAlī to send them into him so that he might interrogate them about ʿAlī's report. So ʿAlī had them—comprising Yaḥyā b. Muʿādh, ʿAbd al-ʿAzīz b. ʿImrān, Mūsā, ʿAlī b. Abī

249. Ibn al-Athīr, *al-Kāmil*, VI, 345–6.

250. Of Khurasanian origin and a supporter of al-Ma'mūn; see Crone, 184. He is not to be confused with the famous ascetic and mystic of a generation later, Yaḥyā b. Muʿādh al-Rāzī, who died in 258 (872).

Saʿīd (the son of al-Faḍl's sister[251]) and Khalaf al-Miṣrī—brought into the Caliph's presence, and al-Ma'mūn asked them about what ʿAlī had said. At first, they refused to say anything until al-Ma'mūn would give them a guarantee of personal safety from possible reprisals against them by al-Faḍl b. Sahl; the Caliph gave them this promise, wrote out for each one of them a guarantee in his own hand and passed it over to them.

Then they told him about the state of civil conflict into which the people had been plunged, giving a clear and detailed exposition of it, and informing him about the anger against him on the part of his own family, his mawlās (clients and freedmen) and his commanders, on account of so many things. (They pointed out) how al-Faḍl had deluded him in the affair of Harthamah, in that the latter had only come to al-Ma'mūn in order to give sincere advice and to explain clearly to him what was being wrought against his interests and how the caliphate would slip out of his hands and those of his family unless al-Ma'mūn reasserted his personal control over affairs of state; and how, nevertheless, al-Faḍl had secretly suborned someone to kill Harthamah, when the latter had only wished to offer wise counsel. (They further told the Caliph) that Ṭāhir b. al-Ḥusayn had exerted himself to the utmost in al-Ma'mūn's service, had made numerous conquests and had secured the caliphate for him, but then when Ṭāhir had made everything smooth for al-Ma'mūn's assumption of power, he was suddenly torn away from everything and dispatched to a distant corner of the empire at Raqqah, with a denial of access to his own wealth and possessions until his position had become enfeebled and his own troops rose in revolt against him. If Ṭāhir had been the Caliph's representative in Baghdad, he would have exercised the governmental power firmly, and the assaults on al-Ḥasan b. Sahl's position would not have been ventured against Ṭāhir. All the different regions of the world had fallen apart, Ṭāhir b. al-Ḥusayn had been deliberately left in obscurity at Raqqah during these years since the killing of Muḥammad (al-Amīn), and his help had never been sought in any of these mili- [1027]

251. According to Yaʿqūbī, *Ta'rīkh*, II, 549, the son of al-Faḍl's maternal aunt.

tary campaigns; indeed, the help of people many times his inferior in worth had been sought. They asked al-Ma'mūn to go to Baghdad, adducing the argument that if the Hāshimites, their mawlās, the commanders and the troops could only see his prestige and might, they would become stilled and quiescent before it and hasten to give him full obedience.[252]

When al-Ma'mūn realized fully the truth of these allegations, he gave orders for departure to Baghdad. But when he issued this command, al-Faḍl b. Sahl realized that at least some of the responsibility for this decision stemmed from the commanders' advice; hence he treated them harshly, even having some of them flogged, jailing some others and having the hairs of the beards of yet others pulled out. ʿAlī b. Mūsā then came to him repeatedly concerning them, and informed him about the guarantee of safety vis-à-vis him which they held; however, he told ʿAlī that he would achieve his own aims anyway, by stealth. Then al-Faḍl set off from Marw, but when he reached Sarakhs,[253] a group of men attacked him when he was in the bath and hacked him to death with their swords. This happened on Friday, the second of Shaʿbān, 202[254] (February 13, 818). They were apprehended, and the assassins proved to be men from al-Ma'mūn's retinue, numbering four persons, Ghālib al-Masʿūdī al-Aswad, Qusṭanṭīn al-Rūmī, Faraj al-Daylamī and Muwaffaq al-Ṣaqlabī. Al-Faḍl was sixty years old when they killed him. They fled, and al-Ma'mūn sent people in pursuit of them, offering a reward of ten thousand dīnārs to whomsoever brought them back. Al-ʿAbbās b. al-Haytham b. Buzurjmihr al-Dīnawarī brought them back. They asserted to al-Ma'mūn, "You yourself ordered us to kill him!" The Caliph, however, ordered their heads to be cut off.[255]

---

252. *ʿUyūn*, 355–6; Ibn al-Athīr, *al-Kāmil*, VI, 346–7.

253. A town of northern Khurasan, on the route through the desert from Marw to Ṭūs; see Yāqūt, *Muʿjam*, III, 208–9; Le Strange, *Lands*, 395–6; *EI*[1] s.v. (J. Ruska).

254. Actually a Saturday. Masʿūdī, *Tanbīh*, 350, tr. 449, has Monday, the fifth of Shaʿbān (actually a Tuesday).

255. Id., *Murūj*, VII, 61 = ed. Pellat, § 2747; Azdī, 343. It was widely believed that the Caliph was behind al-Faḍl's assassination, now that the era of Sahlid ascendancy (marked also by al-Ḥasan's attack of acute melancholia shortly af-

It has been said that, when al-Faḍl's killers were captured, al-Ma'mūn interrogated them, and some of them said that ʿAlī b. Abī Saʿīd, the son of al-Faḍl's sister, had secretly suborned them, whilst others denied this. The Caliph ordered them to be executed, and then summoned ʿAbd al-ʿAzīz b. ʿImrān, ʿAlī, [1028] Mūsā and Khalaf for questioning. They denied having known anything at all about the affair, but he refused to believe them and ordered them to be put to death. He then sent their heads to al-Ḥasan b. Sahl at Wāsiṭ and informed him what a severe misfortune he had suffered through al-Faḍl's murder and how he had appointed al-Ḥasan to take al-Faḍl's place. The letter containing this information reached al-Ḥasan in the month of Ramaḍān (March–April 818).[256]

Al-Ḥasan and his troops continued to remain at Wāsiṭ until the tax collection became due and at least part of the land tax was gathered in. Al-Ma'mūn departed from Sarakhs for Iraq on the day of the breaking of the fast, al-Fiṭr (on the first of Shawwāl, 202 [April 12, 818]). Ibrāhīm b. al-Mahdī was meanwhile at Madā'in, with ʿĪsā, Abū at-Baṭṭ and Saʿīd at Nīl and Ṭarnāyā making repeated military forays (literally: in the evenings and mornings). Al-Muṭṭalib b. ʿAbdallāh b. Mālik b. ʿAbdallāh had set out from Madā'in. He now claimed to be ill, and started secretly acknowledging al-Ma'mūn as Caliph, on the plea that al-Manṣūr b. al-Mahdī was al-Ma'mūn's representative, and throwing off allegiance to Ibrāhīm. Manṣūr, Khuzaymah b. Khāzim and many commanders from the troops of the East Side (of Baghdad) followed his lead here. Al-Muṭṭalib wrote to Ḥumayd and ʿAlī b. Hishām instructing them to move forward and that Ḥumayd should then encamp at the Nahr Ṣarṣar and ʿAlī at Nahrawān.

When Ibrāhīm became fully apprised of this news, he set off from Madā'in to Baghdad and encamped at Zandaward[257] on Sat-

terwards, see below, 85) was coming to an end; cf. Abbott, 224–5; Sourdel, *Vizirat*, I, 208–10.

256. Khalīfah, *Ta'rīkh*, II, 765; Yaʿqūbī, *Ta'rīkh*, II, 549–50; *ʿUyūn*, 355, 356–7; Ibn al-Athīr, *al-Kāmil*, VI, 347–8; Donaldson, 168–9.

257. A place on the East Side of Baghdad, famed for its monastery; see Yāqūt, *Muʿjam*, II, 512–13 (citing a lost part of Shābushtī, see ʿAwwād's edition, 337–8); Le Strange, *Baghdad*, 179; Lassner, *Topography*, 281.

urday, the fourteenth of Ṣafar (203 [August 21, 818]). He sent messages to al-Muṭṭalib, Manṣūr and Khuzaymah, but when his messenger came to them, they made excuses to him. So when Ibrāhīm perceived this, he sent ʿĪsā b. Muḥammad b. Abī Khālid and his brothers to them. Manṣūr and Khuzaymah threw in their hands without a fight, but al-Muṭṭalib's clients and freedmen and his retainers put up a fight in defence of his house until the number of men against them grew too large. Ibrāhīm ordered a herald to proclaim that anyone eager for
[1029] plunder should make his way to al-Muṭṭalib's house. By the time of the noon worship, the mob reached the house; they plundered everything they could find and further ransacked the houses of his kinsmen. They searched for al-Muṭṭalib but were unable to find him. This took place on Tuesday, the sixteenth of Ṣafar[258] (203 [August 23, 818]).

When the news reached Ḥumayd and ʿAlī b. Hishām, Ḥumayd sent a commander who seized Madā'in, cut the route across the bridge and encamped by it. ʿAlī b. Hishām sent a commander who encamped at Madā'in and proceeded to the Nahr Diyālā,[259] and then cut off the route there. Ḥumayd's commanders and their troops remained in Madā'in. Ibrāhīm now regretted what he had done in regard to al-Muṭṭalib, but he was still unable to get his hands on him.[260]

In this year, al-Ma'mūn married Būrān, the daughter of al-Ḥasan b. Sahl.[261]

In this year, al-Ma'mūn married his daughter Umm Ḥabīb to ʿAlī b. Mūsā al-Riḍā and another daughter, Umm al-Faḍl, to Muḥammad b. ʿAlī b. Mūsā.[262]

---

258. Actually a Monday.

259. The Diyālā Canal ran from the Nahrawān Canal southwards to the Tigris below east Baghdad; see Yāqūt, *Muʿjam*, II, 495; Le Strange, *Lands*, 59–61; *EI*[2] s.v. (S.H. Longrigg).

260. Ibn al-Athīr, *al-Kāmil*, VI, 348.

261. Azdī, loc. cit.; *ʿUyūn*, 357; Ibn al-Athīr, *al-Kāmil*, VI, 350. The consummation of the marriage took place in Ramaḍān 210 (December 824-January 825), see below, 153, 158. The reference here is to the Caliph's betrothal to the eight-year-old Būrān, see Abbott, 225.

262. Masʿūdī, *Murūj*, VII, 61–2 = ed. Pellat, § 2747; Iṣfahānī, *Maqātil*, 565; Azdī, loc. cit.; *ʿUyūn*, 357; Ibn al-Athīr, *al-Kāmil*, VI, 350; Donaldson, 167; Abbott, 224–5; Sourdel, "La politique religieuse du calife ʿabbāside al-Ma'-

In this year, Ibrāhīm b. Mūsā b. Jaʿfar b. Muḥammad led the pilgrimage and invoked his brother in the prayers as heir to the caliphate after al-Ma'mūn. Al-Ḥasan b. Sahl had written to ʿĪsā b. Yazīd al-Julūdī, who was at Baṣrah, and the latter came to Mecca with his followers; he participated in the ceremonies of the pilgrimage, and then returned. Ibrāhīm b. Mūsā proceeded to the Yemen, which Ḥamdawayh b. ʿAlī b. ʿĪsā b. Māhān had seized.[263]

---

mūn," 38, noting this as a sign of al-Ma'mūn's veneration for ʿAlī, even after the reversal of these pro-ʿAlid usages after ʿAlī al-Riḍā's death; Marquet, 127–8, also noting the Caliph's continued policy of sympathy for the ʿAlids after ʿAlī al-Riḍā's demise, displayed in several ways.

263. Khalīfah, *Ta'rīkh*, II, 765; Masʿūdī, *Murūj*, IX, 69–70 = ed. Pellat, § 3649; Azdī, 350; Ibn al-Athīr, *al-Kāmil*, loc. cit.; Geddes, 103–4; Marquet, 111.

Events of the Year

203

(JULY 9, 818–JUNE 27, 819)

It is mentioned that one of the events taking place during this year was the death of ʿAlī b. Mūsā b. Jaʿfar.

The Cause of the Death of ʿAlī b. Mūsā b. Jaʿfar

[1030] It is mentioned that al-Maʾmūn set out from Sarakhs until he arrived at Ṭūs. When he came to it, he halted at his father's tomb there for a few days. ʿAlī b. Mūsā then ate an inordinate quantity of grapes and suddenly died, this being at the end of Ṣafar (early September 818). Al-Maʾmūn gave orders, and he was buried at the side of al-Rashīd's grave.[264] In the month of

264. Khalīfah, *Taʾrīkh*, II, 766; Yaʿqūbī, *Taʾrīkh*, II, 551, stating that he died at the village of Nūqān and giving a report that ʿAlī b. Hishām killed him with a poisoned pomegranate (for Yaʿqūbī's general attitude here, see Marquet, 127); Masʿūdī, *Murūj*, VII, 61 = ed. Pellat, § 2747; id., *Tanbīh*, 350, tr. 449, with the date of death given as 1 Ṣafar; Iṣfahānī, *Maqātil*, 565–7, 571–2; Azdī, 352; Donaldson, 169, 171–2; Abbott, 226; Kennedy, 161. However, G.C. Miles, *The numismatic history of Rayy*, 105–8, regards this date of Ṣafar 203 for ʿAlī's death as too early, on numismatic grounds.

Rabīʿ I (September–October 818) al-Ma'mūn wrote to al-Ḥasan b. Sahl informing him that ʿAlī b. Mūsā b. Jaʿfar had died and communicating to him how his death had overwhelmed him with grief and feelings of loss. He also wrote to the members of the ʿAbbāsid family, the clients and freedmen, and the people of Baghdad, announcing to them ʿAlī b. Mūsā's death, stressing that it was only his (al-Ma'mūn's) appointment of ʿAlī as his successor to the throne of which they had disapproved, and asking them to resume now their obedience to him; but they wrote back a reply to him and to al-Ḥasan couched in the toughest terms by which anyone could ever be addressed.[265] The person who led the prayers over ʿAlī b. Mūsā was al-Ma'mūn himself.

In this year, al-Ma'mūn travelled from Ṭūs en route for Baghdad. When he reached Rayy, he lowered its tax assessment by two million dirhams.[266]

In this year, al-Ḥasan b. Sahl was overcome by an attack of melancholia and depression (*al-sawdā'*). The cause of this was said to be that he suffered a severe illness, which subsequently brought about a mental disturbance, to the point that he had to be put in fetters of restraint and locked up in a house. Al-Ḥasan's commanders wrote to al-Ma'mūn about this, and a reply to their letter came back appointing Dīnār b. ʿAbdallāh as supreme commander of al-Ḥasan's army and informing them that the Caliph himself was on his way, close behind the letter.[267]

In this year, Ibrāhīm b. al-Mahdī had ʿĪsā b. Muḥammad b. Abī Khālid beaten and imprisoned.

---

265. Ibn al-Athīr, *al-Kāmil*, VI, 351. The text of this letter is not extant, but what purports to be al-Ma'mūn's answer is reproduced by the much later Shīʿī author Majlisī, apparently going back to the historian Miskawayh; see Madelung, "New documents concerning al-Ma'mūn, al-Faḍl b. Sahl and ʿAlī al-Riḍā," 339–45.

266. Again, Miles, 105, regards this date as too early and would place this event in the year 204 (819/20).

267. *ʿUyūn*, 357; Ibn al-Athīr, *al-Kāmil*, VI, 356. Shortly after this, Dīnār served briefly as governor of Jibāl for al-Ma'mūn; see Yaʿqūbī, *Ta'rīkh*, II, 553, and cf. Sourdel, *Vizirat*, I, 223.

ʿĪsā b. Muḥammad is Beaten and Imprisoned

It is mentioned that ʿĪsā b. Muḥammad b. Abī Khālid had been in constant correspondence with Ḥumayd and al-Ḥasan, the envoy between them being Muḥammad b. Muḥammad al-Maʿbadī al-Hāshimī.[268] At the same time, ʿĪsā was ostensibly displaying his obedience and giving his counsel to Ibrāhīm, but
[1031] was never showing any fight to Ḥumayd nor opposing the latter's actions in any way. Whenever Ibrāhīm instructed him, "Get ready to go out and engage Ḥumayd!" he would make excuses to him that the army was clamoring for its pay allocations, or, on another occasion, he would say, "[Let us wait] till the tax yields are gathered in." He kept on in this vein until finally, when he became fully assured about what he wanted from the negotiations between himself and al-Ḥasan and Ḥumayd, he deserted Ibrāhīm's side, with the understanding that he would hand Ibrāhīm b. al-Mahdī over to them on Friday, the twenty-ninth of Shawwāl (April 29, 819). Information about this reached Ibrāhīm. On the Thursday, ʿĪsā proceeded to the Bāb al-Jisr[269] and proclaimed to the people, "I have come to a peace agreement with Ḥumayd; I have solemnly pledged to him that I shall not trespass upon his administrative charge and he has guaranteed to me that he will not trespass on mine." He then ordered a defensive trench and rampart (*khandaq*) to be dug at the Bāb al-Jisr and the Bāb al-Shām. These words of his reached Ibrāhīm, as did news of what he had been doing. ʿĪsā had previously asked Ibrāhīm if he might lead the Friday worship in the City (of Peace), and Ibrāhīm had assented. Now when ʿĪsā uttered these pronouncements, and news of them was duly reported to Ibrāhīm, together with the

268. I.e., of the branch of the ʿAbbāsid family descended from Maʿbad b. al-ʿAbbās; they owned property in Karkh, after which the Maʿbadī bridge over the ʿĪsā Canal was named; see Le Strange, *Baghdad*, 75; Lassner, *Topography*, 75.

269. Probably the gate leading to the main or upper bridge (*jisr*) constructed by al-Manṣūr to connect the district of the Khuld Palace with Ruṣāfah on the east bank, but the sources are not entirely explicit over the location; see Le Strange, *Baghdad*, 178, 198; Lassner, *Topography*, 151, 281. At all events, the defensive trench and rampart mentioned below would be along the northern perimeter of the Round City.

fact that ʿĪsā was planning to seize him, Ibrāhīm was on his guard.

It is mentioned that Hārūn, ʿĪsā's brother, told Ibrāhīm what ʿĪsā was planning to do to him. Hence when Hārūn passed this information on, Ibrāhīm sent to ʿĪsā ordering him to come to him so that he might harangue and examine him about certain aspects of his intentions, but ʿĪsā adduced various reasons for not coming. Ibrāhīm kept on, repeatedly dispatching messengers to ʿĪsā, until finally he went personally to ʿĪsā's palace in Ruṣāfah.[270] When he went in, all the other people were excluded, and Ibrāhīm and ʿĪsā talked in private. Ibrāhīm started to reproach ʿĪsā, and ʿĪsā began to excuse himself from such reproof and to give the lie to some of the accusations which Ibrāhīm was making. When Ibrāhīm had forced ʿĪsā to admit to various things, he gave orders and ʿĪsā was beaten. He then imprisoned him, and arrested a number of his commanders and jailed them; he sent (men) to ʿĪsā's house and arrested the slave mother of his children and several of his young children and jailed them too. This took place in the night of Thursday (Wednesday–Thursday, the twenty-seventh–)twenty-eighth of Shawwāl (April 28–29, 819). Ibrāhīm searched for one of ʿĪsā's lieutenants called al-ʿAbbās, but the latter concealed himself.

When the news of ʿĪsā's imprisonment reached his family [1032]
and his retainers, groups of them went along to each other, and members of his family and his brothers incited the people against Ibrāhīm. They gathered together under the leadership of (al-) ʿAbbās, ʿĪsā's lieutenant, and attacked Ibrāhīm's financial official at the bridge and drove him out; he crossed over to Ibrāhīm and told him the news, and Ibrāhīm ordered the bridge to be cut. They expelled every single one of Ibrāhīm's financial officials in Karkh and elsewhere. Evildoers and mobsters appeared, and took over the manning of the strong points (*al-masāliḥ*). (Al-)ʿAbbās wrote to Ḥumayd asking him to advance

270. The westernmost quarter of what had been known as ʿAskar al-Mahdī (see above, 42, n. 119) on the east bank of the Tigris; see Yāqūt, *Muʿjam*, III, 46–7; Le Strange, *Baghdad*, 187–98; Lassner, *Topography*, 64–5, 250.

towards them so that they might hand over Baghdad to him.[271] When Friday came, the Friday worship in the mosque of the City (of Peace) comprised only four cycles of inclinations (*raka'āt*); the muezzin led the worship, but there was no sermon.

In this year, the people of Baghdad threw off allegiance to Ibrāhīm b. al-Mahdī and mentioned al-Ma'mūn's name as Caliph in the prayers.

The People of Baghdad Throw off Allegiance to Ibrāhīm

We have just mentioned above the story of Ibrāhīm and 'Īsā b. Muḥammad b. Abī Khālid's relations, Ibrāhīm's imprisoning of 'Īsā, the banding together of 'Īsā's lieutenant (al-) 'Abbās and 'Īsā's brothers against Ibrāhīm and their message to Ḥumayd inviting him to come to them so that they might hand over Baghdad to him. It is further mentioned that this message of theirs, containing the stipulation that Ḥumayd should give each man of the Baghdad troops fifty dirhams, reached Ḥumayd, and he agreed to their terms. He moved forward till he encamped at the Nahr Ṣarṣar on the road to Kūfah on the Sunday, and (al-) 'Abbās and the commanders of the Baghdad troops went out to him. They met him on the Monday morning, and he gave them promises and hopes of reward, which they accepted. He promised them (specifically) that he would hand out the pay allotments to them on the following Saturday at
[1033] Yāsiriyyah,[272] on condition that they would perform the Friday worship and would place al-Ma'mun's name in the bidding prayer and renounce allegiance to Ibrāhīm; to this they agreed.

When the news reached Ibrāhīm, he released 'Īsā and his brothers from jail and asked him to return home and take charge, on his behalf, of that side (of Baghdad); but 'Īsā refused to undertake this for him. When Friday came, (al-) 'Abbās sent

---

271. Ibn al-Athīr, *al-Kāmil*, VI, 351–2.

272. A suburb of western Baghdad lying on the 'Īsā Canal towards Muḥawwal; see Yāqūt, *Mu'jam*, V, 425; Le Strange, *Baghdad*, 151–2; Lassner, *Topography*, 75, 100, 259.

to the legal scholar (*faqīh*) Muḥammad b. Abī Rajā,[273] and the latter led the people in the Friday worship and made the prayers in al-Ma'mūn's name. On the Saturday, Ḥumayd went to Yāsiriyyah, reviewed the army of the Baghdad troops and paid out to them the fifty dirhams which he had promised. They asked him, however, to reduce this sum by ten dirhams each and thereby pay forty dirhams each instead, because of their feeling of ill-omen stemming from the episode of ʿAlī b. Hishām's offering them fifty dirhams and then tricking them by not paying out the allotments. Ḥumayd answered them, "No, I won't; on the contrary, I shall increase your pay and give you each sixty dirhams."

When Ibrāhīm heard the news, he summoned ʿĪsā and asked him to engage Ḥumayd in fighting; he agreed to do this, so Ibrāhīm let him go completely free, having however taken from him guarantors of his good faith. ʿĪsā then addressed the troops and promised them the same as Ḥumayd had given, but they refused to accept this from him. On the Monday, ʿĪsā, his brothers and the commanders of the troops on the East Side crossed over to them and offered the troops on the West Side an amount in excess of what Ḥumayd had given; but they greeted ʿĪsā and his companions with obloquy and expostulated, "We don't want Ibrāhīm!" So ʿĪsā and his companions went forward and entered the City (of Peace); they locked the gates and went up on the walls, and fought the troops for a while. When, however, the numbers opposing them became too great, they retreated till they reached the Bāb Khurāsān, and then they took to boats.[274] ʿĪsā himself went back as if he intended to throw himself into the fight against them once more, but devised a stratagem so that he placed himself into his opponents' hands as if he had been taken prisoner; one of his commanders then took him to his house, whilst the rest of the troops went back to Ibrāhīm and told him what had happened. The news plunged [1034]
Ibrāhīm into deep grief.

Al-Muṭṭalib b. ʿAbdallāh Mālik had concealed himself from Ibrāhīm, so when Ḥumayd drew near, he tried to cross over to

273. Cf. ibid., 69, 255; this scholar is thus identified.
274. I.e., on the Tigris.

him. But the ferry man[275] arrested him and took him along to Ibrāhīm, who imprisoned al-Muṭṭalib in his house for three or four days and then freed him on the night of Monday, the first of Dhū al-Ḥijjah (Sunday–Monday, the twenty-ninth of Dhū al-Qaʿdah-the first of Dhū al-Ḥijjah, 203[May 30, 819]).[276]

In this year, Ibrāhīm b. al-Mahdī concealed himself and disappeared from view after the period of warfare between him and Ḥumayd b. ʿAbd al-Ḥamīd and after he had released Sahl b. Salāmah from prison.[277]

Ibrāhīm Goes into Hiding

It is mentioned that the people used to mention that Sahl b. Salāmah had been killed, when he was (in fact) held in captivity by Ibrāhīm. When Ḥumayd marched on Baghdad and entered it, Ibrāhīm brought Sahl forth, and the latter used to offer up prayers in the mosque of Ruṣāfah as formerly, and then when it was night, Ibrāhīm committed Sahl back to his imprisonment. He remained subject to this procedure for several days. Sahl's partisans came to him with the intention of joining up with him (banding together to release him); but he told them, "Stay in your houses, for I shall obtain something advantageous from this fellow [*arzī hādhā*]," meaning Ibrāhīm. On the night of Monday (Sunday–Monday), the first of Dhū al-Ḥijjah (May 30, 819), Ibrāhīm set him free, and Sahl went off and hid himself. When Ibrāhīm's retainers and commanders saw that Ḥumayd had encamped at the mills of ʿAbdallāh b. Mālik,[278] the greater part of them transferred their allegiance to Ḥumayd, and seized Madā'in on his behalf. When Ibrāhīm real-

275. Reading, with the *Addenda et emendenda*, p. DCCLXVIII, *al-muʿabbir* "ferry man, boatman" (see *Glossarium*, p. CCCL); for the text's dubious *al-m.ʿ.b.d*, which might, nevertheless, refer to the Maʿbadī bridge, see above, 86 and n. 268.

276. Yaʿqūbī, *Ta'rīkh*, II, 548; Ibn al-Athīr, *al-Kāmil*, VI, 353–4.

277. Yaʿqūbī, *Ta'rīkh*, II, 551; Masʿūdī, *Murūj*, VII, 62 = ed. Pellat, § 2748; Barbier de Meynard, 250 ff.

278. ʿAbdallāh b. Mālik's property lay on the eastern bank of the Tigris near Qarn al-Ṣarāt, where the Ṣarāt Canal joined the river near the new bridge; see Lassner, *Topography*, 70, 255.

ized this, he sent all the forces which he had with him forth to fight. The two sides met in battle at the bridge over the Nahr Diyālā and fought together. Ḥumayd defeated Ibrāhīm's forces. They cut the bridge, but Ḥumayd's forces pursued them right into the houses of Baghdad. This was on Thursday, the thirtieth of Dhū al-Qaʿdah,[279] (203 [May 29, 819]).

When it was the day of the Festival of the Sacrifice (ʿĪd al-Aḍḥā) (the tenth of Dhū al-Ḥijjah, 803 [June 8, 819]), Ibrāhīm ordered the judge to lead the people in the worship at ʿĪsābādh;[280] he did this, and then the people returned home. Al-Faḍl b. al-Rabīʿ was in hiding, but then went over to Ḥumayd. ʿAlī b. Rayṭah[281] likewise transferred to Ḥumayd's encampment, and the Hāshimites and the commanders began one-by-one to attach themselves to Ḥumayd's side. When Ibrāhīm perceived this, he was filled with self-reproach and thrown into misery. Al-Muṭṭalib had been in correspondence with Ḥumayd, undertaking to deliver to him control of the East Side of the city, while Saʿīd b. al-Sājūr, Abū al-Baṭṭ and ʿAbdawayh, in company with a host of other commanders, were in correspondence with ʿAlī b. Hishām, undertaking to capture Ibrāhīm for him. When Ibrāhīm got to know about their plans and that all his retainers were plotting against him, he realized that they had surrounded him, and he set about outwitting them. When nightfall came, he went into hiding on the night of Wednesday, the sixteenth of Dhū al-Ḥijjah, 203 (the night of Tuesday–Wednesday,[282] June 13–14, 819)[283] [1035]

Al-Muṭṭalib sent a message to Ḥumayd informing him that he and his followers had surrounded Ibrāhīm's house, and if Ḥumayd was seeking Ibrāhīm, he was to come to him. Also,

279. Actually a Sunday.

280. This is what al-Khaṭīb al-Baghdādī calls al-Mahdī's pleasure palace (*mustaqarr*), actually built for his son ʿĪsā at an unidentified spot in east Baghdad; see Le Strange, *Baghdad*, 194; Lassner, *Topography*, 81, 264.

281. Possibly a son of al-Saffāḥ's daughter Rayṭah, though not by her best-known husband al-Mahdī.

282. Actually the night of Tuesday (i.e., of Monday-Tuesday).

283. Masʿūdī, *Tanbīh*, 350, tr. 449–50, has the eleventh of Dhū al-Ḥijjah; ʿ*Uyūn*, 358, has Tuesday, the seventeenth of Dhū al-Ḥijjah (correctly, the sixteenth of Dhū al-Ḥijjah).

Ibn al-Sājūr and his companions sent a message to ʿAlī b. Hishām. Ḥumayd, who was staying at the mills of ʿAbdallāh (b. Mālik,) rode off immediately, and went to the Bāb al-Jisr. ʿAlī b. Hishām proceeded till he halted at the Nahr Bīn and then advanced to the Kawthar mosque.[284] Ibn al-Sājūr and his companions came out to meet him, and al-Muṭṭalib came to Ḥumayd and met him at the Bāb al-Jisr. Ḥumayd showed them great favor, gave them promises of future beneficence and told them that he was going to inform al-Ma'mūn about what they had done. They came to Ibrāhīm's house and began a search for him there, but without success; Ibrāhīm remained in concealment till al-Ma'mūn arrived and after that, until events turned out for him as they did.

Sahl b. Salāmah had returned from his place of concealment to his own house. He now showed himself openly. Ḥumayd
[1036] sent for him, received him with favor and treated him as an intimate. He had Sahl mounted on a mule and sent him back to his family. Sahl remained there till al-Ma'mūn entered Baghdad; then he came to the Caliph, who rewarded him with favors and presents and ordered him to remain quietly in his house.[285]

In this year, there was an eclipse of the sun on Sunday, the twenty-eighth of Dhū al-Ḥijjah, (203[June 26, 819]), to the extent that the sun's light faded away and over two-thirds of its orb disappeared. The eclipse began when the sun was getting high and continued till it was nearly noon; then it cleared away.[286]

The total length of Ibrāhīm b. al-Mahdī's tenure of power was one year, eleven months and twelve days. ʿAlī b. Hishām secured control of the East Side of Baghdad, and Ḥumayd b. ʿAbd al-Ḥamīd controlled the West Side.[287] Al-Ma'mūn pro-

---

284. Presumably on the property of Kawthar b. al-Yamān in Karkh; see Lassner, *Topography*, 258, n. 58.

285. Ibn al-Athīr, *al-Kāmil*, VI, 354–5.

286. Ibid., VI, 356.

287. *ʿUyūn*, 358; Ibn al-Athīr, *al-Kāmil*, VI, 355.

ceeded as far as Hamadhān by the end of Dhū al-Ḥijjah (203[late June 819]).

In this year, Sulaymān b. ʿAbdallāh b. Sulaymān b. ʿAlī led the pilgrimage.[288]

---

288. Khalīfah, *Taʾrīkh*, II, 766; Azdī, 353. Sulaymān was an ʿAbbāsid prince, descended from ʿAbdallāh b. al-ʿAbbās; subsequently, in 214 (829/30), he became governor of Mecca.

The Events of the Year

204

(JUNE 28, 819–JUNE 16, 820)

The events taking place during this year included al-Ma'mūn's arrival in Iraq and the end of the (previous) increase in civil strife in Baghdad.

Al-Ma'mūn's *Arrival in Iraq and What Happened There*[289]

It is mentioned concerning al-Ma'mūn that when he reached Jurjān[290] he stayed there a month. Then he left and travelled to Rayy in Dhū al-Ḥijjah (203[June 819]), and stayed there for a
[1037] few days.[291] Then he left Rayy and began travelling from one staging post to another, staying one or two days (in each of them) until he reached Nahrawān, this being on a Saturday, and stayed there eight days. The members of his family, the

---

289. The surviving part of Ibn Abī Ṭāhir's *Kitāb Baghdād* begins here.

290. I.e., the southeast Caspian coastland region, Persian Gurgān; see Le Strange, *Lands*, 376–81; Barthold, *An historical geography of Iran*, 115; *EI*[1] s.v. Gurgān (Hartmann—J.A. Boyle).

291. This must be the occasion recorded above, 85, when al-Ma'mūn lightened the assessment of the land-tax of Rayy.

commanders and the leading personalities came out (to meet him) and greeted him. Previous to this, while he was on the road, al-Ma'mūn had written to Ṭāhir b. al-Ḥusayn, who was at that time at Raqqah, telling Ṭāhir to meet him at Nahrawān; and Ṭāhir duly met up with him there. On the next[292] Saturday, al-Ma'mūn entered Baghdad, as the sun was getting high, on the fifteenth of Ṣafar, 204[293] (August 11, 819), with himself and his retinue all wearing short green Persian coats (*aqbiyah*) and tall caps (*qalānis*) and bearing short lances (*ṭarrādāt*) (with green pennants) and green banners (*a'lām*).[294]

When he arrived, he halted and encamped at Ruṣāfah, accompanied by Ṭahir. He ordered Ṭāhir to encamp at Khayzūraniyyah with his troops. Then he transferred his quarters to his palace on the bank of the Tigris. He gave commands to Ḥumayd b. 'Abd al-Ḥamid, 'Alī b. Hishām and every one of the commanders in his army that they should remain in their military encampments. Now these commanders had been resorting to al-Ma'mūn's palace each day, and no one had been able to enter into his presence unless he wore green clothes. The people of Baghdad and the Hāshimites likewise all wore green. Al-Ma'mūn's partisans used to tear off anything black which they observed people wearing, except for caps;[295] isolated individuals used to wear them (black caps), but in fear and trembling; and as for a Persian coat or banner, no one dared to wear one at all or to carry one.

They remained in this state of affairs for eight days, but then the Hāshimites, and the members of the 'Abbāsid family in

---

292. Reading *al-ākharu* for the text's *al-ākhiru*.

293. Actually a Thursday. The date of the fifteenth of Ṣafar for al-Ma'mūn's entry given by Ibn Abī Ṭāhir, 2, n. 3, tr. Keller, 1, n. 1, by Ṭabarī here, by Ibn al-Athīr following them, etc., must really be, relying on other, parallel sources (e.g., Ibn Qutaybah), Sunday, the eleventh of Ṣafar (August 7). Ya'qūbī, *Ta'rīkh*, II, 551, has Rabī' I, i.e., the following month; Mas'ūdī, *Tanbīh*, 351, tr. 450, has Saturday, the eighteenth of Ṣafar (actually a Sunday). Azdī, 353, merely has the month of Ṣafar.

294. Following the *ṭarrād/ṭirād* of Lane's *Lexicon* = *miṭrad*, "short spear;" in Ibn Abī Ṭāhir, tr. 1, Keller has for these last two terms, "Fahnen und Abzeichungen waren grün."

295. This exception is not easily explicable, unless it was that the black cap was so archetypically the 'Abbāsid symbol as to be regarded as sacrosanct.

particular, began to mumur against it and told al-Ma'mūn, "O Commander of the Faithful, you have abandoned the dress of your forefathers, the members of your family and the supporters of their dynasty, and you have adopted green!" The commanders of the Khurasanian troops also wrote to him about this. It is said that al-Ma'mūn instructed Ṭāhir b. al-Ḥusayn to ask him for any of his requirements, and the first matter which Ṭahir raised with him was that he should cast
[1038] aside the wearing of green clothes and revert to wearing black clothes and the traditional apparel of the régime of (ʿAbbāsid) forefathers. So when al-Ma'mūn saw that the people were obediently following his orders and wearing green, but were hating it, and Saturday came along, he took his place among them, still wearing green. When all his followers were gathered round him, he called for black garments and donned them; he then called for a black robe of honor, and presented it to Ṭāhir. Then he summoned forward a number of commanders and gave them black coats and caps to wear. When they came forth from the Caliph's presence wearing black, the rest of the commanders and the army in general threw off their green garments and adopted black ones. This was on Saturday, the twenty-second of Ṣafar[296] (204 [August 18, 819]).[297]

It has been said that al-Ma'mūn wore green garments for twenty-seven[298] days after his entry into Baghdad, and then they were torn up. It is said that he continued to stay in Baghdad at Ruṣāfah until he built residences along the Tigris bank near his own original palace and in the Mūsā garden.[299]

It is mentioned from Ibrāhīm b. al-ʿAbbās (al-Ṣūlī) al-Kātib[300] from ʿAmr b. Masʿadah (al-Ṣūlī)[301] that Aḥmad b. Abī Khālid

296. Actually a Thursday.

297. Yaʿqūbī, *Ta'rīkh*, II, 551; Masʿūdī, *Murūj*, VII, 62 = ed. Pellat, § 2748; *ʿUyūn*, 358–9; Abbott, 226–7.

298. Ibn Abī Ṭāhir, 4, tr. 2: for 29 days.

299. Cf. also ibid., 4, 22, tr. 2, 10. Concerning al-Ma'mūn's palaces, see Lassner, *Topography*, 84, 265–6.

300. Secretary to Aḥmad b. Abī Khālid and subsequently controller of expenditure and chancery head under al-Mutawakkil, and also a poet; see Sourdel, *Vizirat*, I, 10, 221, 266, 274, II, 734; Sezgin, *GAS*, II, 578–80.

301. Cousin of the above and secretary to al-Ma'mūn, and also a poet; see Sourdel, *Vizirat*, I, 234–8; Sezgin, *GAS*, II, 616–17.

al-Aḥwal[302] said: When we travelled from Khurasan with al-Ma'mūn, and we arrived at the pass of Ḥulwān,[303] I myself being his riding-companion, he said to me, "O Aḥmad, I detect the fragrant smell of Iraq!" I answered him with an inappropriate reply and said, "How suitable it is!" And he said, "This is not the answer to my observation, but I assume that you were somehow distracted or were deep in thought." Aḥmad went on to relate: I replied, "Yes, indeed, O Commander of the Faithful." He said, "What were you thinking about?" Aḥmad went on to relate: I said, "O Commander of the Faithful, I was reflecting about our forthcoming attack on the people of Baghdad [or: the troops, *ahl*, of Baghdad], when we have with us only fifty thousand dirhams and there is internecine strife raging in the hearts of the people, to the extent that they positively revel in it. So what will be our position if someone stirs up trouble, or someone makes an untoward move?" Aḥmad went on to relate: He bowed his head and remained silent for quite a while, and then he replied, "O Aḥmad, you are quite right, and how correctly were you thinking! But let me tell you, people in this [1039]
city can be divided into three categories: those who are the oppressors, those who are the oppressed and those who fall into neither category. In regard to the oppressor, he can only expect our forgiveness and our restraint [from punishing him]; in regard to the oppressed person, he can only expect to get justice through ourself; whilst in regard to the person who is neither an oppressor nor oppressed, his house is wide enough for him [that is, he is quite content and has no need of us]." And by God, it proved just as he said.[304]

In this year, al-Ma'mūn ordered that the proportional tax (*muqāsamah*)[305] levied on the produce of the cultivation of the

302. Secretary who became head of al-Ma'mūn's administration after al-Faḍl b. Sahl's death; see Sourdel, *Vizirat*, I, 218–25. As noted by Kennedy, 166, it is not entirely clear whether he was the brother of the Khurasanian military leader in Baghdad, Muḥammad b. Abī Khālid, but Shaban, 51–2, is surely right in stressing his Iranian origin, *pace* Sourdel's suggestion that he was a Syrian.

303. I.e., the Paytak pass through the Zagros mountains; see *EI*[2] s.v. Ḥulwān (Lockhart).

304. Ibn Abī Ṭāhir, 1–6, tr. 1–3; Azdī, 353–5, with further anecdotal material; Ibn al-Athīr, *al-Kāmil*, VI, 357–8.

305. See on this, F. Løkkegaard, *Islamic taxation in the classic period*, 108 ff.

Sawād should be reduced to two-fifths, whereas they had previously been liable for a half of their produce, and he adopted the "bridled" *qafīz* (*al-qafīz al-muljam*), made up of ten *makkūk*s according to the Hārūnī *makkūk*, as the officially authorised measure of capacity.[306]

In this year, Yaḥyā b. Muʿādh gave battle to Bābak, but neither side gained the upper hand over the other.[307]

(In this year,) al-Ma'mūn appointed Ṣāliḥ b. al-Rashīd[308] as governor of Baṣrah, and ʿUbaydallāh b. al-Ḥasan b. ʿUbaydallāh b. al-ʿAbbās b. ʿAlī b. Abī Ṭālib over the two Holy cities (Mecca and Madīnah).[309]

In this year, ʿUbaydallāh b. al-Ḥasan (b. ʿUbaydallāh b. al-ʿAbbās b. ʿAlī b. Abī Ṭālib) led the pilgrimage.[310]

---

306. Ibn Abī Ṭāhir, 22, tr. 10, with a fuller account of this event; Azdī, 353; *ʿUyūn*, 359; Ibn al-Athīr, *al-Kāmil*, VI, 358. For the measures mentioned here, see Ibn Abī Ṭāhir, tr. 10, n. 1; W. Hinz, *Islamische Masse und Gewichte*, 48–9; Bosworth, "Abū ʿAbdallāh al-Khwārazmī on the technical terms of the secretary's art," *JESHO*, XII (1969), 149–50; but note that Ibn Abī Ṭāhir here and also Khwārazmī gives the equivalence in Iraq as being eight *makkūk*s to a *qafīz*.

307. Azdī, loc. cit.; Ibn al-Athīr, *al-Kāmil*, loc. cit.

308. I.e., the son of the Caliph al-Rashīd.

309. Yaʿqūbī, *Ta'rīkh*, II, 553; Ibn al-Athīr, *al-Kāmil*, loc. cit.; Geddes, 104.

310. Khalīfah, *Ta'rīkh*, II, 767; Azdī, loc. cit.; Ibn al-Athīr, *al-Kāmil*, loc. cit.

The Events of the Year

205

(JUNE 17, 820–JUNE 5, 821)

Among the events taking place during this year was al-Ma'mūn's appointment of Ṭāhir b. al-Ḥusayn as governor of the lands from the City of Peace to the farthest province of the East.[311] Previously, the Caliph had appointed him governor of the Jazīrah, commander of the guard (*al-shuraṭ*), (in Baghdad), governor of the two sides of Baghdad and the person responsible for police duties (*maʿāwin*)[312] in the Sawād.[313] Ṭāhir now took up the rôle of receiving people in audience.

311. For the general background to this, see Barthold, *Turkestan down to the Mongol invasion*, 208–9; Bosworth, *Sīstān under the Arabs*, 108–9; id., in *Cambridge history of Iran*, IV, 95–6; Daniel, 181–2.

312. It is not clear from the sources exactly what the *maʿāwin*, sing. *maʿūnah*, literally "assistance," involved; as well as entailing police duties, they seem also to have denoted some kind of financial burdens, perhaps for supporting local officials; see Løkkegaard, 186–7. In some of the Cairo Geniza documents, *maʿūnah* appears as a euphemism for "jail;" see S.D. Goitein, *A Mediterranean society. II. The community*, 368; P. Crone, *EI*² s.v. Maʿūna.

313. Ibn Abī Ṭāhir, 23, tr. 11 (Ṭāhir's appointment to the offices in the Jazīrah and Baghdad, the date for this being given as Sunday, ʿĀshūrā day = the tenth of Muḥarram, 205 [June 26, 820, actually a Thursday]); Yaʿqūbī, *Taʾrīkh*, II, 542, 553–4; Azdī, loc. cit.; *ʿUyūn*, 363; G. Rothstein, "Zu aš-Šābustī's Bericht über die Ṭāhiriden," in *Orientalistische Studien Theodor Nöldeke . . . gewidmet*, I, 159–61.

The Appointment of Ṭāhir b. al-Ḥusayn as Governor of Khurasan

The reason for al-Ma'mūn's appointing Ṭāhir over Khurasan and the East is what is mentioned from Ḥammād b. al-Ḥasan, from Bishr b. Ghiyāth al-Mārisī[314] who related: I, together with Thumāmah (b. Ashras al-Numayrī)[315] and Muḥammad b. Abī al-ʿAbbās (al-Ṭūsī)[316] and ʿAlī b. al-Haytham,[317] was present at
[1040] ʿAbdallāh al-Ma'mūn's court. They were engaged in a disputation about Shīʿism. Muḥammad b. Abī alʿAbbās argued on behalf of the cause of the imāmate (for the Imāmī Shīʿah), whilst ʿAlī b. al-Haytham upheld the cause of the Zaydī Shīʿah. The discussion between the two proceeded, until a point was reached when Muḥammad said to ʿAlī, "You ignorant peasant [*nabaṭī*],[318] what do you know about theological disputation [*kalām*]?" Bishr continued: Al-Ma'mūn, who was at first reclining on a cushion, then sat up and spoke out, "Hurling insults is unseemly, and unpleasant language is reprehensible. We have allowed theological disputation to take place and have staged the open presentation of [religious] viewpoints [*aẓharnā al-maqālāt*]. Now upon whoever speaks the truth, we bestow praise; for whoever does not know the truth, we provide instruction; and in regard to whoever is ignorant of both ways [of disputation], we make a decision as to what is appropriate for him. So, you two, come to an agreement on basic principles [*aṣl*], for *kalām* is concerned with secondary, derivative matters [*furūʿ*], and if you pursue a topic into all its second-

314. Prominent Murji'ite theologian and upholder of the createdness of the Qur'ān, died in 218 (833); see Watt, index; Sezgin, *GAS*, I, 616–17; *EI*² s.v. (Carra de Vaux—Nader—Schacht).

315. Muʿtazilite theologian, highly esteemed at the ʿAbbāsid court, died in 213 (828); see Watt, index; Sezgin, *GAS*, I, 615–16; *EI*¹ s.v. (Horten).

316. Khurasanian commander in al-Ma'mūn's army, from a family which had been prominent in the ʿAbbāsid revolution, and brother-in-law of Tāhir b. al-Ḥusayn; see Crone, 174.

317. Zaydī Shīʿī theologian; cf. Watt, 348.

318. *Nabaṭī* (originally referring to the Aramaic-speaking indigenous populations of Syria and Iraq) was a term of opprobrium in early Islam; see Nöldeke, "Die Namen der aramäischen Nation und Sprache," *ZDMG*, XXV (1817), 124–7.

ary aspects, you nevertheless come back in the end to the basics." He went on to say, "Thus we say, 'There is no god but God, the Unique One, who has no partner, and Muḥammad is His servant and His prophet.'"

The two of them discussed the topic of the divinely-ordained prescriptions and laws (*al-farā'iḍ wa-al-sharā'i'*) in Islam, and argued together after that. Muḥammad pressed 'Alī once more with arguments similar to those used at first, but 'Alī replied, "By God, were it not for the elevated nature of his [the Caliph's] gathering, and the compassion which God has bestowed on him, and were it not a prohibited action, I woud certainly make your forehead run with sweat! Your ignorance is sufficiently demonstrated by your washing down the pulpit in the city [the City of Peace?]!"[319] Bishr continued: Al-Ma'mūn sat up, having been reclining, and said, "What's this about your washing down the pulpit? Was it the result of my falling short in some way in regard to you, or because al-Manṣūr fell similarly short in regard to your father? Were it not that the Caliph, having bestowed something, would be embarassed to take it back, the nearest thing to the ground between the two of us would be your head [cut off]! So arise, and take care not to do it again!" Bishr continued: Muḥammad b. Abī al-'Abbās departed [1041]
and went along to Ṭāhir b. al-Ḥusayn, who happened to be his sister's husband, and said to him, "So-and-so has just happened to me!"

(The eunuch [*al-khādim*][320] Fatḥ used to act as al-Ma'mūn's doorkeeper when the Caliph was involved in his date wine

319. The washing down of the *minbar* in order to get rid of the impurity and pollution left by a previous occupant of it seems to have been not infrequent in early Islamic times. See Ṭabarī, *Glossarium*, p. CCCLXXXVIII, citing Mas'ūdī and Iṣfahānī, when, during 'Uthmān's caliphate, Sa'īd b. al-'Āṣ washed the *minbar* of the mosque at Kūfah when he took over as governor from al-Walīd b. 'Uqbah; and see Crone, 258, n. 606, citing Kindī, on the washing down of the *minbar* at Fusṭāṭ on al-Ma'mūn's orders after the death of the Imām 'Alī b. Mūsā al-Riḍā, whose name had been pronounced from it. The point of the remark in the present context nevertheless remains obscure.

320. Literally "servant," but in this period virtually synonymous with the derogatory term *khaṣī*, "eunuch"; see D. Ayalon, "On the eunuchs in Islam," *JSAI*, I (1979), 67–124; *EI*[2] s.v. Khaṣī (Pellat).

[*nabīdh*][321] drinking sessions; Yāsir was in charge of the robes of honor; Ḥusayn acted as cup-bearer; and Abū Maryam, the slave boy of Saʿīd al-Jawharī, used to go to-and-fro attending to various needs.) Ṭāhir rode up to the palace. Fatḥ went in and announced, "Ṭāhir is at the door." The Caliph replied, "It isn't one of his usual times, [but] let him come in!" So Ṭāhir entered; he greeted al-Ma'mūn, and the Caliph returned the salutation. The Caliph ordered, "Give Ṭāhir a *raṭl* [of wine] to drink." Ṭāhir took it in his right hand. Al-Ma'mūn said to him, "Sit down!" But he went away (from the circle), drained the cup and then came back. Al-Ma'mūn had meanwhile drunk another *raṭl*, so he ordered, "Give him a second draught!" Ṭāhir behaved exactly as when he drained the first draught. Then he came back, and al-Ma'mūn said to him (again), "Sit down!" Ṭāhir replied, however, "O Commander of the Faithful, it is not fitting for the commander of the guard to sit down in his master's presence." Al-Ma'mūn retorted, "That only applies to public sessions at court [*majlis al-ʿāmmah*], whereas in private sessions [*majlis al-khāṣṣah*] it is allowable."

Bishr continued: Al-Ma'mūn wept, and tears welled up in his eyes. Ṭāhir said to him, "O Commander of the Faithful, why are you weeping, may God never cause your eyes to flow with tears! By God, all the lands have submitted to your rule, all the Muslims have acknowledged you as ruler, and you have achieved your desired object in everything you have undertaken." Al-Ma'mūn replied, "I am weeping on account of a matter which is humiliating to mention and whose concealment is a source of grief. No one is free from some care, so tell me about any pressing need which you may have." Ṭāhir said, "O Commander of the Faithful, Muḥammad b. Abī al-ʿAbbās has committed a fault, so please pardon his error and show your favor to him." The Caliph replied, "I have this moment received him back into my favor, I have ordered gifts to be awarded to him and I have restored to him his former position. Moreover, were it not for the fact that he is not the sort of per-

---

321. *Nabīdh* is properly any intoxicating drink fermented from anything but grapes; only the Ḥanafī law school regarded the drinking of it as licit in certain circumstances; see *EI*[1] s.v. (Wensinck); *EI*[2] Khamr. 1 (Wensinck).

son suitable for convivial sessions, I would summon him here to court."

Bishr continued: Ṭāhir went away, and told Ibn Abī al-ʿAbbās about all this. He summoned Hārūn b. Jabghūyah[322] and said to him, "The secretaries have a feeling of mutual professional interest, and the Khurasanians [that is, the military] always stick together and support each other. So take with you three hundred thousand dirhams, and give the eunuch al-Ḥusayn two hundred thousand and his secretary Muḥammad b. Hārūn one hundred thousand, and ask al-Ḥusayn to ask al-Ma'mūn why he was weeping." Bishr relates: He accordingly did that. He continued: When the Caliph had eaten his morning meal, he said, "O [al-] Ḥusayn, pour out a drink for me!" The latter replied, "No, by God, I won't let you have anything to drink unless you tell me why you wept when Ṭāhir came into your presence." Al-Ma'mūn replied, "O [al-] Ḥusayn, why are you so concerned about this, to the point that you have questioned me about it?" He said, "Because of your own grief about that." Al-Ma'mūn replied, "O [al-] Ḥusayn, it is a matter concerning which, if it goes beyond your mouth [literally, "head"], I shall kill you." Al-Ḥusayn said, "O my lord, when did I ever divulge any of your confidences?" Al-Ma'mūn said, "I called to mind my brother Muḥammad [al-Amīn] and the humiliation which he suffered; the tears suffocated me, and I only found release in copious weeping. But Ṭāhir will not escape that from me which he will find unpleasant [because vengeance on him is still due from al-Amīn's killing.]" [1042]

Bishr continued: [Al-] Ḥusayn passed on this information to Ṭāhir. Ṭāhir rode off to Aḥmad b. Abī Khālid and said to him, "Praise addressed to me is not accounted of low value, and a useful act done for me is never wasted. So get me away from the Caliph's gaze [that is, from his possible vengeance]." He re-

---

322. Following the correct reading of this name or title in the *Addenda et emendenda*, p. DCCLXVIII, and in Ibn Abī Ṭāhir, 31. This Hārūn must have been of Turkish extraction, perhaps a descendent of the pre-Islamic Yabghus, or rulers of Ṭukhāristān, on the upper Oxus; see Bosworth and Sir Gerard Clauson, "Al-Xwārazmī on the peoples of Central Asia," *JRAS* (1965), 9–10. In Iṣfahānī, *Aghānī*, XIV, 37, Hārūn is described as a "senior Khurasanian, shrewd and trustworthy."

torted, "I will certainly do that, so come back to me first thing tomorrow morning." Bishr continued: Ibn Abī Khālid rode off to al-Ma'mūn, and when he went into his presence, he said to the Caliph, "I never slept at all last night." Al-Maʿmūn said, "Why was that, you poor fellow?" Ibn Abī Khālid replied, "Because you have appointed Ghassān as governor over Khurasan, and he and his following are weak in numbers. I am afraid lest there be an outbreak of Turkish rebels against him, and they will annihilate him."[323] Al-Ma'mūn said, "You have been thinking on the same lines as myself.[324] Whom do you think is suitable?" He replied, "Ṭāhir b. al-Ḥusayn." The Caliph exclaimed, "I am surprised at you, O Aḥmad; Ṭāhir is, by God, a person who will throw off his obedience [*khalīʿ*]." Aḥmad b. Abī Khālid said, "I will stand guarantor for his loyalty." Al-Ma'mūn said, "Send him forth, then." Bishr continued: So Aḥmad summoned Ṭāhir immediately. Al-Ma'mūn appointed
[1043] him to the command, and Ṭāhir departed instantly.[325] He encamped in the garden of Khalīl b. Hāshim,[326] and every day he remained there a hundred thousand (dirhams) were brought to him. He stayed there for a month, and a total of ten million (dirhams) which were regularly brought for the governor of Khurasan, was brought to him.[327]

Abū Ḥassān al-Ziyādī says: Ṭāhir had been granted Khurasan and Jibāl, from Ḥulwān to (the far borders of) Khurasan, and his departure from Baghdad was on Friday, the twenty-ninth of

---

323. For Ghassān's governorship in Khurasan, see Barthold, *Turkestan*, 208–10; Bosworth, *Sīstān*, 101–2. Ghassān in fact restored order there after a period of disturbance on al-Ma'mūn's departure from Marw, and among other things, appointed members of the Sāmānid family to local governorships. The fears expressed of the Turks doubtless reflect the help given by them to the rebellion in al-Rashīd's reign of Rāfiʿ b. Layth, see Barthold, op. cit., 200–1.

324. Following Keller's vocalization of Ibn Abī Ṭāhir's parallel text, 32 ll. 4–5, rather than that of Ṭabarī's text; the respective meanings amount to the same in any case.

325. *ʿUyūn*, 360–1.

326. Apparently to be identified with the suburb (*rabaḍ*) of Khalīl b. Hāshim al-Bāwardī mentioned by Yaʿqūbī, *Buldān*, 247, tr. G. Wiet, *Les pays*, 27.

327. Ibn Abī Ṭāhir, 28–32, tr. 13–15; Iṣfahānī, *Aghānī*, XIV, 37–8. The arithmetic here seems strange.

Dhū al-Qaʿdah, 205[328](May 6, 821), he having established his encampment[329] two months previously and having remained in his camp continuously. Abū Ḥassān continued: The reason for Ṭahir's appointment as governor, according to the generally-accepted view of people, was that ʿAbd al-Raḥmān al-Muṭṭawwiʿī gathered together forces in Naysābūr with the intention of using them to fight the Ḥarūriyyah[330] but without the governor of Khurasan's permission. People were afraid that this was because of some secret plan or intention which he had worked towards.[331] Ghassān b. ʿAbbād was acting as governor of Khurasan at that time, having been nominated by al-Ḥasan b. Sahl, Ghassān being the paternal cousin of al-Faḍl b. Sahl.[332]

It is mentioned from ʿAlī b. Hārūn that, before Ṭāhir b. al-Ḥusayn's departure for Khurasan and his assumption of the governorship over it, al-Ḥasan b. Sahl urged him to go out and fight Nasr b. Shabath, but Ṭāhir replied, "Have I made war on a caliph, and have I handed over the caliphate to [another] caliph, that I should be given such an order as this? It is only fitting that you should send one of my subordinate commanders for a task like this!"[333] This was the reason for the breach between al-Ḥasan and Ṭāhir. He continued to relate: Ṭāhir set out for

---

328. Actually a Monday; according to Ibn Abī Ṭāhir, 54, tr. 25, Ṭāhir departed on Sunday, the twenty-ninth of Dhū al-Qaʿdah.

329. Or: "he having gathered together his troops," *wa-qad kāna ʿaskara.*

330. Since al-Rashīd's reign, Khurasan and Sīstān had been disturbed by a prolonged Khārijite rebellion under Ḥamzah b. Adharak (died in 213 [828]), and in the past ʿAbd al-Raḥmān had fought the Khārijites in Sīstān; see Bosworth, *Sīstān*, 91–102.

331. The phrase is problematical; it reads, *li-aṣlin ʿamila ʿalayhi.*

332. Ibn Abī Ṭāhir, 32–3, tr. 15; Yaʿqūbī, *Taʾrīkh*, II, 554–5; id., *Buldān*, 307, tr. 136–7, both with the different account of Ṭāhir's appointment as being the result of his friend Aḥmad b. Abī Khālid's intrigue. The divergent accounts on Ṭāhir's appointment and his subsequent act of rebelliousness, seen especially sharply in the account of Yaʿqūbī on one side and that of Ibn Abī Ṭāhir and Ṭabarī on the other, but with significant items of information from further sources, are discussed by Sourdel, "Les circonstances de la mort de Ṭāhir Ier au Ḫurāsān en 207/822," *Arabica*, V (1958), 66–9. It seems likely that Aḥmad b. Abī Khālid, known to have been corruptible and perhaps suborned by Ṭāhir, forged a letter of resignation from his governorship by Ghassān; see Sourdel, *Vizirat*, I, 222–3.

333. Ibn al-Athīr, *al-Kāmil*, VI, 360–2.

[1044] Khurasan as soon as he assumed the governorship, without speaking to al-Ḥasan b. Sahl at all. People reproached him for that, but he replied, "I am not the man to offer a solution to a difficulty [literally, to untie a knot] which he has made for me in his hostility."

In this year, ʿAbdallah b. Ṭāhir reached Baghdad, having returned from Raqqah. His father Ṭāhir had appointed him there as his deputy and had commanded him to make war against Naṣr b. Shabath. Yaḥyā b. Muʿādh arrived, and al-Ma'mūn appointed him governor of the Jazīrah.[334]

In this year, al-Ma'mūn appointed ʿĪsā b. Muḥammad b. Abī Khālid governor of Armenia and Azerbaijan, with responsibility for the war against Bābak.[335]

In this year, al-Sarī b. al-Ḥakam, governor in Egypt, died there.[336]

In this year, Dāwūd b. Yazīd (b. Ḥātim al-Muhallabī), governor and financial administrator (*ʿāmil*) in Sind, died. Hence al-Ma'mūn appointed as governor there Bishr b. Dāwūd (al-Muhallabī), with the stipulation that he should deliver to the Caliph a million dirhams each year.[337]

In this year, al-Ma'mūn appointed ʿĪsā b. Yazīd al-Julūdī to combat the Zuṭṭ.[338]

In this year, Ṭāhir b. al-Ḥusayn set out for Khurasan in Dhū al-Qaʿdah (205[April–May 821]).[339] He remained (in his encampment) for two months until news of ʿAbd al-Raḥmān al-Naysābūrī al-Muṭṭawwiʿī's outbreak (*khurūj*) at Naysābūr

334. Yaʿqūbī, *Ta'rīkh*, II, 554; *ʿUyūn*, 363; Ibn al-Athīr, VI, 362.

335. *ʿUyūn*, 361; Ibn al-Athīr, *al-Kāmil*, loc. cit.

336. Ibid. Al-Sarī had been appointed governor in 200 (816); see Kindī, 161.

337. Ibn al-Athīr, *al-Kāmil*, loc. cit. Bishr remained governor, as his father's successor, till Ghassān b. ʿAbbād was appointed in 213 (828/9), see below, 179–80.

338. Ibid. The Zuṭṭ were peoples from Sind, Jhats and others, established on the Persian Gulf shores since Sāssānid times. The revolt of these Zuṭṭ in the marshlands of lower Iraq was not suppressed till 220 (835); see Pellat, *Le milieu baṣrien*, 37–40; *EI*[1] s.v. Zoṭṭ (G. Ferrand).

339. Cf. Ibn Abī Ṭāhir, 33, 54, tr. 15, 25.

reached him, and then he left. The Toghuz-Oghuz[340] arrived in Ushrūsanah.[341]

In this year, Faraj (b. Ziyād) al-Rukhkhajī[342] seized ʿAbd al-Raḥmān b. ʿAmmār al-Naysābūrī.

In this year, ʿUbaydallāh b. al-Ḥasan (b. ʿUbaydallāh b. ʿAbbās b. ʿAlī), governor of the two Holy Cities, led the pilgrimage.[343]

---

340. A Turkish people of Inner Asia, from whom the Seljuqs were later to arise and who were at this time harrying the fringes of Islamic Transoxiana and assisting rebels there; see Barthold, *Turkestan*, 200–2; Bosworth, *The Ghaznavids, their empire in Afghanistan and eastern Iran*, 210 ff.; *EI*[1] s.v. Toghuzghuz (Barthold); *EI*[2] s.v. Ghuzz. i. Muslim East (Cahen).

341. The region of Transoxiana to the south of the southermost bend of the Syr Darya; see Le Strange, *Lands*, 474–6; Barthold, *Turkestan*, 165–9.

342. A mawlā, originally captured in Sīstān and overseer of the caliphal private domains under Aḥmad b. Abī Khālid; see Bosworth, *Sīstān*, 82–3; Crone, 190.

343. Khalīfah, *Taʾrīkh*, II, 768; Azdī, 359; Ibn al-Athīr, *al-Kāmil*, VI, 362.

The Events of the Year 206

(JUNE 6, 821–MAY 26, 822)

The events taking place during this year included al-Ma'mūn's
[1045] appointment of Dāwūd b. Bānījūr[344] to be in charge of the war against the Zuṭṭ and to be governor of the provinces of Baṣrah, the Tigris districts, Yamāmah and Baḥrayn.[345]

In this year, there occurred the high tide which inundated the Sawād, Kaskar, the land-grant (*qaṭīʿah*) of Umm Jaʿfar and the land-grant of al-ʿAbbās and carried away the greater part of (the topsoil of) them.[346]

In this year, Bābak defeated (literally: cast down) ʿĪsā b. Muḥammad b. Abī Khālid.[347]

In this year, al-Ma'mūn appointed ʿAbdallāh b. Ṭāhir governor of Raqqah with the task of combatting Naṣr b. Shabath and Muḍar.[348]

---

344. Following the reading of the *Addenda et emendanda*, p. DCCLXIX. Dāwūd was apparently a member of the Bānījūrid or Abū Dāwūdid family, later governors of Ṭukhāristān; see *EI*[2] Suppl. s.v. Bānīdjūrids (Bosworth).

345. Ibn al-Athīr, *al-Kāmil*, VI, 379.

346. Azdī, 362; Ibn al-Athīr, *al-Kāmil*, loc. cit.

347. Ibid.

348. Yaʿqūbī, *Ta'rīkh*, II, 555; Azdī, 359; *ʿUyūn*, 362, 363. The North Arabian tribal group of Muḍar (on which see *EI*[1] Suppl. s.v. Rabīʿa and Muḍar [Kindermann]) provided much of Naṣr's support.

Al-Ma'mūn Appoints 'Abdallāh b. Ṭahīr Governor of Raqqah

According to what is mentioned, the reason for this was that al-Ma'mūn had appointed Yaḥyā b. Mu'ādh as governor of the Jazīrah, but then he died in this year, having appointed as successor in his governorship there his own son Aḥmad. It is mentioned from Yaḥyā b. al-Ḥasan b. 'Abd al-Khāliq that al-Ma'mūn summoned 'Abdallāh b. Ṭāhir during the month of Ramaḍān (January–February 822)—some say, however, that this was in the year 205 (820/1), others in the year (200) odd, and yet others in the year (20)7 (822/3). When 'Abdallāh came into his presence, al-Ma'mūn said, "O 'Abdallāh, I have been seeking guidance from God for a month now, and I hope that God is leading me to the right decision. I have observed a man describing his son's characteristics in order to praise the son in glowing terms, because of his own high opinion of him; and in order to exalt his status; but I have noted that you are actually better than your father's description of you. Now Yaḥyā b. Mu'ādh has died, and has appointed as his successor his son Aḥmad b. Yaḥyā, who is a nonentity. I have therefore considered it fit to appoint you governor over Muḍar and the conduct of the war against Naṣr b. Shabath." 'Abdallāh replied, "I hear and obey, O Commander of the Faithful, and I hope that God will vouchsafe His favor for the Commander of the Faithful and the Muslims!"[349]

Yaḥya continues: The Caliph invested him with the insignia of office, and then he ordered the drying lines of the fullers impeding 'Abdallāh's way to be taken down and the awnings against the sunlight to be removed from the streets so that there should be nothing which would catch on 'Abdallāh's banner as he went along them. Then, as part of the insignia of office he presented 'Abdallāh with a banner, which had as its legend, written in gold letters, the wording usually written on banners, to which he further added the phrase "O victorious one [*yā Manṣūr*]!"[350] 'Abdallāh went forth with his retinue and [1046]

349. Ibn Abī Ṭāhir, 34, tr. 16; Ibn al-Athīr, *al-Kāmil*, VI, 363.
350. On the *shi'ār* or *da'wah* "rallying cry in battle," such as this, see Gold-

arrived at his house. The next morning, a host of people rode along to visit him, including al-Faḍl b. al-Rabīʿ. The latter remained with him till nightfall and then got up to go. ʿAbdallāh said, "O Abū al-ʿAbbās, you have been generous and kind, and both my own father and your brother have adjured me not to decide any great matters without your advice. I need to know your views, and I need to find guidance through your good counsels. If you think it possible to remain here in my house till we can break the fast,[351] then please stay!" Al-Faḍl replied to him, "Various circumstances render it impossible for me to break my fast here." ʿAbdallāh said, "If you don't like the cuisine of the Khurasanians, then send along to your own kitchen and they will bring you your usual food." Al-Faḍl told him, "I have to perform several cycles of inclinations between the evening worship and complete darkness." So ʿAbdallāh retorted, "Go, with God's protection!" and went along with him as far as the courtyard of his (al-Faḍl's) house, seeking his advice on various private matters.[352]

Ṭāhir's Advice to his Son

It is said that ʿAbdallāh's actual departure for (the lands of) Muḍar[353] in order to combat Nasr b. Shabath took place six months after his father's departure for Khurasan. When Ṭāhir appointed his son ʿAbdallāh over Diyār Rabīʿah,[354] he sent him an epistle, whose text is as follows:

> Let there be in you the fear of God, He who is one and without associate. Hold Him in awe and reverence and avert his wrath. Look after the interests of your subjects.

---

ziher, *Muhammedanische Studien*, I, 60–3, Eng. tr. *Muslim Studies*, I, 63–5; M. Hinds, "The banners and battle cries of the Arabs at Ṣiffīn (657 AD)," *al-Abḥāth*, XXIV (1971), 12–16.

351. The month being Ramaḍān.

352. Ibn Abī Ṭāhir, 34–5, tr. 16.

353. Diyār Muḍar was the region of the Jazīrah along the middle Euphrates and its tributaries, the lower Khābūr and Balīkh, with Raqqah as its centre; see Le Strange, *Lands*, 101 ff.; Canard, 86–97; *EI*² s.v. (Canard—Cahen).

354. The eastern part of the Jazīrah, centred on Mosul; see Le Strange, *Lands*, 86 ff.; Canard, 97–131; *EI*² s.v. (Canard—Cahen).

Hold fast to all the good fortune which God has bestowed on you, at the same time remembering the ultimate destination [the return to God for judgment] towards which you are inevitably travelling, the duties to which you are obligated and for which you will be held responsible. [Take [1047]
care] to labor at everything in such a way that God will ensure your preservation and will keep you safe from His punishment and painful retribution on the Day of Resurrection.

God has been gracious to you and has accordingly made it incumbent upon you to show tenderness towards those of His creatures over whom He has appointed you shepherd. He has enjoined you to behave justly with them, to maintain His divine truth and His prescribed punishments [*ḥudūd*] amongst them, to protect them, to defend their womenfolk and kindred [*ḥarīmihim wa-bayḍatihim*], to preserve them from bloodshed, to keep the roads safe for them and to create the peaceful conditions in which they can go about their daily work. He holds you fully responsible for all the things enumerated above, whose observance has been laid upon you; He will require from you a reckoning concerning them, will question you about them and will recompense you for the good acts which you have committed and the evil acts which you have refrained from. So let your thoughts, your mind, your sharp-sightedness and your vision be entirely concentrated on these things, and let no one distract or divert you from them; for all this is the basic foundation of your authority and the fundamental support of your ruling position, and is the first thing which God bestows on you for guiding you along the right path.

Now the first thing which you must impose on yourself, and the goal towards which your actions should dispose you, is assiduous observance of the ritual prescriptions laid down by God as mandatory—the five daily acts of worship [*ṣalawāt*], and the assembling of the people together for worship with you at the appointed times and after due performance of the ritual ablutions [*wuḍū'*] required by the religious law. You must begin the ceremony

with the mention of God's name; you must use the correct chant as you recite the words of the worship; you must perform the inclinations and prostrations involved firmly and decisively and pronounce the profession of faith clearly. Also, let your intention in performing the worship be sincere in the sight of your Lord. Furthermore, urge
[1048] those in your retinue and under your command to be assiduous in attendance and always show keenness yourself, for as God says, the worship urges people to what is reputable and restrains [them] from what is disreputable.[355]

You must then follow this up by firm adherence to the practices [*sunan*] laid down by the Messenger of God and by perseverance in imitating his [noble] qualities, and you must imitate the examples left by the Prophet's successors, the virtuous early generation of Muslims [*al-salaf al-ṣāliḥ*]. Whenever you are faced with some problem, seek help over it by desiring God's favor, by showing piety to Him, by adhering to what He has ordained or prohibited, made lawful or forbidden, as revealed in His Book, and by following the trail indicated by the traditions from the Prophet; then act in this matter in accordance with the duties which you owe to God.

Do not incline away from justice according to your own likes and dislikes in favor of someone near to you or someone far away, but choose to be guided by the religious law [*fiqh*] and its practitioners, by religion and its exponents the theologians, and by the Book of God and those who act by it; for the greatest adornments which a man can have are a thorough knowledge of the religion of God, a searching desire for it, a zeal in urging others to follow it and a knowledge of that part of it by which a man is brought closer to God. Indeed, this thorough knowledge guides the way towards all that is good and is the leader thither; it ordains man towards good and restrains people from all acts of rebellion against God and from sins entailing perdition. By means of this, and with the help of God's favor, His ser-

355. Cf. Qur'ān, XXIX, 44/45, and XXXI, 16/17.

vants increase in knowledge of Him, in glorifying Him and in following the right path towards the highest stages in man's journey back to God [*maʿād*, after the Resurrection]. All this in addition to what becomes apparent of the people's regard for your rule, their respect for your authority, their close bond with you and their trust in your justice.

Be careful to observe moderation [*iqtiṣād, qaṣd*][356] in all things, for there is nothing of more obvious value, nothing more conducive to personal security and nothing containing within itself so many merits, as moderation. Moderation is one of the forces predisposing towards right guidance, and right guidance is a guide towards divine fa- [1049]
vor and success; and this last, in turn, leads the way to happiness. Moreover, moderation is a supporting prop for religion and for those usages handed down from the Prophet by which men are guided. So choose moderation as your watchword in all affairs of your present life. Do not, however, fall short in your pursuit of the next world and a heavenly reward, in performing meritorious works, in following the accepted ways of virtuous behavior and in seeking out the waymarks towards righteousness. For the endeavor to increase in piety and the pursuit of good works can have no bounds when God's grace and approval, and the companionship of His saints in the abode of divine felicity, are being sought through them.

Know that moderation in the things of this world brings one increased prestige and preserves one from sinfulness. There is nothing more excellent than moderation as a protection for yourself and your intimates or as a force to improve and put right your affairs. So adopt it as a rule of life, and let yourself be guided by it; if you do, your affairs will all reach satisfactory completion, your power will increase, and both your personal circle of friends and the people in general [or: your personal affairs and public affairs] will benefit from it.

356. These terms here clearly mean "moderation, prudence, circumspection," the golden mean of the Greeks, and Ṭāhir is here echoing Aristotle in urging it as the foundation for all right conduct; see Bosworth, "An early Arabic Mirror for Princes," *JNES*, XXIX (1970), 28.

Keep your mind fixed on God's favor; if you do, your subjects will behave towards you in an honest and upright fashion. In all your affairs, seek to bring yourself closer to God; through this policy, His grace will be vouchsafed to you perpetually. Do not take action against anyone for some offence committed in the official position to which you have appointed him before you have investigated the matter under suspicion, since it is a crime to let suspicions and evil thoughts come down upon innocent people. Adopt as a conscious policy a favorable attitude towards your associates, and set aside and repudiate malevolent thoughts about them. This will assist you in attaching them firmly to your own interest and in managing them. Do not allow Satan, the enemy of God, to be able to find some defect in your conduct. He only needs [to become
[1050] aware of] a minor weakness, and he will be able to introduce an element of grief into your mind through your acquiring a bad opinion [of those around you] which will make the sweetness of life bitter for you.

Know that, in holding a favorable attitude towards people, you will find a source of strength and contentment of mind, and through it you will be able to bring to a satisfactory conclusion any of your affairs you wish; you may also use it to make people love you and behave honestly in all their dealings with you. However, this good opinion of your associates and this tenderness towards your subjects should not prevent you from making use of enquiries and investigations into the way in which your affairs are being conducted, from personally supervising the actions of your agents, from protecting the interests of your subjects and from looking into whatever may be conducive to their welfare and happiness. Indeed, personal supervision of your agents' activities, protection of your subjects' interests, investigation into their needs and shouldering their burdens should be preferred by you over everything else, for they will have more effect in strengthening religion and in breathing life into the *sunna*. Let your intentions in all this be pure; concentrate your efforts on self-reformation, in the same way as does a person who realizes that he will be held responsible for everything which he does, will be recompensed for his good deeds and will be punished for his bad ones. God has made His faith a sure refuge and a source of strength; He exalts those who follow Him and raises them in dignity. Hence lead those over whom you rule, and act as shepherd in the path of true religion and the way of divine guidance!

Be swift to apply the penalties prescribed by God [*ḥudūd*], to criminals, according to their positions in society and according to their deserts. Do not neglect this duty, and do not treat it lightly or be laggardly in punishing those deserving punishment, because if you fall short in this duty, you will surely damage your good reputation in people's eyes. In this matter, always stick determinedly to the well-established practices [*sunan*]. If you avoid all dubious courses and innovations [*al-shubah wa-al-bidaʿāt*], your faith will be preserved unsullied and your nobility of character [*muruwwah*] will be kept intact.

When you make an agreement with someone, keep to it; and when you promise to perform some good deed, make [1051] sure that you fulfill it. Accept a favor gracefully and return it. Close your eyes to the minor shortcomings of petty offenders among your subjects; guard your tongue against uttering falsehood and calumny and show your detestation of those who practice this vice. Banish from your presence all slanderers, because the prime factor which will vitiate your present life and your future one is the encouragement of a notorious liar or a shameless disposition towards lying yourself. Mendacity, indeed, is the beginning of all sins, and calumny and slander set the seal on them. For the person who manufactures slander is not safe himself; nor is any friend of a man who listens to slander[357] safe; and nothing will go right for the person who acts in accordance with slander.

Make friends of the people of sincerity and righteous-

357. Reading *qābiluhā* for the text's *qāʾiluhā*, as according to F. Rosenthal, *The Muqaddimah, an introduction to history*, II, 145, n. 760.

ness. Give succor to the aristocracy [*al-ashrāf*] by allotting them their just due; give material help to the weak; and strengthen the bonds of kinship. In all these things desire the face of God and the strengthening of His power; through them seek a heavenly reward from Him and the abode of eternal life. Shun evil thoughts and oppressive behavior, deflecting your mind completely from them, and demonstrate openly to your subjects your freedom from these defects. Let your rule over them be graced with the exercise of justice; govern them with due equity and with the knowledge which will lead you on the way of divine guidance. Keep a grip on your temper when you are angry, and adopt rather the attitudes of forbearance and magnanimity. Take care not to succumb to hasty temper, frivolous behavior and deception in anything you undertake. Also, take care that you do not say to yourself, "I have been set in authority, I shall do what I like," because that will speedily destroy your judgment, and it further shows a lack of firm belief in God, He who is one and without associate. Make pure to God your intentions in this and your firm belief in Him!

Know that royal authority belongs to God alone; He be-
[1052] stows it upon whom He wills and takes it away from whom He wills. You will not find His favors towards anyone change more completely, nor His vengeance descend more swiftly, than in regard to those holders of power and those set in authority who have been the recipients of His favor, but have shown ingratitude towards God's bounty and benevolence, and who have adopted a high and mighty attitude because of the goodness which He has bestowed on them.[358]

Lay aside any avariciousness which may be in your heart. Let the treasuries and storehouses which you pile up

358. Or: who have used oppressively that which He of His goodness has bestowed on them, *wa-staṭālū bi-mā ātāhum Allāh min faḍlihi*. Keller translated the corresponding passage of Ibn Abī Ṭāhir, 42, tr. 19, "[wenn sie] . . . das, was ihnen Gott in seiner Freigebigkeit verleiht, für ewig halten." The lexica support all these various meanings for *istaṭāla*; see *Lisān al-ʿArab*[1], XIII, 438, and *Tāj al-ʿarūs*[1], VII, 422–3.

and accumulate be composed of piety, fear of God, justice, measures for your subjects' welfare and the prosperity of their land, acquaintance with their affairs, protection for the mass of them and assistance for those who sorrow. Know that wealth which is accumulated and then stored away in treasuries bears no fruit; but when it is expended on the improvement of the conditions of subjects, on the provision of their just dues and on removing burdens from them, it thrives and multiplies. As a result, the common people derive benefit from it, the governors bask in reflected glory from it, the whole age is made bright by it, and strength and defensive power are consolidated through it. Consequently, let the accumulated wealth of your treasuries be expended on making the world of Islam and its populace more prosperous. Further, allot part of it for what is due to those of the Commander of the Faithful's officials who preceded you[359]; and utilise another part of it to fulfill the just claims of your subjects, paying close heed to what will improve their general state and conditions of life. If you do all this, God's favor will be vouchsafed to you and you will have merited an increased reward from Him. Moreover, you will find that all these things will facilitate your levying the land-tax [*jibāyat kharājika*] and your collecting the taxes in kind from your subjects and from the regions under your control [*jamʿ amwāl raʿiyyatika wa-ʿamalika*]. Because of your all-encompassing justice and benevolent rule, the whole of [1053] these will be more obedient to your authority and will be more complaisant towards whatever you desire of them. So strive to the best of your ability to achieve what I have delineated for you under this heading, and let your esteem for it be great; for the only wealth which endures forever is that which is expended in furtherance of God's just dues.[360]

359. Following the preference of Rosenthal, op. cit., II, 146 and n. 766, for *qablaka* rather than the text's *qibalaka*.

360. On the ruler's or governor's relations with his officials and tax collectors, a constant preoccupation of the writers of Mirrors for Princes, see Bosworth, op. cit., 28–9.

Acknowledge the gratitude of those who show thanks and recompense them appropriately for it. Beware lest this present world and its deceptions make you forget due fear for the next world, so that you treat lightly your obligations in this connection; because this insouciance will inevitably breed neglectfulness, and neglectfulness will lead to ruin. Let all your work be undertaken for God and have its being in Him, and hope only for reward. Indeed, it is He who has lavished on you His beneficence in this present world and has shown His grace to you. Accordingly, make yourself secure by showing proper gratitude; trust in Him, and He will increase your share of His goodness and benevolence. God rewards people according to the measure of their gratitude [to Him] and according to the conduct of those who act righteously; He has judged rightfully in regard to the good things which He has brought and the good fortune and exalted status which He has conferred.

Do not treat any sinful deed [*dhanb*] lightly; do not incline towards the envious person; do not show mercy towards the evildoer; do not give presents to an ungrateful person;[361] do not hold culpable relations with [or: treat gently] an enemy; do not give credence to a slanderer; do not trust a treacherous person; do not make friends with an evil-liver; do not follow after someone who will lead you into error; do not give praise to a hypocrite; do not treat any man with contempt; do not send away empty-handed a destitute beggar; do not deign to bandy words with a foolish person; do not pay attention to a buffoon; do not go back on your promises; do not show respect for overweening pride;[362] do not undertake anything while in a state of
[1054] anger; do not go forth exhibiting haughtiness; do not walk along showing an unseemly hilarity [or:displaying arrogance]; do not commit an act of stupidity; do not fall short in your pursuit of the next life; do not pass the days in an

---

361. *Wa-lā taṣilanna kafūran*; Keller's translation in Ibn Abī Ṭāhir, 43, tr. 20, "tritt nicht in Verbindung mit dem Ungläubigen," hardly fits here.
362. Following the *fakhr*[an] of Ibn Abī Ṭāhir, 44, tr. 20, instead of the text's *fajr*[an].

unthankful manner;[363] do not avert your eyes from someone who is behaving tyrannically, either from respect for him or out of fear; and do not seek the rewards of the next world by means of this present life.

Make a habit of consulting the scholars of the religious law [*fuqahā'*] as much as possible, and when exercising your will, show forbearance [*ḥilm*].[364] Learn from people with experience of the world and from people with intelligence, judgment and wisdom. Do not allow into your counsels contemptible and stingy people, and never pay heed to their words, for they will do you more harm than good. There is nothing more likely to bring to disaster any course of action regarding your subjects which you may embark upon than avarice. For know that if you are avaricious, you will want to grab everything and give nothing. If you behave thus, your rule will not go right for very long. Your subjects will only have confidence in your benevolence in as much as you refrain from arbitrary exactions on their wealth and avoid tyrannizing over them, and your subordinates will only remain sincerely devoted to your interests as long as you give them adequate allowances and good pay. Therefore shun avarice, and know that avariciousness was the first act of rebellion raised by man against his Lord, and that the abode of the rebel against God is that of abasement and disgrace, according to what God says [in His Book]; "Those who are protected from niggardliness of soul, they are the ones who prosper."[365] So be really generous. Grant to all the Muslims a share and allotment from the revenue of your captured plunder,[366] and

363. Following the *ʿabām*^{an}. of Ibn Abī Ṭāhir, loc. cit., instead of the text's *ʿiyān*^{an}. Ibn al-Athīr, *al-Kāmil*, VI, 370, has *ʿitāb*^{an}, "in finding fault," which is favored in the *Addenda et emendanda*, p. DCCLXX.

364. The ensemble of qualities which made up *ḥilm*—restraint, moderation, conciliatoriness, statecraft, magnanimity, etc.—were regarded by the early Arabs as the highest attributes for the successful leader; see Bosworth, op. cit., 28, and *EI*^{2} s.v. (Pellat).

365. Qur'ān, LIX, 9, LXIV, 16.

366. Following the reading preferred in the *Addenda et emendanda*, p. DCCLXX.

be sure that liberality is one of the most meritorious acts
[1055] of which God's creatures are capable. Account it as one of your virtues, and regard it with constant favor in your work and practice.

Maintain close supervision of the affairs of your army, the soldiers' pay registers and the government departments concerned with military matters. See that they have adequate salaries and be generous in their living allowances; by this means, God will take away their neediness. Their happy condition will become a source of strength for you, and their hearts will increase by means of it in sincerity and contentedness, in obedience to you and attachment to your cause. It is sufficient felicitousness for a ruler that his army and his subjects should find compassion in his equitable conduct, his protection, his exercise of justice, his concern for people, his solicitude, his benevolent works and his open-handedness. Avoid the unpleasantness of either of the two ways[367] [of erring on the sides of harshness or leniency] by being conscious of the merits of the other alternative and by always acting in accordance with it. You will then, God willing, achieve worldly success, spiritual merit and personal happiness.

Know that the judge's office [*qaḍā'*] enjoys in God's sight an importance exceeding all others. This is because it is God's balance, by means of which the affairs on earth are regulated. When justice prevails in the judge's office and in judicial procedure, the subjects' welfare is assured, the highways are kept safe, those who have been wronged are given just recompense, people receive their due rights, people's ways of life become pleasant and rightful obedience is freely vouchsafed. God gives provision for happiness and preservation of life, religion is firmly maintained, the *sunna* and the religious law are put into practice and, on the basis of their effectiveness, truth and justice are successfully achieved in the judge's office.

---

367. Following the reading preferred in the *Addenda et emendanda*, p. DCCLXX.

Be zealous in carrying on God's work and refrain from corrupt behavior; be assiduous in applying the obligatory legal penalties for offences; never be overhasty in doing things; avoid becoming vexed and disturbed in your mind; and be content with a [moderate] share.[368] In this fashion, your successfulness will be undisturbed and your good fortune firmly established. Profit by your past experience; concentrate your thoughts while you are silent, and then when you speak be cogent and to the point. Be fair to the plaintiff; pause when you are in doubt, but exert yourself in bringing forward relevant evidence. Do not let partiality, claims to protection or fear of anyone's blame sway you in any dealings with one of your subjects. Instead, act with patience and deliberation; keep your eyes open and watch carefully; consider, reflect and ponder over things; adopt an attitude of humility towards your Lord and of clemency towards all your subjects. Make the pursuit of righteousness the dominating principle of your personal conduct and do not hasten to spill blood, for God regards bloodshed all the more seriously when it is spilt with violence and injustice. [1056]

Look carefully into this matter of the land-tax, which the subjects have the obligation to pay.[369] God has made this a source of strength and might for Islam, and a means of support and protection for His people; but He has made it a source of chagrin and vexation for His enemies and the enemies of the Muslims, and for the unbelievers in treaty relationship with the Muslims[370] a source of abasement

---

368. Keller in his translation of Ibn Abī Ṭāhir, 46, tr. 21, interprets the *q.s.m.* of his text and that of Ṭabarī here as *qism*, "begnüge dich mit dem Teile"; Rosenthal, *The Muqaddimah*, II, 149, interprets it as *qasam*, "be satisfied with an oath."

369. From what follows, *kharāj* here seems to have the wide definition so as to include the *jizyah*, normally interpreted as "poll-tax;" concerning the common confusion of terminology here, see Bosworth, op. cit., 37, n. 2.

370. *Ahl al-kufr min muʿāhadatihim*, i.e., the "protected peoples" or Dhimmīs.

and humiliation.[371] Apportion it amongst the taxpayers with justice and fairness, and with equal treatment and universal applicability for all. Do not remove any part of the obligation to pay land-tax from any noble person just because of his nobility; nor from any rich person on account of his richness; nor from any of your secretaries or personal retainers. Do not require from anyone more than he can bear, and do not exact an amount which is in excess of the normal rate.[372] Impose taxation on all the people in an equitable manner, for that is more likely to attach them to your interests and more certain to make the masses contented.

Know that, by your appointment as governor, you have been placed as a custodian of valuables, a watchman and a shepherd; the people in your sphere of administrative jurisdiction are only called "your flock" [*raʿiyyataka*] because you are their shepherd [*rāʿīhim*] and their overseer. Take from them that which they hand over to you from their surplus income and means of subsistence, and expend it on things which will ensure their continued mate-
[1057] rial well-being and welfare and which will provide for their burdens. Within the provinces under your control, appoint over the people officials of clear foresight and judgment, men who are well-tested and experienced in provincial government and who know when to show severity and when to show restraint [or: who know how to exercise statesmanship, *siyāsah*, and moderation]. Pay them adequate salaries, for this is one of the inescapable obligations laid upon you when you took up your governorship and when it was entrusted to your charge. Let no one distract or deflect you from this, for if you choose consciously to follow this path, and fulfill faithfully the attendant obligations, you will gain for yourself additional grace and favor

371. *Dhullᵃⁿ wa-ṣaghārᵃⁿ*, echoing Qur'ān, IX, 29/30, a phrase whose exact interpretation has been much discussed by recent scholars; see the views of Cahen, M. Bravmann and M.J. Kister in *Arabica*, IX (1962), 76–9, X (1963), 94–5, XI (1964), 272–8.

372. *Amrᵃⁿ fīhi shaṭaṭ*, echoing Qur'ān, LXXII, 4.

from your Lord and a favorable reputation within your own province; you will secure as a protection sincere advisers from amongst your people, and you will be helped in following a policy of amelioration. As a consequence, well-being [or: charitable works] will abound in your land and prosperity will be general in your territories. The land under your rule will burgeon with fertility, the yield from the land-tax will increase and your income in kind will be proportionately expanded.[373] By this means, you will be able to strengthen the bonds linking your army to you, and you will bring contentment to the masses by distributing your personal largesse to them. In following these courses your statesmanship will be acclaimed and your justice regarded with satisfaction, even by your enemies. In all your affairs you will be characterized by justice and might, and you will have the equipment and armaments of war. Strive zealously in this, and let nothing come before it; [if you do this,] the successful outcome of your affairs will receive due praise, if God wills.

In every district of your governorship, you should appoint a trusted observer [*amīn*][374] who will keep you informed of the activities of your local officials and will write to you regularly about their way of life and doings, in such a way that you will be, as it were, an eyewitness of every official's complete activities within his sphere of responsibility. If you wish to instruct an official to adopt a certain course of action, have due regard for all the consequences which you expect to follow from that. If you consider it to be a safe and wholesome course of action, and hope to find in it a useful defensive measure, wise counsel or benefit, then put it into practice. But if you find the con-

373. Or: your own personal properties/your wealth in general will become extensive, *wa-tawaffarat amwāluka*.

374. Here obviously the equivalent of the *ṣāḥib al-barīd*, postmaster and intelligence officer, of the ʿAbbāsid caliphate and of the later *mushrif al-mamlakah* of eastern Iranian states; see A. Mez, *The renaissance of Islam*, 495 ff.; Levy, *The social structure of Islam*, 299–302; *EI*² s.v. Barīd (Sourdel); Bosworth, "Abū ʿAbdallāh al-Khwārazmī on the technical terms of the secretary's art," 141–3.

[1058] trary, renounce it, and refer the matter to far-sighted and prudent experts in the question; then make proper provision for putting it into effect. For it often happens that a man examines a certain course of action in his policy and finds it agreeable, because of his personal inclinations, and this accordingly strengthens his resolve and gratifies him; but if he neglects to examine the consequences, it may lead to his destruction or ruin his whole policy.

Employ resolution in all that you purpose to do and, after obtaining God's help, set about it with vigor. Seek to discover by prayer your Lord's will in everything which you undertake. See that you finish the day's stint of work and never leave it to finish the next day. Instead, give it your personal attention, because the morrow always has its own affairs and events, which will divert you from the work left over from the previous day. You must realize that once a day is over, it carries away with it everything which was done during that day; so, when you put off the work belonging to it, you find yourself burdened with two days' work, and this will keep you occupied until you are able to turn aside from it. When you get through each day's work on the same day, you keep your mind and body fresh and at the same time you strengthen the fabric of your rule.[375]

Look to those of noble lineage and gentle birth, and then to those concerning whom you are certain[376] of the sincerity of their intentions, of the genuineness of their love for you, of their open manifestation of good counsel and their warm devotion to your rule. [When you are sure of this,] take them into your personal service and act kindly towards them. Take care of the interests of those members of good families [*ahl al-buyūtāt*] who have fallen on hard

375. This injunction to get through each day's work and not let unsolved problems pile up, is an echo of the injunction attributed to the Caliph ʿUmar b. al-Khaṭṭāb in a letter to the governor of Baṣrah, Abū Mūsā al-Ashʿarī, concerning the judge's duties; see R.B. Serjeant, "The Caliph ʿUmar's letters to Abū Mūsā al-Ashʿarī and Muʿāwiya," *JSS*, XXIX (1984), 69.

376. Following the reading of the *Addenda et emendanda*, p. DCCLXXI.

times; shoulder their burdens and improve their condition, so that they do not, in their distressed state, feel the touch of misfortune so keenly.

Devote yourself to looking after the affairs of the poor and destitute, those who are unable to bring their complaints of ill-treatment to you personally, and those of wretched estate who do not know how to set about claiming their rights. Ask about these people as discreetly as possible; appoint as agents, in this work of seeking out such oppressed persons, reliable people from among your [1059]
subjects, and give them orders to raise before you their needs and conditions, in order that you may examine them and bring such relief as God may provide for their predicaments. Turn your attention to those who have suffered injuries and to their orphans and widows, and provide them with allowances from the state treasury, following the example of the Commander of the Faithful, may God exalt him, in showing compassion for them and in giving them financial subventions, so that God may thereby bring some alleviation into their daily lives and may by means of it bring you the spiritual food of His blessing and an increase in His favor. Give pensions from the state treasury to the blind, and give to those who know the Qur'ān text by heart or the greater part of it higher allowances than to others. Set up hospices where sick Muslims can find shelter, and appoint custodians for these places who will treat the patients with kindness and physicians who will cure their illnesses. Comply with their desires, provided that this does not lead to the state treasury being thereby squandered.

Know that people, even if they are given their due rights and the greater part of their desires, will not be satisfied with these and their minds will not be at peace unless they are able to present their needs to their rulers, in the hope of getting more attention and kinder treatment from them. The man who investigates closely the people's affairs often becomes wearied by all the things which come before him, and the trouble and hardship which he undergoes in chasing them up often completely occupy his mind and thoughts. The person who seeks after justice, and who recognizes his material advantages in this present life and the superiority of the reward which he will enjoy in the next one, is not like the person who sets his face towards that which will bring him closer to God and through it seeks His mercy.[377]

Allow people access to your person as much as possible, and show your face to them as often as you can. Order your guards to treat them peaceably; be humble towards them,
[1060] and show your face of approval to them. When questioning them or speaking with them, be gentle, and grant them a share of your goodness and beneficence. Moreover, when you give, give in a generous and open-hearted manner, seeking to do a good action and to secure a future reward, and not so as to embarrass the recipient or remind him of it [in the hope of a gift or favor in return]; for a gift bestowed according to the first fashion will be regarded as a profitable transaction, if God wills.

Take careful note of everything which you observe in this present world, and consider the examples of your predecessors, the rulers and leaders of past centuries, and of nations [that have] now disappeared from the earth. Then in your affairs hold fast to God's command; keep yourself in the orbit of His love; let your actions be guided by His religious law and the examples laid down by His prophet and the successors, and maintain the supremacy of His faith and His Book. Avoid anything which departs from that or which contradicts it or which arouses[378] God's ire. Be cognizant of the amount of taxation which your officials collect, and of that which they expend of it; do not amass unlawful wealth and do not spend wealth prodigally.

Spend a lot of time with the learned scholars [*'ulamā'*]; seek their advice, and frequent their company. Your desire

---

377. I.e., the first person deserves a greater reward because he is seeking to enforce God's will, here on earth, and is not just seeking his personal salvation in isolation from the needs of this present world.

378. Following the reading of the *Addenda et emendenda*, p. DCCLXXI.

should be that of following the established practices of the faith and of putting them into action, and that of preferring [before all else] the noble and lofty aspects of affairs. The noblest person among all those who join your circle and act as your confidants should be the person who, when he discerns a fault in you, is not held back by awe of you from privately pointing out to you the defect and from telling you about the shortcoming which lies in that defect. Such persons as these are the sincerest of your intimates and supporters in giving disinterested advice.

Keep an eye on the officials at your court and on your secretaries. Allot to each of them a fixed time each day when they can bring you their official correspondence and any documents requiring the affixing of the ruler's mark,[379] and can acquaint you of the officials' various requirements and of all the affairs of your provinces and your subjects. Then devote all your faculties—ears, eyes, understanding and intellect—to the affairs of that sort which they set before you; reflect and pore over it repeatedly. Finally, put [1061] into effect those courses which seem to you to be in accordance with good judgment and justice, and seek to know God's will in them; but where they seem to be opposed to these criteria, put them off for further consideration and more enquiries.

Do not remind your subjects or anyone else, to whom you have granted a favor, about it [in expectation of a gift in return]; accept nothing from anyone except faithfulness, honest dealing and assistance to the Commander of the Faithful's interests; do not grant any favor except on this basis.

Strive to understand this epistle of mine to you; study it at length, and always use it as a guide for your actions. In all your undertakings, ask God for help and seek to know His will, for God is with every good work of righteousness

379. *Mu'āmarah*, originally a financial term, sometimes with the modern meaning of "surcharge," but one which became generalized for any file or inventory of documents requiring the ruler's or governor's signature; see Bosworth, op. cit., 126.

and with those who follow after it. Let your most important conduct and your best desire be what is pleasing to God and what brings order to His faith, strength and steadfastness to His people, and justice and righteousness both for the protected peoples and the community of the Muslims [*al-dhimma wa-al-milla*].

I myself will ask God to favor you with His aid, His help towards success, His right guidance and His safe keeping. Also, [I will ask Him] to grant you His favor and mercy through a bestowal of all His grace and generosity, so that He will make you the most fortunate of all your peers and contemporaries, the richest in possessions and the most elevated in reputation and power. Finally, [I will ask Him] to destroy your enemies, those who rise up against you and those who act wrongfully against you; to bring you prosperity from your subjects; and to keep Satan and his evil promptings away from you. As a result of this, your position will be exalted in power and might and successfulness; indeed, He is always near, always ready to answer.[380]

It is mentioned that when Ṭāhir gave this charge to his son ʿAbdallāh, people struggled amongst themselves (to get a copy), wrote it out and studied it repeatedly. Its fame spread until it reached al-Ma'mūn. He ordered a copy to be brought, and it was read out to him. He exclaimed after this, "Abū al-Ṭayyib has not mentioned anything of the matters concerning the
[1062] faith, the present world, the conduct of public affairs, judgment, statecraft, the improvement of the realm and of the subjects, the safeguarding of the Muslim community, obedience to

380. Qur'ān, XI, 64/61. For the original version of the text of this epistle of Ṭāhir's, see Ibn Abī Ṭāhir, 35–53, tr. 16–25, with an English translation also by Bosworth, "An early Arabic Mirror for Princes," 25–41; Ibn Abī Ṭāhir was of course the basis for Ṭabarī's text. Of later authors, Ibn al-Athīr, *al-Kāmil*, VI, 363–77, used Ṭabarī, and Ibn Khaldūn, tr. Rosenthal, *The Muqaddimah*, II, 139–56, French tr. V. Monteil, *Ibn Khaldûn, discours sur l'histoire universelle (al-Muqaddima)*, II, 616–31, used, according to Rosenthal, II, 139, n. 751, Ibn al-Athīr's text in the first place but revised it in the light of Ṭabarī's. On the place of Ṭāhir's epistle within the genre, see G. Richter, *Studien zur Geschichte der älteren arabischen Fürstenspiegel*, 80–5; Bosworth, op. cit., 25–30; id., "The Ṭāhirids and Arabic culture," *JSS*, XIV (1969), 55–6.

the Caliphs and maintenance of the caliphate, without in fact dealing with them thoroughly, making recommendations about them and giving instructions [for their execution]."[381] Al-Ma'mūn ordered that it should be copied out and sent to all the governors in the various districts ʿAbdallāh then set out to take up his official appointment; he modelled his conduct on that recommended in the epistle, followed its injunctions and acted in accordance with what he had been enjoined to do.[382]

In this year, ʿAbdallāh b. Ṭāhir placed Isḥāq b. Ibrāhīm (al-Muṣʿabī)[383] in charge of the two bridges[384] and appointed Isḥāq as his representative in the offices which his father Ṭāhir had (previously) made ʿAbdallāh himself his representative—the command of the guard at Baghdad and the collection of the tax revenues from there.[385] This was at the time when he set off for Raqqah in order to combat Naṣr b. Shabath.

In this year, ʿUbaydallāh b. al-Ḥasan, governor of the two Holy Cities, led the pilgrimage.[386]

---

381. Supplying, with the text of Ibn Abī Ṭayfūr, 54, *fīhi.*

382. Ibn Abī Ṭāhir, 53–4, tr. 25; Ibn al-Athīr, *al-Kāmil*, VI, 377.

383. Member of the Ṭāhirid family, first cousin of Ṭalḥah and ʿAbdallāh b. Ṭāhir, and holder of the office of governor of Baghdad till his death in 235 (849/50); see Bosworth, "The Ṭāhirids and Arabic culture," 67–8; Sourdel, *Vizirat*, I, 260, 265, 273.

384. The old and new bridges over the Tigris at Baghdad, the former dating back to Sāsānid times and the latter to al-Manṣūr; see Le Strange, *Baghdad*, 60, 91–3; Lassner, *Topography*, 101, 277.

385. See Bosworth, op. cit., 45–6.

386. Khalīfah, *Ta'rīkh*, II, 769; Azdī, 362.

The Events of the Year

207

(May 27, 822–May 15, 823)

The events taking place during this year included the rebellion of ʿAbd al-Raḥmān b. Aḥmad b. ʿAbdallāh b. Muḥammad b. ʿUmar b. ʿAlī b. Abī Ṭālib in the district of the ʿAkk[387] in the Yemen, summoning people in the name of The One Well-pleasing [to God] from the House of Muḥammad.

The Rebellion of ʿAbd al-Raḥmān

The reason for his rebellion was that the tax officials in the Yemen had behaved in an oppressive manner, so the local people gave their allegiance to this ʿAbd al-Raḥmān. When news of this reached al-Maʾmūn, he sent against him Dīnār b. ʿAbdallāh with a powerful army, and sent with him a written promise guaranteeing ʿAbd al-Raḥmān's security. Dīnār b. ʿAbdallāh arrived at the season of the pilgrimage and made the pilgrimage

---

387. The Banū ʿAkk were an old-established South Arabian tribe, dwelling to the north of Zabīd, according to Hamdānī; see *EI*² s.v. (W. Caskel). Five years before this, in 202 (817), the two tribes of ʿAkk and Aʿshar had risen in revolt against al-Maʾmūn's governor in the Yemen, Ḥamdawayh b. ʿAlī b. ʿĪsā b. Māhān; see Geddes, 105–6.

himself. When he had accomplished this, he went on to the Yemen until he made contact with ʿAbd al-Raḥmān. He sent to [1063]
him the guarantee of security from al-Ma'mūn; ʿAbd al-Raḥmān accepted this, coming into Dīnār's presence and clasping hands with him. Dīnār went back with ʿAbd al-Raḥmān to al-Ma'mūn. At this point al-Ma'mūn forbade the Ṭālibids to enter his presence and ordered them to start wearing black garments. This was on Thursday, the twenty-ninth of Dhū al-Qaʿdah (April 15, 823).[388]

In this year, the death of Ṭāhir b. al-Ḥusayn took place.

The Death of Ṭāhir b. al-Ḥusayn[389]

It is related from Muṭahhar b. Ṭāhir[390] that the death of Dhū al-Yamīnayn[391] was the result of a fever and high temperature which attacked him and that he was found dead in his bed. It is also related that his two paternal uncles, ʿAlī b. Muṣʿab and the latter's brother Aḥmad b. Muṣʿab,[392] went to visit him in his sickness. They asked the servant how he was, at the point when the servant was performing the dawn worship. The servant replied that Ṭāhir was sleeping and had not yet awakened. ʿAlī and Aḥmad accordingly waited for a while, but when the dawn had unfolded itself fully and there was still no sign of any movement on Ṭāhir's part at this time when he normally used to rise for the worship, they became disquieted about this and told the servant to wake him up. The latter replied, "I daren't

---

388. Ibn al-Athīr, *al-Kāmil*, VI, 381 (with the date the twenty-eighth of Dhū al-Qaʿdah); Geddes, 106–7. The date the twenty-ninth of Dhū al-Qaʿdah was actually a Wednesday.

389. The historical reports on Ṭāhir's death show considerable divergences; see Barthold, *Turkestan*, 208–9; Rothstein, 161; Sourdel, "Les circonstances de la mort de Ṭāhir Ier," 66–9; Bosworth, in *Cambridge history of Iran*, IV, 95.

390. This son of Ṭāhir is given the *kunyah* or patronymic of Abū Muḥammad in Ibn Abī Ṭāhir, 129, tr. 59.

391. Various explanations are given in the sources for Ṭāhir's sobriquet of "the man with two right hands;" see Goldziher, "Ueber Dualtitel," *WZKM*, XIII (1899), 324; Bosworth, op. cit., 92.

392. It had been this forebear, Muṣʿab b. Ruzayq al-Khuzāʿī, and his brother Ṭalḥah, who had founded the family's fortunes by their rôle in the ʿAbbāsid revolution; see Bosworth, "The Ṭāhirids and Arabic culture," 47–8; M. Kaabi, "Les origines Ṭāhirides dans la *daʿwa* ʿabbāside," *Arabica*, XIX (1972), 158–9.

do that." But they told him to knock at the door on their behalf[393] so that they might enter. Then they went in and found him wrapped in a coverlet which he had tucked underneath himself and with which he had covered himself securely from head to feet. They touched him, but he did not move at all; so they uncovered his face and found him dead. They had no idea exactly when he had died, and none of his servants was aware of his time of death. They questioned the servant about what had happened to him and about last thing which he (the servant) had been aware of from him. He recounted that Ṭāhir had performed the sunset and the final night worships, and then had wrapped himself up in his coverlet. The servant related that he had heard Ṭāhir utter a few words in Persian, "*dar marg nīz mardī wāyadh,*" meaning, "manly fortitude is necessary even in death."[394]

[1064] It is related from Kulthūm b. Thābit b. Abī Saʿd, whose patronymic was Abū Saʿd,[395] that he said: I was in charge of the intelligence and postal service (*barīd*) in Khurasan, and the place where I usually sat each Friday was at the foot of the pulpit. In the year 207 (822/823), two years after Ṭāhir b. al-Ḥusayn had become governor, I was present at the Friday worship. Ṭāhir ascended the pulpit, and then delivered the sermon (*khuṭbah*). When he came to mentioning the Caliph, he refrained from praying for him, and merely said, "O God, secure the welfare of the community of Muḥammad as you have secured it for those who are your close supporters [*awliyā'aka*], and relieve them of the crushing burden of those who would oppress and band together against them by repairing the disorder of affairs, preventing the shedding of blood and restoring harmonious relations between people." Kulthūm went on to relate: I said to myself, "I am going to be the first to be killed, for I cannot con-

393. The text has *uṭruq lanā*; Ibn Abī Ṭāhir, 130, has, alternatively, *ṭarriq lanā*, "clear the way for us."

394. Ibn Abī Ṭāhir, 129–30, tr. 59–60; *ʿUyūn*, 364; Ibn al-Athīr, *al-Kāmil*, VI, 381; cf. Bosworth, op. cit., 48.

395. In Ibn Abī Ṭāhir, 117, tr. 53, Kulthūm is given the *nisbah* or gentilic of al-Nakhaʿī and described as a mawlā of Muḥammad b. ʿImrān of Fūtaq (a village of the Marw oasis, see Yāqūt, *Muʿjam*, IV, 279), who obtained for Kulthūm the office of Ṣāḥib al-Barīd of Khurasan.

ceal this news." Hence I went away, performed the ablutions prescribed before death, put on the waistcloth of those about to die and a robe, and threw a cloak over myself. I took off my (official ʿAbbāsid) black clothing, and wrote to al-Ma'mūn.

He continued: When Ṭāhir had performed the afternoon worship, he sent for me, but at that point he had some sort of attack in his eyelids and the interior corner of his eye, and fell down dead. He continued: Ṭalḥah b. Ṭāhir went forth and shouted, "Bring him back, bring him back!"—I having left—so they brought me back. He asked me, "Have you written a report about what happened [that is, about Ṭāhir's act of rebelliousness]?" I retorted that I had. Then he said, "Write a message about his death," and gave me five hundred thousand (dirhams) and two hundred sets of clothes. I then wrote a report about Ṭāhir's death and Ṭalḥah's assumption of command over the army.

He continued: There reached al-Ma'mūn the dispatch bag (*kharīṭah*) containing the letter announcing Ṭāhir's renunciation of obedience in the morning. He summoned Ibn Abī Khālid and told him, "Set out, and bring Ṭāhir back to me, just as you said you would and just as you guaranteed." Ibn Abī Khālid replied, "Let me stay here just this one night." Al-Ma'- [1065]
mūn swore, "Nay, upon my life, you shall only spend the night on the back of a mount!" Ibn Abī Khālid kept on imploring him to relent, until al-Ma'mūn at last gave him permission to remain for one night. He continued: By night, the dispatch bag arrived bringing news of Ṭāhir's death. Al-Ma'mūn summoned Ibn Abī Khālid and told him, "Ṭāhir is dead; whom do you think [should be his successor]?" Ibn Abī Khālid replied, "His son Ṭalḥah." The Caliph said, "You have spoken correctly. Write out a diploma investing him with the governorship." So he wrote it out. Ṭalḥah remained governor in Khurasan during al-Ma'mūn's caliphate for seven years after Ṭāhir's death, and then he himself died; al-Ma'mūn thereupon appointed ʿAbdallāh governor in Khurasan.[396] The latter was at that time in

---

396. Yaʿqūbī, *Taʾrīkh* II, 557; *ʿUyūn*, 364–5; Barthold, *Turkestan*, 208; Bosworth, in *Cambridge history of Iran*, IV, 98.

charge of the military operations against Babāk. He established his base at Dīnawar and sent out armies from there. The news of Ṭalḥah's death reached al-Ma'mūn; he thereupon sent Yaḥyā b. Aktham[397] with a message of condolences on his brother's death and hailing him with his appointment as governor of Khurasan, and he placed ʿAlī b. Hishām in charge of the war against Bābak.[398]

It is mentioned from al-ʿAbbās[399] that he was present at one of al-Ma'mūn's sessions when the latter had just received the announcement of Ṭāhir's death, and the Caliph exclaimed, "O [my] two hands and mouth![400] Praise to be God, who has sent Ṭāhir on [to the next life] and kept us back!"[401]

An account different from the one above has been mentioned in regard to Ṭalḥah's appointment as governor of Khurasan after his father Ṭāhir. According to what this account says, when Ṭāhir died—this event taking place in Jumādā I (September–October 822)—the army rose up in an émeute and plundered some of his treasuries. The eunuch Sallām al-Abrash assumed leadership of them; he issued an order, and they were given six months' pay allowance. Al-Ma'mūn then entrusted Ṭāhir's governorship to Ṭalḥah, as the deputy of ʿAbdallāh b. Ṭāhir. The point here was that, according to the people who give this variant account, al-Ma'mūn appointed ʿAbdallāh as governor after Ṭāhir's death over the whole of Ṭāhir's former area of responsibility. ʿAbdallāh was at that moment stationed at Raqqah engaged in the war with Naṣr b. Shabath. Al-Ma'mūn added Syria to his responsibilities, and sent him an investiture diploma for Khurasan and his father's (other) administrative

397. Grand judge of Baghdad and counsellor of al-Ma'mūn, but who was later disgraced for his corruption and licentiousness; see Sourdel, *Vizirat*, I, 238–9.

398. Ibn Abī Ṭāhir, 130–2, tr. 60, (see also Rothstein, 161), with another, briefer account of Ṭāhir's act of rebelliousness and death, related from Yaḥyā b. al-Ḥasan, in ibid., 116–17, tr. 53; Yaʿqūbī, *Ta'rīkh* II, 556–7, with the story that Ṭāhir was poisoned by the nephew of his friend Muḥammad b. Farrukh al-ʿAmrakī (see also Rothstein, loc. cit.).

399. I.e., al-Ma'mūn's son.

400. For this proverbial expression, whose exact point is unclear, see Maydānī, *Muʿjam amthāl al-ʿArab*, tr. G.W. Freytag, II, 475, no. 243.

401. Ibn Abī Ṭāhir, 133, tr. 61; *ʿUyūn*, 365; Ibn al-Athīr, *al-Kāmil*, VI, 382.

responsibilities. ʿAbdallāh then sent his brother Ṭalḥah to Khurasan,[402] and appointed as his deputy in the City of Peace Isḥāq b. Ibrāhīm.[403] Ṭalḥah wrote to al-Ma'mūn in his brother's name. Al-Ma'mūn sent Aḥmad b. Abī Khālid to Khurasan in order to take over Ṭalḥah's responsibilities. Aḥmad led an ex- [1066] pedition into Transoxiana; he conquered Ushrūsanah and captured Kāwūs b. Khārākhuruh[404] and his son al-Faḍl, and sent them both to al-Ma'mūn. Ṭalḥah gave Ibn Abī Khālid three million dirhams plus moveable objects excluding gold and silver (*ʿurūḍ*) amounting to one million (dirhams), and gave Ibrāhīm b. al-ʿAbbās, Aḥmad b. Abī Khālid's secretary, five hundred thousand dirhams.[405]

In this year, prices rose high in Baghdad, Baṣrah and Kūfah, until the price of a *hārūnī qafīz* of wheat rose to forty dirhams and the price of a *muljam qafīz* of wheat to fifty.[406]

In this year, Mūsā b. Ḥafṣ was appointed governor of Ṭabaristān, Rūyān and Dunbāwand.[407]

In this year, Abū ʿĪsā b. al-Rashīd led the pilgrimage.[408]

---

402. Cf. above, and Ibn Abī Ṭāhir, 131, tr. 60.

403. Ibid., 35, tr. 16. The accounts of Ṭāhir's death are particularly divergent over chronology; it may be that an interval of several weeks took place between Ṭāhir's act of rebelliousness and his actual death, cf. Sourdel, "Les circonstances de la mort de Ṭāhir Ier," 68–9.

404. The father Khārākhuruh (for this Iranian name, see F. Justi, *Iranisches Namenbuch*, 170) had submitted to al-Faḍl b. Yaḥyā al-Barmakī in 178 (794), see Ṭabarī, III, 631; Kāwūs's other son Ḥaydar was to enter ʿAbbāsid service as the famous general al-Afshīn, on whom see *EI*² s.v. (Barthold—Gibb).

405. *ʿUyūn*, 365; Ibn al-Athīr, *al-Kāmil*, VI, 382–3; Barthold, 210–11; Rothstein, 162; Bosworth, in *Cambridge history of Iran*, IV, 96–7.

406. Ibn Abī Ṭāhir, 134, tr. 61; Azdī, 362; Ibn al-Athīr, *al-Kāmil*, VI, 384. For these measures of capacity, see Bosworth, "Abū ʿAbdallāh al-Khwārazmī on the technical terms of the secretary's art," 148–50.

407. Ibn al-Athīr, *al-Kāmil*, VI, 385; Rabino di Borgomale, "Les préfets du Califat au Ṭabaristān," 262. Rūyān was the westernmost district of Ṭabaristān, see Le Strange, *Lands*, 373–4, and Barthold, *An historical geography of Iran*, 233–4; and Dunbāwand was the highest peak of the Elburz chain, see Le Strange, ibid., 371, Schwarz, 755 ff., and *EI*² s.v. Damāwand (Streck).

408. Khalīfah, *Ta'rīkh*, II, 770; Ibn al-Athīr, *al-Kāmil*, loc. cit.

The Events of the Year
208
(May 16, 823–May 3, 824)

Among the events taking place during this year was al-Ḥasan b. al-Ḥusayn b. Muṣʿab's move from Khurasan to Kirmān, where he then defied the government, and Aḥmad b. Abī Khālid's expedition against him until he seized him and brought him to al-Ma'mūn, who then pardoned him.[409]

In this year, in Muḥarram (May–June 823), al-Ma'mūn appointed Muḥammad b. ʿAbd al-Raḥmān al-Makhzūmī as judge of ʿAskar al-Mahdī (of Ruṣāfah).

In this year, the judge Muḥammad b. Samāʿah asked to be relieved of his office; he was accordingly released from it and Ismāʿīl b. Ḥammād b. Abī Ḥanīfah appointed in his stead.[410]

[1067] In this year, Muḥammad b. ʿAbd al-Raḥmān was dismissed from the office of judge after he had only just been invested

409. Op. cit., VI, 386. The Ṭāhirid al-Ḥasan b. al-Ḥusayn was the uncle of ʿAbdallāh b. Ṭāhir, and subsequently acted as deputy governor for the latter in Ṭabaristān; see Saʿīd Nafīsī, *Ta'rīkh-i khāndān-i Ṭāhirī*, I, 29–30, citing Ẓahīr al-Dīn Marʿashī, *Ta'rīkh-i Ṭabaristān u Rūyān u Māzandarān.*

410. Ibn al-Athīr, *al-Kāmil*, loc. cit. Azdī, 341, gives the name as Muḥammad b. Samāwah in recording his appointment in 201 (816/17) as judge of the West Side of Baghdad.

with it, in the same year, in Rabīʿ I (July–August 823), and Bishr b. al-Walīd al-Kindī was appointed to it. A certain poet has said:

O monarch, who proclaims the unity of his Lord,
 your judge Bishr b. al-Walīd is an ass!

He rejects the legal testimony of the person who holds the faith of what
 the Book has spoken about and what the historical traditions have brought,

And he considers as a reliable legal witness the person who says that
 he is a shaykh who encompasses with his body the regions of the world [that is, a universal sage]![411]

In Shaʿbān (December 823–January 824), Mūsā b. Muhammad al-Makhlūʿ (the son of the deposed Caliph al-Amīn) died, and in Dhū al-Qaʿdah (March–April 824), al-Faḍl b. al-Rabīʿ died.[412]

In this year, Ṣālih b. al-Rashīd led the pilgrimage.[413]

---

411. Azdī, 365; Ibn al-Athīr, *al-Kāmil,* loc. cit.
412. Ibid. Mūsā had been his father al-Amīn's choice as his first heir; see Abbott, 230–1.
413. Khalīfah, *Ta'rīkh,* II, 771; Ibn al-Athīr, *al-Kāmil,* loc. cit.

The Events of the Year

209

(MAY 4, 824–APRIL 23, 825)

Among the events taking place during this year was ʿAbdallāh b. Ṭāhir's exertion of pressure on (or: his surrounding of) Naṣr b. Shabath, driving him into a tight corner so that he had to seek a guarantee of safety.[414] It is mentioned from Jaʿfar b. Muḥammad al-ʿĀmirī that he said: Al-Ma'mūn said to Thumāmah (b. Ashras), "Can't you point out to me a man from the people of the Jazīrah with intelligence, eloquence and knowledge, who can transmit a message from me, which I will dispatch him with, to Naṣr b. Shabath?" He replied, "Certainly, O Commander of the Faithful, [there is] a certain man from the Banū ʿĀmir called Jaʿfar b. Muḥammad." Al-Ma'mūn said, "Bring him to me!" Jaʿfar continued: So Thumāmah summoned me
[1068] and brought me into the Caliph's presence. He spoke to me at great length, and then commanded me to deliver these words to Naṣr b. Shabath. Jaʿfar continued: So I went to Naṣr, who was at that moment at Kafar ʿAzūn in the neighborhood of

414. ʿ*Uyūn*, 365. For Naṣr's final efforts and surrender, see Vasiliev, *Byzance et les Arabes*, I, 91, and cf. Shaban, 52.

Sarūj,[415] and passed on to him al-Ma'mūn's message. He showed himself submissive, but laid down certain conditions, including that he should not be required to step on any of the Caliph's carpets (as a sign of supplication and submission).

Jaʿfar continued: I went back to al-Ma'mūn and gave him the reply. He answered, "By God, I'll never agree to these stipulations of his, even if I reach the point of having to sell my shirt in order to persuade him to step on my carpet! What's the matter with him, shrinking from us in fear?"

Jaʿfar continued: I said, "Because of his offences and all that he has perpetrated up till now." Al-Ma'mūn replied, "Do you imagine that he has committed greater offences, in my sight, than al-Faḍl b. al-Rabīʿ and ʿIsā b. Abī Khālid? Do you know what al-Faḍl did to me? He appropriated my commanders, my troops, my weapons and everything which my father had bequeathed to me, and went off with them to Muḥammad [al-Amīn], leaving me alone and isolated at Marw! He betrayed me, and he turned my brother against me until those events involving him took place as they did. That struck me more harshly than anything else! Do you know what ʿĪsā b. Abī Khālid did to me? He drove my representative out of my own city and the city of my forefathers, went off with my receipts from the land-tax and my revenues from the cultivators of the conquered lands, razed my houses to the ground, set up Ibrāhīm as Caliph in place of me and hailed him with my rightful title!"

Ja'far continued: I said, "O Commander of the Faithful, will you allow me to speak, so that I may say something apposite?" He replied, "Speak on!" I said, "Al-Faḍl b. al-Rabīʿ was your foster-brother and your close associate [mawlā]; the status of his forebears was the same as your, and the status of your forebears the same as his; you can make a claim on him[416] in vari-

415. The village of Kafar ʿAzūn is mentioned later in accounts of Byzantine-Arab warfare in this neighborhood, see Yāqūt, *Muʿjam*, IV, 470, and E. Honigmann, *Die Ostgrenze des byzantinischen Reiches*, 108; Sarūj was a town of the Jazīrah to the west of Ḥarrān and Edessa, see Yāqūt, *Muʿjam*, III, 216–17, and Le Strange, *Lands*, 108.

416. Conjectural restoration of the text here by the editor.

ous ways, all of which connect you with him. As for ʿĪsa b. Abī Khālid, he is a man who comes from the supporters of your dy-
[1069] nasty (the ʿAbbāsids); his precedence [*sābiqah*][417] and the precedence of his forebears, all this constitutes a claim on him through that. Whereas this fellow [Naṣr] has never had any share of power on the basis of which he might achieve eminence, nor have any of his forebears; these last merely came from the troops of the Umayyads." Al-Ma'mun answered, "If what you say is indeed the case, what about all the rancor and ire which is involved? I shall never leave him alone until he steps on my carpet."

Jaʿfar continued: I went back to Naṣr and told him all that. He continued: He shouted loudly for his horses, and they wheeled around. Then he said, "Shame on him! He has not the strength to subdue four hundred frogs on his own doorstep [literally: under his own wing]"—he was referring to the Zuṭṭ—"so can he overcome the assembled cohorts of swift horses of the Arabs?"[418]

Naṣr b. Shabath Seeks a Guarantee of Safety

It is mentioned that when ʿAbdallāh b. Ṭāhir brought his full force to bear on Naṣr in battle and constricted him, and when his request for a guarantee of safety came (to ʿAbdallāh), the latter granted it and then moved out of his military camp to Raqqah in the year 209 (824/5). Naṣr now went to ʿAbdallāh b. Ṭāhir.[419] Previous to this, after ʿAbdallāh had defeated Naṣr's armies, al-Ma'mūn had written a letter to Naṣr summoning him to obedience and the abandonment of his rebellion. However, Naṣr had rejected this. ʿAbdallāh himself then wrote to Naṣr. The text of al-Ma'mūn's letter to Naṣr—indited by ʿAmr b. Masʿadah—was as follows:

---

417. The repeated use here of the term *sābiqah* obviously echoes its importance in earliest Islam in regard to pre-eminence and a preferential rôle in the new *ummah* or Islamic community.

418. Ibn Abī Ṭāhir, 141–3, tr. 64–5.

419. Ibn al-Athīr, *al-Kāmil*, VI, 388–9.

O Naṣr b. Shabath, you know about obedience to authority, its mightiness, the coolness of its shade and the sweet smell of its pasturage; and [on the other hand] the regretfulness and deprivation which result from rejecting this obedience. Even though God may grant you a long respite, He only grants a lengthy period of enjoyment of life in the case of a person whom He wishes to make a publicly-known proof, so that God's warning examples may strike home to the people concerned, according to the de- [1070]
gree of their persistence [in such courses] and their meriting [eventual retribution]. I have deemed it good to give you due warning and to open your eyes, because I hope that what I am writing to you may have an effect on you. For truth is indeed truth, and falsity is falsity, and speech can only be judged according to the times and places of its enunciation [*makhārijihi*] and by those who are concerned with it [that is, have uttered it]. None of the Commander of the Faithful's governors has treated you in a manner more beneficial to your material wealth, your faith and your own person, nor has anyone been more solicitous of drawing you back and rescuing you from your errors than myself.

O Naṣr, by virtue of what first or last reason, or by what means or by what power, have you rebelled against the Commander of the Faithful? Do you seize his property and arrogate to yourself the authority which God has conferred on him, excluding him from it, and expect to remain in a state of security, with peace of mind, quietness, peaceableness and calm? By Him who knows both what is hidden and what is open, if you do not return to obedience, submitting fully to it, you will certainly experience the unpleasantness of retribution, and I shall certainly then concentrate my attention on you before everything else; for if the horns of Satan are not cut off, they are a source of strife and great corruption in the earth. Moreover, I shall certainly, with the supporters of the royal power [or: of the dynasty] who are in my forces, press down on the backs of the necks of the dregs of your followers, those who have [1071]

> come to you in a confused band from the near and distant corners of the lands, with their scum and worst elements, those thieves and robbers who have rallied to your side and those whom their land has spewed forth or whose tribe has expelled them because of their bad reputation within it. He who has delivered a warning is excused [from any of its consequences]! Farewell![420]

According to what has been mentioned, ʿAbdallāh b. Ṭāhir remained engaged in fighting Naṣr b. Shabath for five years, until Naṣr sought a guarantee of safety. ʿAbdallāh then wrote to al-Ma'mūn informing him that he had driven Naṣr into a tight corner and was tightening the screws on him, that he had killed the leaders in his entourage and that Naṣr had sought refuge in a guarantee of safety and had asked for this. Al-Ma'mūn ordered ʿAbdallāh to write a letter to Naṣr promising this guarantee. So he wrote our a guarantee of safety for him, with the following text:

> Vigorous exertion in the cause of what is right is God's decisive proof and one which is linked with success, and conducting one's cause with justice is a call to God with which is connected strength. The one who continuallly strives for what is right and who conducts his cause with justice is always seeking to open the gates of succor and always calling for the means of firm control, until God gives the victory—and He is the best of those who give victory—and establishes people in firm control—and He is the best of those who establish people in firm control. With regard to the course which you have been following, you must inevitably fall into one of three classes: [that of] the one who seeks religion; [that of] the one who desires the present world; or [that of] the one who rushes forward recklessly, seeking dominance through tyrannical behavior.
>
> Now if you are following the way of religion in your

420. Ibn Abī Ṭāhir, 137–8, tr. 63.

conduct, then make this clear to the Commander of the Faithful, who will [immediately] seize the opportunity to accept this, if it is really genuine; for by my life, his supreme intention and farthest aim is to incline towards what is right, whenever he inclines [towards something], and to incline away, with what is just, whenever he inclines away [that is, to make affirmative or negative decisions, according to what is right or just, in their appropriate places]. If you are aiming to follow the way of the present world, then inform the Commander of the Faithful about your aim and about the state of affairs under which you claim an entitlement to it. If you establish a deserving [1072]
claim to it and he is able to grant that, then he will do it for you; for by my life, he does not permit any person to be debarred from what he justly deserves, however great this may be. But if you are rushing forward through life recklessly, then God will relieve the Commander of the Faithful of the burden of you and will speedily bring that about, just as He speedily disposed of the burden of other people who followed the same way as you, who were stronger in resources, with more numerous armies, and extensively endowed with manpower, numbers and support than you; He drove them towards the places where those who have been found wanting are left prostrated, and He brought down on them the calamities merited by those behaving tyrannically. The Commander of the Faithful seals his letter with the declaration of faith that there is no god but God, the Unique One who is without associate, and that Muḥammad is His servant and messenger. His guarantee to you, according to his religion and his protection, is the pardoning of your previous misdeeds and earlier crimes and your being established in the positions of power and exaltedness which you merit, if you come forward and respond [to his invitation], if God wills. Farewell![421]

421. Ibid., 138–40, tr. 63–4.

When Naṣr b. Shabath went forth to ʿAbdallāh b. Ṭāhir with the guarantee of safety, he (ʿAbdallāh) pulled down and destroyed Kaysūm.[422]

In this year, al-Ma'mūn appointed Ṣadaqah b. ʿAlī, known as Zurayq,[423] as governor of Armenia and Azerbaijan, with responsibility for the war against Bābak; Ṣadaqah invited Aḥmad b. al-Junayd b. Farzandī al-Iskāfī to take charge of the actual military operations against Bābak. Aḥmad b. al-Junayd b. Farzandī returned to Baghdad and then came back to (fight) the Khurramiyyah, but Bābak took him captive. The Caliph then appointed Ibrāhīm b. al-Layth b. al-Faḍl al-Tujībī[424] over Azerbaijan.[425]

[1073] In this year, Ṣāliḥ b. al-ʿAbbās b. Muḥammad b. ʿAlī (b. ʿAbdallāh b. al-ʿAbbās), the governor of Mecca, led the pilgrimage.[426]

In this year, there died Michael son of George, emperor of Byzantium, who had reigned for nine years. The Byzantines appointed as ruler over themselves Theophilus son of Michael.[427]

---

422. Yaʿqūbī, *Ta'rīkh*, II, 560; Azdī, 366; Ibn al-Athīr, *al-Kāmil*, VI, 390; Rothstein, 163. Kaysūm lay in the upper Euphrates region, to the southwest of Adiyaman, and is the modern Keysun, Greek Kaisou; see Le Strange, *Lands*, 123; Honigmann, 62.

423. Thus apparently correct, following Balādhurī, *Futūḥ al-buldān*, 330–1: Ṣadaqah b. ʿAlī b. Ṣadaqah b. Dīnār, a mawlā of the Azd tribe, *pace* the Zurayq b. ʿAlī b. Ṣadaqah of Yaʿqūbī, *Ta'rīkh*, II, 564, and Azdī, 366 ff., and the ʿAlī b. Ṣadaqah of other sources, see Ṭabarī, III, 1072, n. *f*.

424. Editor's conjecture for this *nisbah*, written without dots; but we do not otherwise know of the presence of members of Tujīb of Kindah in Azerbaijan; Dr. Hinds accordingly suggests the *nisbah* al-Yaḥmadī (a subdivision of the Azd) as a conceivable reading. Cf. also Azdī, 366.

425. Ibn al-Athīr, *al-Kāmil*, VI, 390.

426. Khalīfah, *Ta'rīkh*, II, 772; Ibn al-Athīr, *al-Kāmil*, loc. cit.

427. As with Ṭabarī's previous recording of the death of Leo V four years too early (above, 45), Ṭabarī is some five years premature here; Michael II, founder of the Amorian line of emperors, actually died in 829, when his son Theophilus succeeded him. See Vasiliev, *Byzance et les Arabes*, I, 272, 280–1; Anastos, in *Cambridge medieval history. IV. The Byzantine empire*, I, 100–2.

The Events of the Year 210

(April 24, 825–April 12, 826)

Among the events taking place during this year was the arrival at Baghdad of Naṣr b. Shabath, whom ʿAbdallāh b. Ṭāhir sent to al-Maʾmūn. He entered the city on Monday, the seventh of Ṣafar, 210[428] (May 30, 825); he was lodged in the City of Abū Jaʿfar (the Round City), with guards appointed to watch over him.[429]

In this year, al-Maʾmūn gained the upper hand over Ibrāhīm b. Muḥammad b. ʿAbd al-Wahhāb b. Ibrāhīm al-Imām, who was known as Ibn ʿĀʾishah,[430] Muḥammad b. Ibrāhīm al-Ifrīqī, Mālik b. Shāhī,[431] Faraj al-Baghwārī[432] and their confederates who had been active in securing allegiance to Ibrāhīm b. al-

428. Actually a Tuesday.
429. Ibn Abī Ṭāhir, 143, tr. 65.
430. Yaʿqūbī, *Taʾrīkh*, II, 558–9, gives his full *nasab*, or lineage, back to al-ʿAbbās through eight generations.
431. Ibid., II, 559, adds Mālik's *nisbah* as al-Niffarī.
432. Reading uncertain, and Samʿānī in his *Kitāb al-Ansāb* does not mention such a *nisbah*; perhaps we should read al-Baghawī, see ibid. (Hyderabad), II, 273–6.

Mahdī. The person who provided al-Ma'mūn with information about them and about what they were plotting was ʿImrān al-Qaṭrabullī. According to what is mentioned, al-Ma'mūn sent officers to arrest them on Saturday, the fifth of Ṣafar, 210[433] (May 28, 825). Al-Ma'mūn ordered Ibrāhīm Ibn al-ʿĀ'ishah to be left (pinioned) in the sun for three days at the gateway of his (al-Ma'mūn's) palace; on Tuesday he had him flogged and then jailed him in the Maṭbaq (or: Muṭbaq) prison.[434] Then he had Mālik b. Shāhī and his confederates flogged. They wrote down
[1074] for al-Ma'mūn the names of all those—commanders, troops and other persons—who had entered into the conspiracy with them. Al-Ma'mūn did not, however, make a move towards any of those who had been delated, since he was not sure that the conspirators were not accusing innocent persons.[435] The conspirators had agreed among themselves that they would cut the bridge when the troops had gone forth to meet Naṣr b. Shabath. But they were delated and then arrested. After this, Naṣr b. Shabath entered Baghdad alone, none of the troops being sent to escort him.[436] First of all, he was lodged with Isḥāq b. Ibrāhīm, and subsequently transferred to the city of Abū Jaʿfar.

Ibrāhīm al-Mahdī Is Arrested

In this year, during the night of Sunday (the night of Saturday-Sunday), the sixteenth of Rabīʿ II (August 5–6, 825),[437] Ibrāhīm b. al-Mahdī was arrested, veiled and dressed like a woman and in the company of two women.[438] A black negro guard stopped

---

433. Actually a Sunday; Ibn Abī Ṭāhir, 176, has the sixth of Ṣafar, corrected by Keller in his tr. 80, to the fifth of Ṣafar.

434. The celebrated jail in the Round City on the street running between the Kūfah and Baṣrah gates; see Le Strange, *Baghdad*, 27; Lassner, *Topography*, 243.

435. Ibn al-Athīr, *al-Kāmil*, VI, 391.

436. Ibn Abī Ṭāhir, 176–7, tr. 80.

437. Inserting, with Ibn Abī Ṭāhir, 185, and the ms. cited in the editor's n. *f*, the word *baqiyat* rather than *khalat*; the date of the sixteenth of Rabīʿ II gives the correct correspondence with Sunday.

438. According to Masʿūdī, *Murūj*, VII, 63 = ed. Pellat, § 2750, in the street called "The Long" (al-Darb al-Ṭawīl); see for this, Le Strange, *Baghdad*, 221. Masʿūdī, *Tanbīh*, 351, tr. 450, confirms this date.

him during the night and demanded, "Who are you, and where are you going at this hour?" According to what is mentioned, Ibrāhīm offered him a ruby ring of high value from his own finger, if he would let them pass and cease questioning them. When the guard looked at the ring, he became suspicious about them and said to himself, "This ring belongs to a man of high social status." Hence, he took them along to the commander of the guard post, and the latter ordered them to unveil their faces. Ibrāhīm refused, but the commander pulled it away,[439] and Ibrāhīm's beard was revealed. He took him to the commandant of the bridge, who recognised him and took him to al-Ma'mūn's gate. The Caliph was informed, and ordered him to be kept in the palace. On the Sunday morning, he was set down in al-Ma'mūn's palace so that the Hāshimites, the commanders and the troops might gaze on him. They put the veil which [1075]
he had been wearing round his neck and the mantle in which he had been wrapped across his breast, so that people might see him and know in what guise he had been taken. When it was Thursday, al-Ma'mūn had him transferred to Aḥmad b. Abī Khālid's house and had him imprisoned in his custody. Then al-Ma'mūn had him brought forth to accompany himself when he went to visit al-Ḥasan b. Sahl at Wāsiṭ. People said that al-Ḥasan spoke to the Caliph about him, and al-Ma'mūn showed his favor towards Ibrāhīm, released him and sent him back to Aḥmad b. Abī Khālid.[440] Along with Ibrāhīm, al-Ma'mūn sent Ibn Yaḥyā b. Muʿādh and Khālid b. Yazīd b. Mazyad[441] to watch over him, except that he was allowed plenty of living space there, having his mother and family with him; he used to ride to al-Ma'mūn's palace with these (two) persons guarding him as an escort.[442]

In this year, al-Ma'mūn had Ibn ʿĀ'ishah killed and gibbeted.

439. One might have here, with the same meaning, the *lectio facilior* of *fa-jadhabahu*.

440. Masʿūdī, *Murūj*, loc. cit.; *ʿUyūn*, 365; Ibn al-Athīr, *al-Kāmil*, VI, 392.

441. Governor of Kūfah and then of Armenia, and member of an Arab family prominent under the early ʿAbbāsids; from his family there later sprang the Yazīdī line of Shīrwān-Shāhs; see Crone, 169–70; V. Minorsky, *A history of Sharvān and Darband*, 22 ff., 116–17.

442. Ibn Abī Ṭāhir, 184–5, tr. 83–4.

Al-Ma'mūn Has Ibn ʿĀ'ishah Killed

The reason for this was that al-Ma'mūn consigned to prison Ibn ʿĀ'ishah, Muḥammad b. Ibrāhīm al-Ifrīqī, two men from the city mobsters called Abū Mismār and ʿAmmār respectively, Faraj al-Baghwārī, Mālik b. Shāhī and also a group of those who had conspired with them to give allegiance to Ibrāhīm (b. al-Mahdī), after they had been flogged, with the exception of ʿAmmār, who was given a guarantee of immunity because he had denounced the plans of the group in the Maṭbaq prison. One of the prisoners in the Maṭbaq reported that the prisoners intended to stir up a riot and bore a way through the walls of the jail. The day before, they had barricaded the door of the prison from the inside and had prevented anyone from getting access in to them. When night fell and people heard the commotion they were making, the news reached al-Ma'mūn. He rode there in person immediately, had these four men brought forth and
[1076] had them beheaded while pinioned. Ibn ʿĀ'ishah hurled savage insults at al-Ma'mūn. Next morning, their corpses were gibbeted on the lower bridge. On the Wednesday morning, Ibrāhīm Ibn al-ʿA'ishah's body was taken down; it was enshrouded, prayers were said over it and it was buried in the cemetery of Quraysh.[443] Ibn al-Ifrīqī's body was taken down and buried in the cemetery of al-Khayzurān, but the rest were left there.[444]

It is mentioned that when Ibrāhīm b. al-Mahdī was captured, he was taken along to the palace of Abū Isḥaq b. al-Rashīd (the later Caliph al-Muʿtaṣim) at a time when Abū Isḥāq himself was with al-Ma'mūn. So Ibrāhīm was borne along, mounted behind Faraj al-Turkī. When he was brought into al-Ma'mūn's presence, the latter said to him, "So we meet again, O Ibrāhīm!" Ibrāhīm said, "O Commander of the Faithful, the

443. On the upper West Side of the city, according to al-Khaṭīb al-Baghdādī; see Le Strange, *Baghdad*, 158, 193–4, and Lassner, *Topography*, 111, 285–6, who suggests that the name was also used for the cemetery of al-Khayzurān on the East Side, see ibid., 114, 287.

444. Ibn Abī Ṭāhir, 178–9, 206, tr. 80–1, 94; Yaʿqūbī, *Ta'rīkh*, II, 558–9; Masʿūdī, *Murūj*, VII, 78 = ed. Pellat, § 2763; Ibn al-Athīr, *al-Kāmil*, VI, 391–2. For the whole episode of Ibn ʿĀ'ishah, see Barbier de Meynard, 251–3; Levy, *A Baghdad chronicle*, 95.

kinsman to whom it falls to exact vengeance [*walī al-tha'r*] is the one who is made to judge in respect of [the nature of] the retaliation, but forgiveness is nearer to piety.[445] The man who is made heedless and hesitant by the causes of difficulty and heart-searching placed in his way [in securing the vengeance] brings down on himself the adverse buffetings of fate.[446] God has set you above every sinner, just as He has placed every sinner below you. If you punish, then it is only in accordance with your right; but if you grant pardon, then it comes from your own graciousness." Al-Ma'mūn replied, "Nay, I pardon you, O Ibrāhīm!" Then Ibrāhīm glorified God and fell down in prostration.[447] It is said that Ibrāhīm wrote these words to al-Ma'mūn while he was still in hiding, and al-Ma'mūn made a note in the margin of his copy to the effect that "power drives away anger; contrition implies repentance; and between the two is God's forgiveness, and this is the greatest thing we can ask of Him."[448]

Ibrāhīm recited, praising al-Ma'mūn:

O best of those after the Messenger [of God] whom a Yamanī she-camel conveys gently along
towards him who is in despair or who is hopeful of bounty!

And [O] most pious of those who worship God with godly fear [1077]
and in earnestness,[449] and most eloquent one of those who proclaim clearly-manifest truth!

The honey of the mountain tops, so long as men give you obedience; but if you are aroused [by opposition],
then you are the colocynth, mingled with deadly poison!

---

445. Qur'ān, II, 238.

446. The exact meaning of this difficult passage is not certain, but the general idea seems to be that the person who neglects his obligations lays himself open to the vicissitudes of fate. The text of Ibn Abī Ṭāhir, 184, has *al-rajā'*, "hope," for *al-shaqā'*, "wretchedness," and Barbier de Meynard and Pavet de Courteille translate this passage in Mas'ūdī (see next note) as "L'homme . . . plein d'une confiance aveugle dans les moyens de révolte qui s'offrent à lui, se livre tout entier aux vicissitudes de la destinée."

447. Mas'ūdī, *Murūj*, VII, 63–4 = ed. Pellat, § 2750.

448. Ibn Abī Ṭāhir, 184, tr. 83; Ya'qūbī, *Ta'rīkh* II, 558; Azdī, 369.

449. An alternative reading for the text's *'ayn*^{an}, "in earnestness, in reality," might be *ghayb*^{an}, "without seeing Him directly."

The ever-wakeful one, the one who remains watchful;
he who remains alert during the periods of sleep of the slumbering night does not have to fear any foe!

People's hearts are filled with awe of you,
and you continue protecting them with a compassionate heart.

May my father, my mother and their sons be your ransom,
against all calamities and vicissitudes which may arise!

[1078] How pleasant is the place in which you have set me down as a homeland,
and how sweet is its herbage for the one seeking pasture! [that is, how pleasant is life for the subjects in your land].

You have become established as an exponent of [literally: brother to] righteous deeds and godly fear,
and a tender father to the humble, destitute person

May my life be your ransom! For my excuses go astray,
and I take refuge from you in the bountifulness of ample beneficence,

In hope of your grace; for bountiful actions are an innate quality [of yours],
which have elevated your character [literally: building] to a lofty place.

For you have lavished outstandingly generous deeds on such a scale
that the widest of hearts [literally: souls] are too narrow to be able to bestow its like,

And you have pardoned a person [that is, himself] with a pardon such as never before been known for such a deed
and [for which] no intercessor has ever pleaded before you previously,

Were it not that loftiness of character [recoils] from vengeance after
your strong arms have seized a humiliated and abased one.

Then you have shown compassion on children, like the sandgrouse's young,
and on the lamentations of a woman past her youth and [1079]
not yet married, [with a sound] like the [release of an] archer's bow.[450]

You have inclined to me with affection, out of a bond of kinship, just as
the bone of one limping from a broken limb heals together again after being broken for a second time.

God knows what I am saying, for it is indeed
the solemnest oath which a true believer, who inclines in worship, can make,

[That] I never became a rebel against you, even when resources and allurements of the erring ones dragged me along,
without retaining the inner intention of remaining obedient,

Until when the cords of my wretched state were suspended,
near to death, over the dark abyss of destruction, a confused and anguished one,

I did not know that a crime like mine could be forgiven,
so I halted there in order to ascertain what mode of death was to strike me down.

The piety of the Imām, the one mighty yet full of humility, [1080]
has given back life to me, after it had gone.

---

450. Barbier de Meynard, 259, translates, "d'une jeune fille gémissante que la douleur avait courbée comme un arc;" but the comparison of lamentation with the twanging sound made by bows is not infrequent in ancient Arabic poetry.

May He who has appointed you to the position of rulership grant you life for the longest possible period,
and may He strike your enemy with an incisive blade in the vein of the heart!

How many benefits from you, which my heart [literally: soul] has been unable to recount [or: did not mention] to me
when I saw myself disappointed in my desires,

Have you conferred on me as an act of pardon to me and as an act of grace,
hence I have given thanks to one who offers favors for the noblest of doers,

Except that it was a small thing when you granted it to me,
but it is a great deal as far as I was concerned, which will never be lost.

If you are generous to me over it [the act of pardoning], well, such liberality is only fitting for you;
and if you withhold it, well, you are the most just of those who withhold [benefits].

The one who allotted noble characteristics[451] gathered them all up
in the loins of Adam for the seventh Imām [that is, for al-Ma'mūn, the seventh ʿAbbāsid Caliph].

The One who controls people's affairs has gathered together hearts around you,
and your cloak has gathered together all goodness which brings [men] together.[452]

---

451. Following the reading *al-faḍā'il* of Ibn Abī Ṭāhir, the *Kitāb al-Aghānī*, Azdī and Ibn al-Athīr rather than Ṭabarī's *al-khilāfa*, the former one being in fact indicated in the editor's n. *i* as preferable.

452. Three of these last verses are given in Ibn Abī Ṭāhir, 204, tr. 93, and, apparently from there, in Azdī, 371, and four are given in Masʿūdī, *Murūj*, VII, 64 = ed. Pellat, § 2751.

It is mentioned that, when Ibrāhīm recited this ode to al-Ma'mūn, the latter exclaimed, "I can only say what Joseph said to his brothers,[453] 'There is no reproach upon you today; God will forgive you, and He is the most merciful of those showing mercy.' "[454] [1081]

In this year, in the month of Ramaḍān (December 825–January 826), al-Ma'mūn consummated his marriage with Būrān, the daughter of al-Ḥasan b. Sahl.

Al-Ma'mūn's Marriage with Būrān

It is mentioned that when al-Ma'mūn proceeded to Fam al-Ṣilḥ to al-Ḥasan b. Sahl's military encampment, he took with him Ibrāhīm b. al-Mahdī. Setting off for the ceremony there for the consummation of his marriage with Būrān, al-Ma'mūn left Baghdad in a skiff (*zawraq*),[455] (and sailed) until he anchored at al-Ḥasan's gate. Al-ʿAbbās b. al-Ma'mūn had preceded his father, travelling on a mount, and al-Ḥasan met him outside his military encampment in a place which had been specially chosen for him on the banks of the Tigris where a pavilion had been erected for him. When al-ʿAbbās saw him, he bent his leg (over the saddle) in order to dismount, but al-Ḥasan adjured him not to do so. Then when he had straightened it, al-Ḥasan lifted his own leg in order to dismount, but al-ʿAbbās exclaimed, "By the Commander of the Faithful's rights, don't get down!" whereupon al-Ḥasan embraced him while still mounted. Then he ordered that al-ʿAbbās's riding beast should be given precedence before him, and the two of them entered al-Ḥasan's house together. Al-Ma'mūn arrived at the time of the evening worship, this being in Ramaḍān 210 (December

453. Qur'ān, XII, 92.

454. Ibn Abī Ṭāhir, 186–8, tr. 84–5, giving twenty-nine verses of the poem, as opposed to Ṭabarī's twenty-seven, and with three of them further repeated, see the previous note; Iṣfahānī, *Aghānī*, IX, 60, giving seventeen verses; Masʿūdī, *Murūj*, loc. cit.; *ʿUyūn*, 366–7; Ibn al-Athīr, *al-Kāmil*, IV, 392–5; Barbier de Meynard, 257–60.

455. See Kindermann, *"Schiff" in arabischen. Untersuchung über Vorkommen und Bedeutung der Termini*, 37–8; cf. Mez, *The renaissance of Islam*, 486 ff.

825–January 826). He, al-Ḥasan and al-ʿAbbās broke their fast,
[1082] while Dīnār b. ʿAbdallāh was still standing (in attendance on them), until they had finished the meal and had washed their hands. Al-Ma'mūn then called for some wine; a golden goblet was brought in and the wine poured into it. Al-Ma'mūn drank from it, and then held out his hand with the goblet containing wine to al-Ḥasan. Al-Ḥasan held back from it, since he had never drunk wine before then. Dīnār b. ʿAbdallāh made a discreet sign to al-Ḥasan, and al-Ḥasan said to the Caliph, "O Commander of the Faithful, I am drinking it with your permission and at your command!" Al-Ma'mūn told him, "If this were not my command, I would not hold out my hand to you!" So al-Ḥasan took the goblet and drank from it.[456]

On the second night, he brought together (in marriage) Muḥammad b. al-Ḥasan b. Sahl and al-ʿAbbāsah, daughter of al-Faḍl Dhū al-Ri'āsatayn.[457] On the third night, he consummated his marriage with Būrān, who had with her (during the preceding preparations and festivities) Ḥamdūnah,[458] Umm Jaʿfar[459] and her grandmother. When al-Ma'mūn sat down with her, her grandmother scattered over her a thousand pearls which were on a golden platter. Al-Ma'mūn ordered them to be collected up and asked her how many pearls there were. She replied, "A thousand." He ordered them to be counted, and ten were missing. He said, "Whoever has taken them must give them back." They said, "[It was] Ḥusayn Z.j.lah."[460] He commanded him to return them, but Ḥusayn protested, "O Commander of the Faithful, the pearls were only scattered so that we might take them [or: were not the pearls scattered just so that we might take them?]! Al-Ma'mūn insisted, "Give them back, and I will give you their equivalent." So Ḥusayn returned them. Al-Ma'-

456. Ibn Abī Ṭāhir, 206–7, tr. 94.

457. On this *laqab*, "the man with the two authorities," given to al-Faḍl in 196 (812), see Sourdel, *Vizirat*, I, 201, II, 678, 681, and on this type of title in general, Goldziher, "Ueber Dualtitel," 321–9.

458. Daughter of Hārūn al-Rashīd, married to Jaʿfar b. al-Hādī, hence half-sister to al-Ma'mūn; see Abbott, 157.

459. I.e., Zubaydah bt. Jaʿfar b. al-Manṣūr, wife of Hārūn and step-mother of al-Ma'mūn; see Abbott, 137 ff.

460. Keller, Ibn Abī Ṭāhir, tr. 95, vocalizes Zujlah.

mūn placed all the pearls together in the vessel, as they had originally been, and they were placed in her bosom. He said, "This is your wedding present, and now, ask me for any of your requests." However, she remained silent. Her grandmother said to her, "Speak to your lord and ask him for your requests, since he has commanded you to do so." Hence she asked him to show his favor to Ibrāhīm b. al-Mahdī. He replied, "I grant [1083]
this." She also asked his permission for Umm Ja'far to go on the pilgrimage, and this he granted also.[461] Umm Ja'far presented her with the (formerly) Umayyad seamless jacket.[462] Al-Ma'mūn consummated his union with her that night, (and the same night) a candle of ambergris, weighing forty *manns* (3.25 kg.), in a golden vessel, was lit. Al-Ma'mūn criticized them for that, saying that it was an act of extravagance.[463]

The next morning, he sent for Ibrāhīm b. al-Mahdī, and he appeared walking from the banks of the Tigris, wearing a fur-lined robe made from cloth with a silk thread warp (*mubaṭṭanah mulḥam*)[464] and with a turban round his head, until he entered (the Caliph's abode). When the curtain was removed from before al-Ma'mūn, Ibrāhīm threw himself on the ground. Al-Ma'mūn cried out, "O my uncle, do not worry any more!" So Ibrāhīm came forward, greeted him in the fashion appropriate to caliphs, kissed his hand and recited his (own) poetry. Al-Ma'mūn called for robes of honor and presented him with a second robe; he summoned a mount for him and girded him with a sword. Ibrāhīm then went out, greeted the assembled people and was escorted back to his place.[465]

It is mentioned that al-Ma'mūn stayed with al-Ḥasan b. Sahl for seventeen days, and all the requirements, each day, for the Caliph and for the whole of his retinue, were taken care of (by

---

461. Abbott, 235, notes that al-Ma'mūn may have discouraged his stepmother from revisiting the scenes in the Hijaz of her philanthropic activities of previous years.

462. This was a special heirloom of the royal harem, formerly the property of the wives of the Umayyad Caliphs 'Abd al-Malik and Hishām; see Abbott, 12, 234.

463. Ibn Abī Ṭāhir, 207–9, tr. 94–5; *'Uyūn*, 365–6.

464. Cf. R. Dozy, *Supplément aux dictionnaires arabes*, II, 522a. *Mulḥam* cloth was a speciality of Marw.

465. Ibn Abī Ṭāhir, 209, tr. 95.

al-Ḥasan's munificence).[466] Al-Ḥasan also presented robes of honor to the commanders, according to their ranks, gave them mounts and rewarded them with presents. The total sum expended on them was fifty million dirhams. The narrator says: When he was about to depart, al-Ma'mūn ordered Ghassān b. ʿAbbād (al-Ḥasan's cousin) to hand over to al-Ḥasan ten million (dirhams) from the taxation of Fārs, and he granted Ṣilḥ to him as an assignment of land. This sum was brought to him on the spot, and was laid out (or: was counted out) in Ghassān b. ʿAbbād's presence. Al-Ḥasan then sat down and divided it up among his commanders, his companions, his retinue and his servants. When al-Ma'mūn departed, al-Ḥasan accompanied him (for the first part of his journey) and then returned to Fam al-Ṣilḥ.[467]

It is mentioned from Aḥmad b. al-Ḥasan b. Sahl, who said that his family used to talk about how al-Ḥasan b. Sahl wrote
[1084] out pieces of paper with the names of his estates on them and scattered them among his commanders and among the Hāshimites, and whoever got hold of one of these pieces of paper with the name of an estate written on it, sent (to there) and took possession of it.[468]

It is mentioned from Abū al-Ḥasan ʿAlī b. al-Ḥusayn b. ʿAbd al-Aʿlā al-Kātib, who said that al-Ḥasan b. Sahl spoke to him one day about various things relating to Umm Jaʿfar, and described the weightiness of her intelligence and understanding. Then al-Ḥasan said: Al-Ma'mūn questioned her one day at Fam al-Ṣilḥ, when he came to visit us, regarding how much the expenditure on Būrān's festivities had amounted to, and he questioned Ḥamdūnah bt. Ghaḍīḍ about the amount which she had spent on that affair. The narrator (al-Ḥasan b. Sahl) continued: Ḥamdūnah replied, "I spent twenty-five million [dirhams]!" The narrator continued: Umm Jaʿfar then exclaimed, "You

466. Masʿūdī, *Murūj*, VII, 66 = ed. Pellat, § 2752.

467. Ibn Abī Ṭāhir, 209–10, tr. 95.

468. Ibid., 210, tr. 95; Yaʿqūbī, *Ta'rīkh*, II, 559; Masʿūdī, *Murūj*, VII, 65–6 = ed. Pellat, § 2752; *ʿUyūn*, 367; Thaʿālibī, *Laṭā'if al-maʿārif*, 120–2, tr. Bosworth, *The Book of curious and entertaining information*, 99–100. This episode especially caught the fancy of later *adab* writers, see e.g., Niẓāmī ʿArūḍī Samarqandī, *Chahār maqāla*, *maqāla* i, anecdote 7.

didn't do anything at all! I spent between thirty-five and thirty-seven million dirhams!" The narrator continued: We prepared for al-Ma'mūn two candles of ambergris. He continued: Al-Ma'mūn consummated his marriage with Būrān by night, and the two candles were lit in his presence. But they smoked badly, so that he said, "Take them away, the smoke is bothering us, and bring ordinary [wax] candles." The narrator continued: That day, Umm Jaʿfar gave her as a wedding present Ṣilḥ. He continued: This was how Ṣilḥ reverted to my possession. I had owned it previously. Then one day, Ḥumayd al-Ṭūsī came into my presence and recited to me four verses of poetry in which he eulogized Dhū al-Ri'āsatayn (al-Ḥasan's brother al-Faḍl b. Sahl). I said to him, "We will pass on the verses to Dhū al-Ri'āsatayn on your behalf, and I myself will make you a grant of Ṣilḥ as an interim measure until you get your full reward directly from him." Thus I made him a grant of Ṣilḥ. Then al-Ma'mūn gave it to Umm Jaʿfar, and she gave it as a wedding present to Būrān.[469]

ʿAlī b. al-Ḥusayn relates that al-Ḥasan b. Sahl used not to have the curtains taken away from round him, nor were the candles removed from his presence, until the sun rose and he could distinguish it clearly when he looked at it. Also, he was superstitious and believed in omens (*kāna mutaṭayyiran*). He used to like people to say to him, when someone came into his presence, "We have left happiness and enjoyment behind;"[470] and he used to dislike being told about a funeral bier or someone's death. [1085]

The narrator (ʿAlī b. al-Ḥusayn) continued: I went into his[471] presence one day, and someone had told him that ʿAlī b. al-Ḥusayn (the narrator) had sent his son al-Ḥasan to the Qur'ān school that day. He continued: He expressed his felicitations to me, and I went away and found in my house a gift of twenty

469. Ibn Abī Ṭāhir, 210–11, tr. 95–6; cf. Abbott, 230–4.

470. I.e., we are awe-stricken and feel completely at his mercy.

471. The most natural referent of the pronoun would be al-Ḥasan b. Sahl, mentioned immediately previously by name; Keller, however, takes it in Ibn Abī Ṭāhir's text—as ambiguous as Ṭabarī's—as referring to the Caliph al-Ma'mūn, and this seems the more suitable inference in the general context.

thousand dirhams for (my son) al-Ḥasan and a draft for twenty thousand more. He continued: He had already given me as a present an estate from his own lands at Baṣrah valued at fifty thousand dīnārs, but (subsequently) Bughā al-Kabīr[472] deprived me of it and added it to his own lands.[473]

It is mentioned from Abū Ḥassān al-Ziyādī[474] that he said that when al-Ma'mūn visited al-Ḥasan b. Sahl, he stayed with him for several days after the consummation of his marriage with Būrān. The total time which he spent on his stay and on the journey, both the outward journey and the return amounted to forty days, and he re-entered Baghdad on Thursday, the eighteenth of Shawwāl (210 [February 1, 826]). It is mentioned from Muḥammad b. Mūsā al-Khwārazmī[475] that he stated that al-Ma'mūn set out for Fam al-Ṣilḥ to visit al-Ḥasan b. Sahl on the eighth of Ramaḍān, (210 [December 23, 825]) and journeyed back from Fam al-Ṣilḥ on the twentieth of Shawwāl, 210 (February 3, 826).[476]

In this year, Ḥumayd b. ʿAbd al-Ḥamīd (al-Ṭūsī) perished on the day of the breaking of the fast (on the first of Shawwāl [January 15, 826]). His slave girl ʿAdhal recited:

[1086] He who set out on the morning of the day of the breaking of the fast with a light heart,
at a time when we had no envious feelings towards him, God be praised!

---

472. The Turkish slave commander who played a great rôle in politics and military affairs during the middle years of the third/ninth century; see *EI*² s.v. (Sourdel).

473. Ibn Abī Ṭāhir, 211, tr. 96.

474. A judge by profession who was later involved in the *miḥnah* (see below, 210, 211), and who was also a significant historical source for Ibn Abī Ṭāhir; see Keller, II, Intro., pp. XIV–XVII.

475. The famous mathematician and astronomer, who in his youth worked in al-Ma'mūn's research and translation center, the Bayt al-Ḥikmah, see *EI*² s.v. al-Khʷārazmī, Abū Djaʿfar Muḥammad b. Mūsā (J. Vernet); but he was also a historian and a source for Ibn Abī Ṭāhir, see Keller, loc. cit.

476. The reading adopted here of the eighteenth of Shawwāl follows the text of Ibn Abī Ṭāhir, 212, against Ṭabarī's text with the eleventh of Shawwāl (*baqiyat* against *khalat*); as Keller points out, tr. 96, n.1, the date of the eighteenth of Shawwāl gives a period of forty days from the departure date of the eighth of Ramaḍān. Yaʿqūbī, *Ta'rīkh*, II, 559, simply mentions al-Ma'mūn's total absence as being forty days.

Or else he was waiting for his master at the time of the breaking of the fast,
while our master was in fact already laid in his sepulchre in the earth.

In this year, ʿAbdallāh b. Ṭāhir conquered Egypt and ʿUbaydallāh b. al-Sarī b. al-Ḥakam[477] sought a guarantee of security under his protection.

ʿAbdallāh b. Ṭāhir Goes Forth from Raqqah to Egypt; Ibn al-Sarī Goes Out to Him under a Guarantee of Security

It is mentioned that when ʿAbdallāh b. Ṭāhir had finished with the campaign against Naṣr b. Shabath al-ʿUqaylī and had sent him on to al-Maʾmūn, letters from al-Maʾmūn reached him at Baghdad ordering him to march to Egypt. Aḥmad b. Muḥammad b. Makhlad[478] related to me that he was at that time in Egypt and that when ʿAbdallāh b. Ṭāhir drew near to it and was only one stage's journey away, he sent out one of his commanders in order to reconnoitre for a good place in which his army could encamp. Ibn al-Sarī had dug a defensive trench round it (the capital Fusṭāṭ).[479] The latter got news about ʿAbdallāh's commander's reconnaissance to the close vicinity of the capital, hence he marched out with a force of supporters who had flocked to his standard against the commander whom ʿAbdallāh b. Ṭāhir had deputed to find a camping-place for his army. Ibn al-Sarī's army and ʿAbdallāh's commander and his accompanying force, which was only a small one, made battle

477. ʿUbaydallāh had been *ṣāḥib al-shurṭah* in Egypt since 205 (820/1) under his brother Abū Naṣr and then himself governor in Shaʿbān 206 (January 822), resisting attempts by al-Maʾmūn to replace him; see Kindī, 172–4; Ibn Taghrībirdī, *al-Nujūm al-zāhirah*, II, 178, 181 ff.

478. Presumably a member of the family of secretaries and viziers, of Christian origin, who served the caliphs in the second half of the century; see Sourdel, *Vizirat*, I, 309 ff., 316 ff; EI^2 s.v. Ibn al-Makhlad (id.).

479. From Kindī, 180, it appears that ʿAbdallāh b. Ṭāhir encamped at Bilbays on entering Egypt and then moved to Zufaytā some twenty miles north of Fusṭāṭ (modern Zifta), whilst ʿUbaydallāh fortified himself within Fusṭāṭ by building the ditch and rampart (*khandaq*) further referred to in ibid., 174.

contact. ʿAbdallāh's commander and his troops wheeled away in an evasive action, and he sent a dispatch by mounted mes-
[1087] senger to ʿAbdallāh informing him about what he had been doing and about Ibn al-Sarī's actions. ʿAbdallāh mounted his foot soldiers on mules, two men on each mule, with all their arms and equipment. They led the horses along by the side of the mules and travelled as speedily as possible till they caught up with ʿAbdallāh's commander and Ibn al-Sarī. ʿAbdallāh and his troops only had to make a single charge and Ibn al-Sarī and his forces were routed. Most of Ibn al-Sarī's forces fell successively into the ditch, and more of them perished in the trench by their bodies falling one on top of another than were killed by the swords of the opposing army. Ibn al-Sarī himself fled; he retired into Fusṭāṭ and closed the gate, with himself, his followers and the resident population all inside it. ʿAbdallāh b. Ṭāhir besieged him, but Ibn al-Sarī did not continue fighting back against him after this; in the end, he came forth to ʿAbdallāh under a guarantee of safety.

It is mentioned from Ibn Dhī al-Qalamayn[480] (the son of ʿAlī b. Abī Saʿīd, cousin of al-Faḍl b. Sahl), who stated that when ʿAbdallāh b. Ṭāhir came to the capital of Egypt and Ibn al-Sarī barred him from entry, Ibn al-Sarī sent him a thousand male and female slaves, each slave boy having with him a thousand dīnārs in a silken purse; these he sent by night. The narrator continued: However, ʿAbdallāh sent all these back to him and wrote, "If I were able to accept your present by day, then I would
certainly accept it by night, but 'Nay, it is you who rejoice in your gift. Return to them; indeed, we shall come to them with hosts which they will have no power to withstand and we shall certainly expel them from it abased and in a state of humiliation'"[481] The narrator continued: At that point, Ibn al-Sarī sought a guarantee of security from 'Abdallāh and went forth to him.[482]

---

480. For suggestions on the meaning of this honorific, see Sourdel, *Vizirat*, I, 202–3.

481. Qur'ān, XXVII, 36–7.

482. In Abī Ṭāhir, 148–9, tr. 67–8; Yaʿqūbī, *Ta'rīkh*, II, 560–1; Kindī, 180–3, giving the date of ʿUbaydallāh b. al-Sarī's submission to ʿAbdallāh b. Ṭāhir as in

Aḥmad b. Ḥafṣ b. ʿUmar mentioned from Abū al-Samrāʾ, who said: We set out with the amīr ʿAbdallāh b. Ṭāhir, travelling in the direction of Egypt. When we were at a point between Ramlah and Damascus, a tribesman suddenly appeared before us. He turned out to be an old man, of obvious intelligence and piety (*baqiyyah*),[483] mounted on a greyish-colored camel. He greeted us, and we returned the greeting. Abū al-Samrāʾ continued: I was with Isḥāq b. Ibrāhīm al-Rāfiqī and Isḥāq b. Abī Ribʿī, and we were accompanying the amīr in his journey. It happened that on that particular day we had more spirited mounts than he, and we were wearing finer-quality clothes. He continued: The tribesman started peering intently at our faces. He continued: I therefore said, "O shaykh, you are eyeing us very persistently; have you recognized something, or is there something of which you disapprove?" He replied, "No, by God, I never knew you before today, and I have not discerned in you any evil characteristic which I should condemn; but I possess a very keen ability of knowing people's character and fates through physiognomy [*firāsah*],[484] and am able to discern a great deal about them." He continued: I then pointed out Isḥāq b. Abī Ribʿī to him and said, "What can you say about this man?" He thereupon recited: [1088]

I see a secretary, whose skill in the secretary's art is clearly to be discerned,
and with his training in Iraq shining forth.[485]

The movements which he makes amply bear witness to the fact that he is
knowledgeable and far-sighted about the assessment of the land-tax.

Ṣafar 211 (May–June 826); *ʿUyūn*, 367–8; Ibn al-Athīr, *al-Kāmil*, VI, 396–7; Ibn Taghrībirdī, *al-Nujūm*, II, 181, 191–2. On al-Maʾmūn's Egyptian policy in general, see Shaban, 52–3, 59–61.

483. This is the meaning which this word acquired from the traditional interpretation of the phrase *ūlū baqiyyah* in Qurʾān, XI, 118/116; see Lane, *Arabic-English lexicon*, Part 1, 238c.

484. On this skill, see EI^2 s.v. (T. Fahd).

485. The complexity of the administrative and fiscal system of the Sawād of Iraq made it the training ground par excellence for secretaries.

Then he looked at Isḥāq b. Ibrāhīm al-Rāfiqī and recited:

Many a person who outwardly manifests piety does not reveal externally his inner character,
loves presents [that is, he is corrupt] and acts deceitfully with men.

I discern in him cowardliness, avarice and a personal character
which tells one about him that he is indeed a vizier.

Then he looked at me and began to recite:

This man is one of the amīr's boon companions and confidants,
from whose intimacy the amīr derives joy.

I recognise him as a transmitter of poetry and the religious sciences,
and also at times a boon companion and storyteller at nocturnal literary sessions.

Then he looked at the amīr and began to recite:

This one is the amīr, the bounty of whose hands is hoped for;
among all those I have ever seen, there is none like him.

He wears a cloak of seemliness and dignity,
and has a face which bears the good tidings of the attainment of success.

Through him, Islam has been made secure from the outset;
through him, goodness has flourished and evil has withered away.

Is not ʿAbdallāh b. Ṭāhir
indeed a father to us, a benefit for us as well as being an amīr?

He continued to relate: All this made an extremely favorable impression on ʿAbdallāh. The shaykh's words delighted him, so he ordered that he should be given five hundred dīnārs and that he should accompany him.[486] [1090]

It is mentioned from al-Ḥasan b. Yaḥyā al-Fihrī, who said: We met al-Buṭayn, the poet of Ḥimṣ,[487] while we were accompanying ʿAbdallāh b. Ṭāhir, at a spot between Salamiyyah[488] and Ḥimṣ. He halted in the roadway and recited to ʿAbdallāh b. Ṭāhir:

A twofold welcome and greetings
to the son of the munificent one, Ṭāhir b. al-Ḥusayn!

A twofold welcome and greetings
to the son of the man with two noble characteristics [*ghurratayn*] in the two missions [*daʿwatayn*]![489]

A twofold welcome to the one whose palm is a sea [of bounty]
when it overflows like the foaming waters over the two sides of a well!

Al-Ma'mūn, may God strengthen him, does not have to worry
as long as he has the two of you [Ṭāhir and ʿAbdallāh] remaining in his service.

You are a West, and he is an East, established there
against whatever breach may occur from the two sides [of the empire].

It is only right, since the two of you are from a long time back
the descendants of Ruzayq,[490] Muṣʿab and Ḥusayn,

---

486. Ibn Abī Ṭāhir, 158–60, tr. 71–2; Ibn al-Athīr, *al-Kāmil*, VI, 397–8; Ibn Taghrībirdī, *al-Nujūm*, II, 193–4.

487. Al-Buṭayn b. Umayyah al-Bajalī; see Sezgin, *GAS*, II, 477.

488. A town to the northeast of Ḥimṣ; see Yāqūt, *Muʿjam*, III, 240–1; Le Strange, *Palestine under the Moslems*, 510, 528; R. Dussaud, *Topographie historique de la Syrie antique et médiévale*, 272–3; *EI*[1] s.v. Salamīya (Kramers).

489. I.e., the ʿAbbāsid revolution and the movement to place al-Ma'mūn on the throne, sometimes referred to by contemporaries as *al-daʿwah al-thāniyah*; cf. on the latter, Daniel, 177–80.

490. Both Ṭabarī's text and that of Ibn Abī Ṭāhir, loc. cit., have, wrongly,

That you should both reach the peak of glory which you have in fact reached
and that you should attain a position of superiority over the two heavy creations [men and jinn].[491]

[1091] ʿAbdallāh said, "Who are you, may your mother be bereft of you?" He replied, "I am al-Buṭayn, the poet of Ḥimṣ." ʿAbdallāh said, "Ride with us, lad, and reflect how may lines of verse you have just recited." He replied, "Seven." So ʿAbdallāh ordered that he should be given seven thousand dirhams or seven hundred dīnārs. Al-Buṭayn journeyed with ʿAbdallāh all the way to Egypt and Alexandria, until the time when a drainage outlet (*makhraj*) opened up in the ground and swallowed him and his mount, and he died in it at Alexandria[492]

In this year, ʿAbdallāh b. Ṭāhir captured Alexandria—according to other reports, in the year 211 (826/7)—and expelled from it the Andalusians who had taken the city over.[493]

The Activities of ʿAbdallāh and the Andalusians

Several of the people of Egypt related to me that some ships approached on the Mediterranean (Baḥr al-Rūm) from the direction of Andalus, containing a large number of men, at the time when the local people were distracted from their approach by the insurrection of al-Jarawī[494] and Ibn al-Sarī. Finally, they an-

---

Zurayq. The ancestor Ruzayq had been a mawlā of the Umayyad governor of Sīstān Ṭalḥah b. ʿAbdallāh al-Khuzāʿī; see Bosworth, "The Ṭāhirids and Arabic culture," 47; Kaabi, 148–51.

491. See Bosworth, op. cit., 60–1.

492. Ibn Abī Ṭāhir, 160–1, tr. 72–3; Ibn Taghrībirdī, *al-Nujūm*, II, 194–5.

493. These Andalusian corsairs and adventurers included considerable elements from the rebels expelled from the suburb of Cordova in 202 (818) by the Umayyad amīr, al-Ḥakam I, the so-called al-Rabaḍiyyūn; see E. Lévi-Provençal, *Histoire de l'Espagne musulmane*, I, 165–73.

494. Yaʿqūbī, *Taʾrīkh*, II, 555–6, Kindī, 169 ff., and Severus b. al-Muqaffaʿ, *Taʾrīkh Baṭāriqat al-kanīsah al-miṣriyyah*, ed. and tr. B. Evetts, *History of the Patriarchs of the Coptic Church of Alexandria*, IV, 428, give accounts of ʿAlī b. ʿAbd al-ʿAzīz al-Jarawī's revolt in lower Egypt and then his submission to al-Maʾmūn's commanders, sent to Egypt to re-establish caliphal authority, Khālid b. Yazīd b. Mazyad al-Shaybānī (see above, 147) and ʿUmar b. Faraj al-Rukhkhajī.

chored their ships at Alexandria, their leader at that time being a man called Abū Ḥafṣ (ʿUmar b. Ḥafṣ al-Ballūṭī), and they remained there till ʿAbdallāh b. Ṭāhir entered Egypt.[495]

Yūnus b. ʿAbd al-Aʿlā told me: A young man—he meant ʿAbdallāh b. Ṭāhir—came to us from the direction of the east at a time when our whole world had been plunged into strife; various usurpers had seized power in every part of the land, and had terrorized the people; but he set the world to rights, brought peace and security to the innocent and struck fear into the evil-minded, and the subjects flocked to him tendering their obedience. Then he continued: ʿAbdallāh b. Wahb related [1092] to us from ʿAbdallāh b. Lahīʿah, who said (I do not know whether he carried the transmission back to an earlier generation or not; we have not found [it] in any of the books which we have read): God has an army in the east, and none of His creation has rebelled against Him without His having sent this army against them and His having wrought vengeance on them by means of it (or some other form of words with this meaning).

When ʿAbdallāh b. Ṭāhir b. al-Ḥusayn entered Egypt, he sent a message to the Andalusians there and to those who had joined up with them, announcing that he was going to attack them unless they submitted. They (that is, the authorities on events in Egypt) related to me that the Andalusians agreed to submit, and sought a guarantee of safe-conduct from him, on condition that they were to depart from Alexandria to some other region of the land of Rūm (the Byzantine territories) which was not part of the lands of Islam. ʿAbdallāh granted them a guarantee on this condition, hence they set sail from Alexandria and landed on one of the islands in the (Mediterranean) Sea called Crete. They established a colony and settled there, and there are the remains of their progeny on that island to this day.[496]

495. Yaʿqūbī, *Taʾrīkh*, II, 541–2, Kindī, 158, 161–5, 169–70, and Severus, IV, 429 ff., give the circumstances of the Andalusians' seizure of the city from the Banū Mudlij and the Lakhm in 199 (814/15).

496. Yaʿqūbī, *Taʾrīkh*, II, 560–1; Kindī, 183–4 (both placing ʿAbdallāh's recovery of Alexandria in the early part of 212 [summer 827]; Severus, IV, 455 ff.,

In this year, the people of Qumm threw off their allegiance to the ruling authority and withheld payment of the land-tax.

The People of Qumm Throw off the Ruling Authority

It is mentioned that the reason for their renunciation of it was that they considered the burden of the land-tax imposed on them as being excessively high. The tax required amounted to two million dirhams. Al-Ma'mūn had reduced the people of Rayy's assessment when he had entered the city on his journey from Khurasan to Iraq by the amount which I mentioned previously. Hence the people of Qumm were eager for al-Ma'mūn to lighten their burden and decrease their taxation just as he had done for the people of Rayy. They made petition to him, requesting a reduction in taxation and complaining of its heavi-
[1093] ness upon them. But al-Ma'mūn refused to grant their request. Thereupon they withheld payment of taxes, so al-Ma'mūn sent against them ʿAlī b. Hishām and then reinforced him with ʿUjayf b. ʿAnbasah. One of Ḥumayd's commanders called Muḥammad b. Yūsuf al-K.ḥ b.q.w.ṣ[497] came from Khurasan, and al-Ma'mūn wrote to him to head towards Qumm and attack its people in concert with ʿAlī b. Hishām. ʿAlī fought with them and gained a victory over them, killing Yaḥyā b. ʿImrān and razing the town walls of Qumm. He imposed on them a tax assessment of seven million dirhams, after they had (previously) complained of two millions.[498]

In this year, Shahriyār, the son of Sharwīn, died. His son Sābūr took his place, but Māzyār b. Qārin disputed the succes-

---

465 ff.; *ʿUyūn*, 369; Ibn al-Athīr, *al-Kāmil*, VI, 398–9; Ibn Taghrībirdī, *al-Nujūm*, II, 192. The Andalusian control over Crete, under members of the family of Abū Ḥafṣ ʿUmar, lasted until the Byzantine reconquest of 961; see Canard, in *Cambridge medieval history. IV. The Byzantine empire. I*, 709; Vasiliev, *Byzance et les Arabes*, I, 49–61, 287; EI^2 s.v. Iḳrīṭish (Canard).

497. Reading uncertain here, and equally so in the death notice (year 236 [850/1]) of this commander in Ṭabarī, III, 1407 (where he is given the *nisbah* of al-Marwazī).

498. Ibn al-Athīr, *al-Kāmil*, VI, 399; Shaban, 55. Al-Ma'mūn's destruction of the town walls is noted in Ḥasan b. Muḥammad Qummī, *Ta'rīkh-i Qum*, 35, 163, 189–90.

sion with him, and captured and killed him. The mountain region (the inland parts of Ṭabaristān) now passed into the hands of Māzyār b. Qārin.[499]

In this year, Ṣāliḥ b. al-ʿAbbās b. Muḥammad, the governor of Mecca at that time, led the pilgrimage.[500]

---

499. Ibn al-Athīr, *al-Kāmil,* VI, 401; *EI*[1] s.v. Māzyār (Minorsky); *EI*[2] s.v. Ḳārinids (Rekaya).

500. Khalīfah, *Ta'rīkh,* II, 773; Azdī, 372.

The Events of the Year 211

(APRIL 13, 826–APRIL 1, 827)

Among the events taking place during this year was ʿUbaydallāh b. al-Sarī's journeying forth to ʿAbdallāh b. Ṭāhir under a guarantee of safe-conduct and ʿAbdallāh b. Ṭāhir's entering Egypt. It is said that this (actually) took place in the year 210 (825/6). A certain authority mentions that Ibn al-Sarī went forth to ʿAbdallāh b. Ṭāhir on Saturday, the twenty-fourth of Ṣafar 211[501] (June 5, 826),[502] was brought to Baghdad on the twenty-third of Rajab, 211 (October 29, 826) and lodged in the
[1094] City of Abū Jaʿfar.[503] ʿAbdallāh b. Ṭāhir remained in Egypt as

501. Actually a Monday.

502. Keller, Ibn Abī Ṭāhir, tr. 68, n.1, points out that, from mentions elsewhere (e.g., text 145, tr. 66) of this author's concern with Egyptian events in 210, the date of ʿUbaydallāh's going forth to ʿAbdallāh must have been on Saturday, the twenty-sixth of Rajab, 210 (November 12, 825—but this was actually a Sunday). Ṭabarī's ms. O has Rajab, and the preferable date 210 of mss. C and O was rejected by the editor as wrong. But Kindī, 182, in a detailed account of events, with several circumstantial dates, has Ṣafar 211 as the date for ʿUbaydallāh's formal acceptance of the *amān*.

503. Yaʿqūbī, *Taʾrīkh*, II, 561, says that ʿAbdallāh appointed ʿUbaydallāh over upper Egypt for two months before sending him to Baghdad.

governor of the province and over the whole (*sā'ir*) of Syria and the Jazirah.[504] It is mentioned from Ṭāhir b. Khālid b. Nizār al-Ghassānī, who said that al-Ma'mūn wrote to ʿAbdallāh b. Ṭāhir when the latter was in Egypt at the time of his conquest of the province, and at the foot of one of his letters (were the words):

> You are my brother and my friend (*mawlāyā*),
> and the one for whose benefits I give thanks.
>
> Whatever thing you may love,
> I will show my desire for it eternally.
>
> While whatever thing you may dislike,
> I shall find it displeasing.
>
> You have God's word for this,
> you have God's word, you have God's word!

Al-Ma'mūn Tests ʿAbdallāh b. Ṭāhir

It is mentioned from ʿAṭā', the official charged with hearing complaints (*ṣāḥib al-maẓālim*)[505] for ʿAbdallāh b. Ṭāhir, who related that one of al-Ma'mūn's brothers spoke to al-Ma'mūn thus, "O Commander of the Faithful, ʿAbdallāh b. Ṭāhir has an inclination towards the progeny of Abū Ṭālib, just as his father had before him." He continued: Al-Ma'mūn pushed this suggestion aside and gave it no credence. Then the brother came back and repeated the same allegation. So al-Ma'mūn sent a man secretly to ʿAbdallāh instructing him, "Go forth to Egypt in the guise of one of the Qur'ān reciters[506] and ascetics, and summon a group of the great men of state there to the alle-

504. Ibn Abī Ṭāhir, 149, tr. 68; Azdī, 368, 373; Ibn al-Athīr, *al-Kāmil*, VI, 402.
505. Concerning this function, see H.F. Amedroz, "The mazālim jurisdiction in the Ahkam Sultaniyya of Mawardi," *JRAS* (1911), 635–74; Levy, *The social structure of Islam*, 348–51; *EI*[2] s.v. Maẓālim (J.S. Nielsen).
506. *al-qurrā'*, also in Ibn al-Athīr, *al-Kāmil*, VI, 402; Ibn Abī Ṭahir, 146, tr. 66, and *ʿUyūn*, 369, have *al-ghuzāt*, "frontier warriors for the faith."

giance of al-Qāsim b. Ibrāhīm b. Ṭabāṭabā (al-Rassī),[507] recounting his virtues, his learning and his merits. After that, get in touch with one of ʿAbdallāh b. Ṭāhir's confidants and then go to ʿAbdallāh himself, summoning him and making attractive to him the giving of allegiance to the ʿAlid. Ferret out in a manner which dispels doubt about his innermost intentions, and report back to me what you hear from him."

He continued to relate: The man did what al-Ma'mūn had told and instructed him to do. He summoned to allegiance a group of the leading men and notables, and then he sat down one day at ʿAbdallāh b. Ṭāhir's gate, at a moment when the latter had ridden to visit ʿUbaydallāh b. al-Sarī after he had made peace with him and granted him a guarantee of security. When ʿAbdallāh returned, the man rose up before him and brought
[1095] out of his sleeve a paper, and handed it to him. ʿAbdallāh took it in his hand. ʿAbdallāh had hardly gone in, when the chamberlain came out to the man and escorted him inside, where he found ʿAbdallāh seated on his carpet with nothing else between it and the ground, with his legs stretched out and his boots still on. ʿAbdallāh said to him, "I have understood what is in your paper, the whole of what you have said—so out with what you really mean!" The man said, "Do I have your guarantee of safety and the protection of God in regard to you?" He replied, "Certainly."

He related: He then revealed to ʿAbdallāh his intention, and summoned him to give allegiance to al-Qāsim, telling him all about his merits, his learning and his ascetic way of life. ʿAbdallāh asked him, "Will you give me a fair hearing?" He replied that he would. ʿAbdallāh then asked him, "Is gratitude to God incumbent on all His servants?" He agreed that it was. He further asked, "Is gratitude incumbent on one person to another in return for beneficence, favors and acts of kindness?" He agreed that it was. ʿAbdallāh said, "Yet you come to me, when I am in this exalted position which you see, with my seal effica-

507. Brother of the Ḥasanid Ibn Ṭabāṭabā whose revolt in Kūfah in 199 (815) was managed by Abū al-Sarāyā, see above, 13 ff., and founder of the Rassid line of Zaydī Imāms in the Yemen, died in 246 (860), see *EI*[1] s.v. Rassids (A.S. Tritton).

cious in the East as in the West, and my command obeyed and my word accepted in the lands between? I have only to turn to my right or left, or to look behind me or before me, and I see manifestations of acts of liberality from a man who has heaped them upon me, favor with which he has laid a seal on my neck, and unsolicited, clear beneficence [literally: a white, shining hand, *yad lā'iḥah bayḍā'*] which he bestowed upon me from the outset of graciousness and nobility of character! And you now invite me to display ingratitude for favor and for this beneficence, and you say, 'Betray the one who was the first and the last mover in all this, and bend your efforts to sever the vital cord of his neck and shed his blood!'? Do you yourself think that, even if you were to invite me directly into the Garden of Paradise, so that I could see it before my very eyes, as I know Paradise to be, God would like me to betray him, display ingratitude for his beneficence and favors, and break my oath of allegiance to him?"

The man remained silent. Then ʿAbdallāh said to him, "Moreover, I have heard all about your activities, and by God, I am only afraid for your life. So depart from this land, for if the supreme ruling authority gets to hear about your doings—and I [1096] cannot give you a guarantee of security concerning that—you will bring down disaster on both yourself and others."

Thus when the man had despaired of acheiving anything of his intentions, he came to al-Ma'mūn and told him the whole story. The Caliph rejoiced greatly and exclaimed, "That man is the tender shoot nurtured by my own hand, the intimate companion from my process of upbringing and the sprig of my fertilization and grafting!" He never divulged anything of this to anyone, and ʿAbdallāh only knew about it after al-Ma'mūn's death.[508]

It is mentioned from (or: concerning, *ʿan*) ʿAbdallāh b. Ṭāhir that, while he was besieging ʿUbaydallāh b. al-Sarī in Egypt, he recited these verses:

508. Ibn Abī Ṭāhir, 145–8, tr. 66–7; *ʿUyūn*, 369–70; Ibn al-Athīr, *al-Kāmil*, VI, 402–3, identifying the brother who denounced ʿAbdallāh as al-Muʿtaṣim.

She shed copious tears in the morning,
when she saw how near was the moment of my departure,

And I exchanged by richly-embroidered sash
for a gleaming Yemeni sword,

And spent a long time in journeying
both in the mornings and the evening [that is, in perpetual travelling].

She considered it foolish, in that
I was weary and without rest,

[But I said to her,] Cut short your dalliance with me, for I am setting out on the road in search of my fortune.

I am one of al-Ma'mūn's servants,
in the shadow of [his] protective wing.

If God one day grants success,
then the attainment of my place of refreshment and repose will be near;

But if it be destruction, then proclaim
with lamentation and cries,

"A slain one has found his last resting-place in Egypt,"
and leave off your complaining and querulousness.[509]

It is mentioned from ʿAbdallāh b. Aḥmad b. Yūsuf that his father[510] wrote to ʿAbdallāh b. Ṭāhir at the point when ʿUbaydallāh b. al-Sarī submitted to him congratulating him on that success (in the following words):

509. Ibn Abī Ṭāhir, 148, tr. 67.

510. Aḥmad b. Yūsuf was a secretary and confidant of al-Ma'mūn, occupying in effect the position of vizier after the death in 211 (827) of Aḥmad b. Abī Khālid; see Sourdel, *Vizirat*, I, 225–31.

I have heard the news, may God strengthen the amīr, of the victory which God has granted you and Ibn al-Sarī's submission to you. So praise be to God, who upholds the cause of His faith, who strengthens the secular power of His Caliph appointed over His servants, and who humbles [1097] the one who deviates from His way and His rightful due and who throws off obedience to Him! We implore God to strengthen him with acts of favor and to assist him in conquering the lands of polytheism. Praise be to God for the authority which he has given to you[511] since you departed from your specified purpose! Indeed, we and all our dependents remind ourselves with pride of your conduct in engaging in battle and granting peace, and we show immense wonder at the qualities bestowed on him [ʿAbdallāh] [by God] of severity and leniency in their appropriate places. We do not know of any ruler over a body of soldiers or subjects who acts so equitably between them as you do, nor of anyone who grants forgiveness, to persons who have caused harm or shown rancor towards him, from a position of superior strength as you do. How rarely do we see a nobly-descended person who does not give up control of his affairs [that is, throw away his own personal talent or potential], relying rather upon what his forefathers have passed on to him! And the one who is given good fortune, material sufficiency, ruling authority and governmental power does not simply cleave to[512] what has fallen to his share in abundant quantity,[513] so that he falls short in being able to cope with what is before him.[514] Furthermore, we do

511. This seems to be the sense, and Keller, Ibn Abī Ṭāhir, tr. 68, adopts a similar interpretation of the parallel passage in this author, "was er dir erwiesen hat."

512. *Lam yukhlid,* following the sense of *akhlada ilā al-arḍ,* "he clung to the ground," in Qur'ān, VII, 175/176.

513. *Mā ʿafā lahu,* echoing the sense of *ʿafā* given by some commentators, "be luxuriant," where it occurs in Qur'ān, VII, 93/95.

514. This seems to be the sense of a difficult passage with tortuous syntax, whose general meaning depends largely on the interpretation of the phrase *lam yulqi bi-yadihi,* here translated as "does not cast away by his own hand," following Dozy, II, 547a.

not know any person exercising power who deserves success on account of his good conduct and his restraining of the arbitrary conduct of his retainers as you do. Nor does any one of our dependants consider it appropriate that he should prefer before you anyone whom he would like to have in the face of affliction or some calamitous happening. So may God's beneficence and His augmentation of favor reward you, and may God grant you this favor which He has brought together for you, by keeping firm hold of that by means of which the bond with your Imām and master and the master of all the Muslims will be completely strengthened for you. May He also grant you and us perpetuation of life! For you yourself well know that you have never ceased to be, in our eyes and in those of our dependents, in an honored status, assured of primacy and magnified in our sight. God has bestowed on you an increase of glory and honor in the eyes of the high and the
[1098] low, so that they focus all their personal hopes on you and regard you as their bulwark against the adverse events and vicissitudes which come upon them. I hope that God will guide you to those things which He loves, just as His benefits and favor have helped you to success. Indeed, you have comported yourself well in achieving the protection of divine favor; for it has not led you into arrogance and presumption, and you have only grown in humility and self-abasement. So praise be to God for what He has secured for you, has conferred on you of benefits and has entrusted to you! Farewell![515]

In this year, ʿAbdallāh b. Ṭāhir b. al-Ḥusayn arrived in the City of Peace from the western lands,[516] and al-ʿAbbās b. al-Ma'mūn,[517] Abū Isḥāq al-Muʿtaṣim and the rest of the men of

515. Ibn Abī Ṭāhir, 150–1, tr. 68–9.

516. Kindī, 184, says that ʿAbdallāh sailed down the Nile from Fusṭāṭ, en route for Iraq, on the twenty-fifth Rajab, 212 (October 20, 827).

517. Claimant to the caliphate after his father's death in 218 (833) and especially during the rebellion of 223 (838) against his uncle al-Muʿtaṣim; see Ṭabarī, III, 1249–50, 1257–68, tr. E. Marin, *The reign of al-Muʿtaṣim (833–842)*, 71, 76–85.

state came out to meet him. He brought with him the rebels who had previously seized control over Syria, such as Ibn al-Sarj, Ibn Abī al-Jamal and Ibn Abī al-Ṣaqr.[518]

(In this year,) Mūsā b. Ḥafṣ died, and Muḥammad b. Mūsā took over the governorship of Ṭabaristān in his father's stead.[519]

(In this year,) Ḥājib b. Ṣāliḥ became governor of India, but Bishr b. Dāwūd (al-Muhallabī) defeated him in battle and he retreated to Kirmān.[520]

In this year, al-Ma'mūn ordered a herald to proclaim, "No protection for anyone who mentions the name of Muʿāwiyah favorably or who accords him superiority over any one of the Messenger of God's Companions."[521]

In this year, Ṣāliḥ b. al-ʿAbbās, governor of Mecca, led the pilgrimage.[522]

In this year, the poet Abū al-ʿAtāhiyah died.[523]

---

518. Ibn Abī Ṭāhir, 149, tr. 68; Azdī, 378; *ʿUyūn*, 370; Ibn al-Athīr, *al-Kāmil.*, VI, 406.

519. Ibid.; Rabino di Borgomale, "Les préfets du Califat au Ṭabaristān," 264.

520. Ibn al-Athīr, *al-Kāmil*, loc. cit.; Yaʿqūbī, *Ta'rīkh*, II, 557, records that Ḥājib b. Ṣāliḥ was originally sent out by al-Ma'mūn to quell the rebellious Bishr.

521. Masʿūdī, *Murūj*, VII, 90–1 = ed. Pellat, § 2775; *ʿUyūn*, loc. cit.; Ibn al-Athīr, *al-Kāmil*, loc. cit.; Goldziher, *Muhammedanische Studien*, II, 46–7, Eng. tr. II, 54; Pellat, "Le culte de Muʿâwiya au IIIe siècle," *SI*, VI (1956), 55. According to Masʿūdī, *Murūj*, VII, 93 = ed. Pellat, § 2776, cf. Sourdel, "La politique religieuse du calife ʿabbāside al-Ma'mūn," 39, the Caliph was dissuaded from this course on the grounds that it would cause discontent among the people.

522. Khalīfah, *Ta'rīkh*, II, 774; Azdī, loc. cit.; Ibn al-Athīr, *al-Kāmil*, loc. cit.

523. Ibid.; Sezgin, *GAS*, II, 534–5; *EI*^{2} s.v. (A. Guillaume).

[1099] # The Events of the Year

212

(APRIL 2, 827–MARCH 21, 828)

Among the events taking place during this year was al-Ma'mūn's dispatching Muḥammad b. Ḥumayd al-Ṭūsī[524] via the Mosul Road to campaign against Bābak, and his reinforcing Muḥammad b. Ḥumayd for this purpose. Muḥammad b. Ḥumayd seized Yaʿlā b. Murrah and other rebels like him in Azerbaijan and sent them back to al-Ma'mūn.[525]

In this year, Aḥmad b. Muḥammad al-ʿUmarī, known as the Red-eyed One, rebelled in the Yemen.[526]

In this year, al-Ma'mūn appointed as governor in the Yemen Muḥammad b. ʿAbd al-Ḥamīd, known as Abū al-Rāzī.[527]

In this year, al-Ma'mūn proclaimed the doctrine of the

524. Son of Ḥumayd b. ʿAbd al-Ḥamīd, and a poet as well as a soldier, cf. Sezgin, *GAS*, II, 583.

525. Yaʿqūbī, *Ta'rīkh*, II, 564 ff., with a very detailed account of events in Arrān, Azerbaijan and Armenia and the war against Bābak; Azdī, 378 ff., with a detailed account of events in the region of Mosul; *ʿUyūn*, 373; Ibn al-Athīr, *al-Kāmil*, VI, 407; Shaban, 56–9.

526. Yaʿqūbi, *Ta'rīkh*, II, 561–2; Ibn al-Athīr, *al-Kāmil*, VI, 408.

527. Yaʿqūbī, *Ta'rīkh*, II, loc. cit.; Ibn al-Athīr, *al-Kāmil*, loc. cit.

createdness of the Qur'ān and the pre-eminence (*tafḍīl*) of ʿAlī b. Abī Ṭālib, saying that he was the best of mankind after the Messenger of God. This was in the month of Rabīʿ I (June 827).[528]

In this year, ʿAbdallāh b. ʿUbaydallāh b. al-ʿAbbās b. Muḥammad led the pilgrimage.[529]

---

528. ʿ*Uyūn*, 370; Ibn al-Athīr, *al-Kāmil*, loc. cit.; Sourdel, op. cit., 38–41; cf. Marquet, 127.

529. Khalīfah, *Taʾrīkh*, II, 775; Azdī, 385; Ibn al-Athīr, *al-Kāmil*, loc. cit.

The Events of the Year

213

(MARCH 22, 828–MARCH 10, 829)

Among the events taking place during this year was the renunciation of allegiance by ʿAbd al-Salām (or: al-Sallām) and Ibn Jalīs in Egypt with a throng of Qaysīs and Yamanīs and their rebellion there.[530]

In this year, Ṭalḥah b. Ṭāhir died in Khurasan.[531]

[1100] In this year, al-Maʾmūn appointed his brother Abū Isḥāq as governor of Syria and Egypt, and his son al-ʿAbbās b. al-Maʾmūn over the Jazīrah, the frontier regions and the defensive fortresses (*al-thughūr wa-al-ʿawāṣim*),[532] and he ordered five hundred thousand dīnārs to be given to each of them and to

530. Yaʿqūbī, *Taʾrīkh*, II, 567, and Kindī, 185–6, give ʿAbdallāh b. Jalīs al-Hilālī as the leader of the Qays and ʿAbd al-Salām b. Abī al-Māḍī al-Judhāmī al-Jarawī as leader of the Yaman.

531. Ibn Abī Ṭāhir, 173–4, tr. 78, with a much fuller account; *ʿUyūn*, 371; Ibn al-Athīr, *al-Kāmil*, VI, 409; Rothstein, 162; Bosworth, in *Cambridge history of Iran*, IV, 98.

532. I.e., the much fought-over frontier zone of northern Syria and the Jazīrah separating the Dār al-Islām from Byzantium; see Vasiliev, *Byzance et les Arabes*, I, 94 ff.; *EI*² s.v. al-ʿAwāṣim (Canard).

ʿAbdallāh b. Ṭāhir. It is said that he had never before divided out a sum of money of this magnitude in a single day.[533]

In this year, he appointed Ghassān b. ʿAbbād as governor of Sind.

Al-Maʾmūn Appoints Ghassān b. ʿAbbād Governor over Sind

According to the reports which have reached me, the reason for that was that Bishr b. Dāwūd b. Yazīd (al-Muhallabī)[534] rebelled against al-Maʾmūn. He levied the land-tax, but did not forward any of it to al-Maʾmūn. It is mentioned that al-Maʾmūn said to his courtiers one day, "Tell me about Ghassān b. ʿAbbād, for I want him for an important office;" he had, in fact, already decided to appoint him governor of Sind because of the rebelliousness of Bishr b. Dāwūd. Those present spoke and went on at great length in Ghassān's praise. Then al-Maʾmūn looked towards Aḥmad b. Yūsuf, who remained silent, and said to him, "What do you say, O Aḥmad?" The latter replied, "O Commander of the Faithful, here is a man whose virtues are more numerous than his bad qualities. He is not sent[535] to any class of people without his rendering justice to them. Whatever fears you may have regarding him, he will never embark on any affair which needs excusing [or: from which he has to exculpate himself];[536] for he has divided up his days into days of beneficence [*al-faḍl*] [or possibly: he has divided up his time in the service of al-Faḍl (b. Sahl)], and for every person he allots a special time [for approaching him with petitions or complaints]. When you examine his conduct, you do not know which of his personal modes of conduct is the more remarkable—that

533. Yaʿqūbī, *Taʾrīkh*, II, loc. cit.; Azdī, loc. cit.; *ʿUyūn*, 371, 373; Thaʿālibī, *Laṭāʾif al-maʿārif*, 141, tr. 110; Ibn al-Athīr, *al-Kāmil*, VI, 409.

534. Son of the former governor of Sind Dāwūd, and great-great-great-grandson of the famous Umayyad general al-Muhallab b. Abī Ṣufrah.

535. Interpreting the consonant ductus here as *lā yuṣrafa bihi*, as seems allowable by n. *g*.

536. The text given here by the editor is very conjectural, hence the present translation must be equally so; furthermore, there is a variant text in Ibn Abī Ṭāhir, 238, tr. 109.

which his intelligence directs him towards, or that which he acquires through his education." Al-Ma'mūn said, "You have
[1101] eulogized him, despite your personally unfavorable opinion of him." Aḥmad b. Yūsuf replied, "[That is] because he is, in regard to what I have just stated, like what the poet has said:

May it be sufficient thanks for what you have bestowed on me
that I have praised you in regard to both friends and enemies.[537]

He related: Al-Ma'mūn was delighted at his words and found his learning and wit impressive.[538]

In this year, ʿAbdallāh b. ʿUbaydallāh b. al-ʿAbbās b. Muḥammad led the pilgrimage.[539]

---

537. Reading here, with ibid., 239, and the *Addenda et emendanda*, p. DCCLXXII, *ʿudātī*.

538. Ibn Abī Ṭāhir, 238–9, tr. 108–9, adding a second verse; Yaʿqūbī, *Ta'rīkh*, II, 557; Ibn al-Athīr, *al-Kāmil*, VI, 409–10.

539. Khalīfah, *Ta'rīkh*, II, 776; Ibn al-Athīr, *al-Kāmil*, VI, 410.

The Events of the Year 214

(MARCH 11, 829–FEBRUARY 27, 830)

Among the events taking place in this year was the killing of Muḥammad b. Ḥumayd al-Ṭūsī by Bābak at Hashtādsar[540] on Saturday the twenty-fifth of Rabīʿ I[541] (June 2, 829); Bābak scattered Muḥammad's army and killed a large number of his troops.[542]

In this year, Abū al-Rāzī was killed in Yemen.[543]

In this year, ʿUmayr b. al-Walīd al-Bādhghīsī, financial administrator (*ʿāmil*) in Egypt for Abū Isḥāq b. al-Rashīd, was

---

540. Literally, "the eighty peaks;" apparently this lay in northern Azerbaijan, in the mountainous region south of the Araxes, where lay also Babak's headquarters of al-Badhdh; see Schwarz, 970–1.

541. Actually a Wednesday.

542. *ʿUyūn*, 373–4, and Ibn al-Athīr, *al-Kāmil*, VI, 412–13, with a much more detailed account of these events; Vasiliev, op. cit., I, 92–3.

543. Yaʿqūbī, *Taʾrīkh*, II, 561–2, with a detailed account of how Abū al-Rāzī captured the rebel al-ʿUmarī but was himself subsequently killed by Ibrāhīm b. Abī Jaʿfar al-Ḥimyarī, called al-Manākhi, who seized power in the Yemen; Ibn al-Athīr, *al-Kāmil*, VI, 415.

killed in the Ḥawf[544] in the month of Rabīʿ I (May-June 829).[545] Abū Isḥāq marched into Egypt and brought it into submission. He seized ʿAbd al-Salām and Ibn Jalīs and executed them,[546] while al-Ma'mūn had Ibn al-Jarawī[547] beaten and then sent him back to Egypt.[548]

In this year, Bilāl al-Ḍabābī al-Shārī (the Khārijite) came out in revolt. Al-Ma'mūn set off for al-ʿAlth,[549] and then returned to Baghdad, and sent (instead) his son ʿAbbās, together with a
[1102] body of commanders, including ʿAlī b. Hishām, ʿUjayf (b. ʿAnbasah) and Hārūn b. Muḥammad b. Abī Khālid. Hārūn then killed Bilāl.[550]

In this year, ʿAbdallāh b. Ṭāhir set out for Dīnawar.[551] Al-Ma'mūn dispatched to him Isḥāq b. Ibrāhīm (al-Muṣʿabī) and Yaḥyā b. Aktham, who offered him the choice between Khurasan on the one hand, and Jibāl, Armenia, Azerbaijan and the conduct of the war against Bābak on the other; ʿAbdallāh chose Khurasan, and set off towards it.[552]

In this year, Jaʿfar b. Dāwūd al-Qummī became active (that is, became rebellious), but ʿAzīz the freedman of ʿAbdallāh b. Ṭāhir seized him; Jaʿfar had fled from Egypt, but was now sent back to there.[553]

---

544. Literally "flank," the region stretching from the eastern Nile delta to the fringes of Sinai; see Yāqūt, *Muʿjam*, II, 322.

545. Kindī, 186, gives the date of the battle in which the rebels (see above, 178) killed ʿUmayr as Tuesday, the thirteenth of Rabīʿ II, 814 (June 20, 829: actually a Sunday).

546. Yaʿqūbī, *Ta'rīkh*, II, 567; Kindī, 185–9, giving the date of the rebels' execution as Monday, the eighteenth of Dhū al-Qaʿdah, 214 (January 17, 830); Ibn al-Athīr, *al-Kāmil*, VI, 409.

547. Text, al-Ḥarūrī, but see above, 178 and n. 530.

548. According to Kindī, 189–90, ʿAlī b. ʿAbd al-ʿAzīz al-Jarawī was tortured by al-Ma'mūn's general, the Afshīn Ḥaydar, to make him disgorge his wealth, but held out and was therefore executed on the fourteenth of Dhū al-Ḥijjah, 215 (February, 1, 831).

549. A town on the Tigris above ʿUkbarā; see Yāqūt, *Muʿjam*, IV, 145–6; Le Strange, *Lands*, 50.

550. Ibn al-Athīr, *al-Kāmil*, VI, 415. Azdī, 395, gives this rebel's name as al-Ṣanābī.

551. Cf. Ibn Abī Ṭāhir, 268–9, tr. 122.

552. Azdī, loc. cit.

553. Ibn al-Athīr, *al-Kāmil*, loc. cit.

In this year, al-Ma'mūn appointed ʿAlī b. Hishām as governor of Jabal, Qumm, Iṣfahān and Azerbaijan.[554]

In this year, Isḥāq b. al-ʿAbbās b. Muḥammad led the pilgrimage.[555]

---

554. Ibid.
555. Khalīfah, *Ta'rīkh*, II, 777; Ibn al-Athīr, *al-Kāmil*, VI, 416.

The Events of the Year 215

(FEBRUARY 28, 830–FEBRUARY 17, 831)

Among the events taking place during this year was al-Ma'mūn's setting out from the City of Peace to raid the Byzantines, this being, reportedly, on Saturday, the twenty-seventh of Muḥarram (March 26, 830). Other reports say that he travelled from Shammāsiyyah[556] to Baradān[557] on Thursday, after the noon worship, the twenty-fourth of Muḥarram, 215[558] (March 23, 830). When al-Ma'mūn departed from the City of Peace, he appointed as his deputy over it Isḥāq b. Ibrāhīm b. Muṣʿab, who was further entrusted with the Sawād, Ḥulwān and the districts of the Tigris. When al-Ma'mūn arrived at Takrīt,[559]

556. The quarter of East Baghdad northeast of Ruṣāfah; see Le Strange, *Baghdad*, 199–216.

557. A town lying just to the north of Baghdad, which gave its name to the Baradān Gate leading out of Shammāsiyyah; see Yāqūt, *Muʿjam*, I, 375–6; Le Strange, *Lands*, 32.

558. Actually a Wednesday.

559. A town on the Tigris above Sāmarrā; see Yāqūt, *Muʿjam*, II, 38–9; Le Strange, *Lands*, 57; Barthold, *A historical geography of Iran*, 205–6; *EI*[1] s.v. (Kramers).

Muḥammad b. ʿAlī b. Mūsā b. Jaʿfar b. Muḥammad b. ʿAlī b. al-Ḥusayn b. ʿAlī b. Abī Ṭālib (the son of the Imām ʿAlī al-Riḍā) arrived from Madīnah in Ṣafar, during the night of Friday (Thursday-Friday night), in the same year, and met the Caliph there. Al-Ma'mūn bestowed gifts on him, and ordered him to consummate his union with his (al-Ma'mūn's) daughter [1103]
Umm al-Faḍl, whom he had (previously) given in marriage to Muḥammad b. ʿAlī. She was brought into his presence in the house of Aḥmad b. Yūsuf, which was situated on the banks of the Tigris. Muḥammad b. ʿAlī remained there. When the time of the pilgrimage came round, he set off with his household and family back to Mecca; then he went on to his house at Madīnah, and remained there.[560]

After this, al-Ma'mūn took the road for Mosul until he got as far as Manbij,[561] and then went on to Dābiq,[562] to Antioch and to Maṣṣīṣah.[563] Then he set off from there for Tarsus,[564] and then into the land of the Byzantines in the middle of Jumādā I (July 10, 830), while al-ʿAbbās b. al-Ma'mūn set out from Malaṭyah.[565] Al-Ma'mūn next besieged a fortress called Qurrah[566] until he captured it by storm and ordered the fortress to be destroyed, this being on Sunday, the twenty-sixth of Jumādā I (July 21, 830).[567] Previous to this, he had conquered a fortress called Mājidah,[568] but had spared its occupants. It is said that when al-Ma'mūn halted before Qurrah and then attacked

560. Ibn Abī Ṭāhir, 262–3, tr. 119.

561. A town on the Euphrates above Raqqah where there was a bridge of boats; see Yāqūt, *Muʿjam*, V, 205–7; Le Strange, *Lands*, 107; id., *Palestine*, 501–2; Canard, 87–8; *EI*[1] s.v. Manbidj (Honigmann).

562. A town in northern Syria on the road from Manbij to Antioch; see Yāqūt, *Muʿjam*, II, 416–17; Le Strange, *Palestine*, 426, 503; *EI*[2] s.v. (Sourdel).

563. A town in Cilicia, classical Mopsuestia; see Yāqūt, *Muʿjam*, V, 144–5; Le Strange, *Lands*, 130–2; id., *Palestine*, 505–6; *EI*[1] s.v. Miṣṣīṣ (Honigmann).

564. The town, famed since classical times, in Cilicia; see Yāqūt, *Muʿjam*, IV, 28–9; Le Strange, *Lands*, 132–4; *EI*[1] s.v. Ṭarsūs (F. Buhl).

565. A frontier fortress near the course of the upper Euphrates, classical Melitene; see Yāqūt, *Muʿjam*, V, 192–3; Le Strange, *Lands*, 120; Honigmann, 58–9, 72 ff.; *EI*[2] s.v. (Honigmann—S. Faroqhi).

566. A fortress in Cappadocia, Greek Koron; see Vasiliev, *Byzance et les Arabes*, I, 101–2; Honigmann, 45.

567. Ibn Abī Ṭāhir, 263, tr. 119.

568. A fortress in Cappadocia; see Vasiliev, op. cit., I, 101; Honigmann, 46.

its defending garrison, they sought a guarantee of security. Al-Ma'mūn granted this to them, and he then sent Ashinās to the fortress of Sundus,[569] and Ashinās brought back to the Caliph its commander. He further sent ʿUjayf and Jaʿfar al-Khayyāṭ to the commander of the fortress of Sinān,[570] and the latter harkened to the Caliph and gave his obedience.[571]

In this year, Abū Isḥāq b. al-Rashīd returned from Egypt. He met up with al-Ma'mūn before the latter reached Mosul, and Manuel[572] and his (al-Ma'mūn's) son ʿAbbās met up with him at Ra's al-ʿAyn.[573]

In this year, after leaving the land of the Byzantines, al-Ma'mūn set off for Damascus.[574]

In this year, ʿAbdallāh b. ʿUbaydallāh b. al-ʿAbbās b. Muḥammad led the pilgrimage.[575]

---

569. The Greek Soanda, perhaps the modern Turkish town of Nevşehir, according to Vasiliev, op. cit., I, 102.

570. A fortress which probably lay near Heracleia and Tyana; see ibid., I, 103.

571. Azdī, 399; *ʿUyūn*, 374; Ibn al-Athīr, *al-Kāmil*, VI, 417. For the whole campaign, see Vasiliev, op. cit., I, 94–103, 287–8, 370, 391–2.

572. Byzantine *patricius* who had fled to the Muslims in the reign of the Emperor Michael II; see Canard, in *Cambridge medieval history. IV. The Byzantine empire*, I, 709–10.

573. Ibn Abī Ṭāhir, 264, tr. 120, with a much fuller account; Ibn al-Athīr, *al-Kāmil*, VI, 418; Vasiliev, op. cit., I, 288, 392.

574. Ibn Abī Ṭāhir, loc. cit.; Ibn al-Athīr, *al-Kāmil*, loc. cit.

575. Khalīfah, *Ta'rīkh* (Damascus), II, 778; Azdī, 405; Ibn al-Athīr, *al-Kāmil*, loc. cit.

The Events of the Year 216 [1104]

(FEBRUARY 18, 831–FEBRUARY 6, 832)

The events taking place during this year included al-Ma'mūn's return to the land of the Byzantines.

Al-Ma'mūn's Return to the Land of the Byzantines

There are varying reports about this. It is said, the reason for it was that al-Ma'mūn received reports about the king of Byzantium's slaughter of people of Tarsus and Maṣṣīṣah—according to what has been mentioned, amounting to sixteen hundred in all.[576] When he got this news, he set off on an expedition till he entered the land of the Byzantines on Monday, the nineteenth of Jumādā I of this year[577] (July 4, 831), and he remained there till the middle of Sha'bān (September 26 or 27). But it is also said that the reason for it was that Theophilus son of Michael wrote to al-Ma'mūn and put his own name first in his letter

576. According to the *'Uyūn*, 374, two thousand were killed. Cf. Vasiliev, *Byzance et les Arabes*, I, 103–4.
577. Actually a Tuesday.

(*bada'a bi-nafsihi*). When the letter reached al-Ma'mūn, he did not read it, and set off for the land of the Byzantines. The envoys of Theophilus, son of Michael, met him at Adana, and Theophilus sent along to al-Ma'mūn five hundred Muslim captives. When al-Ma'mūn entered the Byzantine lands, he halted before Anṭīghū[578] and besieged it, and its garrison marched out to him after securing peace terms (without fighting). Al-Ma'mūn then proceeded to Heraclia,[579] and its garrison marched out to him after securing peace terms. He sent off his brother Abū Isḥāq, who captured thirty fortresses and subterranean strongholds and storehouses (*maṭmūrah*),[580] and he sent off from Ṭuwānah[581] Yaḥyā b. Aktham, who raided, killed, burned, seized and enslaved captives, and then returned to the main body of the army. Al-Ma'mūn next set off towards Kaysūm, and remained there for two or three days and then turned back to Damascus.[582]

[1105] In this year, ʿAbdūs al-Fihrī rose in rebellion, and he and his partisans attacked Abū Isḥāq's tax officials and killed several of them, this being in Shaʿbān (September-October 831). Al-Ma'mūn set out from Damascus for Egypt on Wednesday, the fifteenth of Dhū al-Ḥijjah[583] (January 23, 832).[584]

In this year, al-Afshīn arrived from Barqah,[585] on his way back from there, and remained in Egypt.[586]

---

578. A fortress in Cappadocia; see Vasiliev, op. cit., I, 111–12; Honigmann, 46.

579. Arabic Hiraqlah, modern Eregli, a town in the Taurus region; see Yāqūt, *Muʿjam*, V, 398–9; Vasiliev, op. cit., I, 110; *EI*² s.v. Eregli (J.H. Mordtmann—Taeschner).

580. Pl. *maṭāmīr*, subterranean grottoes or emplacements, placed by Le Strange, *Lands*, 138, in the region of Malacopia, Arabic Malaqūbiyah; see also Vasiliev, op. cit., I, 112; Honigmann, loc. cit.; *EI*² s.v. Maṭmūra (Pellat).

581. The town in Cilicia, classical Tyana; see Yāqūt, *Muʿjam*, IV, 45–6; Le Strange, *Palestine*, 547; id., *Lands*, 139.

582. Ibn Abī Ṭāhir, 264–5, tr. 120; Yaʿqūbī, *Ta'rīkh*, II, 567–8; Azdī, loc. cit.; *ʿUyūn*, 374–5; Ibn al-Athīr, *al-Kāmil*, VI, 419. For this campaign, see Canard, in *Cambridge medieval history. IV. The Byzantine empire*, I, 710; Vasiliev. op. cit., I, 109–14, 272–3, 288–9, 371, 409.

583. Actually a Tuesday.

584. Ibn Abī Ṭāhir, 265, tr. 120; Kindī, 192; Azdī, 406; Ibn al-Athīr, *al-Kāmil*, VI, 419.

585. The port in modern Cyrenaica; see *EI*² s.v. Barḳa (J. Despois).

586. According to Yaʿqūbī, *Ta'rīkh*, II, 568, he had been suppressing a re-

In this year, al-Ma'mūn wrote to Isḥāq b. Ibrāhīm (al-Muṣʿabī) ordering him to oblige the troops to pronounce the *takbīr*[587] when they performed the worship. So they first put this into practice in the mosque of the City (of Peace) and at Ruṣāfah on Friday, the sixteenth of Ramaḍān of this year (October 27, 832), at the moment when they had completed the worship; they all remained standing and pronounced the *takbīr* three times. Subsequently, they followed this procedure at every prescribed session of the worship.[588]

In this year, al-Ma'mūn became angry with ʿAlī b. Hishām; he sent ʿUjayf b. ʿAnbasah and Aḥmad b. Hishām to him, and ordered the confiscation of his property and weapons.[589]

In this year, Umm Jaʿfar (Zubaydah, mother of al-Amīn) died at Baghdad in Jumādā I (June–July 831).[590]

In this year, Ghassān b. ʿAbbād arrived from Sind, after Bishr b. Dāwūd al-Muhallabī had come to him seeking a guarantee of security. Ghassān restored order in Sind, and appointed as chief financial officer (*istaʿmala*) there ʿImrān b. Mūsā al-Barmakī.[591] A poet said:

The gleam of battle is in Ghassān's sword,
  and a deadly fate lies in two edges of its point.

When he brings it along to the land of Sind, [1106]
  Bishr shows his submission [literally: lets himself be led] to him,

---

bellion at Barqah; see also Kindī, 190–1; Ibn al-Athīr, *al-Kāmil*, VI, 420; Ibn Taghrībirdī, *al-Nujūm*, II, 212. Al-Afshīn remained in Egypt, suppressing unrest among the Arabs of the Ḥawf and in Alexandria.

587. I.e., the formula *Allāh akbar*, "God is most great."

588. Ibn Abī Ṭāhir, 265–6, tr. 120; Azdī, 405; Ibn al-Athīr, *al-Kāmil*, loc. cit. The ordering of supplementary *takbīr*s was apparently in accordance with Shīʿī practice, and is considered by later Sunnī historians as one of al-Ma'mūn's *bidaʿ* or heretical innovations; see Sourdel, "La politique religieuse du calife ʿabbāside al-Ma'mūn," 41–2, 46.

589. Ibn al-Athīr, *al-Kāmil*, loc. cit.

590. Yaʿqūbī, *Ta'rīkh*, II, 568; Ibn al-Athīr, *al-Kāmil*, loc. cit.; Abbott, 247.

591. Yaʿqūbī, *Ta'rīkh*, II, 557–8, giving considerable detail, including about Ghassān's first appointing Mūsā b. Yaḥyā al-Barmakī as his deputy there after Bishr, then Mūsā's death and the appointment of his son ʿImrān; Ibn al-Athīr, *al-Kāmil*, loc. cit.

Swearing that he will never again, while ever any worshipper makes the pilgrimage in duty to God
and hurls his pebbles from the two [*sic*] piles of stones [actually, three piles, in the *rajm* of Satan at Minā],

Act treacherously, throwing off allegiance to rulers and suddenly attacking
troops which seek refuge in his nobility [*dhurwatayhi*, literally, "his two peaks"].

Ghassān then came back to al-Ma'mūn.

(In this year,) Ja'far b. Dāwūd al-Qummī fled to Qumm and threw off his allegiance there.[592]

In this year, there was an excessively cold spell.

In this year, according to what some people say, Sulaymān b. 'Abdallāh b. Sulaymān b. 'Alī b. 'Abdallāh b. 'Abbās led the pilgrimage, but according to what others assert, it was 'Abdallāh b. 'Ubaydallāh b. al-'Abbās b. Muḥammad b. 'Alī b. 'Abdallāh b. al-'Abbās who led the pilgrimage this year; al-Ma'mūn had appointed him governor of the Yemen and had given him the governorship of all the regions which he would pass through till he reached the Yemen. Accordingly 'Abdallāh b. 'Ubaydallāh left Damascus and came to Baghdad; he led the people in the worship there on the day of the breaking of the fast (the first of Shawwāl [November 11, 831]), and then set off from Baghdad on Monday the second of Dhū al-Qa'dah (December 11, 831) and performed the rites of the pilgrimage for the people.[593]

---

592. Ibid.

593. Ibn Abī Ṭāhir, 266, tr. 120, giving 'Abdallāh b. 'Ubaydallāh b. al-'Abbās as leader of the pilgrimage, and Monday, the first of Dhū al-Qa'dah (actually a Sunday) as the date of his departure from Baghdad; Khalīfah, *Ta'rīkh*, II, 779, also naming him; Azdī, 407, naming Sulaymān; Ibn al-Athīr, *al-Kāmil*, loc. cit.

The Events of the Year

217

(FEBRUARY 7, 832–JANUARY 26, 833)

The events taking place during this year included al-Afshīn's victory at Bīmā, a place in the land of Egypt. Its people came forth under a guarantee of security granted on al-Ma'mūn's authority. [1107] The proclamation announcing its capture was read out on the twenty-eighth of Rabīʿ II (June 2, 832).[594]

In this year, al-Ma'mūn came to Egypt during Muḥarram (February–March 832). ʿAbdūs al-Fihrī was brought before him and executed, and then he returned to Syria.[595]

---

594. Ibn Abī Ṭāhir, 267, tr. 120; Yaʿqūbī, *Ta'rīkh*, II, 569; Ibn al-Athīr, *al-Kāmil*, VI, 421. This is presumably al-Afshīn's quelling of a rebellion of the Copts at Basharūd in the Lower Delta, described by Kindī, 192, and Severus, IV, 486–502. Yāqūt, *Muʿjam*, I, 534, however, describes Bīmā as a place on the borders of Upper Egypt and the lands of the infidels. See also Vasiliev, *Byzance et les Arabes*, I, 114–15.

595. Yaʿqūbī, *Ta'rīkh*, loc. cit., giving the exact dates for al-Ma'mūn's stay of forty-seven days in Egypt as being from the tenth of Muḥarram to the twenty-sixth of Ṣafar, 217; Kindī, loc. cit., making it forty-nine days; Masʿūdī, *Murūj*, VII, 94 = ed. Pellat, § 2778; *ʿUyūn*, 376; Ibn al-Athīr, *al-Kāmil*, loc. cit. ʿAbdūs was leader of the Coptic revolt.

In this year, al-Ma'mūn had the two sons of Hishām, ʿAlī and Ḥusayn,[596] killed at Adana[597] in Jumādā I (June–July 832).

Al-Ma'mūn Has ʿAlī Killed

The reason for this was because reports reached al-Ma'mūn about ʿAlī's tyrannical conduct with the people within the governorship entrusted to him by al-Ma'mūn—the regions of Jibāl—including his killing of people and his seizure of property. ʿUjayf was therefore sent against him. ʿAlī hoped to fall upon him suddenly and then join up with Bābak, but ʿUjayf got hold of him and sent him back to al-Ma'mūn. The Caliph ordered him to be decapitated. Ibn al-Jalīl was in charge of ʿAlī's execution and Muḥammad b. Yūsuf, his brother's (ʿAlī's) son,[598] was in charge of al-Ḥusayn's decapitation at Adana on Wednesday, the sixteenth of Jumādā I (June 19, 832). ʿAlī b. Hishām's head was sent (first) to Baghdad and Khurasan, where it was paraded in the streets; then it was sent back to Syria and the Jazīrah, where it was publicly paraded in district after district. After this, it was brought to Damascus during Dhū al-Ḥijjah (December 832–January 833), and then it was sent to Egypt, where it was finally thrown into the Nile (or: the sea, *al-baḥr*).[599]

It is mentioned that, when al-Ma'mūn had ʿAlī b. Hishām executed, he ordered a paper to be written out and hung from his head so that the people might read it. He had the following words written:

[1108] In the past, the Commander of the Faithful summoned ʿAlī b. Hishām among the group of Khurasanians whom he summoned to give support and to establish his rightful claims during the time of the deposed one [al-Amīn]. ʿAlī

596. Ibn Abī Ṭāhir, 267, tr. 121, gives their *nisbah* or gentilic of al-Marwazī.

597. The modern capital of Cilicia; see Yāqūt, *Muʿjam*, I, 133; Le Strange, *Lands*, 131; *EI*[2] s.v. (R. Anhegger).

598. I.e., Abū Saʿīd Muḥammad b. Yūsuf al-Marwazī, often mentioned in the pages of Ṭabarī.

599. Ibn Abī Ṭāhir, 267–8, tr. 121; Yaʿqūbī, *Ta'rīkh*, II, 570–1, mentioning that ʿAlī's head was finally sent to Barqah and then hurled by catapult into the sea; Ibn al-Athīr, *al-Kāmil*, loc. cit.

was one of those who responded, answered the call speedily and gave help enthusiastically. Hence, the Commander of the Faithful acknowledged this to his credit and took him into his service as his protégé, thinking that ʿAlī was filled with the fear of God and obedience to Him, and would be whole-heartedly devoted to the interests of the Commander of the Faithful in any administrative office if it were entrusted to him, displaying praiseworthy conduct and incorruptibility in regard to the mode of gain. The Commander of the Faithful heaped favors on him from the outset, and conferred on him the governorship of prestigious provinces, and showered on him munificent gifts, regarding whose value the Commander of the Faithful ordered an enquiry; he found that they amounted to more than fifty million dirhams. Yet ʿAlī stretched out his hand into treachery and reckless wastefulness in regard to the office which the Caliph had asked him to watch over in a trustworthy manner. The Caliph therefore removed him from office and banished him from his presence to a remote spot. But then ʿAlī besought the Commander of the Faithful to overlook his misdeeds, so the latter vouchsafed to him his forgiveness for them, and appointed him as governor of Jibāl, Azerbaijan and the districts of Armenia, and gave him responsibility for carrying on the war against God's enemies the Khurramiyyah on condition that he did not revert to his former misdeeds. Yet he returned to his old ways more violently than before by his preferring dīnārs and dirhams to actions pleasing to God and to His religion; he behaved tyrannically and oppressed the subject population, and he shed prohibited blood. So the Commander of the Faithful sent ʿUjayf b. ʿAnbasah with full responsibility to deal with his affair and with a call to restore the situation which ʿAlī had brought about. ʿAlī attacked ʿUjayf and tried to kill him, but God gave ʿUjayf strength because of his pure-hearted devotion in service to the Commander of the Faithful, so that he was able to ward him off. If ʿAlī had been able successfully to wreak what he intended on ʿUjayf, there would have arisen a situation which could not have been put right or reversed.

However, when God desires a matter, it is as good as done. When the Commander of the Faithful put into effect God's
[1109] decree concerning ʿAlī b. Hishām, he realized that he ought not to punish ʿAlī's offspring for his offences, so he ordered that the same sums as had been paid during ʿAlī 's lifetime to his children, his family, all those in their household and those to whom he used to give allowances, should continue to be paid out to them. If it had not been that ʿAlī b. Hishām intended the gravest onslaught on ʿUjayf, he would merely have been counted amongst those of al-Ma'-mūn's army who had rebelled and acted treacherously like ʿĪsā b. Manṣūr[600] and his ilk.[601] Farewell![602]

In this year, al-Ma'mūn invaded the Byzantine lands, and halted before and besieged Lu'lu'ah[603] for a hundred days. Then he withdrew from there and left as his deputy for the siege ʿUjayf, but the people of Lu'lu'ah outwitted ʿUjayf and captured him, so that he remained a prisoner in their hands for eight days until they set him free. (The Emperor) Theophilus[604] advanced on Lu'lu'ah and surrounded ʿUjayf; but al-Ma'mūn dispatched further troops to Lu'lu'ah, and Theophilus fell back before making any contact with the Muslim army. So the people of Lu'lu'ah marched forth to ʿUjayf under a guarantee of security.[605]

---

600. Presumably ʿĪsā b. Manṣūr al-Rāfiʿī, governor of Egypt in 216 (831) and again in 229 (843); see Kindī, 189–93, 196.

601. I.e., and possibly would have been pardoned.

602. Ibn Abī Ṭāhir, 269–70, tr. 122.

603. The Greek Loulon, on the ancient site of Faustinopolis, a fortress whose site is marked today by Ulu Kişla northwest of Adana; see Vasiliev, op. cit., I, 116–17; Honigmann, 44–5.

604. The second ruler of the Amorian line, who reigned 829–42; see Vasiliev, *History of the Byzantine empire*, I, 276.

605. Yaʿqūbī, *Ta'rīkh*, II, 570–1; Azdī, 408; *ʿUyūn*, 375–6; Ibn al-Athīr, *al-Kāmil*, VI, 421; Vasiliev, *Byzance et les Arabes*, I, 115–18, 273–4, 289, 371; Canard, in *Cambridge medieval history. IV. The Byzantine empire*, I, 710.

The Ruler of Byzantium Asks for Peace

In this year, the ruler of Byzantium, Theophilus, wrote to al-Ma'mūn asking for peace.[606] He put his own name first in his letter, and al-F.ṣ.l[607] the vizier of Theophilus brought the letter, seeking peace and offering a tribute (literally: a ransom). The actual text of Theophilus's letter to al-Ma'mūn was as follows:

> It seems more sensible that the two opposing sides should come together over their respective shares [of good fortune] than adopt courses injurious to themselves. You are not the sort of person who would relinquish such a share which you possess for yourself in favor of a share which might pass to another person. You already know this well enough without my having to tell you. I have written to you inviting you to make a peace agreement and as one desirous of the advantage of a truce in military operations, so that you may remove the burdens of war from upon us and so that we may be to each other friends and a band of associates, in addition to the accruing of benefits [1110] and widened scope for trading through commercial outlets, the release of those who have been carried off into captivity and the security of the highways and heartlands of the realms. If you reject this [peace offer], I shall not bamboozle you [literally: creep up on you secretly in an ambush[608]], nor shall I speak to you in an ingratiating, misleading manner; but I shall penetrate into the innermost recesses of your land, take over against you its barriers and scatter its cavalry and infantry alike. And if I do this, it will only be after setting forth a valid excuse [for adopting this course of action] and after setting up between us the standard of decisive argument. Farewell![609]

606. Ibn al-Athīr, *al-Kāmil,* loc. cit., adding, "but did not succeed in getting it."
607. For this cryptic name, Canard, in Vasiliev, op. cit., I, 289 n. 1, suggests a deformation of Syncellus, originally perhaps written "al-S.q.l."
608. A proverbial saying, see Maydānī, tr. II, 913.
609. Ibn Abī Ṭāhir, 284, tr. 128–9.

Al-Ma'mūn wrote back to him as follows:

There has reached me your letter, in which you ask for a truce in the fighting and call for the making of a mutual peace treaty. In your letter also, you mingle soft words with harsh ones in that you are seeking to achieve conciliation [with me] in regard to the opening-up of commercial outlets, the achieving of advantageous dealings, the release of captives and the cessation of killing and fighting. If it were not that what I am working towards involves proceeding with deliberation and seizing a favorable opportunity through turning things over in the mind, and were it not that I do not formulate any opinion [*ra'y*] on a future contingency except on a basis of an informed opinion taking into account the welfare of the community [*istiṣlāḥ*] as to what I prefer in regard to its outcome,[610] I should make the answer to your letter [the dispatch of] cavalry horses bearing steadfast, courageous and keen-sighted riders, who would contend with you over your destruction [*thuklikum*], to seek God's favor by spilling your blood and to make light, as a means of obtaining nearness to God, of the suffering which they will have endured from your military might. Then I should provide them with reinforcements and send them a sufficiency of matériel and military equipment. They are more eager to go forward to the
[1111] watering-places of death than you are to preserve yourselves from the fearful threat of their onslaught upon you. They have the promise of one of the two best things:[611] a speedy victory or a glorious return [to God as martyrs in battle]. But I consider that I should proffer you a warning, with which God establishes clearly for you the decisive proof [of Islam], involving the summoning of you and your supporters to knowledge of the divine unity and the divine law of the religion of the *ḥanīfs*.[612] If you refuse [to accept

610. This passage of the letter seems to echo legal terminology.

611. Cf. Qur'ān, IX, 52.

612. *al-Sharīʿah al-ḥanīfiyyah*, i.e., the religion of the *ḥanīf*s or pre-Islamic monotheist seekers after righteousness, regarded as proto-Muslims, so that *al-dīn al-ḥanīfī*/*al-sharīʿah al-ḥanīfiyyah* = Islam; see *EI*^{2} s.v. Ḥanīf (Watt).

this offer], then you can hand over tribute [literally: a ransom] which will entail the obligation of protection [*dhimmah*] and make incumbent a respite [from further warfare]. But if you choose not to make that [payment or ransom], then you will clearly experience face-to-face our [martial] qualities to an extent which will make any effort [on my part] of eloquent speaking and an exhaustive attempt at description superfluous. Peace be upon him who follows the divine guidance![613]

In this year, al-Ma'mūn went to Salaghūs[614]

In this year, ʿAlī b. ʿĪsā al-Qummī sent along Jaʿfar b. Dāwūd al-Qummī, and Abū Isḥāq b. al-Rashīd had him executed.[615]

In this year, Sulaymān b. ʿAbdallāh b. Sulaymān b. ʿAlī led the pilgrimage.[616]

---

613. Ibn Abī Ṭāhir, 285, tr. 129, Yaʿqūbī, *Ta'rīkh*, II, 568; Vasiliev, op. cit., I, 118–21, 289–91; Canard, in *Cambridge medieval history. IV. The Byzantine empire*, I, loc. cit.; Shaban, 56, 61.

614. *ʿUyūn*, 375; Ibn al-Athīr, *al-Kāmil*, VI, 422. Salaghūs was a fortress beyond Tarsus; see Yāqūt, *Muʿjam*, II, 238; Le Strange, *Palestine*, 528.

615. Ibn al-Athīr, *al-Kāmil*, loc. cit.

616. Khalīfah, *Ta'rīkh*, II, 780; Azdī, 411; Ibn al-Athīr, *al-Kāmil*, loc. cit.

The
Events of the Year
218
(January 27, 833–January 15, 834

The events taking place during this year included al-Ma'mūn's journeying from Salaghūs to Raqqah and his executing there Ibn Ukht al-Dārī.

In this year, he ordered the clearing of the population from Rāfiqah so that he might quarter his personal entourage (*ḥasham*) there; but the people there raised an outcry, so al-Ma'mūn allowed them to stay.[617]

In this year, al-Ma'mūn sent his son al-ʿAbbās to the Byzantine lands and ordered him to encamp at Ṭuwānah and to embark on a building program there. He had already dispatched thither workmen and detachments of regularly-paid troops (*furūḍ*).[618] He set to work on this building program, and con-

617. Azdī, 412. Rāfiqah was the new garrison town just outside Raqqah (hence its name, "the companion") built by al-Manṣūr on the pattern of the Round City at Baghdad; see Yāqūt, *Muʿjam*, III, 15; Le Strange, *Lands*, 100–1; Canard, *H'amdânides*, 90–1. The two places are sometimes referred to by the geographers as "the two Raqqahs."

618. For this sense of *farḍ*, pl. *furūḍ*, see Lane, 2374b.

structured it to occupy a mile square.[619] He made its wall three *farsakhs* (eighteen km) in circumference, with four gates, each gate having a fortified tower. Al-Ma'mūn's dispatch of his son al-ʿAbbās for this purpose was on the first of Jumādā (I [May 25, 833]).[620] He also wrote to his brother Abū Isḥāq b. al-Rashīd to the effect that he had made a levy on the armies of Damascus, Ḥimṣ, Urdunn and Filasṭīn of four thousand men, with the pay allocations of one hundred dirhams for each cavalryman and forty dirhams for each infantryman.[621] He further made a levy on the troops of Egypt, and he wrote to al-ʿAbbās about the numbers of troops which he had levied from (the armies of) Qinnasrīn and the Jazīrah, and to Isḥāq b. Ibrāhīm (al-Muṣʿabī) about those levied from the army of Baghdad, these last amounting to two thousand men. Some of them marched off till they reached Ṭuwānah and encamped there with al-ʿAbbās.[622] [1112]

The Interrogation of the Judges and Traditionists

In this year, al-Ma'mūn wrote to Isḥāq b. Ibrāhīm that he should interrogate the judges and traditionists, and he ordered a group of them to be sent to him at Raqqah.[623] This was the first letter which he issued on this topic, and the text of his letter to Isḥāq was as follows:

God has made incumbent upon the imāms and caliphs of the Muslims that they should be zealous in establishing

---

619. The Arab mile (*mīl*) has been variously estimated, but was probably just over two thousand yards, and three of these made up a *farsakh* (six km). The wall three *farsakhs* in circumference must accordingly have been an outer wall, and not that of the *madīnah* itself; at all events, these operations must have been on an enormous scale.

620. Masʿūdī, *Murūj*, VII, 94 = ed. Pellat, § 2778; Azdī, 412.

621. Ibid.; Ibn al-Athīr, *al-Kāmil*, VI, 440–1.

622. Azdī, loc. cit.; Vasiliev, op. cit., I, 121–2, 291.

623. See in general on the *miḥnah*: Yaʿqūbī, *Ta'rīkh*, II, 572–3; Azdī, 412–14; Abū al-ʿArab al-Tamīmī, *Kitāb al-Miḥan*, 436–53; *ʿUyūn*, 376–7; Ibn al-Athīr, *al-Kāmil*, VI, 423–7; W.M. Patton, *Aḥmed ibn Ḥanbal and the Miḥna*; Goldziher, *Introduction to Islamic theology and law*, 98–100; Sourdel, "La politique religieuse du calife ʿabbāside al-Ma'mūn," 42–4; Watt, 178–9, 242–5, 253, 280–1, 292; *EI*[1] s.v. (Wensinck); *EI*[2] s.v. (Hinds).

God's religion, which He has asked them to guard faithfully; in the heritage of prophethood of which He has made them inheritors; in the tradition of knowledge which He has entrusted to their keeping; in acting justly with the government of their subjects; and in being diligent in obeying God's will in their conduct towards those subjects. Now the Commander of the Faithful asks God to direct him to firmness and resolution in the right way, and to just actions in the exercise of political authority over his people which God, with His compassion and grace, has entrusted to him.[624]

The Commander of the Faithful has realized that the broad mass and the overwhelming concentration of the base elements of the ordinary people[625] and the lower strata
[1113] of the commonalty are those who, in all the regions and far horizons of the world, have no farsightedness, or vision, or faculty of reasoning by means of such evidential proofs as God approves along the right way which He provides, or faculty of seeking illumination by means of the light of knowledge and God's decisive proofs. [These persons are] a people sunk in ignorance and in blindness about God, plunged into error regarding the true nature of His religion and His unity and faith in Him; [they are] too far off the right track from His clear marks for guidance and the obligation of following in His way; [they are] a people who fall short of being able to grasp the reality of God as He should be recognized, to acknowledge Him exactly as He should be acknowledged and to distinguish between Him and His creation.[626] This is because of the feebleness of their judg-

624. The Caliph, while avoiding the claims to infallibility and immaculateness (*ʿiṣmah*) of the Shīʿī Imāms, nevertheless claims a high status for himself as bearer of the Prophet's charge to guide his people; see Sourdel, op. cit., 44.

625. *Ḥashw al-raʿiyyah*. F. Steppat sees here a possible influence from the terminology of one Middle Persian wisdom text, as known from its later Arabic version, and more generally a strand in al-Ma'mūn's religious policy here deriving from earlier Persian imperial governmental attitudes; see "From *ʿahd Ardasīr* to al-Ma'mūn: a Persian element in the policy of the *Miḥna*," in *Studia arabica et islamica, Festschrift for Iḥsān ʿAbbās*, 451–4.

626. Here the Caliph's contempt for the intellectual powers and judgment of the masses of his subjects distances him from the Sunnī veneration for the

ment, the deficiency of their intellects and their lack of facility in reflecting upon things and calling them to mind; all this arises from the fact that they consider as perfectly equal God Himself and the Qur'ān which He has revealed; they have agreed with one voice and have asserted unequivocally that it is eternal and primordial, not created nor originated nor invented in any way by God. Yet God has said in the clear and unambiguous parts of His Book, which He has set forth as a healing for what there is [of anguish] in people's breasts and as an act of mercy and guidance for the believers, "Indeed, we have made it an Arabic Qur'ān."[627] Now everything which God made He must have created. He has also said, "Praise be to God who has created the heavens and earth and has made the darkness and the light."[628] He has further said, "In this way, We recount to you some of the stories of the past,"[629] and He gives the information that this is an account of events which He brought into existence subsequently to those events happening, and with it He followed up the begin- [1114]
nings of the events. He has also said, "*Alif, lām, rā'*. A book, whose miraculous signs have been clearly set forth and then made distinct, from One wise and well-informed."[630] Now everything which has been clearly set forth and made distinct must necessarily have an agent who brings these actions to pass; God is the One who has clearly set forth His Book and made it distinct, and He is its creator and originator.

Furthermore, those are the people who dispute about vain and useless things and then invite others to adopt their views.[631] They consider themselves adherents of the *sunnah*, whereas in every section of the Book of God there

community, *jamā'ah*, and its corporate will or validatory consensus, *ijmā'*, and approaches him in some measure towards the Shī'ī stress on the need for an authoritative Imām.

627. Qur'ān, XLIII, 2/3.

628. Qur'ān, VI, 1.

629. Qur'ān, XX, 99.

630. Qur'ān, XI, 1.

631. I.e., those who should give instruction and provide a lead for the masses are themselves purveyors of false teaching.

is an account related by Him which invalidates their words and gives the lie to their claims, turning their sayings and their call to adopt their professed beliefs back on themselves. Despite all this, they go on to make an outward show of being people of the divine truth, the [real] religion and the community of Muslims, and assert that all others are people of false beliefs, infidelity and schism. They raise themselves up importunately against the people with these assertions, and thereby deliberately lead astray the ignorant, to the point that a group of adherents of the false way, who display submissiveness to someone other than God and who lead an ascetic life—but for another cause and not the true faith—have inclined towards agreement with them and accordance with their evil opinions, thereby acquiring for themselves glory in their eyes and securing for themselves leadership and a reputation for probity amongst them. These people have forsaken the divine truth for their own delusions and have adopted for themselves a supporter for their error to the exclusion of God. Thus their testimony had been accepted because they [the ignorant ones or the people of the false way] have declared them [those who claim to be the people of truth] to be veracious witnesses, and the prescriptions of the Book have been put into effect through them [those who claim to be the people of truth], despite the suspect nature of their religion, the corruptness of their honor and the depraved nature of their intentions and their faith.

That has been their ultimate aim, to which they have urged others and which they have sought after in their own course of action and in their mendaciousness towards their Lord, even though the solemn covenant of the Book has been laid upon them, that they should not say any-
[1115] thing against God except what is true, and even though they have studied intently its contents. These are the people whom "God has made deaf and has blinded their eyes. Do they not consider the Qur'ān, or are there locks on their hearts?"[632]

632. Qur'ān, XLVII, 25–6/23–4.

The Commander of the Faithful considers that these people are the worst of the Muslim community and the chief ones in error, the ones who are defective in their belief in the divine unity and who have an imperfect share in the faith. They are vessels of ignorance, banners [or: milestones, *aʿlām*] of mendaciousness and the tongue of Iblīs, who speaks through his companions and strikes terror into the hearts of his adversaries, the people of God's own religion. They are the ones most fittingly considered as suspect in their truthfulness, whose witness is to be discarded and whose words and deeds are alike to be mistrusted. For there can be no good works except after sure faith, and no sure faith except after fully apprehending the true nature of Islam and a sincere profession of faith in the divine unity. Whoever is too blind to perceive his own right course and his share of faith in God and in His unity has, in other respects in regard to his conduct and endeavors to bear witness to the faith, become even more blind and even more errant from the right road.

By the life of the Commander of the Faithful! The person who most properly deserves to be branded as a liar in his utterances and as a forger of false testimony is the one who utters lies against God and His divine revelation and who does not recognize God as He really is. Indeed, the person who most appropriately deserves to be rejected when he bears witness about what God ordains and about His religion is the one who rejects God's testimony to His Book and who makes slanderous statements about God's truth through his vain lying.

Therefore, summon together all the judges in your sphere of jurisdiction and read out to them this letter from the Commander of the Faithful to you. Begin by testing them out concerning what they say and by finding out from them their beliefs about God's creating and originating the Qur'ān in time. [1116] Inform them too that the Commander of the Faithful will not seek the assistance in any of his administrative tasks of anyone whose religion, whose sincerity of faith in God's unity and whose own religious beliefs are not deemed trustworthy, nor will he place any reliance on such a man in the responsibilities laid on him by God and in the affairs of his subjects which have been entrusted to him. Then when they have publicly declared that [the Qur'ān is created] and have shown full agreement with the Commander of the Faithful concerning it, and are on the road of right guidance and salvation, order them to interrogate closely the legal witnesses within their sphere of jurisdiction and to question them about their knowledge of the Qur'ān; then [they are] no longer to recognize the validity of the testimony of those failing to affirm or hold the view that the Qur'ān was created and originated in time, and [they are] to prevent the admission and countersigning of such testimony in the judge's own court. Write back to the Commander of the Faithful what you learn from the judges over the people within your administrative province as to the results of their enquiries and their ordering these processes to be set in motion. Then keep a close oversight of them and search out what they have been doing, to such a point that God's decrees are only put into execution on the testimony of people clear-sighted in religion and wholly sincere in belief in the divine unity. Write to the Commander of the Faithful about what happens in regard to all this, if God wills.

He wrote this in Rabīʿ I 218 (March–April 833).[633]

Al-Ma'mūn wrote to Isḥāq b. Ibrāhīm about sending (to him) seven persons, including Muḥammad b. Saʿd,[634] the secretary of al-Wāqidī;[635] Abū Muslim, the one charged with the task of writing down dictated information (*mustamlī*) from Yazīd b. Hārūn;[636] Yaḥyā b. Maʿīn;[637] Abū Khaythamah Zuhayr b. Ḥarb;[638]

633. Ibn Abī Ṭāhir, 338–43, tr. 153–5; Patton, 56–61.

634. The historian and traditionist, died in 230 (845); see *EI*² s.v. Ibn Saʿd (J.W. Fück); Sezgin, *GAS*, I, 300–1.

635. The historian Muḥammad b. ʿUmar, died in 207 (823); see *EI*¹ s.v. (J. Horovitz); Sezgin, *GAS*, I, 294–7.

636. Qur'ān commentator and traditionist, died in 206 (821); see ibid., I, 40.

637. Traditionist, died in 233 (847); see ibid., I, 106–7.

638. Traditionist, died in 234 (848); see ibid., I, 107.

Ismāʿīl b. Dāwūd; Ismāʿīl b. Abī Masʿūd; and Aḥmad b. (Ibrāhīm) al-Dawraqī.[639] These seven persons were sent to him (at Raqqah),[640] and he put them to the test (*imtaḥanahum*) and interrogated them about the creation of the Qur'ān. They all replied to him that the Qur'ān was created. Hence he dispatched them to the City of Peace, and Isḥāq b. Ibrāhīm sum- [1117] moned them together at his house. He announced publicly their opinion and their judgement to a gathering of experts in the religious law (*fuqahā'*) and senior traditionists, and they affirmed exactly what the seven persons had replied to al-Ma'mūn. So Isḥāq let them go. What Isḥāq b. Ibrāhīm did in this matter was by the command of al-Ma'mūn.[641]

After this, al-Ma'mūn wrote to Isḥāq b. Ibrāhīm as follows:

That which God has a right to expect from His representatives [or: caliphs, *khulafā'*] on earth and from those entrusted by Him with authority over His servants, upon whom He has been pleased to lay the setting up of His religion and upon whom He has laid the burden of caring for His creatures, the putting into effect of His ordinance and His laws (*sunanihi*), and the conscious imitation of His justice among His creation, is that they should exert themselves earnestly for God; render Him sincere service in that which He has asked them to keep safe and has laid upon them; make Him known through that excellence of learning which He has entrusted to them and the knowledge which He has placed within them; guide back to Him the one who has turned aside from Him and bring back the one who has turned his back from His command; trace out for their subjects the way of salvation for them; draw their attention to the limits of their faith and the way to their heavenly success and protection from sin; and reveal to them those of their affairs which are hidden from them and those which are dubious and obscure by means of what will remove doubt from them and bring back illumi-

639. Traditionist, died in 246 (860); see ibid., I, 112.

640. See above, 198.

641. Ibn Abī Ṭāhir, 343–4, tr. 155–6; Patton, 64–5.

nation and clear knowledge to them all. [God also claims from them as of right] that they should bring this about by guiding the subjects aright and giving them clear vision, since this involves all the different kinds of their actions and systematically gathers together their shares of fortune in this present life and in the next. They [God's representatives, the caliphs] should reflect how God is the one who holds himself ready to question them about what they have been made responsible for, and to reward them for what they have done in advance and have laid up with Him. The Commander of the Faithful's way to success comes through God alone, and his sufficiency is in God, who is all-sufficient for him.

Among those things which the Commander of the Faithful has made plain to himself by reflection, and has
[1118] studied intently by his thinking so that the great danger attending it has become obvious, as well as the seriousness of the corruption and harm which will rebound on religion, are the sayings which the Muslims are passing round among themselves about the Qur'ān, which God has established as an exemplar for them and an enduring legacy to them of the Messenger of God and His chosen one, Muḥammad. [Another thing is] the confusedness of opinion about the Qur'ān in the minds of many people, to the point that it has seemed good to them and attractive to their intellects that it is not created. They thereby lay themselves open to the risk of rejecting God's creative power, by which He is distinguished from His creation and remains apart in His splendor in the bringing into existence of all things by means of His wisdom and their being originated by His power, and in His priority in time over them by reason of His primordial existence, whose beginning cannot be attained and whose extent cannot be comprehended. Everything apart from Him is a created object from His creation and a new thing which He has brought into existence. [They hold this erroneous view about the uncreatedness of the Qur'ān] even though the Qur'ān itself speaks about God's creating power, sets forth its proof and decisively confutes all difference of opinion about it.

[These people] talk just like the Christians when they claim that Jesus son of Mary was not created, because he was the Word of God.[642] But God says, "Indeed, We have made it an Arabic Qur'ān,"[643] meaning, "We have created it," just as He also says,[644] "And He made from him his spouse, that he might dwell with her."[645] He also says, "We have made the night a garment and have made the daylight as a means of sustenance,"[646] and, "We have made every living thing from water."[647] Thus God places the Qur'ān and these created things, which He mentions with the [1119]
indications of the act of making, on an equal footing, and He gives the information that He alone is the one who made it, saying, "Indeed, it is a glorious Qur'ān, [recorded] on a preserved tablet."[648] Now He says that on the supposition that the tablet encompasses the Qur'ān, and only something which is created can be encompassed by something else. He likewise says to His prophet, "Do not move your tongue in it in order to get through it quickly,"[649] and also, "No new reminder comes to them from their Lord."[650] He further says, "Who does greater wrong than the one who forges a lie against God or accounts His miraculous signs false?"[651] He speaks too about a group of people whom He blames for their mendacity, in that they have said, "God has not sent down anything to a human being."[652] Then, by the tongue of His messenger, He brands

642. Cf. Qur'ān, CXII.
643. Qur'ān, XLII, 2/3.
644. Ibn Abī Ṭāhir, 344–6, tr. 156–7 (here the manuscript of Ibn Abī Ṭāhir breaks off at f. 130b, with a lacuna, resuming at f. 131a with a short section of similar theological polemic regarding the createdness of the Qur'ān, not in Ṭabarī; the lacuna caused by the lost folios is obviously a considerable one, and the text of Ṭabarī corresponding with Ibn Abī Ṭāhir does not resume till p. 1134, l.2. See Keller's Introduction to his vol. II, pp. XV–XVI).
645. Qur'ān, VII, 189.
646. Qur'ān, LXXVIII, 10.
647. Qur'ān, XXI, 31/30.
648. Qur'ān, LXXXV, 21–2.
649. Qur'ān, LXXV, 16.
650. Qur'ān, XXI, 2.
651. Qur'ān, VI, 21.
652. Qur'ān, VI, 91.

them as liars, and says to His messenger, "Say, who has sent down the Book which Moses brought?"[653] Hence God calls the Qur'ān a collection to be recited, a reminder, and item of faith, a light, a right guidance, a blessed thing, a composition in Arabic and a story. For He says, "We shall narrate to you the finest of stories, in that We have revealed to you by inspiration this Qur'ān."[654] He also says, "Say, indeed, if men and jinn agree together to produce a Qur'ān like this one, they will not be able to produce its like."[655] He says additionally, "Say, bring forth ten *sūras* like it which have been invented,"[656] and, "Falsehood does not come to it either from before or from behind it."[657]

In this way, God places [at least putatively] something before it and after it, and indicates that it is finite and created. But by their utterances concerning the Qur'ān, these ignorant people have enlarged the breach in their religion and the defect in their truthworthiness; they have made the way easy for the enemy of Islam, and have confessed perversion of the Qur'ānic text and heresy against their
[1120] own hearts; they have made known and described God's work of creation and His action by that form of description which belongs to God alone and have compared Him with it, whereas it is only His creation that is the fitting subject of comparison. The Commander of the Faithful does not consider that the person professing this doctrine has any share in the true religion, nor any part in the real faith and the certainty of revealed truth. Nor does he consider that he should regard any of them as suitable for an office of confidence like that of trusted depository, person in good legal standing, legal witness, person veracious in speech or report, or one involving the exercise of any aspect of authority over the subjects. Moreover, even if any of them is outwardly known for his equitable behavior and is

653. Ibid.
654. Qur'ān, XII, 13.
655. Qur'ān, XVII, 90/88.
656. Qur'ān, XI, 16/13.
657. Qur'ān, XLI, 42.

recognised for his straightforwardness, as one who pursues a just course among the subjects, nevertheless, the branches must be traced back to their roots and must be classified among the categories of praise or blame according to these roots. A man who is ignorant in the matter of his religion, that which God has commanded him in regard to His divine unity, is even more sunk in ignorance in regard to other things, more blind in finding right guidance concerning other matters and more erring from the right road.

So read out the Commander of the Faithful's letter, and what he has instructed you in it, to Ja'far b. 'Īsā and the judge 'Abd al-Raḥmān b. Isḥāq,[658] and question them both about their knowledge of the Qur'ān. Inform them that the Commander of the Faithful will not seek the aid, in any affairs of the Muslims, of anyone except those in whose sincerity of faith and belief in God's unity he has full trust, and that belief in God's unity cannot be imputed to anyone who does not affirm that the Qur'ān is created. If Ja'far b. 'Īsā and 'Abd al-Raḥmān b. Isḥāq profess the Commander of the Faithful's view in this regard, then command them both to test those who are in their courts for purposes of giving evidence about claimant's rights and to cite them to answer for their professions regarding the Qur'ān. If any of them will not profess that the Qur'ān is created, then the two of them are to declare that person's legal witness invalid and to refrain from pronouncing sentence on a basis of what he says, even though his probity of life be firmly established by his equity and straightforwardness. Do this with all the judges in the remainder of your sphere of administrative authority and watch over them with such a careful watch as God may by means of it [1121]
cause an increase in the clearsightedness of the clearsighted person and may prevent the one in doubt from neglecting his religion. Then, if God wills, write to the Commander of the Faithful what you are doing in this matter.[659]

658. Scholar of the Ḥanafī law school; see Watt, 286.
659. Patton, 65–9.

He continued to relate: Acting on these instructions, Isḥāq b. Ibrāhīm summoned to his presence a number of the *faqīhs,* judges (*ḥukkām*) and traditionists. These included Abū Ḥassān al-Ziyādī, Bishr b. al-Walīd al-Kindī, ʿAlī b. Abī Muqātil, al-Faḍl b. Ghānim, al-Dhayyāl b. al-Haytham, (al-Ḥasan b. Ḥammād) Sajjādah, (ʿUbaydallāh b. ʿUmar) al-Qawārīrī, Aḥmad b. Ḥanbal, Qutaybah (b. Saʿīd), Saʿdawayh al-Wāsiṭī, ʿAlī b. al-Jaʿd, Isḥāq b. Abī Isrāʾīl, Ibn al-Hirsh, Ibn ʿUlayyah al-Akbar, Yaḥyā b. ʿAbd al-Raḥmān al-ʿUmarī and another shaykh from the progeny of ʿUmar b. al-Khaṭṭāb who was judge of Raqqah, Abū Naṣr al-Tammār, Abū Maʿmar al-Qaṭīʿī, Muḥammad b. Ḥātim b. Maymūn, Muḥammad b. Nūḥ al-Maḍrūb and Ibn al-Farrukhān. He further summoned another group, which included al-Naḍr b. Shumayl, Ibn ʿAlī b. ʿĀṣim, Abū al-ʿAwwām al-Bazzāz, Ibn Shujāʿ and ʿAbd al-Raḥmān b. Isḥāq.[660] All of these were brought into Isḥāq's presence en masse, and he read out to them twice this letter of al-Ma'mūn's until they comprehended it. Then he asked Bishr b. al-Walīd,[661] "What is your view about the Qur'ān?" He replied, "I have acquainted the Commander of the Faithful with my views about this on more than one occasion." Isḥāq replied, "But this letter from the Commander of the Faithful is something new, as you can see." Bishr retorted, "I say that the Qur'ān is the word of God." Is-
[1122] ḥāq said, "I didn't ask you about this. Is it created?" Bishr responded, "God is the creator of everything." Isḥāq said, "Is not the Qur'ān a thing?" Bishr replied, "It is a thing." Isḥāq said, "Then it must be created?" Bishr replied, "It is not a creator." Isḥāq said, "I didn't ask you about this; is it created?" Bishr replied, "I cannot do better than what I have said to you, and I have already secured from the Caliph a promise that I do not have to speak about it; I have no views other than what I have told you." Isḥāq b. Ibrāhīm took up a document which lay before him and read it out and explained it to him. Then he went on to say, "Bear witness that there is no god but God, the One, the Solitary, before whom there was nothing and after whom

660. See concerning various of these figures, ibid., 70; Watt, 281, 286.
661. See ibid., 281; Sezgin, *GAS*, I, 438.

there shall be nothing, and whom nothing of His creation resembles in any meaning or sense whatsoever." Bishr retorted, "I bear witness to that, and I have been having people beaten for less than that [*ʿalā dūni hādhā*]." Isḥāq turned to the clerk and said, "Set down what he has said."

Then Isḥāq said to ʿAlī b. Muqātil "What do you say, O ʿAlī?" ʿAlī replied, "I have let the Commander of the Faithful hear my words about this on several occasions, and I have nothing to add to what he has already heard." Isḥāq then put ʿAlī to the test with the document, and ʿAlī gave his assent to its contents. Then Isḥāq said, "Is the Qur'ān created?" ʿAlī replied, "The Qur'ān is the word of God." Isḥāq said, "I didn't ask you about this." ʿAlī responded, "It is the word of God, but if the Commander of the Faithful commands us with the doing of a thing, we hear and obey." Isḥāq said to the clerk, "Set down his views." Then he said to al-Dhayyāl more or less what he had said to ʿAlī b. Abī Muqātil, and al-Dhayyāl replied in the same vein.

Then Isḥāq said to Abū Ḥassān al-Ziyādī,[662] "What is your opinion?" He replied, "Ask about anything you like." Then Isḥāq read out the document and explained it to him, and Abū Ḥassān gave his assent to the contents. Then Isḥāq said, "Any person who does not agree with these doctrines is an unbeliever," and asked him, "Is the Qur'ān itself created?" Abū Ḥassān replied, "The Qur'ān is the word of God, and God is the [1123]
creator of everything; all things apart from him are created. But the Commander of the Faithful is our Imām, and by means of him we have heard the whole sum of knowledge. He has heard what we have not heard, and he knows what we do not know. God has invested him with the rule over us; he upholds the pilgrimage and the worship for us, we hand over to him the poor-tax levied on our wealth, we fight at his side in the holy war and we recognize his imāmate as a true one. So if he commands us, we obey his orders; if he forbids us from doing something, we desist; and if he calls upon us, we respond to him." Isḥāq

662. Judge and traditionist who died in 243 (857/8) and who is frequently quoted by Ibn Abī Ṭāhir (see concerning this, above, 158 n. 474); see Ibn al-Nadīm, *Fihrist*, tr. B. Dodge, I, 241–2.

said, "Is the Qur'ān itself created?" In answer, Abū Ḥassān repeated his views as given above. Isḥāq said, "This is the Commander of the Faithful's doctrine." Abū Ḥassān retorted, "But sometimes the Commander of the Faithful's view is one concerning which he gives the people no explicit command and does not call upon them to adopt it. If, however, you tell me that the Commander of the Faithful has commanded you that I should say this, I will say whatever you command me to say, for you are a trustworthy person, one on whom reliance is to be placed regarding anything which you convey to me from him; hence if you convey to me any command from him about anything, I will hasten to do it." Isḥāq said, "He has not given me the order to convey anything to you." ʿAlī b. Abī Muqātil said, "The Commander of the Faithful's words may conceivably be like the variation in views amongst the Companions of the Messenger of God concerning the obligatory shares [*farāʾiḍ*] and inheritances,[663] and he has not given any injunction to the people about them." Abū Ḥassān said to him, "I have no idea but to hear and obey; command me, and I shall obey his orders." Isḥāq said, "The Commander of the Faithful has not commanded me to give you any orders, but only that I should put you to the test."

He then came back to Aḥmad b. Ḥanbal[664] and said to him, "What is your view concerning the Qur'ān?" Aḥmad replied, "It is the word of God." Isḥāq said, "Is it created?" Aḥmad retorted, "It is the word of God; I cannot add any more to these words." Isḥāq then put him to the test with the contents of the document. When he came to the words "There is nothing like Him, and He is the hearing and seeing one," he held back from the phrase " . . . whom nothing of His creation resembles in
[1124] any meaning or sense whatsoever." Ibn al-Bakkāʾ al-Aṣghar interrupted him and said, "May God grant you righteousness! It speaks of 'a hearing one' because of ears and 'a seeing one' be-

663. See J. Schacht, *An introduction to Islamic law,* 170 ff.; *EI*² s.v. Farāʾiḍ (T.W. Juynboll).

664. Spearhead of the conservative and traditionalist opposition to al-Maʾmūn's religious policy here and founder of the subsequent Ḥanbalī law school; see Patton, *passim*; Watt, index; *EI*² s.v. (H. Laoust).

cause of eyes!" Isḥāq said to Aḥmad b. Ḥanbal, "What do the words 'a hearing and seeing one' mean?" Aḥmad replied, "God is even as He has described Himself." Isḥāq said, "But what does it mean?" Aḥmad responded, "I don't know; He is even as He has described Himself." Then Isḥāq summoned them, one by one, and they all said that the Qur'ān was the word of God except for this group of people: Qutaybah, 'Ubaydallāh b. Muḥammad b. al-Ḥasan, Ibn 'Ulayyah al-Akbar, Ibn al-Bakkā', 'Abd al-Mun'im b. Idrīs b. Bint Wahb b. Munabbih, al-Muẓaffar b. Murajjā, a blind man who was not a *faqīh* and about whom nothing was known except that he had been introduced into there, the judge of Raqqah who was descended from 'Umar b. al-Khaṭṭāb and Ibn al-Aḥmar. In regard to Ibn al-Bakkā' al-Akbar, he replied that the Qur'ān was something made (*maj'ūl*) because of God's words, "Indeed, we have made it [*ja'alnāhu*] an Arabic Qur'ān,"[665] and something originated (*muḥdath*) because of His words,"No recently-originated [*muḥdath*] warning has come to them from their Lord."[666] Isḥāq said to him, "Is, then, what is made, created?" Ibn al-Bakkā' replied, "Yes." Isḥāq said, "So the Qur'ān is created?" Ibn al-Bakkā' replied, "I don't say that it is created, but that it is something made." Isḥāq then wrote down what he had said.[667]

When he had finished putting the members of the group to the test and had recorded their replies, Ibn al-Bakkā' al-Aṣghar broke in, saying, "May God grant you righteousness! These two judges are leading scholars, why don't you order them [to affirm their views on the Qur'ān?" He kept on urging this. Isḥāq said to him, "These two men are the ones who held their position through the Commander of the Faithful's nomination." Ibn al-Bakkā' kept on, "Why don't you order them to let us hear their views, so that we might pass these down directly from them?" Isḥāq replied, "If you will serve as a witness before them, you will know their views, if God wills." He wrote [1125]
down the views of all the group one after the other, and these were sent to al-Ma'mūn. The group remained there for nine

665. Qur'ān, XLIII, 2/3.
666. Qur'ān, XXI, 2.
667. Patton, 69–74.

days.[668] Then Isḥāq summoned them together again, the Caliph's letter having arrived in answer to Isḥāq b. Ibrāhīm's communication regarding the affair. Its text was as follows:

In the name of God, the Merciful, the Compassionate. There has reached the Commander of the Faithful your letter, comprising an answer to his letter sent to you about that doctrine which the ostentatious ones among the people of *qiblah* [the Muslims] and those among the people of the faith who seek a leadership for which they are not qualified, profess about the creation of the Qur'ān. The Commander of the Faithful also commanded you in that letter to put them to the test, investigate their various positions and set them down in their appropriate places. You mention summoning to your presence Ja'far b. 'Īsā and 'Abd al-Raḥmān b. Isḥāq on the arrival of the Commander of the Faithful's letter, together with your summoning those who have been classed as experts on the religious law, who have been recognized as transmitters of tradition and who have set themselves up as competent to give judicial decisions in the City of Peace; [you mention] your reading the Commander of the Faithful's letter out to the assembled group; [you mention] interrogating them about their religious convictions regarding the Qur'ān; [you mention] pointing out to them how they could best serve their own interests; [you mention] their agreement to reject anthropomorphism [*tashbīh*][669] and their differences of view concerning the Qur'ān. [You also mention] your giving orders to those of them who would not profess that the Qur'ān was created to refrain from transmitting traditions and from giving judicial decisions, whether in private or in public; and [you mention] your giving instructions to al-Sindī and to 'Abbās, the Commander of the Faithful's client, to the same effect as the instructions concerning them which you gave to the two judges, even the same

668. Ibid., 74.
669. See for this, also called *tajsīm*, Watt, 246–9, 290, 295; *EI*[1] s.v. Tashbīh (R. Strothmann).

which the Commander of the Faithful prescribed to you, namely, the testing of the legal witnesses who attend their courts. [You also mention] the dispatch of letters to the judges in the outlying parts of the areas of your administrative jurisdiction, instructing them to come to you so that you might constrain them and test them according to what the Commander of the Faithful has defined; and [you mention] your listing at the end of your letter the names of those who were present and their professed doctrines.

The Commander of the Faithful has understood what you have recounted, and he gives God abundant praise, as indeed befits Him, and asks Him to grant a blessing upon His servant and His messenger Muḥammad, and he desires earnestly of God success in obeying Him and, through his mercifulness, effective aid to realize his good intentions. The Commander of the Faithful has also pondered over what you have written to him concerning the names of those whom you interrogated about the Qur'ān, the replies which you got back from each one of those persons in regard to it, and the explanations which you have given of their views. [1126]

As for what the deluded Bishr b. al-Walīd has said about rejecting anthropomorphic conceptions and as for what he has held back from in connection with the createdness of the Qur'ān, and also what he has claimed concerning his not having to speak about that and his having obtained an agreement to this effect from the Commander of the Faithful—he has lied about it and shown himself an unbeliever, and has uttered deceit and falsehood. For there has not passed between him and the Commander of the Faithful any agreement or exchange of views on this topic or on any other beyond his telling the Commander of the Faithful that he believed in the doctrine of exclusive devotion to God [*ikhlāṣ*][670] and profession of the Qur'ān's createdness. So summon him before you and tell him what the Commander of the Faithful has just told you about this

670. See for this, *EI*^{2} s.v. (L. Gardet).

matter; require him to answer about what he has said regarding the Qur'ān and ask him to recant his beliefs. For indeed, the Commander of the Faithful believes that you should ask someone who holds views like his to recant, since such views are unalloyed infidelity and sheer polytheism in the Commander of the Faithful's opinion. If he then repents of these views, proclaim his action publicly and leave him alone; but if he persists in his polytheism and refuses, in his unbelief and heresy, to admit that the Qur'ān is created, then have him decapitated and, if God wills, send his head along to the Commander of the Faithful. Do likewise with Ibrāhīm b. al-Mahdī. Test him in the same terms as you tested Bishr, for he used to profess
[1127] Bishr's views, and reports about him have reached the Commander of the Faithful. If he acknowledges that the Qur'ān is created, proclaim his action publicly and disclose it fully; but if not, then have him decapitated and, if God wills, send his head along to the Commander of the Faithful.

As for ʿAlī b. Abī Muqātil, say to him, "Are you not the person who said to the Commander of the Faithful, 'You are the one who declares what is permissible and what is not permissible,' and who spoke to him about what you have spoke to him about." The recollection of this cannot yet have left him. As for al-Dhayyāl b. al-Haytham, tell him that what should occupy his mind is the corn which he used to steal at Anbār and what he used to appropriate for himself in the city of the Commander of the Faithful Abū al-ʿAbbās [al-Saffāḥ], and that if he were a follower in the footsteps of his forefathers, walking in their ways and keeping to their identical tracks,[671] he would certainly not go off into polytheism after having believed. As for Aḥmad b. Yazīd, known as Abū al-ʿAwwām, and his saying that he cannot answer well regarding the Qur'ān, tell him that he is a child in intellect, if not one in years, and an ignoramus, and that unless he sees his way to answer properly about the Qur'ān, he will certainly see his way to do it properly when

671. Following the reading of the *Addenda et emendanda.*, p. DCCLXXII.

punishment befalls him; then if he still does not do it, there is the sword beyond that, if God wills. As for Aḥmad b. Ḥanbal and what you write about him, tell him that the Commander of the Faithful has understood the significance of that view and his conduct regarding it, and from it he deduces as proven his ignorance and defective intelligence. As for al-Faḍl b. Ghānim, tell him that what he did in Egypt and the riches which he amassed for himself in less than one year have not been hidden from the Commander of the Faithful, nor has the legal imbroglio over those doings which went on between him and al-Muṭṭalib b. ʿAbdallāh;[672] for one cannot but believe that a man who behaved as he did, and who showed himself as avid [1128] for dīnārs and dirhams as he did, would barter his faith out of lust for money and out of a preference for deriving an immediate advantage from it. [Remind him,] moreover, that he is the one who said to ʿAlī b. Hishām what he said and who opposed him in that in which he opposed him, and [remind him] what it was that caused him to abandon that doctrine and brought him over to another one. As for al-Ziyādī, tell him that he is alleging a connection with the first false claimant over lineage in Islam, in whose case the Messenger of God's ordinance was set aside;[673] it is only fitting that he should behave as he does. [But Abū Ḥassān denied that he was a client of Ziyād (b. Abīhi),[674] or indeed that he was anyone's client, and stated that he simply had a *nisbah* relating to Ziyād for some other reason.] As for the person known as Abū Naṣr al-Tammār, the Commander of the Faithful compares the insignificance of his intellect with the insignificance of his trade.[675]

As for al-Faḍl b. al-Farrukhān, tell him that, through the doctrine which he professes on the Qur'ān, he has tried to appro-

672. Al-Faḍl was appointed chief judge in Egypt by the governor al-Muṭṭalib b. ʿAbdallāh al-Khuzāʿī in 198 (813), but was dismissed after ten months in office; see Kindī, 422–3.

673. I.e., a connection with Ziyād b. Abīhi, who claimed to be a son of the Meccan leader Abū Sufyān by the notorious whore Sumayyah and whom the Caliph Muʿāwiyah b. Abī Sufyān endeavored to adopt into the Umayyad family; see H. Lammens, *Etudes sur le siècle des Omayyades*, 27–161; *EI*[1] s.v. (Lammens).

674. I.e., that a forebear of his had been a client of Ziyād b. Abīhi.

675. *Tammār* = "seller of dates" (*tamr*).

priate the deposits which ʿAbd al-Raḥmān b. Isḥāq and others entrusted to him, waiting for a favorable moment when someone will ask him to act as a depository and hoping to add to what has already come into his hands; furthermore, there is no way of securing redress from him, because of the extended duration of the agreement and the prolongation of the period of its existence. But say to ʿAbd al-Raḥmān b. Isḥāq, "May God not recompense you with good for your giving strength to a man like this and your reposing trust in him, seeing that he is firmly bound up with polytheism and has completely thrown off belief in God's unity." As for Muḥammad b. Ḥātim, Ibn Nūḥ and the man known as Abū Maʿmar, tell them that they
[1129] are too much occupied with devouring usury properly to grasp the concept of the divine unity and that, if the Commander of the Faithful had sought legal justification in combatting them for the sake of God and launching a holy war against them solely on the grounds of their taking usury and that which has been revealed in the Qur'ān regarding their likes, he would surely have found it lawful. How will it be with them now, when they have added polytheism to their practice of usury and have become just like the Christians? As for Aḥmad b. Shujāʿ, tell him that you were in close contact with him only recently and extracted from him what he himself had confiscated as being licit of ʿAlī b. Hishām's wealth, and [tell him] that he is one of those people whose religion is made up of dīnārs and dirhams. As for Saʿdawayh al-Wāsiṭī, say to him, "May God make vile a man whose ostentatious preparation of himself for transmitting traditions, his self-glorification by means of it and his avidity in seeking a leading position in that field have reached such a pitch that he looks forward to the coming of the *miḥnah* and proclaims his desire to ingratiate himself with me through it. Let him be put to the test, and [if he assents to the createdness of the Qur'ān,] he may still teach traditions.

As for the person who is known as Sajjādah and his denial that he has ever heard the doctrine that the Qur'ān is created from any of the traditionists and *faqīhs* with whom he used to study, tell him that, in his concern to prepare datestones and his rubbing [his forehead] in order to make the callosity on his forehead [*sajjāda*] look more imposing,[676] and similarly in his care for the deposits which ʿAlī b. Yaḥyā and others commited to his keeping, lies that which has diverted his attention from the idea of God's unity and made him unmindful of it. Then ask him about what Yūsuf b. Abī Yūsuf and Muḥammad b. al-Ḥasan used to say, if he really did have contact with them and attend their sessions for study. As for al-Qawārīrī, what shows up clearly his real beliefs, his evil conduct and the feebleness of his intellect and religion can be discerned in what has become open and notorious about his proclivities and his taking of bribes and presents offered to influence his decision favorably. It has also reached the Commander of the Faithful that he has taken upon himself responsibility for [the settling of] legal questions for Jaʿfar b. ʿĪsā al-Ḥasanī; so command Jaʿfar b. ʿĪsā to set him aside and no longer place any reliance on him [1130] or confidence in him. As for Yaḥyā b. ʿAbd al-Raḥmān al-ʿUmarī, if he were genuinely from the progeny of ʿUmar b. al-Khaṭṭāb, it is well-known how he would answer. As for Muḥammad b. al-Ḥasan b. ʿAlī b. ʿĀṣim, if only he really did imitate his ancestors,[677] he would not profess that spurious doctrine which has been related of him. He is still a child who needs instruction.

Now the Commander of the Faithful has also sent to you a certain person called Abū Mus'hir after the Commander of the Faithful had required him to answer in his testing about the Qur'ān. He mumbled indistinctly over it and kept on repeating himself in it, until the Commander of the Faithful ordered the sword to be brought out for him; then he made his profession in the manner of one worthy of censure. So require him to make his affirmation about it, and if he stands fast in it, proclaim it publicly and divulge it openly, if God wills. But those

676. Such a callosity when caused by repeated prostration (*sujūd*) was regarded as a sign of great piety, but could be fabricated by rubbing the forehead.

677. Muḥammad was presumably either the descendant of the traditionist and author on the Prophet's *maghāzī*, or raids, ʿĀṣim b. ʿUmar b. Qatādah, died in 120 (738) (see A.A. Duri, *The rise of historical writing among the Arabs*, 27, 34) or else of ʿĀṣim b. Bahdalah al-Asadī, Kūfan author of one of the seven canonical systems of Qur'ān reading, died in 127 or 128 (745) (see *EI*[2] s.v. [A. Jeffery]).

who refuse to abandon their polytheism, from amongst those whom you named to the Commander of the Faithful in your letter and whom the Commander of the Faithful has either mentioned to you or else has refrained from mentioning in this letter of his, and who will not profess that the Qur'ān is created, with the exceptions of Bishr b. al-Walīd and Ibrāhīm b. al-Mahdī, send them all in bonds to the Commander of the Faithful's encampment, together with someone who will be responsible for watching over and guarding them on the journey; then bring them to the Commander of the Faithful's encampment and hand them over to the person to whom their delivery has been entrusted, so that the Commander of the Faithful may require them to give their answer. If they do not then recant and repent of their errors, he will consign them en bloc to the sword, if God wills; and there is no power except in God. The Commander of the Faithful has dispatched this letter by a special courier's letter bag [*kharīṭah bundāriyyah*],[678] and has
[1131] not considered [awaiting] the collection of letters for the regular letter bag service [*kutub kharā'iṭiyyah*], thereby expediting it and seeking to advance in God's favor through the decree which he has issued, expecting to achieve his purpose and thereby gaining a hoped-for generous reward from God. So put into effect the Commander of the Faithful's order which comes to you, and hasten to give a reply to him about what you are doing by special courier's letter bag, sent separately from the rest of the letter bags, so that you may inform the Commander of the Faithful what they are doing, if God wills.

(This) was written in the year 218 (833).[679]

When Isḥāq b. Ibrāhīm put the question to them again, all of the group now confessed that the Qur'ān was created, except for four of them—Aḥmad b. Ḥanbal, Sajjādah, al-Qawārīrī and Muḥammad b. Nūḥ al-Maḍrūb. Accordingly, Isḥāq b. Ibrāhīm ordered these last to be loaded with iron fetters. The next day, he sent for (the four of) them together, and they were thrust

---

678. I.e., by express courier service. For the Persian term *bundār*, here meaning "rapid courier," see Ṭabarī, *Glossarium*, pp. CXLI–CXLII.

679. Patton, 74–80.

forward in irons. He put them to the test once more, and this time Sajjādah responded that the Qur'ān was indeed created. Isḥāq therefore ordered his fetters to be struck off and set him free. The others, however, maintained their original position. On the day after that, he had (the three of) them brought out once more and repeated the question. This time, al-Qawārīrī acknowledged that the Qur'ān was created, so Isḥāq ordered his fetters to be struck off and set him free. But Aḥmad b. Ḥanbal and Muḥammad b. Nūḥ persisted in their original profession and would not recant. Hence they were both loaded with fetters and sent to Tarsus, accompanied by a letter from Isḥāq with instructions that they should be sent onwards. He further wrote a separate letter giving an explanation of what the group had finally assented to. The group remained (in Baghdad) for a few days, and then Isḥāq summoned them. At this juncture, a letter had just reached him from al-Ma'mūn to the effect that:

> The Commander of the Faithful has understood what the group assented to. The postmaster and intelligence agent [*ṣāḥib al-khabar*] Sulaymān b. Ya'qūb has reported that [1132] Bishr b. al-Walīd has furnished an interpretation of the verse which God Most High revealed in connection with 'Ammār b. Yāsir,[680] ". . . except him who is compelled, while his heart is still at peace in belief,"[681] but his interpretation is erroneous; God merely refers in this verse to the person who holds fast [in his heart] to the faith, while outwardly professing polytheism. As for the person who holds fast [in his heart] to polytheism, while outwardly showing the faith, the verse does not refer to him at all. Hence, send them all to Tarsus, where they are to wait until the time when the Commander of the Faithful will leave the Byzantine lands.

Isḥāq b. Ibrāhīm took guarantors from the group, that they would meet up at the army camp at Tarsus, and accordingly

680. Companion of the Prophet, famed for his piety and knowledge of traditions; see *EI*² s.v. (H. Reckendorff), noting that various passages of the Qur'ān were interpreted by anti-Umayyad polemicists as referring to 'Ammār.

681. Qur'ān, XVI, 108/106.

sent forward Abū Ḥassān, Bishr b. al-Walīd, al-Faḍl b. Ghānim, ʿAlī b. Abī Muqātil, al-Dhayyāl b. al-Haytham, Yaḥyā b. ʿAbd al-Raḥmān al-ʿUmarī, ʿAlī b. al-Jaʿd, Abū al-ʿAwwām, Sajjādah, al-Qawārīrī, Ibn al-Ḥasan b. ʿAlī b. ʿĀṣim, Isḥāq b. Abī Isrāʾīl, al-Naḍr b. Shumayl, Abū Naṣr al-Tammār, Saʿdawayh al-Wāsiṭī, Muḥammad b. Ḥātim b. Maymūn, Abū Maʿmar, Ibn al-Hirsh, Ibn al-Farrukhān, Aḥmad b. Shujāʿ and Abū Hārūn b. al-Bakkāʾ. When they approached Raqqah, the news of al-Ma'mūn's death reached them, and the governor of Raqqah, ʿAnbasah b. Isḥāq, ordered them to enter the town; but then he sent them back to Isḥāq b. Ibrāhīm at the City of Peace in the company of the envoy who had been charged with escorting them to the Commander of the Faithful. The envoy delivered them to Isḥāq, who instructed them to remain in their houses. He subsequently relented towards them and allowed them to go out. However, Bishr b. al-Walīd, al-Dhayyāl, Abū al-ʿAwwām and ʿAlī b. Abī Muqātil set out (from Raqqah) without having obtained permission, and reached Baghdad. As a penalty
[1133] for that, they received punishment from Isḥāq b. Ibrāhīm. The rest of the group arrived with Isḥāq b. Ibrāhīm's envoy, and he then set them free.[682]

In this year, letters from al-Ma'mūn were dispatched to his governors in the provinces, (with the heading,) "From the slave of God ʿAbdallāh, the Imām al-Ma'mūn, Commander of the Faithful, and his brother, the Caliph in succession to him, Abū Isḥāq, son of the Commander of the Faithful al-Rashīd."[683] It is also said that al-Ma'mūn did not have it written just like that, and that it was only set down in a period of lucidity which al-Ma'mūn regained from the general state of unconsciousness which came over him during his illness at Budandūn,[684] on al-Ma'mūn's instructions to al-ʿAbbās b. al-Ma'mūn, to Isḥāq (b. Ibrāhīm al-Muṣʿabī) and to ʿAbdallāh b. Ṭāhir, to the effect that, if death should supervene during this illness of his, then

682. Patton, 83–4.
683. *ʿUyūn*, 377.
684. A river and place in Cilicia to the north of Tarsus, Greek Podandos; see Honigmann, 44–5, 82.

the next Caliph in succession to him should be Abū Isḥāq, son of the Commander of the Faithful al-Rashīd. Muḥammad b. Dāwūd wrote that out, sealed the letters and dispatched them.

Abū Isḥāq wrote to his governors, (with the heading,) "From Abū Isḥāq, brother of the Commander of the Faithful and Caliph after the Commander of the Faithful." Then there arrived a letter from Abū Isḥāq Muḥammad b. Hārūn al-Rashīd to Isḥāq b. Yaḥyā b. Muʿādh, his governor over the *jund*[685] of Damascus, on Sunday, the thirteenth of Rajab[686] (August 4, 833). Its heading was: "From the slave of God ʿAbdallāh, the Imām al-Ma'mūn, Commander of the Faithful, and the Caliph in succession to the Commander of the Faithful [al-Ma'mūn], Abū Isḥāq, son of the Commander of the Faithful al-Rashīd," (and its text was as follows,) "The Commander of the Faithful has commanded in the letter to you that you should instruct your [subordinate] governors [*ʿummāl*] that they should conduct themselves well, lighten the financial burdens and avoid harming the people within your administrative district. So in- [1134] struct your governors concerning this in the strongest possible terms, and write to the officials charged with levying and collecting the land-tax [*ʿummāl al-kharāj*] in the same vein." He wrote a similar letter to all his governors in the various *jund*s of Syria—those of Ḥimṣ, Urdunn and Filasṭīn—and then when Friday, the nineteenth of Rajab[687] (August 10, 833), came round, Isḥāq b. Yaḥyā b. Muʿādh led the Friday worship in the mosque at Damascus and proclaimed in his *khuṭbah*, after prayers for the Commander of the Faithful, "O God, grant righteousness to the Amīr, the brother of the Commander of the Faithful Abū Isḥāq, son of the Commander of the Faithful al-Rashīd."

In this year, al-Ma'mūn died.

---

685. Here with the meaning of the administrative region around Damascus, originally settled in the conquest period by an Arab army group (*jund*); see *EI*^{2} s.v. Djund (Sourdel).

686. Actually a Monday.

687. Actually a Sunday.

The Cause of al-Ma'mūn's Fatal Illness

It is mentioned from Saʿīd al-ʿAllāf the Qur'ān reciter, who related: Al-Ma'mūn sent for me, at the time when he was in the Byzantine lands, having entered them from Tarsus on Wednesday, the sixteenth of Jumādā II (July 9, 833).[688] I was brought to him at Budandūn. He used often to ask me to recite, and one day he summoned me. I found him sitting on the bank (of the river) of Budandūn with Abū Isḥāq al-Muʿtaṣim seated at his right hand. He bade me, and I sat down near him, and behold, at that moment, he and Abū Isḥāq were dangling their feet in
[1135] the water (of the river) of Budandūn. He said to me, "O Saʿīd, dangle your feet in this water too, and taste it; have you ever seen water more cool, more sweet and more clear than this?" I did (as he instructed), and replied, "O Commander of the Faithful, I have never seen its like." He said, "What comestible would go well with this water, to follow it?" I replied, "The Commander of the Faithful knows best." He said, "Fresh green dates of the *āzādh* variety!"[689]

At the very moment when he was uttering these words, the clinking noise of the bridles of the mounts of the postal and intelligence service (*barīd*) could be heard. He turned round and looked, and behold, there were some of the mules of the postal and intelligence service with panniers over their hindquarters in which were gifts. He said to one of his servants, "Go and see if there are any fresh dates amongst these gifts, and if there are in fact any fresh dates, see whether there are any of the *āzādh* variety and bring them here." The servant came hurrying back with two baskets of fresh *āzādh* dates, as if they had been gathered from the palm tree that very moment. He vouchsafed thanks to God Most High, and we were most astonished at all this. Al-Ma'mūn said, "Come forward and eat some!" He and

688. Masʿūdī, *Murūj*, VII, 94–6 = ed. Pellat, §§ 2778–9, cf. Vasiliev, *Byzance et les Arabes*, I, 122–3, describes the coming of an envoy from the Emperor Theophilus to al-Ma'mūn, seeking to buy him off with tribute and an exchange of captives, but failing in his mission, after which the Caliph invaded Byzantine territory, returning to Budandūn.

689. *Āzādh* = Persian "free, noble," hence here "excellent;" see Dozy, I, 19a-b.

Abū Isḥaq ate some, and I ate with them, and we all drank some of that water; but by the time we got up, each one of us had contracted a fever. That illness proved fatal for al-Ma'mūn; al-Muʿtaṣim continued to be ill till he reached Iraq; but I myself remained ill only for a short while.[690]

When al-Ma'mūn's illness grew worse, he sent for his son al-ʿAbbās, although he imagined that he would not arrive (in time). But al-ʿAbbās came to him, by which time al-Ma'mūn was extremely ill, with mind impaired; the letters containing his instructions regarding Abū Isḥāq b. al-Rashīd had already been sent off. Al-ʿAbbās stayed with his father for some days, al-Ma'mūn having already made his last testament, concerning the succession, to his brother Abū Isḥāq previously to that. [1136] Others say that he did not make this testament until al-ʿAbbās, the judges, the *faqīhs*, the army commanders and the secretaries were all present.

(The text of) his last testament was as follows:

This is what ʿAbdallāh b. Hārūn, the Commander of the Faithful, asks witness to be borne to, in the presence of those who have gathered round him. He asks all of them to bear witness to himself, that he and those present testify that God is one, that He has no associate in His power and no controller sharing His authority except Himself, and that He is the creator, and everything else apart from Him is created, so that the Qur'ān must be a thing which can have a likeness, whereas there is nothing resembling God. Also, that death, the physical resurrection and the final reckoning are realities, and that the reward of him who does good will be Paradise but the punishment of him who does evil will be hell fire. Also, that Muḥammad has delivered from his Lord the prescriptions of His religion and has conveyed His wise counsels to His community, until the

690. Ibn Abī Ṭāhir, 349–50, tr. 157–8 (the surviving part of Abī Ṭāhir's historical narrative ends here); Azdī, 414–15; *ʿUyūn*, 377–8; Vasiliev, op. cit., I, 291–2. In Masʿūdī, *Murūj*, VII, 94–101 = ed. Pellat, §§ 2779–83, cf. Vasiliev, op. cit., I, 329–30, a different, equally anecdotal account of al-Ma'mūn's fatal illness on the banks of the Budandūn is given, on the authority of the judge Abū Muḥammad ʿAbdallāh b. Aḥmad b. Zayd al-Dimashqī.

time when God took him to Himself—may God bless him with the finest of blessings which He has ever given to those angels of His brought near to His presence and the prophets whom He has sent as messengers. Also, that I confess freely my sinfulness, and I both hope [for forgiveness] and fear [the divine punishment],[691] except that when I mention God's forgiveness, I am filled with hope.

When I die, turn my face [towards God], close my eyes, perform the lesser ablution and the rites of purification over me, and see that I am properly shrouded. Then give repeated promises to God for the Islamic faith and for the knowledge of His necessary beneficence to you concerning Muḥammad, when he made us part of his community, meriting God's mercy. Then lay me on my side in my litter and hasten along with me, and when you set me down for the worship,[692] let the one among you who is nearest to me in kinship and the eldest in years come forward to lead the worship. Let the leader utter the *takbīr* five times, and on the first occasion begin with the formula, "Praise be to God and eulogies on Him, and blessing upon our master and the master of all the messengers who have been sent," as the opening words. Then should come a prayer for the men and the women believers, those still alive and those now dead; and then a prayer for those who have preceded
[1137] us in the faith. Then let him utter the *takbīr* for the fourth time, and then let him praise God, proclaim the confession of faith to Him, magnify Him and ask Him to grant peace on the fifth occasion. Then load my corpse on your shoulders and bear me along to my grave; once there, let the one of you nearest in kinship to me and the one who has the deepest feeling of affection go down into the grave. Render profuse praises to God and mentions of His name. Place me on my right side and turn me in the direction of the

691. *Arjū wa-akhāfu*, echoing Qur'ān, XVII, 57/55. On the concept of contrasting hope and fear (*rajā' wa-khawf*) as a factor in human behaviour and human religious consciousness, see Rosenthal, *"Sweeter than hope", complaint and hope in medieval Islam*, 79, 141 ff.

692. I.e., for the *ṣalāt al-mawt*; see *EI*[1] s.v. Ṣalāt. IV (Wensinck).

qiblah. Unwind my shroud from my head and feet, and then wall up the niche with mud bricks and sprinkle earth over me.[693] [Finally,] depart from me and leave me with my own affair. For indeed, none of you will avail me at all, nor will you be able to keep back from me anything unpleasant which may befall me.

Then all of you together are to stand there, and to say good things [about me], if you know of any, but refrain from mentioning unfavorable things if you have known about any of them, for I [alone] among you shall be held responsible for what you may say and what you may enunciate.[694] Do not allow any weeping woman to be near me, for the person who is lamented over is thereby troubled. May God have mercy on a man who takes heed of warnings and who reflects on the annihilation which God inevitably brings down on all His creation and the inescapable death which He decrees for them! So praise be to God who has made eternal existence a quality solely for Himself alone and has decreed annihilation for the whole of His creation! Next, let [such a heedful man] consider what my own state once was, with the might of the caliphate—has that been of any avail for me when God's command has come for me? No, by God! Indeed, I shall have to give a double accounting [at the last day] because of this responsibility. So would that ʿAbdallāh b. Hārūn [that is, himself] had not been created as a human being, yea, would that he had not been created at all! O Abū Isḥāq, come close to me and derive a warning from what you see!

Follow your brother's policy regarding the Qur'ān, and when God invests you with the caliphate, strive in it as one earnestly desiring God's favor and as one fearing His retribution and punishment. Do not be deluded in regard to God and the respite [from death and judgment] which He grants, for death has already established itself within you. Do not neglect the affairs of the subjects; keep your

693. For these burial practices, see T.P. Hughes, *A dictionary of Islam*, 44–7; *EI*^{2} s.v. Djanāza (Tritton).

694. I.e., don't say anything detrimental to me, which might send me to hell!

[1138] subjects and the common people perpetually in mind! For the maintenance of royal power comes only through them and through your continual concern for the Muslims and their welfare. So watch over them and the other Muslims, and do not let any matter which involves any advantage or benefit for the Muslims come along without giving it a priority and preference over any other of your inclinations. Take from the powerful subjects and give to the weak ones. Do not impose any intolerable burden upon them, and ensure that justice is meted out between all individuals with fairness; keep them near to you and treat them in a gentle manner.

Hurry away from me quickly on your journey and head speedily for the seat of your authority in Iraq. Look to these people in whose land you find yourself, and do not neglect them at any time. Launch against the Khurramiyyah expeditions led by a commander who is resolute, fierce and firm, and support him with finance, arms and troops, both cavalry and infantry. If they are away campaigning for a long time, concentrate your attention on them and send them reinforcements from the auxiliaries and retainers whom you have around you. In all this, act just like a person putting his whole heart into it, hoping for God's reward in return for it. Know, too, that exhortation, when it becomes prolonged, renders obligatory a demonstrable justification for it on the one who hears it and one the one giving the exhortation. Fear God in all your affairs and do not be seduced [from the path of duty]![695]

Then after a while, when his affliction grew intense and he felt the imminence of God's command (that is, death), al-Ma'mūn summoned Abū Isḥāq and he said to him:

695. Sourdel, "La politique religieuse du calife ʿabbāside al-Ma'mūn," 44–5, has underlined the importance of this *waṣiyyah* or testament as an exposition of several pro-Shīʿī and Muʿtazilī attitudes, such as the need to show kindness to the ʿAlids, the emphasis on the divine unity (*tawḥīd*), the use of the Shīʿī quintuple *takbīr* during his obsequies, etc.

O Abū Isḥāq, take care to observe God's covenant and contractual agreement, and the Messenger of God's protection, in order that you may maintain God's right among His servants and that you may choose obedience to Him in preference to disobedience, since I have conveyed it [the Messenger of God's protection] to you from someone else.

Abū Isḥāq replied, "By God, I certainly will." Al-Ma'mūn said:

Also, look to the person whom you have heard me putting forward [giving preferment] in my express words, and increase his prominent position [or, less probably: double [1139] the financial reward for him, *al-taqdimah*], that is, ʿAbdallāh b. Ṭāhir. Confirm him in his governorship and do not disquiet him in any way, for you have recognized what the two of you achieved in the past during my own lifetime and at my court. Endeavor to conciliate him with all your heart and single him out with your benevolence, for you have known well his bravery and his ability to be able to do without your brother [that is, his ability to act independently and his freedom from entanglements]. [In regard to] Isḥāq b. Ibrāhīm [al-Muṣʿabī], associate him in the above policy also, since he is indeed worthy of it. [In regard to] your own family [the ʿAbbāsids], you have well realized that there are no outstanding qualities [*baqiyyah*][696] among them, even though an odd one of them retain a regard for personal honor [*al-ṣiyānah li-nafsihi*]. [In regard to] ʿAbd al-Wahhāb,[697] pay particular attention to him among the members of your family; make him their leader, and entrust all matters concerning them to him. [In regard to] Abū ʿAbdallāh b. Abī Duwād,[698] make sure that he does not abandon your side, and associate him as an adviser in all

696. Cf. Qur'ān, XI, 118/116.
697. Presumably ʿAbd al-Wahhāb b. Ibrāhīm al-Imām b. Abī ʿAbdallāh Muḥammad, nephew of al-Saffāḥ and governor of Syria in the time of al-Manṣūr, although by now he must have been extremely old.
698. The Muʿtazilī scholar, chief judge for al-Muʿtaṣim and head of the *miḥnah* under him; see Sourdel, *Vizirat*, I, 258–60; *EI*² s.v. Aḥmad b. Abī Du'ād (K.V. Zettersteén—Pellat).

your affairs, for he is indeed a repository of good advice for you. After I am gone, do not take for yourself any vizier to whom you might impute any fault [who has not got an unimpeachable reputation], for you have known with what troubles Yaḥyā b. Aktham burdened me through his treatment of the people and his infamous conduct, to the point when God made these activities of his clear to me, my own integrity remaining intact [*fī ṣiḥḥah minnī*], and I then proceeded to dispense with him, feeling detestation and disapproval towards him for what he had done with the money meant for God and the alms collected on His behalf. May God not reward him with any goodness from Islam! [In regard to] these, your paternal cousins who are the descendants of the Commander of the Faithful ʿAlī b. Abī Ṭālib [the ʿAlids], make them welcome in your court circle, overlook the transgressions of those who act wrongfully and welcome those who act honestly. Do not neglect giving them presents each year on the appropriate occasions, for the rights due to them demand recognition on several grounds of consideration. "Fear God, your Lord, with the respect due to Him, and do not die except as Muslims."[699] Fear God, and labor on his behalf. Fear God in all your affairs. I commend you, as also myself, to God. I seek pardon from God for what has gone before, and I further seek pardon from Him for what I myself have committed; indeed, He is the all-forgiving one. Of a certainty, He
[1140] knows the extent of my contrition for my sins; hence I place my confidence in Him from [the effects of] the worst of these sins, and to Him I turn in repentance. There is no strength except in God; God is my sufficiency, and how excellent He is as an advocate! May God grant blessings on Muḥammad the prophet of right guidance and mercifulness![700]

699. Qur'ān, III, 97/102.
700. Ibn al-Athīr, *al-Kāmil*, VI, 428–31.

The Time of al-Ma'mūn's Death, the Place where He Was Buried, the Person Who Prayed over Him, His Age and the Duration of His Caliphate

In regard to the time of his death, there have been varying reports. Some authorities have said that his term of life expired on Wednesday the eighteenth of Rajab, 218[701] (August 9, 833) after the afternoon worship. Others have denied this, and say that his term of life came to an end on that same day at the time of the midday worship. When he expired, his son al-ʿAbbās and his brother Abū Isḥāq Muḥammad b. al-Rashīd bore him to Tarsus and buried him in a house belonging to Khāqān, al-Rashīd's eunuch (*khādim*), and his brother Abū Isḥāq al-Muʿtaṣim prayed over him. Then they entrusted the task of watching over him to a guard composed of men from the garrison of Abnā' (Khurasanians) in Tarsus and others, a hundred men all told, each man being allotted ninety dirhams.[702]

His caliphate lasted for twenty years, five months and thirteen days, excluding the two years when he was hailed as ruler in the *khuṭbah* of Mecca and while his brother Muḥammad al-Amīn b. al-Rashīd was being besieged in Baghdad. He was born in the middle of Rabīʿ I (on the 15th) 170 (September 14, 786) and given the patronymic, according to Ibn al-Kalbī,[703] of Abū al-ʿAbbās.[704] He was of middle stature, pale-complexioned, handsome and with a long beard which had become whitened with advancing age. It has (also) been said that

701. Actually a Saturday.

702. Yaʿqūbī, *Ta'rīkh*, II, 573, placing his death on Thursday, the seventeenth of Rajab; Dīnawarī, *al-Akhbār al-ṭiwāl*, I, 396, placing his death on Wednesday, the eighth of Rajab, aged forty-nine; Masʿūdī, *Murūj*, VII, 2, 101 = ed. Pellat, §§ 2694, 2783; id., *Tanbīh*, 351, tr. 450 (with date given wrongly here); *ʿUyūn*, 378, placing his death on the eighth of Rajab, aged forty-eight; Vasiliev, *Byzance et les Arabes*, I, 123–4.

703. The historian Hishām b. Muḥammad al-Kalbī (died in 204 [819] or two years later), an important source for Ṭabarī, or else his son ʿAbbās; see Sezgin, *GAS*, I, 268–71; *EI*[2] s.v. al-Kalbī (W. Atallah).

704. Yaʿqūbī, *Ta'rīkh*, II, 573–4, states that he died aged forty-eight years, four months, and that his caliphate lasted twenty-two years, with twenty years five, months and twenty-five days since the death of al-Amīn; Masʿūdī, *Murūj*, VII, 1–2 = ed. Pellat, § 2694, that he died at the age of forty-nine.

[1141] he was swarthy-complexioned, but with a yellowish tinge, with a bowed back, with large, dark pupils to his eyes, a long beard with the thinner parts growing white, a narrow forehead and with a black mole on his cheek.[705] He was hailed as Caliph on Wednesday, the twenty-fifth of Muḥarram, (198 [September 25, 813]).[706]

Some of the Stories about al-Ma'mūn and His Conduct[707]

It is mentioned from Muḥammad b. al-Haytham b. ʿAdī[708] that Ibrāhīm b. ʿĪsā b. Burayhah b. al-Manṣūr[709] said: When al-Ma'mūn wanted to set out for Damascus, I prepared a speech to be delivered to him which occupied me for two whole days and part of a third one. When I stood respectfully before him, I said:

> May God prolong the days of the Commander of the Faithful in the most enduring state of might and most ample state of nobility, and may he make me his ransom against any evil which may befall him! The person who goes about early and late [literally, in the evening and in the morning, that is, continuously] discovering for himself God's favor [may He be abundantly praised!] through the Commander of the Faithful's [may God strengthen him!] favorable opinion of him and affability towards him, must necessarily seek the prolongation of this favor and ask for an increase in it, with gratitude to God and to the Commander of the Faithful [may God extend his life in that state of fa-

705. ʿ*Uyūn*, 378–9; Ibn al-Athīr, *al-Kāmil*, VI, 431–2.

706. Yaʿqūbī, *Ta'rīkh*, II, 538–9, with details of the astral conjunctions at this moment.

707. Various anecdotal details about al-Ma'mūn and his confidants, with emphasis on their great liberality, are given by Yaʿqūbī in his *Mushākalat al-nās li-zamānihim*, ed. W. Millward, 27–31, tr. id., "The adaptation of men to their time," *JAOS*, LXXXIV (1964), 340–2.

708. Son of the Kūfan historian, who died in or after 206 (821) and was a prime source for historians like Ṭabarī, Yaʿqūbī and Masʿūdī; see Sezgin, *GAS*, I, 272; *EI*^{2} s.v. al-Haytham b. ʿAdī (Pellat).

709. A second cousin of al-Ma'mūn's.

vor!] [Such a person] has furthermore earnestly wanted the Commander of the Faithful to know that I do not desire for myself any letting-up or ease of life which might distract me from my service to the Commander of the Faithful, since he takes upon himself the burden of rough travelling conditions and painful journeyings. The most suitable of all persons to share these hardships with him and to devote his life to him is myself, for God has given me knowledge of his state of mind, and has given me a sense of obedience to him and a knowledge of the recognition of his rights which God necessarily requires. Hence, if the Commander of the Faithful [may God make him noble!] sees fit to honor me by taking me into his service as a permanent companion and letting me be with him, let him so ordain!

Al-Ma'mūn answered me, speaking immediately and without pausing to reflect:

The Commander of the Faithful has not yet come to any decision at all in regard to that, but if he chooses anyone from the members of your family as a travelling companion, he will select you in the first place and you will be the person put forward to be at his side for that, above all if you willingly let yourself be set down in the same place as the Commander of the Faithful chooses to place you in relationship to him [that is, if you show yourself as adaptable]. And if he does not fulfill this intention, this will not imply any dissatisfaction with your position and capabilities, but because he has need of you [elsewhere]. [1142]

Ibrāhīm b. ʿĪsā commented, "By God, the Caliph's words delivered on the spur of the moment were more incisive than my carefully-prepared speech."[710]

It is mentioned from Muḥammad b. ʿAlī b. Ṣāliḥ al-Sarakhsī, who related: A man thrust himself forward on several occasions before al-Ma'mūn when the latter was in Syria and said to the Caliph, "O Commander of the Faithful, look after the interests of the Arabs of Syria just as you look after the inter-

710. Ibn Abī Ṭāhir, 261–2, tr. 118–19.

ests of the Persians from the people of Khurasan." Al-Ma'mūn replied, "O brother from the people of Syria, you have reproached me in strong terms! By God, I have never made Qays dismount from the backs of their horses [that is, dismissed them from service] except at times when I saw that there was not a single dirham left in the public treasury [in times of great financial stringency]. As for Yaman, I have never liked them and they have never liked me. As for Quḍāʿah, their chiefs live in the messianic expectation of the Sufyānī and his appearance, so that they might join his party.[711] As for Rabīʿah, they have been angry with God ever since He sent His prophet from Muḍar,[712] and there have never been two of them going out [in rebellion] without one of them being a Khārijite [*Shārī*]. Now get out, may God wreak [evil] on you!"[713]

It is mentioned from Saʿīd b. Ziyād that when he went into al-Ma'mūn's presence at Damascus, the Caliph said to him, "Show me the document which the Messenger of God wrote out for your family." He related: So I showed it to him. He related: Al-Ma'mūn said, "I should very much like to know what this covering is over this seal." He related: Abū Isḥāq said to him, "Untie this knot so that you may know what it is." He related: But al-Ma'mūn then said, "I do not doubt that the
[1143] Prophet tied this knot himself, and I am not the person who is going to unloose a knot tied by the Messenger of God." Then he said to (his nephew) al-Wāthiq, "Take it and lay it on your eye; perhaps God will heal you." He related: Al-Ma'mūn began to lay it on his eye and to weep.[714]

It is mentioned from al-ʿAyshī, the confidant of Isḥāq b. Ibrāhīm, that he said: I was with al-Ma'mūn at Damascus, at a time when the amount of money which he had with him had

711. Cf. Ṭabarī, III, 830, year 195 (810/11), recording the revolt in Syria in Dhū al-Ḥijjah 195 (August–September 811) of the Sufyānid ʿAlī b. ʿAbdallāh b. Khālid b. Yazīd b. Muʿāwiyah, expelling al-Amīn's governor Sulaymān b. Abī Jaʿfar al-Manṣūr from Damascus; Lammens, "Le 'Sofiānī', héros national des Arabes syriens," in *Etudes sur le siècle des Omayyades*, 391–408.

712. Quraysh and Kinānah were considered as part of the Muḍar branch of the North Arabs.

713. Ibn Abī Ṭāhir, 266–7, tr. 121; Azdī, 408–9; Ibn al-Athīr, *al-Kāmil*, VI, 342–3.

714. Ibn Abī Ṭāhir, 271, tr. 123; Ibn al-Athīr, *al-Kāmil*, VI, 433.

become very low, until he found himself in a tight spot. He complained about this to Abū Isḥāq al-Muʿtaṣim, and the latter said to him, "O Commander of the Faithful, you have as good as got money; it will have reached you after Friday." He related: There was brought to him the sum of thirty million (dirhams) from the land-tax for whose collection, on his behalf, Abū Isḥāq al-Muʿtaṣim was responsible. He related: When that sum of money reached him, al-Ma'mūn said to Yaḥyā b. Aktham, "Let us go along and look at this wealth." He related: So the two of them set off until they came to an open space and halted to look at it. It had been arranged in the most attractive way possible: the camels carrying the money were adorned with figured silk saddle cloths and caparisons dyed in rich colors, and with woollen streamers draped round their necks. The money bags were made from Chinese silk, red, green and yellow, and their necks were sticking out (from under the cover). He related: Al-Ma'mūn looked at what was a fine sight and accounted it a splendid amount of wealth. It made a great impression on him, and the people (with him) strained their gaze at it, looking at it and marvelling at it. Then al-Ma'mūn said to Yaḥyā, "O Abū Muḥammad, are these companions of ours, whom you have seen just a moment ago [wondering at the sight], to go back to their homes disappointed, while we are going back with all this wealth which has come into our possession but to their exclusion? In such circumstances, we would indeed be contemptible persons." He thereupon summoned Muḥammad b. Yazdād[715] and told him, "Set down in the register a million [dirhams] for the family of so-and-so, and the same for the family of so-and-so and for the family of so-and-so." He related: By God, he kept on in this fashion until he [1144]
had allocated twenty-four million dirhams, while his very foot was in the stirrup. Then he said, "Hand over the remainder to al-Muʿallā[716] for him to pay our troops." Al-*'Ayshī related*: I went along until I stood before his eyes, and I did not take away

715. The Khurasanian official and secretary who was, in effect, the chief executive for al-Ma'mūn at the time of his death; see Sourdel, *Vizirat*, I, 214, 232–4.

716. The secretary al-Muʿallā b. Ayyūb.

my gaze from his eyes. He did not notice me till he saw me thus. Then he said, "O Abū Muḥammad, set down in the register for this man fifty thousand dirhams out of the six millions, and then I will not be deprived of my sight!" He related: Before two nights had elapsed, I had received the money.[717]

It is mentioned from Muḥammad b. Ayyūb b. Jaʿfar b. Sulaymān[718] that there lived in Baṣrah a man from the Banū Tamīm who was a poet and wit, but who used unseemly language[719] and did not enjoy any fame. I was at that time the governor of Baṣrah, in close contact with him, and I found him pleasant company. I wanted to deceive him and to bring him down a peg or two.[720] So I said to him, "You are a poet and wit, and al-Ma'mūn is more generous than an abundantly-flowing rain cloud and a rain-bearing wind; what then keeps you away from him?" He replied, "I do not possess means to transport me[721] [thither]." I said, "I will give you a sprightly, nobly-bred horse and an ample sum for living expenses, and you can go to him. You have already praised al-Ma'mūn, and if you obtain favor through your encounter with him, you will have attained your desire." He replied, "By God, O Amīr, I think you are not far from the truth! So get ready for me what you have promised." He related: I called for a noble, high-spirited horse to be brought for him and told him, "This is yours to do as you like with it, so ride off on it." He replied, "This is just one of the two pieces of bounty [which you promised to me]; what about the other?" So I then called for three hundred dirhams to be brought for him and told him that these were his living expenses. But he complained, "O Amīr, you have been stingy over these!" I protested, "No, these are adequate, even though I
[1145] have stopped short at being extravagant." He replied, "When

717. Ibn Abī Ṭāhir, 271–3, tr. 123; Ibn al-Athīr, *al-Kāmil*, VI, 434.

718. Mentioned in Iṣfahānī, *Aghānī*, XII, 129–30.

719. *Kāna shāʿir*^{an} . . . *khabīth*^{an}, presumably in the sense of "foul-mouthed;" cf. ibid., XX, 183, where ʿUmārah b. ʿAqīl is characterised similarly as *khabīth al-lisān*.

720. *Astanzilahu*. This seems to give the best sense. Ṭabarī, *Glossarium*, p. DX, suggests, less fittingly, "he tried to persuade him," for *istanzalahu*, presumably with the meaning that he could expect no further bounty from the governor (!).

721. *Mā yuqillunī*, following ibid., p. CDXXXI

do you see extravagance among the great men of the [Banū] Saʿd?[722] You only see that among the lesser of them." He thereupon took the horse and the money, and then composed a poem in *rajaz* metre which was not very long and recited it to me, but omitted any mention of me or praise for me and showed himself as discontented. So I told him, "You haven't composed anything [worthwhile]!" He enquired, "How is that?" I said, "You are going to the Caliph, but you don't have a word of praise for your Amīr!" He replied, "O Amīr, you wanted to deceive me, but you have found me to be a deceiver [in showing myself discontented and not praising and thanking you adequately]! The proverbial saying 'He who copulates with a wild ass copulates with one who is a really experienced copulator'[723] [that is, he meets more than he has bargained for] was coined for an occasion like this. For by God, it wasn't out of honor for me that you gave me your noble horse as a mount, nor were you generous to me with your money, [a sum] which no one would ever desire unless God had made his rank in society the lowest [totally down-and-out and grateful for anything]. Nevertheless, I will certainly mention you in my poetry and praise you before the Caliph; be certain of this!" I said, "Have you spoken truly?" He replied, "Since you have revealed what was in your mind, I have [now] mentioned your name and praised you." I said, "Recite to me what you have composed." He then recited it, and I congratulated him on it. Thereupon he bade me farewell and set off.

He came to Syria, at a time when al-Ma'mūn was at Salaghūs. Muḥammad b. Ayyūb related: The poet (subsequently) told me the story, saying: I was joining up with the Qurrah campaign, riding that noble horse of mine and wearing my ordinary garments (*muqaṭṭaʿātī*),[724] and I was heading for the

722. Keller, Ibn Abī Ṭāhir, tr. 124, erroneously sees here *saʿd* as a common noun; but the Tamīmī poet's affiliation to the component Banū Saʿd is explicitly mentioned below, 238.

723. Maydānī, *Amthāl al-ʿArab*, tr., II, 674–5, no. 293.

724. Literally, "Garments sewn together from several pieces," perhaps here with the denotation of non-military dress. Cf. Ṭabarī, *Glossarium*, p. CDXXIX, "garments which are sewn together like the *qamīṣ, jubbah, sarāwīl*;" Dozy, II, 375a, "worn, used clothes."

army camp, when I suddenly found myself with an elderly man on a high-spirited mule which was too restive to stand still and which could not be overtaken in its swift flight. He related: While I was reciting to myself my *rajaz* poem, he met me brow-to-brow and face-to-face. He greeted me with the words, "Peace be upon you!" in a loud voice and with an unforced mode of expression. I returned the greeting, "Upon you be peace, and the mercy and blessings of God!" He said, "Halt
[1146] there, if you please," so I halted. There diffused from him a sweet perfume of amber and pungent-odored musk. He said, "What is your first [genealogical name]?" I replied, "I am a man of Muḍar." He said, "We come from Muḍar too." Then he said, "And after that, what?" I replied, "I am a man of the Banū Tamīm." He said, "And after Tamīm, what?" I replied, "From the Banū Sa'd." He replied, "Tell me more! What has impelled you to come to this land?" He related: I said, "I have headed for this kingdom, of whose like I have never heard for abundance of sweet odors, wideness of living space, richness in resources of power and extensiveness of hills." He replied, "What have you brought with you to this land?" I said, "Some fine poetry which is pleasant on the lips, which the rhapsodists can repeat and which is sweet in the ears of its hearers." He said, "Recite some of it to me, then." Thereupon I grew angry with him and said, "O ignoble fellow, limited in your mind [*yā rakīk*]! I have told you that I am making my way towards the Caliph with a poem which I have composed and a eulogy which I have put together with skill, and you ask me to recite it to you?" He related: He gave the appearance, by God, of not having heard my words, and remained with lowered eyes at them, making no answer. Then he said, "What do you hope to gain by means of it?" I replied, "If the state of affairs is as it has been reported to me, then one thousand dīnārs." He said, "I will give you one thousand dīnārs if I consider the poetry to be good and the speech sweet, and I will spare you the trouble and the continued repetition [of the verses] and the fact that, when you arrive at the Caliph's presence, [you will find there] ten thousand spearmen and archers between you and him!" I interjected, "Do I have your word that you will do that?" He retorted, "Yes, you do have my word." Then I said, "Do you have the money

with you at this precise moment?" He replied, "This is my [1147]
mule, which is worth more than one thousand dīnārs; I will dismount from its back and hand it over to you." He related: I grew angry again, and there came over me the hasty temper of the Banū Sa'd and their quickspiritedness; I told him that this mule was not equal in value to my noble horse. He replied, "Leave the mule, then, and I undertake before God as witness against me on your behalf to give you the one thousand dīnārs immediately."

He related: So I then recited to him:

O Ma'mūn, bestower of exalted favors
  and occupier of the loftiest rank,

Commander of the most numerous military forces,
  would you like to hear an elegant *rajaz* poem?

One more elegantly-constructed than the legal system of Abū Ḥanīfah?
  Nay, by Him whose deputy [*khalīfah*] you are,

No weak female person suffers oppression in our land,
  and the burdens laid on us by our amīr are light.

He does not exact for himself anything above the official rate of taxation,

  so that the wolf and the ewe can remain under one roof,

  And the thief and the merchant can lie down together under one coverlet.

He related: By God, I had hardly finished reciting it when suddenly a host of around ten thousand cavalrymen filled the horizon, crying, "Peace and the mercy and blessings of God be upon you, O Commander of the Faithful!" He related: Terror gripped me, and he saw me in that state and said, "No harm will come to you, my brother!" I replied, "O Commander of [1148]
the Faithful, may God make me your ransom, do you know the various modes of speech of the Arabs?" He replied, "Yes, by

God's life." I said, "And those of them who pronounce the *kāf* in place of *qāf*?" He replied, "These are the Ḥimyar." I said, "May God curse them and anyone who uses this mode of speech after today!"[725] Al-Ma'mūn laughed at this, and realized what I wanted; he turned to the servant at his side and said, "Give him all that you have with you here." The servant pulled out for me a bag containing three thousand dīnārs. Al-Ma'mūn said, "Take it!" Then he said, "Peace be with you," and went on his way; and that was the last contact I ever had with him.[726]

Abū Sa'īd al-Makhzūmī[727] recited:

Have you seen that the stars were of any use to al-Ma'mūn
or to his solidly-based royal power?

[On the contrary,] they left him at the two open spaces of Tarsus,
just as they left his father at Ṭūs.[728]

'Alī b. 'Ubaydah al-Rayḥānī[729] recited:

How inadequate are tears for al-Ma'mūn!
I am not satisfied with anything but blood dripping from my eyelids.

Abū Mūsā Hārūn b. Muḥammad b. Ismā'īl b. Mūsā al-Hādī[730]
[1149] has mentioned that 'Alī b. Ṣāliḥ[731] related to him as follows: One day, al-Ma'mūn said to me, "Obtain for me a man from

725. Ibn al-Athīr, *al-Kāmil*, VI, 436, adds a gloss to this: that he meant to say *yā raqīq*, "O tender, elegant one!" but said *yā rakīk*, "O feeble, vile one!" (i.e., the poet is exonerating himself from having unwittingly stigmatised al-Ma'mūn previously as "ignoble, limited in mind" [above, 238] and implying that he really meant to describe him in favorable terms as "tender, elegant").

726. Ibn Abī Ṭāhir, 273–8, tr. 123–5; Ibn al-Athīr, *al-Kāmil*, VI, 434–6.

727. Abū Sa'd (thus in Sezgin, *GAS*, II, 575) 'Īsā b. Khālid al-Makhzūmī was a poet of al-Ma'mūn's court circle.

728. Mas'ūdī, *Murūj*, VII, 101–2 = ed. Pellat, § 2784. Al-Rashīd had died near Ṭūs in Khurasan.

729. The author of works on rhetoric and belles-lettres, who died in 219 (834); see Sezgin, *GAS*, II, 58, 83.

730. I.e., a descendant of the fourth 'Abbāsid caliph.

731. A poet of al-Ma'mūn's time; see I. Guidi, *Tables alphabétiques du Kitâb al-Aġânî*, II, 497.

the people of Syria who has the ways of polite society [*adab*] and who can act as my intimate companion and provide conversation for me." So I made enquiries about such a person and found him. I then summoned him and told him, "I am going to bring you into the Commander of the Faithful's presence. You are not to ask him for anything until he has himself taken the initiative in speaking; for indeed, I am very well acquainted with your importunings, O people of Syria!" He replied, "I shall not overstep the bounds which you have commanded me to observe." Then I went in to al-Ma'mūn's presence and informed him, "I have found the required person, O Commander of the Faithful!" He said, "Bring him in!" At that the man entered and gave a greeting. Then al-Ma'mūn invited him to draw near; he was at that moment involved in a drinking session. Then he said to the man, "I would like you to be one of my intimates and to converse with me." The Syrian said, "O Commander of the Faithful, when a boon-companion's clothes are inferior to those of his associate, this gives him a feeling of inferiority." He related: So al-Ma'mūn ordered him to be given a robe of honor. He related: At that, a feeling came over me such as God only knows! He related: When the Syrian had put on the robe of honor and gone back to his place in the circle, he said, "O Commander of the Faithful, since my mind is preoccupied with my family, you will not derive much benefit from conversation with me." Al-Ma'mūn said, "Fifty thousand [dirhams] are to be conveyed to his house!" Then the Syrian said, "O Commander of the Faithful, and a third thing . . . ". Al-Ma'mūn replied, "And what is that?" The Syrian said, "You have introduced something which interposes between a man and his understanding [to rob him of his peace of mind.] If I should have committed any minor fault, please forgive it." Al-Ma'mūn replied, "That also [will be done]." ʿAlī said: It was as if this third thing dispelled from my mind what I had been apprehensive about (and I breathed more easily now that nothing further was to be asked for by the Syrian).[732]

Abū Ḥashīshah Muḥammad b. ʿAlī b. Umayyah b. ʿAmr[733] has

732. Ibn Abī Ṭāhir, 279–80, tr. 126–7.
733. A secretary, poet and musician of the third (ninth) century, who had

mentioned: We were at Damascus, before the presence of the Commander of the Faithful, and ʿAllawayh[734] sang,

[1150] May I renounce the Islamic faith [or alternatively: I will
renounce . . .], if that which
my traducers report to you is as they allege;

But when they have seen how swift you are to [reward] me,
they have urged each other to slanderous talk and have
devised trickery.

Al-Ma'mūn said, "O ʿAllawayh, who is this poetry by?" He said, "By the judge." Al-Ma'mūn said, "Which judge, shame on you?" ʿAllawayh said, "The judge of Damascus." Al-Ma'mūn said, "O Abū Isḥāq [al-Muʿtaṣim], dismiss him from office!" Abū Isḥāq replied, "I will do this immediately." Al-Ma'mūn said, "Let him be brought in straight away." He related: An old man, short of stature, his hair and beard dyed with henna, was brought in. Al-Ma'mūn said to him, "Who are you?" He replied, "So-and-so, son of so-and-so, with so-and-so *nisbah*." Al-Ma'mūn said, "Are you a poet?" He replied, "I used to be a poet." Al-Ma'mūn said, "O ʿAllawayh, recite the verses to him." So ʿAllawayh recited them. Al-Ma'mūn said, "Are these verses by you?" He replied, "Yes, O Commander of the Faithful, but may the poet's wives all be divorced, and may he give all his possessions away for pious purposes, if he has composed any poetry during the last thirty years except on the theme of asceticism or in order gently to reproach a friend." Al-Ma'mūn said, "O Abū Isḥāq, dismiss him from his job; I am not going to give power over the necks of the Muslims to a man who begins, in his jesting, to speak about throwing off the Islamic faith." Then he continued, "Give him something to drink," And they brought the poet-judge a beaker of wine. He took it, all the time trembling with fear, but then protested,

---

the *nisbah* of al-Ṭunbūrī; see H.G. Farmer, *A history of Arabian music*, 158; Sezgin, *GAS*, II, 608.

734. A musician who flourished at the caliphal courts from al-Rashīd's time onwards, and who was originally a mawlā of the Umayyads (see below, 243–4); see Farmer, 123; *EI*² Suppl. s.v. (E. Neubauer).

"O Commander of the Faithful, I have never tasted it before." Al-Ma'mūn said, "Would you perhaps prefer another kind [of wine]?" The judge said, "I have never touched any of it before." Al-Ma'mūn said, "Is it forbidden, then?" He replied, "Certainly, O Commander of the Faithful!" Al-Ma'mūn said, "Good for you! Through this answer you have escaped [punishment for an infringement of the *sharī'ah*]. Be off with you!"[735] Then al-Ma'mūn said, "O 'Allawayh, do not say the words, 'May I renounce the Islamic faith . . . ', but say instead:

May I be deprived of the object of my desires in you [that is, of
your love; or alternatively: I will be deprived . . .], if that which
my traducers report to you is as they allege.[736]

He related: We were with al-Ma'mūn at Damascus. He rode off, with the intention of going to Mount Hermon,[737] and passed by a large cistern, one of those constructed by the Umayyads. On its banks stood four cypresses and the water would flow up to them and then flow back. Al-Ma'mūn found the spot pleasing, and called for *bazmāward*[738] and a *raṭl* (of wine). He mentioned the Umayyads, and then spoke of them in a deprecatory fashion and belittled them. Then 'Allawayh came forward with his lute ('*ūd*) and began to sing: [1151]

These are my people; after being once powerful and rich,
they have all passed to destruction. Should I not therefore
let my eyes weep, and feel sadness?

At this, al-Ma'mūn lashed out at the food with his foot and sprang up, saying to 'Allawayh, "O son of a whore, was there no other suitable time than this for you to mention your ancient masters [*mawālīka*]?" 'Allawayh replied, "Your client

735. Iṣfahānī, *Aghānī*, X, 124, gives three verses as sung by 'Allawayh.
736. Ibn Abī Ṭāhir, 281–3, tr. 127–8; Iṣfahānī, *Aghānī*, X, 123–4; Azdī, 409–10.
737. The Arabic *Jabal al-Thalj*; see Le Strange, *Palestine*, 79–80, 418–19.
738. Cf. Ṭabarī, *Glossarium*, p. CXXXIII, defining it as a Persian term (*bazmāward*, "what is brought away from a feast") denoting a kind of confection of pastry, meat, etc., *pace* Keller's translation, 128, "eine Flasche Rosenwasser."

[*mawlākum*] Ziryāb[739] is at this moment with my masters [*mawāliyya*],[740] riding with an escort of a hundred slave boys, while I am dying of hunger here with you." Al-Ma'mūn was angry with him for twenty days, but then took him back into favor. The narrator says: Ziryāb was originally the client of al-Mahdī who went first to Syria and then to the Western lands (al-Maghrib) and joined the Umayyads there.[741]

Abū ʿAlī al-Salīṭī has mentioned from ʿUmārah b. ʿAqīl,[742] who said: I once recited to al-Ma'mūn an ode containing a eulogy of him and comprising a hundred verses. I began with the first hemistich, but he quickly forestalled me (in adding the remaining hemistich of each verse) right up to the rhyme letter, exactly as I myself had completed the rhyme. I accordingly commented, "By God, O Commander of the Faithful, no one has ever heard this ode from me before." He replied, "It must nevertheless be thus." Then he came up to me and said, "Have you not heard that ʿUmar b. Abī Rabīʿah[743] recited to ʿAbdallāh b. al-ʿAbbās his ode in which he said:

In the morning, the encampment of our neighbours will be far away

[1152] and Ibn al-ʿAbbās continued (and completed the verse),
. . . and the day after that it will be even further away

until ʿUmar had recited to Ibn al-ʿAbbās the whole ode, with the latter completing each second hemistich." Then al-Ma'mūn remarked, "I am the successor [literally: the son] of that one [Ibn al-ʿAbbās]."[744]

---

739. The famed musician who, during al-Ma'mūn's reign, entered the service of the Umayyad amīrs of Spain; see Farmer, 128–30; *EI*[1] Suppl. s.v. (id).

740. I.e., the Spanish Umayyads.

741. Ibn Abī Ṭāhir, 283–4, tr. 128; Iṣfahānī, *Aghānī*, X, 131–2.

742. A tribal poet of northeastern Arabia, the great-grandson of Jarīr, who also frequented the courts of al-Ma'mūn and his successors; see Iṣfahānī, *Aghānī*, XX, 183–8; Sezgin, *GAS*, II, 559–60.

743. The famed lyric poet of Mecca and Madīnah in the Umayyad period; see ibid., II, 415–17; *EI*[1] s.v. ʿOmar b. Abī Rabīʿa (I. Kratschkowsky).

744. Ibn Abī Ṭāhir, 289–90, tr. 131; Ibn al-Athīr, *al-Kāmil*, VI, 436. Al-Ma'mūn was of course the direct physical descendant of Ibn al-ʿAbbās as well as being, as he claimed, the inheritor of this feel for poetry.

It is mentioned from Abū Marwān Kāriz[745] b. Hārūn that Al-Ma'mūn once recited:

I sent to you, out of passion, so that you had the good fortune
to gain a glance,
and then you neglected me, until I acquired a bad opinion
of you.

Then you were in intimate contact with the one whom I love,
while I was far away;
so would that I knew what would relieve me of wanting
you near!

I see a clear trace of him in your eyes;
your eyes have indeed taken beauty from his eye!

Abū Marwān related: In expressing this meaning in his verses, al-Ma'mūn relied upon (that is, was alluding to) the poem of al-ʿAbbās b. Aḥnaf,[746] who produced the following:

If my eye is afflicted because of her, the eye of my messenger
has become happy,
and I have experienced good fortune from his news.

Whenever the messenger from her comes to me,
I deliberately direct my gaze again and again at his glance.

Her beauties are revealed in his face;
they have left on it the most beautiful of impressions.

O messenger, take freely my eye's orb,
look with it and give judgement with my glance![747]

Abū al-ʿAtāhiyah related: Al-Ma'mūn sent for me one day. I [1153]
went along to him, and found him with bowed head and sunk

745. Following the correct reading of Ibn Abī Ṭāhir, 290, *pace* the text's Kāzir.

746. A court poet of al-Rashīd; see Sezgin, *GAS*, II, 513–14; *EI*[2] s.v. (Blachère).

747. Ibn Abī Ṭāhir, 290–1, tr. 131–2; Ibn al-Athīr, *al-Kāmil*, VI, 436–7.

in thought. I accordingly refrained from approaching him while he was in that state. Then he raised his head, looked at me and beckoned me with his hand to come near; so I drew near. He remained downcast for a considerable while, and then raised his head and said, "O Abū Isḥāq, the natural state of the soul is a feeling of tedium and a love of something strange and new; it comes to find solitude congenial just as it does sociability." I replied, "Assuredly, O Commander of the Faithful, and I have composed a verse on this theme." He said, "What is that?" I then recited:

When the soul is disquieted, the only remedy for it
 is changing from one state of mind to another.[748]

It is mentioned from the poet Abū Nizār al-Ḍarīr,[749] that he said: ʿAlī b. Jabalah[750] told me: I once said to Ḥumayd b. ʿAbd al-Ḥamid, "O Abū Ghānim, I have praised the Commander of the Faithful with a eulogy so fine that no one on the whole earth could produce its like; so mention my name to the Commander of the Faithful." Ḥumayd said, "Recite it to me!" So I recited it to him. Ḥumayd exclaimed, "I bear witness that you are speaking the truth!" So he took the panegyric and presented it to al-Ma'mūn. Al-Ma'mūn said, "O Abū Ghānim, the answer to all this is clear. If he wishes, we will pardon him and consider this as a reward for his panegyric. But if he wishes otherwise, we will bring together for comparison his poetry on you and on Abū Dulaf al-Qāsim b. ʿĪsā [al-ʿIjlī].[751] If what he has written on you and on Abū Dulaf is finer than his eulogy on us, we will flog him on his back and prolong his imprisonment. But if what he has written is finer, I will reward him with a thousand dirhams for every verse of his panegyric, and if he

748. Ibn Abī Ṭāhir, 293, tr. 133; Masʿūdī, *Murūj*, VII, 31–2 = ed. Pellat, § 2720.

749. This blind poet is mentioned in conjunction with ʿAlī b. Jabalah in Iṣfahānī, *Aghānī*, XVIII, 105.

750. A poet of the time of al-Rashīd and al-Ma'mūn, known as al-ʿAkawwak; see Sezgin, *GAS*, II, 572–3; *EI*² s.v. al-ʿAkawwak (Blachère).

751. Famed contemporary military leader, poet and patron of the arts; see Sezgin, *GAS*, II, 632–3; *EI*² s.v. al-Ḳāsim b. ʿĪsā (J.E. Bencheikh).

wishes, we will let him go free."[752] I replied, "O my master, who are Abū Dulaf and myself, that he should eulogize us [1154] in finer words than those in your praise?" Al-Ma'mūn said, "These words are no answer at all to the question; lay my propositions before the man." ʿAlī b. Jabalah related: Ḥumayd said to me, "What do you think about it?" I replied, "In my estimation, being pardoned is better." This was reported to al-Ma'mūn, and he commented, "He knows best [what he is doing!]!" Ḥumayd related: I said to ʿAlī b. Jabalah, "What words was the Caliph thinking of in your eulogies of Abū Dulaf and of myself?" He replied, "About my words on Abū Dulaf,

The present world is nothing but Abū Dulaf,
[in the time which is] between his coming into the world naked and his being at the point of death.

So when Abū Dulaf turns his back [on life],
the world turns its back [on life] also, following in his track.

and about my words on you,

If it were not for Ḥumayd,
no outstanding merit or noble lineage could be enumerated.

O unique one of the Arabs,
through whose greatness the Arabs have become great!"

ʿAlī b. Jabalah related: Ḥumayd remained with bowed head for a while, and then said, "O Abū al-Ḥasan, the Commander of the Faithful has already allotted a sum of money for you, and has ordered me [to give you] ten thousand dirhams, a beast for bearing these presents, a robe of honor and a slave." Abū Dulaf

752. *Wa-in shā'a, aqalnāhu.* This translation gives good parallelism with the phrase *in shā'a, ʿafawnā ʿanhu,* "if he wishes, he will pardon him," a few lines further up. Keller's translation of Ibn Abī Ṭāhir's parallel text, 133, "Will er dies, so lasse er uns wissen," seems to take *aqāla* here as form IV of root *q-w-l* and not of *q-y-l* and seems less plausible.

heard about this, and doubled the gift to me. Both of them did this in secret, and no one has ever known about it, O Abū Nizār, until I have told you about this.

Abū Nizār related: I imagined that al-Ma'mūn viewed ʿAlī b. Jabalah with disfavor[753] because of this verse on Abū Dulaf:

[1155] The water of liberality flowed down from Adam's loins,[754]
and then the Merciful One fixed it in the loins of [Abū Dulaf al-] Qāsim.[755]

It is mentioned from Sulaymān b. Razīn al-Khuzāʿī,[756] the nephew of Diʿbil,[757] as follows. He said: Diʿbil once satirized al-Ma'mūn, saying:

Al-Ma'mūn is imposing on me the office of diviner;
did he not see only yesterday the head of Muḥammad [al-Amīn, his brother]?

He looks down on the skulls of the caliphs[758] just as
the mountains look down on the low-lying hills,

And he lurks in the refuge-places of every inaccessible spot,
until he brings low a lofty mountain, which has never before been ascended.

The one who seeks revenge is kept awake at nights and is sleepless;
so keep your spittle away from the spittle of the black one [the venomous viper]![759]

---

753. See for this sense of *taʿaqqada*, Ṭabarī, *Glossarium*, p. CCCLXX

754. Cf. Qur'ān, LXXXVI, 6–7.

755. Ibn Abī Ṭāhir, 294–6, tr. 133–4.

756. Cf. Iṣfahānī, *Aghānī*, XVIII, 36.

757. The Shīʿī poet and satirist, hence generally hostile to the ʿAbbāsids and Ṭāhirids; see Bosworth, "The Ṭāhirids and Arabic culture," 52–4; Sezgin, *GAS*, II, 529–32; *EI*² s.v. (L. Zolondek).

758. The *Dīwān* of Diʿbil, 145, has the inferior reading *khalāʾiq*, "creatures," for the *khalāʾif* of Ibn Abī Ṭāhir and Ṭabarī.

759. Ibn Abī Ṭāhir, 296, tr. 134; Diʿbil, *Dīwān*, 144–5 (fragment of seven verses); Iṣfahānī, *Aghānī*, XVIII, 55 (the first verse only).

Someone said to al-Ma'mūn, "Diʿbil has satirized you." Al-Ma'mūn replied, "[No,] he is satirizing Abū ʿAbbād [Thābit b. Yaḥyā],[760] and not me," alluding to Abū ʿAbbād's passionate temper. Whenever Abū ʿAbbād went into al-Ma'mūn's presence, the latter would frequently laugh and say to him, "What did Diʿbil really mean regarding you when he was saying:

It is as if he had escaped from the Dayr Hizqil,[761] [1156]
a deranged and violent one, who still drags along the chains of his fetters."[762]

Al-Ma'mūn used to say to Ibrāhīm b. Shaklah (Ibrāhim b. al-Mahdī)[763] when the latter came into his presence, "Diʿbil has caused you pain when he says,

If Ibrāhīm is able to bear the burden of it [the caliphate],
then it will certainly be suitable for al-Mukhāriq after him,

And it will certainly be suitable after that one for Zulzul,
and likewise after Zulzul for al-Māriqī.[764]

How can it be? Nay, it cannot be and it never has been possible
for an evildoer [*fāsiq*] to take over from [another, previous] evildoer."[765]

Muḥammad b. Haytham al-Ṭā'ī has mentioned that al-Qāsim b. Muḥammad al-Ṭayfūrī related to him saying: (Abū Mu-

---

760. Al-Ma'mūn's secretary; see ibid., XVIII, 39; Sourdel, *Vizirat*, I, 214, 231–2.

761. The principal madhouse in Baghdad; see Yāqūt, *Muʿjam*, II, 540–1; A. Mez, *Abulk̦âsim, ein bagdader Sittenbild*, p. XLVIII and the references there.

762. Diʿbil, *Dīwān*, 148; Iṣfahānī, *Aghānī*, XVIII, 30.

763. Ibrāhīm b. al-Mahdī is frequently referred to pejoratively in the sources as the son of his black slave mother Shaklah, from whom he acquired his swarthy visage; see Ibn Khallikān *Wafayāt al-aʿyān*, I, 39, tr. de Slane, I, 17.

764. The text here and Ibn Khallikān have al-Māriq, but Ibn Abī Ṭāhir and Iṣfahānī, *Aghānī*, VI, 20–1, XIII, 31, have the apparently more correct al-Māriqī. For the singers and musicians mentioned here, see Farmer, 118–19, 121.

765. Ibn Abī Ṭāhir, 296–7, tr. 134, with the first three of the latter verses also at 194, tr. 88, with a variant third verse; Iṣfahānī, *Aghānī*, XVIII, 58, with verses one and three; Ibn Khallikān, I, 40, tr. 18, with all four of these verses.

ḥammad) al-Yazīdī[766] complained to al-Ma'mūn about a financial loss which he had suffered and about some debt which he was now required to settle. Al-Ma'mūn said, "We do not have by us at this moment a sum which, if we handed it over to you, would be sufficient for your needs." Al-Yazīdī replied, "O Commander of the Faithful, I am in straitened circumstances just now, and my creditors are pressing me hard." Al-Ma'mūn said, "Suggest a way out for yourself, from which you might derive advantage." He replied, "Among your boon-companions is one from whom, if I move him to respond, I will get what I desire; so give me free rein to devise a stratagem with them." Al-Ma'mūn said, "Say what you have in mind." He replied, "When both they and I are present [in the Caliph's palace], order your servant so-and-so to bring you my petition, and when
[1157] you have read it, send back to me the message 'Your entry at this moment [into the Caliph's circle of boon-companions] is not possible; but choose for yourself [as a companion] whomsoever you like.'" He related: When Abū Muḥammad (al-Yazīdī) knew that al-Ma'mūn was holding a convivial session, with his boon-companions gathered round him, and when he was certain that they were befuddled from their wine drinking, he came to the door and handed over to that servant a petition which he had written out. The servant conveyed it to the Caliph on his behalf, and the Caliph read it out, and behold, it contained the words,

O best of my brothers and companions,
this intruder at the feast is at the door!

He has been told that the members of the circle are all in a state of enjoyment,
in which every comer yearns to share.

So make me one of your number,
or else let one of my equals come out to me!

766. Presumably Yaḥyā b. al-Mubārak, a poet from this well-known family; see Sezgin, *GAS*, II, 610; M. Fleischhammer, in *ZDMG*, CXII (1962), 299–308.

He related: Al-Ma'mūn read these words out to those assembled round him, and they said, "It is not fitting that this parasite should come in under the present circumstances." So al-Ma'mūn sent back to him, "Your entry at this moment is not possible; but choose for yourself whomsoever you would like to make your companion." He said, "I don't consider that there is anyone whom I would like to choose except ʿAbdallah b. Ṭāhir." Al-Ma'mūn said to ʿAbdallāh b. Tāhir, "His choice has fallen on you, so off you go to him!" ʿAbdallāh protested, "O Commander of the Faithful, must I be the parasite's companion?" Al-Ma'mūn replied, "Abū Muḥammad cannot be refused both of his requests. If you wish to go out [and join him, well and good]; but if not, then purchase your freedom [from this commitment]." He related: ʿAbdallāh said, "O Commander of the Faithful, I will pay him ten thousand dirhams." [1158]
Al-Ma'mūn replied, "I don't think that that sum from you will satisfy his claim on you, nor compensate for companionship with you." He related: ʿAbdallāh kept on increasing the sum offered by ten thousand dirhams at a time, with al-Ma'mūn telling him each time, "I am not satisfied with that for him." Finally, he reached the figure of a hundred thousand (dirhams). He related: Al-Ma'mūn then told him, "Hand it over to him immediately!" He related: He thereupon wrote out for him an order to his financial intendant for the money, and sent a messenger along with him. Al-Ma'mūn wrote a message to al-Yazīdī, "In your present circumstances, getting this sum of money is better to you than enjoying the companionship of him in his kind of position, and has a more useful end-product!"[767]

It is mentioned from Muḥammad b. ʿAbdallāh, the master of the caliphal stables and conveyances (*ṣāḥib al-marākib*), that he said: My father related to me from Ṣāliḥ b. al-Rashīd, who said: I once went into al-Ma'mūn's presence, having with me two verses by al-Ḥusayn b. al-Ḍaḥḥāk.[768] I said, "O Commander

767. Ibn Abī Ṭāhir, 303–5, tr. 137–8; Ibn al-Athīr, *al-Kāmil*, VI, 467–8.

768. Court poet of various ʿAbbasid caliphs of the time, who was called al-Khalīʿ, "The Debauched One"; see Sezgin, *GAS*, II, 518–19; *EI*² s.v. (Pellat).

of the Faithful, I should like you to hear from me two verses." He said, "Recite them." He related: Ṣāliḥ then recited to him:

We praise God, O Commander of the Faithful,
out of thankfulness, since He has bestowed on us your help.

You are truly the representative [*khalīfah*] of the Merciful One,
and have united in yourself generosity and religion.

Al-Ma'mūn found them to be good, and asked, "O Ṣāliḥ, who is the author of these two verses?" I replied, "Your servant, O Commander of the Faithful, al-Ḥusayn b. al-Ḍaḥḥāk." He said, "He has done well." I replied, "But he has written even better poetry than this, O Commander of the Faithful!" He said, "Such as?" So I recited to him:

Can the one whose goodness is unique, and whose [noble] characteristics are unique, be miserly
[1159] towards me, when I have devoted to him exclusively a unique love?

God has seen that ʿAbdallāh [al-Ma'mūn] is the best of His servants,
hence has given him kingly power—and God is the most knowing one about His servant.[769]

It is mentioned from ʿUmārah b. ʿAqīl that he related: ʿAbdallāh b. Abī al-Simṭ[770] said to me, "Did you know that al-Ma'mūn has little taste for poetry?" He related: I replied, "But who is there, nevertheless, who is more knowledgeable about poetry than him? By God, you shall see us recite the first part of a verse to him, and he will complete its latter part before we ourselves can." He said, "I once recited a verse to him, which I had composed very well, but I could not detect any re-

769. Ibn Abī Ṭāhir, 312, tr. 141; Iṣfahānī, *Aghānī*, VI, 72 (where, however, it is stated that these verses did not counterbalance, in al-Ma'mūn's eyes, the poet's previous eulogies of his brother al-Amīn and satires on himself).

770. Apparently a member of the famous Abū Ḥafṣah poetic family; see Sezgin, *GAS*, II, 583.

action to it on his part." He related: I said, "What was it you recited to him?" He said, "I recited to him,

The Imām of right guidance, al-Ma'mūn, has become fully occupied
with religion, whereas the people devote themselves to the affairs of the present world."

He related: I said to him, "By God, what you have composed is worthless! Have you added anything [to his status] in making him [like] an old woman in her prayer niche, with her rosary in her hand? Who can be responsible for the affairs of the world, when he has been invested [by God] with its direction, if he is unconcerned about it? Why didn't you say of him like your forebear [literally: your paternal uncle] Jarīr[771] said of ʿAbd al-ʿAzīz b. al-Walīd,[772]

He does not let his share in this present world go to waste,
yet on the other hand, the concerns of this world do not deflect him from religion.

He commented: At that moment, I realized that I had made an error.[773]

It is mentioned from Muḥammad b. Ibrāhīm al-Sabārī[774] that he said: When (Kulthūm b. ʿAmr) al-ʿAttābī[775] came to al-Ma'mūn in the City of Peace, he was given permission to enter. [1160] So he went into the Caliph's presence, the latter having with him at that time Isḥāq b. Ibrāhīm al-Mawṣilī.[776] Al-ʿAttābī was at this time a highly-respected elderly man. He greeted the Caliph, who returned the greeting and ordered al-ʿAttābī to approach him, and brought him near until he was close to him. Al-ʿAttābī kissed his hand. The Caliph then ordered him to

771. See above, 244 and n. 742.

772. The Umayyad prince, son of al-Walīd I.

773. Ibn Abī Ṭāhir, 313, tr. 141–2; Ibn al-Athīr, *al-Kāmil*, VI, 438.

774. The correct reading for this *nisbah* is unclear; al-Sayyārī would be possible, whilst Iṣfahānī, *Aghānī*, XII, 3, has al-Yasārī. Samʿānī (Hyderabad), VII, 22, connects al-Sabārī with a village of the Bukhara oasis.

775. The secretary and poet, eulogist of al-Rashīd and al-Ma'mūn; see Sezgin, *GAS*, II, 540–1; *EI*² s.v. al-ʿAttābī (Blachère).

776. The great musician, singer and poet, and favorite of al-Ma'mūn; see Farmer, 124–6; Sezgin, *GAS*, II, 578; *EI*² s.v. (Fück).

be seated, so he sat down, and then the Caliph came up to al-ʿAttābī and questioned him about his present circumstances. Al-ʿAttābī began to answer him in an eloquent voice, which al-Ma'mūn found pleasing, and he came up to al-ʿAttābī, making jests and pleasantries. The old man thought that al-Ma'mūn was mocking him, and exclaimed, "O Commander of the Faithful, does assembling beasts for milking come before making yourself familiar to them?"[777] He related: Al-Ma'mūn did not comprehend the allusion to "assembling beasts for milking" (*al-ibsās*); he looked at Isḥāq b. Ibrāhīm, and then said, "Yes! O slave boy, [bring] one thousand dīnārs!" The sum was brought and then poured out in front of al-ʿAttābī.

They then began to talk together and tell stories. Isḥāq b. Ibrāhīm made a surreptitious sign with his eye to al-Ma'mūn. He would not allow al-ʿAttābī to embark on any topic without starting to dispute with him over the greater part of it. Al-ʿAttābī was left mystified by this, but then said, "O Commander of the Faithful, give me permission to ask this old man what his name is!" Al-Ma'mūn answered, "Certainly, do ask him." Al-ʿAttābī said, "O old man, who are you, and what is your name?" Isḥāq replied, "I am a human being and my name is Kul baṣal."[778] Al-ʿAttābī said, "As for the name of attribution [*nisbah*], that is known, but with regard to the name proper [*ism*], that is still unknown [to me]; Kul baṣal is not a recognized name." Isḥāq answered him, "You are quite unjust here! Is not Kul thūm a recognized name, then? Onions are pleasanter than garlic!" Al-ʿAttābī said, "What an excellent fellow you are! How persuasively you have argued! O Commander of the Faithful, I have never before seen an old man like this one! Would you permit me to make him a gift of what
[1161] the Commander of the Faithful bestowed on me [earlier]? For by God, he has got the better of me!" Al-Ma'mūn retorted, "Nay, you shall keep the whole of it, and I shall order him to be given an equivalent sum." Isḥāq then said to al-ʿAttābī, "Since

777. An allusion to the proverb, "Make yourself known to beasts before milking them," cf. Maydānī, tr. I, 94.

778. *Kul baṣal*, literally, "eat onions!"—al-ʿAttābī's *ism* being interpretable as *kul thūm* "eat garlic!"

you have acknowledged this [superiority of mine in debate], make a guess about me, and you will find me out!" He said, "By God, you must be none other than the shaykh, concerning whom reports reach us from Iraq and who is known as Ibn al-Mawṣilī." Isḥāq replied, "I am that person, just as you imagined." He then went up to him to give him the greetings of long life and of peace. Al-Ma'mūn commented, after the conversation between the two shaykhs had gone on for a considerable time, "Since the two of you have come to a peaceful and amicable understanding, arise, and go off together as boon-companions!" So al-ʿAttābī went off to Isḥāq's house and stayed there with him.[779]

It is mentioned from Muḥammad b. ʿAbdallāh b. Jasham al-Ribʿī that ʿUmārah b. ʿAqīl said: One day, when I was drinking with him, al-Ma'mūn said to me, "What poor company you are, O bedouin!" He related: I protested, "That is not the case, O Commander of the Faithful, but my heart is troubled." He enquired, "How is that?" I replied:

Mufaddāt said, when she saw that I was sleepless
and that the phantom of care was visiting me repeatedly, as an obsession,

You have dissipated your wealth on acts of favor to people both near
and far, to the point that indigence now encompasses you.

Seek out these people, and you will see what a fine state you once enjoyed;
you shower them with gifts, so that they have now already got whole herds of camels!

But I replied, Away with your reproaches! You have blamed me too much; [1162]
neither Ḥātim nor Harim died from extreme poverty.

779. Ibn Abī Ṭāhir, 316–17, tr. 143; Masʿūdī, *Murūj*, VII, 26–8 = ed. Pellat, § 2715; Iṣfahānī, *Aghānī*, XII, 3–4.

Al-Ma'mūn said to me, "What are you thinking of, setting yourself up in comparison with Harim b. Sinān, the lord of the Arabs, and Ḥātim al-Ṭā'ī?[780] They did so-and-so and so-and-so," and he began to overwhelm me with a heap of examples of their generosity. He related: I replied, however, "O Commander of the Faithful, I am better than both of them, because I am a Muslim and they were infidels, and I am an Arab as well."[781]

It is mentioned from Muḥammad b. Zakariyyā' b. Maymūn al-Farghānī that he said: Al-Ma'mūn said to Muḥammad b. al-Jahm,[782] "Recite to me three verses of poetry which are on the respective themes of eulogy, satire and elegy, and I will give you a tract of land for each verse." So he recited to him as an example of eulogy:

He yields up his life, when even the [ordinary] generous person is tenacious of it;
giving up one's life is the highest point of generosity.

He recited to him as an example of satire:

Their external appearance is hateful, but when you get to know them,
their external appearance appears beautiful because of the extreme hatefulness of their inner character.

He recited to him as an example of elegy:

They wished to conceal his grave,
but the sweet odor of the grave's earth indicated the way to the tomb.[783]

It is mentioned from al-ʿAbbās b. Aḥmad b. Abān b. al-Qāsim[784] al-Kātib, who said, al-Ḥusayn b. al-Ḍaḥḥāk related to me,

780. The two tribal chiefs, of Dhubyān and Ṭayyi' respectively, who were famed in pre-Islamic times for their liberality; see R.A. Nicholson, *A literary history of the Arabs*, 85–7, 116–17, cf. 288.

781. Ibn Abī Ṭāhir, 317–18, tr. 144; Iṣfahānī, *Aghānī*, XX, 184–5.

782. Apparently a client of the Barmakīs; see Guidi, II, 598; G. Lecomte, "Muḥammad b. al-Ǧahm al-Barmakī . . . ," *Arabica*, V (1958), 263–71.

783. Ibn Abī Ṭāhir, 318–19, tr. 144.

784. Ibn Abī Ṭāhir, 320, has here Abū al-Qāsim.

saying: ʿAllawayh said to me, I will tell you about an episode that once happened to me when I would have despaired of continuing in al-Maʾmūn's favor had it not been for his nobility of character. He summoned us, and when the effects of the wine had got a hold of him, he said, "Sing to me!" Mukhāriq preceded me, and started off by singing a melody by Ibn Surayj[785] to a poem by Jarīr, [1163]

When I recalled to mind the two monasteries,
where the noise of the domestic fowls and the beating of the wooden clappers kept me awake,

I said to the party of riders, at a time when we were weary from the journey
"How far is Yabrīn[786] from the gates of the gardens of paradise!"

He related: I was given the instruction to start singing at that moment, when al-Maʾmūn had in fact just had the idea of setting out for Damascus with the intention of proceeding to the (Byzantine) frontier region,

The moment of time has urged [us] on to Damascus, even though
Damascus is no fitting place for our people.[787]

He thereupon dashed his drinking-cup to the ground and exclaimed, "What's the matter with you? May God's curse be upon you!" Then he said, "O slave boy, give Mukhāriq three thousand dirhams!" I was taken by the hand and set down in my place, whilst his eyes were overflowing with tears and he was saying to al-Muʿtaṣim, "This is, by God, my last expedition and I don't think that I shall ever see Iraq again." He related: By God, it was indeed his last contact with Iraq, at the time of this expedition, just as he said.[788]

---

785. Famed singer in the Hijaz during the Umayyad period; see Farmer, 79–80; *EI*² s.v. (Fück).
786. According to Yāqūt, *Muʿjam*, V, 427, a sand dune region of eastern Arabia.
787. Following the *li-ahlinā* of Ibn Abī Ṭāhir, 320, and Iṣfahānī, *Aghānī*, X, 132, instead of the text's *li-ahlihā*.
788. Ibn Abī Ṭāhir, 320–1, tr. 145.

Bibliography

(I. Primary Sources: Texts and Translations)

al-Azdī, Abū al-Muṭahhar Muḥammad b. Aḥmad. *Ḥikāyat Abī al-Qāsim al-Baghdādī*. Edited by A. Mez under the title *Abulḳâsim, ein bagdâder Sittlenbild*. Heidelberg, 1902.

al-Azdī, Abū Zakariyyā' Yazīd b. Muḥammad. *Ta'rīkh al-Mawṣil*. Edited by ʿAlī Ḥabībah. Cairo, 1387 (1967).

al-Azraqī, Abū al-Walīd Muḥammad b. ʿAbdallāh. *Akhbār Makkah*. 2 vols. Edited by Rushdī al-Ṣāliḥ Malḥas. Riyadh, 1385 (1965–6).

al-Bakrī, Abū ʿUbayd ʿAbdallāh b. ʿAbd al-ʿAzīz. *Muʿjam mā 'staʿjam min asmā' al-bilād wa-al-mawāḍiʿ*. 4 vols. Edited by Muṣṭafā al-Saqqā. Cairo, 1364–71 (1945–51).

al-Baladhūrī, Abū al-Ḥasan Aḥmad b. Yaḥyā. *Futūḥ al-buldān*. Edited by M. J. de Geeje under the title *Liber expugnationis regionum*. Leiden, 1866.

Diʿbil b. ʿAlī al-Khuzāʿī. *Dīwān*. Edited by ʿAbd al-Ṣāḥib ʿUmrān al-Dujaylī. Najaf, 1382 (1962).

al-Dīnawarī, Abū Ḥanīfah Aḥmad b. Dāwūd. *Kitāb al-Akhbār al-ṭiwāl*. 2 vols. Edited by W. Guirgass and I. Kratchkovsky. Leiden, 1888–1912.

Ibn Abī Ṭāhir, Abū al-Faḍl Aḥmad Ṭayfūr. *Kitāb Baghdād*. 2 vols. Edited and translated by H. Keller under the title *Sechster Band des Kitâb Bagdâd*. Leipzig, 1908.

Ibn al-Athīr, ʿIzz al-Dīn Abū al-Ḥasan ʿAlī b. Muḥammad. *al-Kāmil fī al-ta'rīkh*. 13 vols. Beirut, 1385–7 (1965–7).

Ibn Khaldūn, Walī al-Dīn Abū Zayd ʿAbd al-Raḥmān b. Muḥammad. *al-Muqaddimah*. Translated by F. Rosenthal under the title *The*

Muqaddimah, an introduction to history. 3 vols. New York, 1958. Translated by V. Monteil under the title *Discours sur l'histoire universelle (al-Muqaddima).* 3 vols. Beirut, 1967–8.

Ibn Khallikān, Abū al-ʿAbbās Aḥmad b. Muḥammad al-Irbilī. *Wafayāt al-aʿyān wa-anbāʾ abnāʾ al-zamān.* 8 vols. Edited by Iḥsān ʿAbbās. Beirut, 1968–72. Translated by Baron McGuckin de Slane under the title *Ibn Khallikan's biographical dictionary.* 4 vols. Paris, 1842–71.

Ibn Manẓūr, Jamāl al-Dīn Abū al-Faḍl Muḥammad b. Mukarram al-Anṣārī. *Lisān al-ʿArab.* 20 vols. Būlāq, 1300–8 (1883–91).

Ibn al-Nadīm, Abū al-Faraj Muḥammad b. Isḥāq al-Warrāq. *Kitab al-Fihrist.* Translated by B. Dodge under the title *The Fihrist of al-Nadīm, a tenth century survey of Muslim culture.* 2 vols. New York and London, 1970.

Ibn Taghrībirdī, Jamāl al-Dīn Abū al-Maḥāsin Yūsuf. *al-Nujūm al-zāhirah fī mulūk Miṣr wa-al-Qāhirah.* 16 vols. Edited by Jamāl Muḥarriz *et alii.* Cairo, 1383–92 (1963–72).

al-Iṣfahānī, Abū al-Faraj ʿAlī b. al-Ḥusayn. *Kitāb al-Aghānī.* 20 vols. Būlāq, 1285–6 (1868–70).

———. *Maqātil al-Ṭālibiyyīn.* Edited by Aḥmad Ṣaqr. Cairo, 1368 (1949).

al-Jahshiyārī, Abū ʿAbdallāh Muḥammad b. Abdūs. *Kitāb al-Wuzarāʾ wa-al-kuttāb.* Edited by ʿAbdallāh Ismāʿīl al-Ṣawī. Baghdad, 1357 (1938).

al-Khalīfah, Abū ʿAmr b. Khayyāṭ. *Taʾrīkh.* 2 vols. Edited by Suhayl Zakkār. Damascus, (1967–8).

al-Kindī, Abū ʿUmar Muḥammad b. Yūsuf. *Kitāb al-Wulāt wa-Kitāb al-Quḍāt.* Edited by R. Guest under the title *The governors and judges of Egypt.* GMS XIX. Leiden and London, 1912.

al-Masʿūdī, Abū al-Ḥasan ʿAlī b. al-Ḥusayn. *Murūj al-dhahab wa-maʿādin al-jawhar.* Edited and translated by C. Barbier de Meynard and Pavet de Courteille under the title *Les prairies d'or.* 9 vols. Paris, 1861–77. Edited and translated by Ch. Pellat under the title *Les prairies d'or.* Paris and Beirut, 1962–79.

———. *Kitāb al-Tanbīh wa-al-ishrāf.* Edited by M.J. de Goeje. BGA VIII. Leiden, 1894. Translated by Baron Carra de Vaux under the title *Le livre de l'avertissement et de la revision.* Paris, 1897.

al-Māwardī, Abū al-Ḥasan ʿAlī b. Muḥammad. *al-Aḥkām al-sulṭāniyyah.* Translated by E. Fagnan under the title *Les statuts gouvernementaux ou règles de droit public et administratif.* Algiers, 1915.

al-Maydānī, Abū al-Faḍl Aḥmad b. Muḥammad. *Majmaʿ amthāl*

al-ʿArab. 3 vols. Translated by G.W. Freytag under the title *Arabum proverba.* Bonn, 1838–43.

Niẓāmī ʿArūḍī Samarqandī. *Chahār maqāla.* Translated by E.G. Browne under the title *The four discourses.* GMS XI,2. Leiden and London, 1921.

Qummī, Ḥasan b. Muḥammad. *Ta'rīkh-i Qum.* Edited by Jalāl al-Dīn Ṭihrānī. Tehran, 1353 (1313 *sh.* [1934/5]).

al-Samʿānī, Abū Saʿd ʿAbd al-Karīm b. Muḥammad. *Kitāb al-Ansāb.* 13 vols. Edited by M. ʿAbd al-Muʿīd Khān *et alii.* Hyderabad, Dn., 1382–1402 (1962–82).

Severus (Sawīrus) b. al-Muqaffaʿ. *Ta'rīkh Baṭāriqat al-kanīsah al-miṣriyyah.* Edited and translated by B. Evetts under the title *History of the Patriarchs of the Coptic Church of Alexandria. IV. Mennas I to Joseph (849).* In *Patrologia orientalis,* X, no. 5. Paris, 1915.

al-Shābushtī, Abū al-Ḥasan ʿAlī b. Muḥammad. *Kitāb al-Diyārāt.* Edited by Gurgīs ʿAwwād. Baghdad, 1370 (1951).

al-Ṭabarī, Abū Jaʿfar Muḥammad b. Jarīr. *Ta'rīkh al-rusul wa-al mulūk.* Partially translated by Th. Nöldeke under the title *Geschichte der Perser und Araber zur Zeit der Sassaniden.* Leiden, 1879. Partially translated by E. Marin under the title *The reign of al-Muʿtaṣim (833–842)* New Haven, 1951.

al-Tamīmī, Abū al-ʿArab Muḥammad b. Aḥmad. *Kitāb al-Miḥan.* Edited by Yaḥyā Wahīb al-Jabbūrī. Beirut 1403 [1983].

al-Thaʿālibī, Abū Manṣūr ʿAbd al-Malik b. Muḥammad. *Laṭā'if al-maʿārif.* Edited by Ibrāhīm al-Abyārī and Ḥasan Kāmil al-Ṣayrafī. Cairo, 1960. Translated by C.E. Bosworth under the title *The book of curious and entertaining information.* Edinburgh, 1968.

al-Yaʿqūbī, Abū al-ʿAbbās Aḥmad b. Isḥāq, called Ibn Wāḍiḥ. *Kitāb al-Buldān.* Edited by de Goeje. BGA VII. Leiden, 1892. Translated by G. Wiet under the title *Les pays.* Cairo, 1937.

———. *Mushākalat al-nās li-zamānihim.* Edited by W. Milward. Beirut, 1962. Translated by Milward under the title "The adaptation of men to their time: an historical essay by al-Yaʿqūbī." *JAOS* LXXXIV (1964): 329–44.

———. *Ta'rīkh.* Edited by M.Th. Houtsma under the title *Historiae.* 2 vols. Leiden, 1883.

Yāqūt, Abū ʿAbdallāh Yaʿqūb b. ʿAbdallāh al-Ḥamawī al-Rūmī. *Muʿjam al-buldān.* 5 vols. Beirut, 1374–6 (1955–7).

al-Zabīdī, Abū al-Fayḍ Muḥammad Murtaḍā b. Muḥammad. *Tāj*

al-ʿarūs min jawāhir al-qāmūs. 10 vols. Būlāq, 1306–7 (1889–90).

(II. Secondary Sources and Reference Works)

Abbott, Nabia. *Two queens of Baghdad: mother and wife of Hārūn al-Rashīd.* Chicago, 1946.
Adams, R. Mc C. *Land behind Baghdad. A history of settlement on the Diyala plains.* Chicago, 1965.
Amedroz, H.R. "The Mazālim jurisdiction in the Ahkam Sultaniyya of Mawardi," *JRAS* (1911): 635–74.
Anastos, M.V. "Iconoclasm and imperial rule 717–842." In *The Cambridge medieval history.* Vol. IV, *The Byzantine empire.* Part I, *Byzantium and its neighbours,* edited by J.M. Hussey, 61–104. Cambridge, 1966.
Arioli, A. "La rivolta di Abū Sarāyā: appunti per una tipologia del leader islamico." *Annali di Ca' Foscari* V (1974): 189–97.
Ayalon, D. "On the eunuchs in Islam." *JSAI* I (1979): 67–124.
Barbier de Meynard, C. "Ibrahim, fils de Mehdi. Fragments historiques. Scènes de la vie d'artiste au IIIe siècle de l'hégire (778–839 de notre ère)." *JA,* ser. 6, vol. XIII (1869): 201–342.
Barthold, W. *Turkestan down to the Mongol invasion.* GMS, n.s. V. London, 1968.
———. *An historical geography of Iran.* Translated by S. Soucek. Edited by C.E. Bosworth. Princeton, 1984.
Bosworth, C.E. *The Ghaznavids: their empire in Afghanistan and eastern Iran 994–1040.* Edinburgh, 1963.
———. *Sīstān under the Arabs, from the Islamic conquest to the rise of the Ṣaffārids (30–250/651–864).* Rome, 1968.
———. "Abū ʿAbdallāh al-Khwārazmī on the technical terms of the secretary's art: a contribution to the administrative history of mediaeval Islam." *JESHO* XII (1969): 113–64. Also in *Medieval Arabic culture and administration.* [London, 1982].
———. "The Ṭāhirids and Arabic culture." *JSS* XIV (1969): 45–79. Also in *Medieval Arabic culture and administration.* London, 1982.
———. "An early Islamic Mirror for Princess: Ṭāhir Dhū l-Yamīnain's epistle to his son ʿAbdallāh (206/821)." *JNES* XXIX (1970): 25–41.
———. "Recruitment, muster and review in medieval Islamic ar-

mies." In *War, technology and society in the Middle East*, edited by V.J. Parry and M.E. Yapp, 59–77. London, 1975.

———. "The Ṭāhirids and Ṣaffārids." In *The Cambridge history of Iran*. Vol. IV, *The period from the Arab invasion to the Saljuqs*, edited by R.N. Frye, 90–135. Cambridge, 1975.

Bosworth, C.E. and Clauson, Sir Gerard. "Al-Xwārazmī on the peoples of Central Asia." *JRAS* (1965), 2–12. Also in *The medieval history of Iran, Afghanistan and Central Asia*. London, 1977.

Bravmann, M.M. "À propos de Qur'ān IX–29: *ḥattā yuʿṭū l-ǧizyata ʿan yadin wa-hum ṣāǧirūna*." *Arabica* X (1963): 94–5.

Cahen, Cl. *Mouvements populaires et autonomisme urbain dans l'Asie musulmane du Moyen Âge*. Leiden, 1959. Originally in *Arabica* V (1958): 225–50: VI (1959): 25–56, 223–65.

———. "Coran IX–29: *ḥattā yuʿṭū l-ǧizyata ʿan yadin wa-hum ṣāǧirūna*." *Arabica* IX (1962): 76–9.

Canard, M. *Histoire de la dynastie des H'amdânides de Jazîra et de Syrie* I. Algiers, 1951.

———. "Byzantium and the Muslim world to the middle of the eleventh century." In *The Cambridge medieval history*. Vol. IV, *The Byzantine empire*. Part I, *Byzantium and its neighbours*, 696–735.

Chejne, A.J. "Al-Faḍl b. al-Rabīʿ—a politician of the early ʿAbbāsid period." *IC* XXXVI (1962): 167–81.

Crone, Patricia. *Slaves on horses. The evolution of the Islamic polity*. Cambridge, 1980.

Daniel, E. *The political and social history of Khurasan under Abbasid rule 747–820*. Minneapolis and Chicago, 1979.

De Goeje, M.J. *Annales . . . at-Tabari. Introductio, glossarium, addenda et emendanda*. Leiden, 1901.

Dickson, H.R.P. *The Arab of the desert, a glimpse into Badawin life in Kuwait and Sau'di Arabia*. London, 1949.

Donaldson, D.M. *The Shi'ite religion. A history of Islam in Persia and Iraḳ*. London, 1933.

Dozy, R. *Supplément aux dictionnaires arabes*. 2 vols. Leiden, 1881.

Duri, A.A. *The rise of historical writing among the Arabs*. Edited and translated by L.I. Conrad. Princeton, 1983.

Dussaud, R. *Topographie historique de la Syrie antique et médiévale*. Paris, 1927.

Encyclopaedia of Islām. First edition. 4 vols. and Supplement. Leiden 1913–42.

Encyclopaedia of Islām. New edition. 5 vols. and Supplement. Leiden and London, 1960–.

Farmer, H.G. *A History of Arabian music to the XIIIth century*. London, 1929.

Gabrieli, F. "La successione di Hārūn ar-Rašīd e la guerra fra al-Amīn e al-Ma'mūn." *RSO* XI (1926–8): 341–97.

———. *Al-Ma'mun e gli Alidi*. Leipzig, 1929.

Geddes, C.L. "Al-Ma'mūn's Šī'ite policy in Yemen." *WZKM* LIX–LX (1963–4):99–107.

Goitein, S.D. *A Mediterranean society. The Jewish communities of the Arab world as portrayed in the documents of the Cairo Geniza*. Vol. II, *The community*. Berkeley, Los Angeles and London, 1971.

Goldziher, I. *Muhammedanische Studien*. 2 vols. Halle, 1889–90. Translated by C.R. Barber and S.M. Stern and edited by Stern under the title *Muslim studies*. 2 vols. London 1967–71.

———. "Ueber Dualtitel." *WZKM* XIII (1899): 321–9. Also in *Gesammelte Schriften*, vol. IV edited by J. Desomogyi, 195–203. Hildesheim, 1969–73.

———. *Introduction to Islamic theology and law*. Translated by A. and Ruth Hamori. Edited by B. Lewis. Princeton, 1981.

Grunebaum, G.E. von. "Three Arabic poets of the early Abbasid age (the collected fragments of Muṭī' b. Iyâs, Salm al-Ḫâsir and Abû 'š-Šamaqmaq). V. Salm al-Ḫâsir." *Orientalia* XIX (1950): 53–80. Also in *Themes in medieval Arabic literature*. London, 1981.

Guidi, I. *Tables alphabétiques du Kitâb al-Aġânî* 2 vols. Leiden, 1900.

Hinds, M. "The banners and battle cries of the Arabs at Ṣiffīn (657 AD)." *al-Abḥāth* XXIV (1971): 3–42.

Hinz, W. *Islamische Masse und Gewichte umgerechnet ins metrische System*. Handbuch der Orientalistik, Erganzungsband 1, Heft 1. Leiden, 1955.

Honigmann, E. *Die Ostgrenze des Byzantinischen Reiches von 363 bis 1071 nach griechischen, arabischen, syrischen und armenischen Quellen*. In *Byzance et les Arabes*. Vol. III, edited by A.A. Vasiliev. Brussels, 1935.

Hughes, T.P. *A dictionary of Islam, being a cyclopaedia of the doctrines, rites, ceremonies, and customs, together with the technical and theological terms, of the Muhammadan religion*. London, 1885.

Justi, F. *Iranisches Namenbuch*. Marburg, 1895.

Kaabi, M. "Les origines ṭāhirides dans la *da'wa* 'abbāside."*Arabica* XIX (1972): 145–64.

Kennedy, H. *The early Abbasid Caliphate, a political history*. London and Totowa, N.J., 1981.

Kindermann, H. *"Schiff" im Arabischen. Untersuchung über Vorkommen und Bedeutung der Termini.* Zwickau-im-Sa., 1934.
Kister, M.J. "*'an yadin*' (Qur'ān, IX/29), an attempt at interpretation." *Arabica* XI (1964): 272–8.
Lammens, H. *La Mecque à la veille de l'hégire.* Beirut, 1924.
———. *Etudes sur le siècle des Omayyades.* Beirut, 1930.
Lane, E.W. *An Arabic-English lexicon, derived from the best and most copious Eastern sources.* 8 vols. London, 1863–93.
Lapidus, I.M. "The separation of state and religion in the development of early Islamic society." *IJMES* VI (1975): 363–85.
Lassner, J. *The topography of Baghdad in the early Middle Ages. Text and studies.* Detroit, 1970.
———. *The shaping of 'Abbāsid rule.* Princeton, 1980.
Le Strange, G. *Palestine under the Moslems, a description of Syria and the Holy Land from A.D. 650 to 1500.* London, 1890.
———. *Baghdad under the Abbasid Caliphate from contemporary Arabic and Persian sources.* Oxford, 1900.
———. *The lands of the Eastern Caliphate, Mesopotamia, Persia, and Central Asia from the Moslem conquest to the time of Timur.* Cambridge, 1905.
Lecomte, G. "Muḥammad b. al-Ǧahm al-Barmakī, gouverneur, philosophe, jugé par Ibn Qutayba."*Arabica* V (1958): 263–71.
Lévi-Provençal, E. *Histoire de l'Espagne musulmane.* Vol. I, *La conquête et l'émirat hispano-umaiyade (710–912).* Paris and Leiden, 1950.
Levy, R. *A Baghdad chronicle.* Cambridge, 1929.
———. *The social structure of Islam.* Cambridge, 1957.
Løkkegaard, F. *Islamic taxation in the classic period, with special reference to circumstances in Iraq.* Copenhagen, 1950.
Madelung, W. "The minor dynasties of northern Iran." In *The Cambridge history of Iran.* Vol. IV,*The period from the Arab invasion to the Saljuqs,* 198–249.
———. "New documents concerning al-Ma'mūn, al-Faḍl b. Sahl and 'Alī al-Riḍā." In *Studia arabica et islamica, Festschrift for Iḥsān 'Abbās on his sixtieth birthday,* edited by Wadād al-Qāḍī, 333–46. Beirut, 1981.
Makdisi, G. "Notes on Ḥilla and the Mazyadids in medieval Islam." *JAOS* LXXIV (1954): 249–62.
Marin, E. See under *Primary sources,* s.v. al-Ṭabarī.
Marquart, J. *Ērānšahr nach der Geographie des Ps. Moses Xorenac'i.* In *Abhandlungen der Königl. Gesell. der Wiss. zu Göttingen,* n.s. III, 2. Berlin, 1901.

Marquet, Y. "Le Šīʿisme au IXe siècle á travers l'histoire de Yaʿqūbī." *Arabica* XIX (1972): 1–45, 101–38.
Mez, A. *The renaissance of Islam.* Translated by S. Khuda Bakhsh and D.S. Margoliouth. Patna, 1937.
Miles, G.C. *The numismatic history of Rayy.* New York, 1938.
Minorsky, V. *A history of Sharvān and Darband in the 10th–11th centuries.* Cambridge, 1958.
Mottahedeh, R.P. *Loyalty and leadership in an early Islamic society.* Princeton, 1980.
Nafīsī, Saʿīd. *Ta'rīkh-i khāndān-i Ṭāhirī. I. Ṭāhir b. Ḥusayn.* Tehran, 1335 *sh.* (1956).
Nicholson, R.A. *A literary history of the Arabs.* London, 1907.
Nöldeke, Th. "Die Namen der aramäischen Nation und Sprache." *ZDMG* XXV (1871): 113–31.
———. See under *Primary sources,* s.v. al-Ṭabarī.
———. "Zur Ausbreitung des Schiitismus." *Isl.* XIII (1923): 70–81.
Omar, Farouk. *ʿAbbāsiyyāt, studies in the history of the early ʿAbbāsids.* Baghdad, 1976.
Patton, W.M. *Aḥmed ibn Ḥanbal and the Miḥna. A biography of the Imām including an account of the Moḥammedan inquisition called the Miḥna, 218–234 A.H.* Leiden, 1897.
Pellat, Ch. *Le milieu baṣrien at la formation de Ǧāḥiẓ.* Paris, 1953.
———. "Le culte de Muʿâwiya au IIIe siècle." *SI* VI (1956): 53–66.
Rabino di Borgomale, H.L. *Mázandarán and Astarábád.* GMS n.s. VII. London, 1928.
———. "Les préfets du Califat au Ṭabaristān, de 18 à 328/639 à 939–40." *JA* CCXXXI (1939): 237–74.
Richter, G. *Studien zur Geschichte der älteren arabischen Fürstenspiegel.* Leipzig, 1932.
Rosenthal, F. *"Sweeter than hope." Complaint and hope in mediaeval Islam.* Leiden, 1983.
Rothstein, G. "Zu aš-Šābuštī's Bericht über die Ṭāhiriden (Ms. Wetzstein II, 1100 fol. 44^a–64^a)." *Orientalistische Studien Theodor Nöldeke . . . gewidmet* I, edited by C. Bezold, 155–70. Giessen, 1906.
Sabari, S. *Mouvements populaires à Bagdad a l'époque ʿabbaside IXe–XIe siècles.* Paris, 1981.
Sadan, J. "Kings and craftsmen—a pattern of contrasts. On the history of a medieval Arabic humoristic form." *SI* LVI (1982): 5–49.
Sadighi, G.-H. *Les mouvements religieux iraniens au IIe et au IIIe siècle de l'hégire.* Paris, 1938.
Scarcia Amoretti, B. "Sects and heresies." In *The Cambridge history*

of Iran. Vol. IV. *From the Arab invasion to the Saljuqs*, 481–519.
Schacht, J. *An introduction to Islamic law*. Oxford, 1964.
Schwarz, P. *Iran im Mittelalter nach den arabischen Geographen*. 9 parts. Leipzig, Stuttgart and Berlin, 1896–1936.
Serjeant, R.B. "The Caliph ʿUmar's letters to Abū Mūsā al-Ashʿarī and Muʿāwiya." *JSS* XXIX (1984):65–79.
Sezgin, F. *Geschichte des arabischen Schrifttums*. Vol. I, *Qur'ānwissenschaften, Ḥadīṯ, Geschichte, Fiqh, Dogmatik, Mystik bis ca. 430 H*. Leiden, 1967. Vol. II, *Poesie bis ca. 430 H*. Leiden, 1975.
Shaban, M.A. *Islamic history. A new interpretation. 2. A.D.750–1055 (A.H. 132–448)*. Cambridge, 1976.
Sourdel, D. "Les circonstances de la mort de Ṭāhir Ier au Hurāsān en 207/822." *Arabica* V (1958): 66–9.
———. *Le vizirat ʿabbāside de 749 à 936 (132 à 324 de l'Hégire)*. 2 vols. Damascus, 1959–60.
———. "Questions de cérémonial ʿabbaside." *REI* XXVIII (1960): 121–48.
———. "La politique religieuse du calife ʿabbāside al-Ma'mun", *REI* XXX (1962): 27–48.
Steppat, F. "From ʿahd Ardašīr to al-Ma'mūn: a Persian element in the policy of the *Miḥna*." In *Studia arabica et islamica, Festschrift for Iḥsān ʿAbbās*. 451–4.
Tornberg, C.J. "Ueber muhammedanische Revolutions-Münzen." *ZDMG* XXII (1868): 700–7.
Vasiliev, A.A. *Byzance et les Arabes*. Vol. I, *I. La dynastie d'Amorium (820–867)*. Brussels, 1935.
———. *History of the Byzantine empire 324–1453*. Madison and Milwaukee, 1952.
Watt, W. Montgomery. *The formative period of Islamic thought*. Edinburgh, 1973.
Al-Wohaibi, Abdullah. *The Northern Hijaz in the writings of the Arab geographers 800–1150*. Beirut, 1973.
Wright, E.M. "Bābak of Badhdh and Al-Afshīn during the years 816–41 A.D., symbols of Iranian persistence against Islamic penetration in North Iran." *MW* XXXVIII (1948): 43–59, 124–31.
Zambaur, E. de. *Manuel de généalogie et de chronologie pour l'histoire de l'Islam*. Hanover, 1927.

Index

The index contains all proper names of persons, places, tribal and other groups, as well as topographical data, occurring in the introduction, the text, and the footnotes, together with some technical terms. However, as far as the footnotes are concerned, only those names that belong to the medieval or earlier periods are listed.

The definite article, the abbreviation b. (for ibn, son) and bt. (for bint, daughter), and everything in parentheses are disregarded for the purposes of alphabetization. Where a name occurs in both the text and the footnotes on the same page, only the page number is given.

A

al-ʿAbbās, officer of ʿĪsā b. Muḥammad b. Abī Khālid 87-8
ʿAbbās, mawlā of al-Ma'mūn 214
al-ʿAbbās, *qaṭīʿah* or fief of 108
al-ʿAbbās b. Aḥnaf, poet 245
al-ʿAbbās b. al-Haytham al-Dīnawarī 80
al-ʿAbbās b. Jaʿfar al-Khuzāʿī 43
al-ʿAbbās b. al-Ma'mūn 134, 153-4, 174, 182, 185-6, 198-9, 222, 231
al-ʿAbbās b. Mūsā al-Hādī 67
al-ʿAbbās b. Mūsā b. ʿĪsā, ʿAbbāsid 11
al-ʿAbbās b. Mūsā b. Jaʿfar, ʿAlid 71-4
ʿAbbāsah bt. al-Faḍl b. Sahl 154
ʿAbbāsids (see also Hāshimites) 45, 57, 72, 74, 77, 85, 95
ʿAbdallāh b. al-ʿAbbās 244
ʿAbdallāh b. Abī al-Simṭ, poet 252-3
ʿAbdallāh b. Aḥmad b. Yūsuf, *rāwī* 172
ʿAbdallāh b. Aḥmad b. Zayd al-Dimashqī, judge 225
ʿAbdallāh b. ʿAlī b. ʿĪsā b. Māhān 47
ʿAbdallāh b. Jalīs al-Hilālī, rebel in Egypt 178, 182
ʿAbdallāh b. Khurradādhbih 64
ʿAbdallāh b. Lahīʿah, *rāwī* 165
ʿAbdallāh b. Saʿīd al-Ḥarashī 16
ʿAbdallāh b. Ṭāhir b. al-Ḥusayn 3, 7, 106, 108-10, 128-9, 134-5, 138, 140, 142-5, 159-65, 168-74, 183, 222, 229, 251
ʿAbdallāh b. ʿUbaydallāh b. al-ʿAbbās, ʿAbbāsid 177, 180, 186, 190
ʿAbdallāh b. Wahb, *rāwī* 165

ʿAbd al-ʿAzīz b. ʿImrān 78, 81
ʿAbd al-ʿAzīz b. al-Walīd, Umayyad 253
ʿAbd al-Munʿim b. Idrīs b. Bint Wahb b. Munabbih 213
ʿAbd al-Raḥmān b. ʿAlī b. ʿAbdallāh, ʿAlid 130-1
ʿAbd al-Raḥmān b. ʿAmmār al-Naysābūrī al-Muṭṭawwic 105-7
ʿAbd al-Raḥmān b. Isḥāq 209, 210, 214, 218
ʿAbd al-Sal(l)ām al-Judhamī, rebel in Egypt 178, 182
ʿAbd al-Wahhāb b. Ibrāhīm, ʿAbbāsid 229
ʿAbdasī 25
ʿAbdawayh 91
ʿAbdūs al-Fihrī, rebel in Egypt 188, 191
ʿAbdūs b. Muḥammad b. Abī Khālid 15-16
Abnā' 2, 9, 45, 47, 54, 231
Abū ʿAbdallāh, brother of Abū al-Sarāyā 44, 68-9, 72, 74
Abū ʿAlī al-Salīṭī, *rāwī* 244
Abū al-ʿAtāhiyah, poet 175, 245-6
Abū al-ʿAwwām, Aḥmad b. Yazīd al-Bazzāz 210, 216, 222
Abū al-Baṭṭ 51, 68, 69, 70, 72, 74, 75, 81, 91
Abū Dulaf al-Qāsim al-ʿIjlī 246-8
Abū Ḥanīfah, legist 239
Abū Hārūn b. al-Bakkāʾ al-Aṣghar 212-13, 222
Abū Ḥassān al-Ziyādī 104-5, 158, 210-12, 217, 222
Abū Ibrāhīm b. Ghassān, see Ghassān b. Abī al-Faraj, Abū Ibrāhīm
Abū ʿĪsā b. Hārūn al-Rashīd 135
Abū Laylā, king of Daylam 64
Abū Maʿmar al-Qaṭīʿī 210, 218, 222
Abū Marwān Kāriz b. Hārūn, *rāwī* 245
Abū Maryam, slave of Saʿīd al-Jawharī 102
Abū Mismār, Baghdad mobster 148
Abū Mūsā al-Ashʿarī 124
Abū Mus'hir 219
Abū Muslim, *mustamlī* of Yazīd b. Hārūn 204
Abū Naṣr al-Tammār 210, 217, 222
Abū Nizār al-Ḍarīr, poet 246, 248
Abū Quaraysh, village 48-9
Abū al-Samrāʾ, *rāwī* 161
Abū al-Sarāyā, al-Sarī b. Manṣūr, al-Aṣfar 1, 13, 14-19, 23-7, 29, 40
Abū al-Shaddākh, poet 54
Abū al-Shawk 25
Abū Sufyān b. Ḥarb 217
Abū Zanbīl b. Muḥammad b. Abī Khālid 50-2
Adana 188, 192
ʿAdhal, slave girl of Ḥumayd b. ʿAbd al-Ḥamīd al-Ṭūsī 158

afḍal 61
al-Afshīn, Ḥaydar 135, 182, 188-9, 191
Ahl al-Bayt (see also ʿAlids, Ṭālibids) 26, 37
Aḥmad b. Adī Duwād 229
Aḥmad b. Abī Khālid al-Aḥwal 96-7, 103-4, 105, 133, 135, 147
Aḥmad b. Abī Ṭāhir Ṭayfūr 3, 7-8, 95n., 116n., 117n., 118n., 119n.
Aḥmad b. Ḥafṣ b. ʿUmar, *rāwī* 161
Aḥmad b. Ḥanbal 210, 212-13, 217, 220-1
Aḥmad b. al-Ḥasan b. Sahl, *rāwī* 156
Aḥmad b. Hishām 189
Aḥmad b. Ibrāhīm al-Dawraqī 205
Aḥmad b. al-Junayd al-Iskāfī 144
Aḥmad b. Muḥammad b. Makhlad 7, 159
Aḥmad b. Muḥammad al-ʿUmarī, rebel in Yemen 176, 181
Aḥmad b. Muḥammad b. al-Walīd al-Radmī 21
Aḥmad b. Naṣr al-Khuzāʿī 47
Aḥmad b. Shujāc 210, 218, 222
Aḥmad b. Yaḥyā b. Muʿādh 109, 147
Aḥmad b. Yūsuf 3, 179-80, 185
Ahwāz 10, 25
al-ʿAkawwak, see ʿAlī b. Jabalah al-ʿAkawwak
ʿAkk, Banū 130
Alexandria 164-5, 189
ʿAlī b. ʿAbdallāh b. Khālid b. Yazīd, Sufyānid rebel 234
ʿAlī b. ʿAbd al-ʿAzīz al-Jarawī 164-5, 182
ʿAlī b. Abī Muqātil 210-11, 216, 222
ʿAlī b. Abī Saʿīd, Dhū al-Qalamayn 10, 18, 23, 26, 27, 39, 44, 78-9, 81
ʿAlī b. Abī Ṭālib, caliph 177, 230
ʿAlī b. Hārūn, *rāwī* 105
ʿAlī b. al-Haytham 100-1
ʿAlī b. Hishām al-Marwazī 3, 42-4, 46-7, 81-2, 84, 91-2 95, 134, 166, 182-3, 189, 192-4, 217, 218
ʿAlī b. al-Ḥusayn b. ʿAbd al-Aʿlā al-Kātib 156-7
ʿAlī b. ʿĪsā al-Qummī 197
ʿAlī b. Jabalah al-ʿAkawwak, poet and *rāwī* 246-8
ʿAlī b. al-Jaʿd 210, 222
ʿAlī b. Muḥammad b. Jaʿfar, ʿAlid 31-3, 72
ʿAlī b. Mūsā al-Riḍā, Eighth Imām of the Shīʿah 2, 39, 45, 60-3, 69, 71, 78, 80, 82, 84-5, 101
ʿAlī b. Muṣʿab b. Ruzayq 131
ʿAlī b. Rayṭah 91
ʿAlī b. Ṣāliḥ, poet and rāwī 240
ʿAlī b. ʿUbaydah al-Rayḥānī, poet 240
ʿAlī b. Yaḥyā 219
ʿAlids (see also Ahl al-Bayt, Ṭālibids) 67, 72, 230

ʿAllawayh, musician 242-3, 257
al-ʿAlth 182
al-Amīn, Muḥammad, Caliph 9, 10, 36, 49, 79, 103, 192, 231, 248
ʿAmmār, Baghdad mobster 148
ʿAmmār b. Yāsir 221
ʿAmr b. Masʿadah al-Ṣūlī 96, 140
Anbār 216
Anbār Road district of Baghdad 56-7
Andalusians, in Egypt 164-5
Anṭīghū 188
ʿAqarqūf 39
Aqdhā al-Ḥarūrī 68
al-ʿAqīlī, descendant of ʿAqīl b. Abī Ṭālib 37-9
al-Aʿrābī, ʿ.r.kū 51
ʿArafah 21-2
Armenia 106, 144, 182, 193
Asad b. Abī al-Asad 42
Aṣfar, Banū al- 29
Ashinās, Abū Jaʿfar 68, 186
ʿĀṣim b. Bahdalah al-Asadī 219
ʿĀṣim b. ʿUmar b. Qatādah 219
ʿAskar al-Mahdī quarter of Baghdad 42-3, 47, 59, 87, 136
ʿAṭā', *ṣāḥib al-maẓālim, rāwī* 169
al-ʿAttābī, see Kulthūm b. ʿAmr al-ʿAttābī
al-ʿAyshī, *rāwī* 234-5
ʿayyārūn 55
āzādh dates 224
Azd, Banū 144
Azerbaijan 106, 144, 176, 182, 183, 193
Azhar b. Zuhayr b. al-Musayyab 12
ʿAzīz mawlā of ʿAbdallāh b. Ṭāhir 182

B

Bāb al-Jisr, gate of Baghdad 86, 92
Bāb al-Karkh, gate of Baghdad 43
Bāb Khurāsān, gate of Baghdad 89
Bāb al-Kūfah, gate of Baghdad 51
Bāb al-Muḥawwal, gate of Baghdad 43
Bāb al-Shām, gate of Baghdad 51, 76, 86
Bābak al-Khurramī (see also Khurramiyyah) 65, 98, 106, 108, 134, 144, 176, 181, 182, 192
Badhdh 65
Baghdad, Madīnat al-Salām or City of Peace 10, 19, 26, 41-4, 46-7, 51-2, 55-60, 68, 75-7, 80-1, 85, 92, 95-7, 99, 135, 144-6, 158, 159, 182, 184, 189, 190, 192, 199, 205, 221, 231, 253
Baḥrayn 108
baqiyyah 161
Baradān 39, 184
barīd 132, 224
Barmakīs 256
Barqah 188, 192
Bāsalāmā 47
Baṣrah 10, 16, 17, 23, 25, 26-7, 44, 83, 98, 108, 135, 158, 236
Bayt al-Ḥikmah 158n.

bazmāward 243
Bilāl al-Ḍabābī, Khārijite rebel 182
Bilbays 159
Bīmā 191
Bi'r Maymūn 32, 33-4
Bishr b. Dāwūd al-Muhallabī 106, 175, 179, 189
Bishr b. Ghiyāth al-Mārisī 100-1, 103-4
Bishr b. al-Walīd al-Kindī, judge 137, 210-11, 215-16, 220-2
Budandūn 222, 224
Bughā al-Kabīr 158
Būrān bt. al-Ḥasan b. Sahl 3, 82, 153-8
al-Buṭayn b. Umayyah al-Bajalī al-Ḥimṣī, poet 163-4
Bustān Ibn ʿĀmir or Bustān Ibn Maʿmar 21, 38
Buzurjshābūr 67
Byzantium, Byzantines (see also Rūm) 45, 144, 184-5, 187-8, 194-7, 198-9, 224, 257

C

Cappadocia 185n.
Crete 165

D

Damascus 161, 186, 188, 190, 192, 199, 223, 232, 234, 242, 243, 257
dār khāliṣah 30
dār al-qawārīr 38
Dāwūd b. Banījūr 108
Dāwūd b. ʿĪsā b. Mūsā, ʿAbbāsid 19-21, 28, 32
Dāwūd b. Yazīd al-Muhallabī 106
Daylam 64
Dayr al-ʿĀqūl 48-9, 59
Dayr al-Aʿwar 72
Dayr Hizqil, in Baghdad 249
al-Dhayyāl b. al-Haytham 210-11, 216, 222
Dhubyan, Banū 256n.
Diʿbil b. ʿAlī al-Khuzāʿī, poet 248-9
Dīnār b. ʿAbdallāh 85, 130-1, 154
Dīnawar 134, 182
Diyār Muḍar 10, 110
Diyār Rabīʿah 110
Dujayl 43
Dunbāwand 135

E

Egypt 106, 159-61, 164-5, 168-9, 178, 182, 188, 191, 192, 199

F

al-Faḍl b. al-Farrukhān 210, 217-18, 222
al-Faḍl b. Ghānim 210, 217, 222
al-Faḍl b. Kāwūs b. Khārakhuruh 135
al-Faḍl b. Muḥammad b. al-Ṣabbāḥ al-Kindī al-Kūfī 70, 74
al-Faḍl b. al-Rabīʿ 48-9, 59, 91, 110, 137, 139-40
al-Faḍl b. Sahl, Dhū al-Rh'āsatayn 2, 13-14, 35, 40-1, 59, 62, 69, 78-81, 105, 156, 179
Fam al-Ṣarāt 51
Fam al-Ṣilḥ 3, 49-50, 153, 156-8

Faraj al-Baghwārī 145, 148
Faraj al-Daylamī 80
Faraj al-Turkī 148
Faraj b. Ziyād al-Rukhkhajī 107
Fārs 10
Fatḥ al-Khādim 101-2
Fihr, Banū 31, 67
Filasṭīn 199, 223
Firnās al-Khādim 45
al-F.ṣ.l (? Syncellus), minister of the Emperor Theophilus 195
fussāq, sing. *fāsiq* 55, 76
Fusṭāṭ 159

G

Ghālib al-Mas'ūdī al-Aswad 80
al-Ghāliyah 72
Ghassān b. 'Abbād 53, 104-5, 156, 179-80, 189-90
Ghassān b. Abī al-Faraj, Abū Ibrāhīm, or Abū Ibrāhīm b. Ghassān 24-5, 53, 69, 74

H

Ḥājib b. Ṣāliḥ 175
al-Ḥakīm al-Ḥārithī 71
Hamadhān 93
Ḥamdawayh b. 'Alī b. 'Īsā b. Māhān 27, 38, 83
Ḥamdūnah bt. Hārūn al-Rashīd and Ghaḍīḍ 154, 156
Ḥammād al-Kundughūsh 26
Ḥammād b. al-Ḥasan, *rāwī* 100
Ḥamzah b. Ādharak, Khārijite rebel 105
Hāni' b. Qabīṣah al-Shaybānī 13
Ḥarb b. 'Abdallāh 41
Ḥarbiyyah quarter of Baghdad and its troops 41-4, 47-8, 55, 57-9, 77
Harim b. Sinān 255-6
Harthamah b. A'yan 11, 12, 17-19, 23-4, 39-42, 44, 72, 79
Hārūn b. Jabghūyah 103
Hārūn b. Muḥammad b. Abī Khālid 16, 26, 49, 51, 87, 182
Hārūn b. Muḥammad b. Ismā'īl b. Mūsā al-Hādī, *rāwī* 240
Hārūn b. al-Musayyab 27, 35
Hārūn al-Rashīd, caliph 36, 84
al-Ḥasan al-Hirsh 9, 12
al-Ḥasan b. 'Alī al-Bādhghīsī al-Ma'mūnī 25
al-Ḥasan b. Ḥammād Sajjādah 210, 218-19, 220-2
al-Ḥasan b. al-Ḥusayn b. Muṣ'ab 136
al-Ḥasan b. Sahl 2, 3, 9-10, 12, 13-14, 15, 17, 26-7, 37, 38, 39, 42-3, 47-54, 59, 61-3, 69-71, 75, 78-9, 81, 82, 83, 85, 105-6, 147, 153-8
al-Ḥasan b. Yaḥyā al-Fihrī, *rāwī* 163
Hāshimites (see also 'Abbāsids) 2, 13, 50, 52-3, 61, 66, 80, 91, 95
Hashtādsar 181
Ḥātim al-Ṭā'ī 255-6
ḥawā'iṭ, sing. *ḥā'iṭ* 20

Ḥawf, the 182, 189
al-Ḥawl, nephew of Saʿīd b. Sājūr 74
Ḥawlāyā 68
Heraclia, Hiraqlah 188
Hermon, Mount, Jabal al-Thalj 243
Ḥijāz 10
Ḥimṣ 163-4, 199, 223
Ḥimyar 240
Ḥīrah 72, 73
Hishām b. Muḥammad al-Kalbī 231
Ḥiṣn Sinan 186
Ḥulwān 97, 104, 184
Ḥumayd b. ʿAbd al-Ḥamīd al-Ṭūsī 51-2, 53, 54, 60, 69-72, 74, 81-2, 86, 87, 89-92, 95, 157-8, 166, 246-7
Ḥusayn, eunuch of al-Ma'mūn
Ḥusayn Z.j.lah 154
al-Ḥusayn b. al-Ḍaḥḥāk, poet 251-2, 256
Ḥusayn b. Ḥasan al-Afṭas, ʿAlid 19, 22, 29-32
Ḥusayn b. Hishām al-Marwazī 192
al-Ḥusayn b. Ruzayq 163

I

Ibn Abī al-Jamal, rebel in Syria 175
Ibn Abī Khālid, see Muḥammad b. Abī Khālid al-Marwarrūdhī
Ibn Abī al-Ṣaqr, rebel in Syria 175
Ibn al-Aḥmar 213
Ibn al-Bakkā' al-Aṣghar, see Abū Hārūn b. al-Bakkā' al-Aṣghar
Ibn ʿĀ'ishah, Ibrāhīm b. Muḥammad b. ʿAbd al-Wahhāb, ʿAbbāsid 3, 75, 145, 148
Ibn Dhī al-Qalamayn ʿAlī b. Abī Saʿīd 160
Ibn al-Hirsh 210, 222
Ibn al-Jalīl 192
Ibn al-Kalbī, see Hishām b. Muḥammad al-Kalbī
Ibn al-Nadīm 7
Ibn al-Sarī, see ʿUbaydallāh b. al-Sarī b. al-Ḥakam
Ibn al-Sarj, rebel in Syria 175
Ibn Surayj, singer 257
Ibn Ṭabāṭabā, Muḥammad b. Ibrāhīm b. Ismāʿīl, ʿAlid 12-15, 170
Ibn Ukht al-Dārī, rebel in Syria 198
Ibn ʿUlayyah al-Akbar 210, 213
Ibrāhīm b. al-ʿAbbās, secretary to Aḥmad b. Abī Khālid 135
Ibrāhīm b. al-ʿAbbās al-Ṣūlī al-Kātib 96
Ibrāhīm b. Abī Jaʿfar al-Ḥimyarī, rebel in Yemen 181
Ibrāhīm b. ʿĪsā b. Burayhah, ʿAbbāsid 232-3
Ibrāhīm b. al-Layth al-Tujībī (?) 144
Ibrāhīm b. al-Mahdī, Ibn Shaklah, al-Mubārak 2, 7, 62-3, 66-9, 73, 74, 75-8, 81, 85-92, 146-9, 153, 155, 216,220, 249

Ibrāhīm b. Mūsā b. Jaʿfar al-Jazzār, ʿAlid 28-9, 37-8, 83
Imāmī Shīʿah 100
ʿImrān b. Mūsā al-Barmakī 189
ʿĪsā b. Khālid al-Makhzūmī, Abū Saʿīd, poet 240
ʿĪsā b. Manṣūr al-Rāfiʿī 194
ʿĪsā b. Muḥammad b. Abī Khālid 12, 48, 51, 52, 54-5, 58-63, 70-6, 81, 82, 86-9, 106, 108, 139
ʿĪsā b. Yazīd al-Julūdī 27, 33, 35-7, 38-9, 49, 83
ʿĪsābādh 91
Iṣfahān 65, 183
Isḥāq b. al-ʿAbbās b. Muḥammad, ʿAbbāsid 53, 183
Isḥāq b. Abī Ribʿī 161
Isḥāq b. Ibrāhīm al-Mawṣilī, poet and singer 253-5
Isḥāq b. Ibrāhīm al-Muṣʿabī 3, 129, 135, 182, 184, 189, 199, 204-5, 210-14, 220-2, 229, 234
Isḥāq b. Ibrāhīm al-Rāfiqī 161-2
Isḥāq b. Muḥammad, judge of Mecca 32, 34
Isḥāq b. Mūsā b. ʿĪsā, ʿAbbāsid 28, 33-4, 65
Isḥāq b. Mūsā al-Hādī b. al-Mahdī 42-3, 63, 67, 72, 77
Isḥāq b. Yaḥyā b. Muʿādh 223
Iskāf Banī al-Junayd 48
Ismāʿīl b. Abī Masʿūd 205
Ismāʿīl b. Dāwūd 205
Ismāʿīl b. Ḥammād b. Abī Ḥanīfah, judge 136

J

Jabbul 50, 52, 58
Jaʿfar al-Khayyāṭ 186
Jaʿfar b. Dāwūd al-Qummī 182, 190, 197
Jaʿfar b. ʿĪsā al-Ḥasanī 209, 214, 218
Jaʿfar b. Muḥammad b. Abī Khālid 49, 50
Jaʿfar b. Muḥammad al-ʿĀmirī, *rāwī* 138
Jaʿfar b. Muḥammad, al-Ṣādiq, Sixth Imām of the Shīʿah 31
Jalūlā 26
Jāmiʿ (ayn) (= al-Ḥillah) 16
al-Jarawī, see ʿAlī b. ʿAbd al-ʿAzīz al-Jarawī
Jarīr, powt 244, 253, 257
Jarjarāyā 47, 49, 50
Jāwīdhān b. Sahl 65
Jāwīdhāniyyah 65
al-Jazīrah 10, 19, 25, 106, 109, 169, 192, 199
al-Jibāl, al-Jabal 10, 19, 104, 183, 192, 193
Juddah 34
Juhaynah, Banū 35
Juḥfah 34
Jūkhā 48
Jurjān, Gurgān 37, 94

K

Kaʿbah 29-30, 32, 36, 38
Kafar ʿAzūn 138-9
Kalwādhā 18, 53, 70
Karkh quarter of Baghdad 43,

51, 55, 76, 87
Kaskar 108
Kawthar Mosque, Baghdad 92
Kāwūs b. Khārākhuruh, ruler of Ushrūsanah 135
Kaysūm 144, 188
khādim = *khaṣī* 101
Khalaf al-Miṣrī 79, 81
Khālid al-Daryūsh 2, 55, 57-8
Khālid b. Yazīd b. Mazyad 147
Khalīl b. Hāshim al-Bāwardī, Garden of 104
Khāqān al-Khādim 231
Khārijites, Ḥarūriyyah, Muḥakkimah, Shurāt 67-8, 76, 105, 234
kharīṭah 133, 220
al-Khayzurān bt. ʿAṭāʾ al-Jurashiyyah, wife of al-Mahdī and mother of Hārūn al-Rashīd 47
al-Khayzurān, Cemetery of 148
Khayzurāniyyah quarter of Baghdad 47, 95
khifārah 58
Khuld Palace, in Baghdad 86
Khurāsān 17, 19, 27, 65, 97, 100, 104-6, 133-5, 136, 166, 182, 192, 234
Khurramiyyah (see also Bābak) 193
Khuzaymah b. Khāzim al-Tamīmī 47-8, 50, 53, 59, 81, 82
al-Khwārazmī, see Muḥammad b. Mūsā al-Khwārazmī
Kirmān 175
Kūfah 10, 14, 17, 19, 23, 24, 39, 49, 53, 60, 67, 68, 70-4, 135
Kulthūm b. ʿAmr al-ʿAttābī 253-5
Kulthūm b. Thābit b. Abī Saʿīd, *rāwī* 132
al-Kunāsah quarter of Kūfah 73-4
Kūthā Rabba 16, 54

L

Lārīz, ? Lārījān 64
Leo V the Armenian, Byzantine Emperor 45, 144n.
Lu'lu'ah 194

M

maʿāwīn, sing. *maʿūnah* 99
Maʿbad b. al-ʿAbbās 86
Maʿbadī bridge, in Baghdad 86, 90
Madā'in 17, 18, 23, 51, 53, 59, 67, 70, 77, 81-2, 90
al-Madīnah 19, 22, 98, 185
al-Maghrib 10, 244
Mahdī b. ʿAlwān al-Dihqān al-Ḥarūrī 67-8
Mājidah 185
Makhzūm, Banū 31
Malaṭiyah 185
Mālik b. Shāhī al-Niffarī 145-6, 148
al-Ma'mūn, ʿAbdallah, Caliph 9, 17, 20, 36-7, 39-41, 46, 52, 59, 61-3, 64, 66-7, 71-3, 78-82, 84-5, 88-9, 94-8, 100-4, 108-9, 128-9, 130-1, 136, 138-40, 142, 144, 145-9, 152, 153-9, 166,

169-71, 175, 176, 184-6, 187-90, 191-7, 198-209, 220-21, 231-2, 232-57
Manbij 185
al-Manṣūr b. al-Mahdī 2, 18, 23-4, 46-8, 52-3, 58-9, 62, 66, 73, 81, 82
Manuel, Byzantine *patricius* 186
maqām Ibrāhīm, in Mecca 29, 36
al-Māriqī 249
Marw 37, 39, 41, 78, 80
Marwah 22
Masrūr al-Kabīr al-Khādim 20-1
Maṣṣīṣah 187
al-Mas'ūdī 7
maṭmūrah, pl. *maṭāmīr* 188
Mayzār b. Qārin 64, 166-7
Mecca 19-22, 28-39, 83, 98, 144, 185, 231
Michael II the Stammerer, Byzantine Emperor 45, 144
miḥnah 3, 47, 199-223, 229
Mills of 'Abdallāh b. Mālik, near Baghdad 90, 92
Mills of the Patricius, near Baghdad 43n.
Minā 20-1, 22, 32, 35
minbar 101n.
Minjab 66
Moses 208
Mosul 10, 176, 185, 186
Mu'ādh b. 'Abdallāh 70
al-Mu'allā b. Ayyūb, secretary 235
Mu'āwiyah, Caliph 175, 217
Mubārak, village 50, 51, 52, 69
Muḍar 108, 110, 234, 238
Mufaddāt 255
al-Muhallab b. Abī Ṣufrah 179
Muḥammad al-Rawwā'ī 77
Muḥammad b. 'Abdallāh, *ṣāḥib al-marākib* 251
Muḥammad b. 'Abdallāh b. Jasham al-Rib'ī, *rāwī* 255
Muḥammad b. 'Abdallāh al-Ḥammād, Abū al-Rāzī 176, 181
Muḥammad b. 'Abd al-Raḥmān al-Makhzūmī, judge 21, 136-7
Muḥammad b. Abī al-'Abbās al-Ṭūsī 100-3
Muḥammad b. Abī Khālid al-Marwarrūdhī 42-4, 47-52
Muḥammad b. Abī Rajā, *faqīh* 89
Muḥammad b. 'Alī b. Mūsā al-Imām 82, 185
Muḥammad b. 'Alī b. Ṣāliḥ al-Sarakhsī, *rāwī* 233
Muḥammad b. 'Alī al-Ṭunbūrī, poet, musician and *rāwī* 241
Muḥammad b. Ayyūb b. Ja'far b. Sulaymān, *rāwī* 236
Muḥammad b. Dāwūd b. 'Īsā, 'Abbāsid 20-1
Muḥammad b. Ḥakīm b. Marwān, mawlā of the 'Abbāsids 34

Muḥammad b. b. Hārūn, secretary of al-Ma'mūn 103
Muḥammad b. al-Ḥasan 219
Muḥammad b. al-Ḥasan b. ʿAlī b. ʿĀṣim 210, 219, 222
Muḥammad b. al-Ḥasan b. Sahl 154
Muḥammad b. Ḥātim b. Maymūn 211, 218, 222
Muḥammad b. al-Haytham b. ʿAdī al-Ṭā'ī, *rāwī* 232, 249
Muḥammad b. Ḥumayd al-Ṭūsī 176, 181
Muḥammad b. Ibrāhīm al-Ifrīqī 51, 69, 75, 145, 148
Muḥammad b. Ibrāhīm al-Sabārī, *rāwī* 253
Muḥammad b. ʿImrān al-Fūtaqī 132
Muḥammad b. ʿĪsā b. Yazīd al-Julūdī 37
Muḥammad b. Jaʿfar b. Muḥammad b. ʿAlī, al-Dībājah, ʿAlid 31-7, 45, 49
Muḥammad b. al-Jahm al-Barmakī 256
Muḥammad b. Maslamah 30
Muḥammad b. Muḥammad al-Maʿbad, ʿAbbāsid 86
Muḥammad b. Muḥammad b. Zayd b. ʿAlī, ʿAlid 15, 25, 27, 64
Muḥammad b. Mūsā al-Khwārazmī 158
Muḥammad b. Mūsā b. Ḥafṣ 175
Muḥammad b. Nūḥ al-Maḍrūb 210, 218, 220-1
Muḥammad b. Saʿd, secretary of al-Wāqidī 204
Muḥammad b. Samāʿah, judge 136
Muḥammad b. Sulaymān b. Dāwūd, ʿAlid 19, 22
Muḥammad b. Yaqṭīn b. Mūsā 54
Muḥammad b. Yazdād, secretary 235
Muḥammad b. Yūsuf b. Hishām al-Marwazī 192
Muḥammad b. Yūsuf al-Kh.ḥ.b.q.w.ṣ 166
Muḥammad b. Zakariyyā' b. Maymūn al-Farghānī, *rāwī* 256
Muḥawwal 43
Mukhāriq, singer 257
muqāsamah 97
Mūsā, ʿAbbāsid commander 78, 81
Mūsā garden, Baghdad 96
Mūsā b. Ḥafṣ 135, 175
Mūsā b. Muḥammad al-Amīn 137
Mūsā b. Yaḥyā al-Barmakī 189
Muṣʿab b. Ruzayq al-Khuzāʿī 131, 163
muṣallā (see also Ṣāliḥ, *ṣāḥib al-muṣallā*) 17, 66
Musawwidah 27, 30
Mushāsh 20, 21, 28, 33
Muṭahhar b. Ṭāhir b. al-Ḥusayn 131
al-Muʿtaṣim, Abū

Isḥāq b. Hārūn al-Rashīd, subsequently Caliph 3, 37, 45, 68, 148, 171, 174, 181-2, 186, 188, 197, 199, 222-5, 227-9, 231, 235, 242, 257
Muṭṭalib b. ʿAbdallāh b. Mālik al-Khuzāʿī 47, 59-60, 66, 68, 81, 82, 89-92, 217
muṭṭawwiʿah 55
Muwaffaq al-Ṣaqlabī 80
al-Muẓaffar b. Murajjā 213
Muzdalifah 22

N

Nabaṭī 100n.
nabīdh 102
al-Naḍr b. Shumayl 210, 222
Nahr Bīn 92
Nahr Būq 67
Nahr Diyālā 82, 91
Nahr ʿĪsā 18, 86
Nahr al-Malik 16
Nahr Ṣarṣār 18, 39, 43, 44, 53, 54, 88
Nahrawān 40, 81, 94, 95
Naṣr b. Ḥamzah b. Mālik al-Khuzāʿī 47
Naṣr b. Shabath al-ʿUqaylī 2, 3, 10, 105, 106, 108, 110, 129, 134, 138-44, 145-6, 159
Naysābūr 105-6
Nīl 9, 49-54, 70-2, 75, 81
Nuʿaym b. Khāzim 69, 75
Nūqān 84
Nuṣayr al-Waṣīf 66

Q

qāḍī al-jamāʿah 21
Qādisiyyah 24-5
qafīz 98, 135
Qanṭarah, Qanṭarat al-Kūfah, al-Qanāṭir 72
Qaryat al-Aʿrāb 70
Qaryat Shāhī 14, 23, 72
al-Qāsim b. Ibrāhīm b. Ṭabāṭabā al-Rassī 170
al-Qāsim b. Muḥammad al-Ṭayfūrī 249
Qaṣr Ibn Hubayrah 15, 16, 17, 18, 53, 54, 60, 69, 70, 71
Qaṣr al-Waḍḍāḥ, palace in Baghdad 43
Qaṭrabbul 56
Qays 178, 234
Qinnasrīn 199
Quḍāʿah 234
Qumm 166, 183, 190
Qurrah 185, 237
Qusṭanṭīn al-Rūmī 80
Qutaybah b. Saʿīd 210, 213
Quzaḥ 22

R

Rabaḍiyyūn 164n.
Rabīʿah 234
Rādhānayn 67
radm 21n.
Radm Banī Jumaḥ 21n.
Rāfiʿ b. Layth 104
Rāfiḍah 72
Rāfiqah 198
Rajāʾ b. Abī al-Ḍaḥḥāk 35, 37, 44

Ramlah 261
Raqqah 48, 79, 95, 106, 108-9, 129, 134, 140, 159, 198, 199, 205, 210, 222
Ra's al-ʿAyn 25, 186
Rayy 65, 85, 94, 166
Round City (Madīnat Abī Jaʿfar) of Baghdad 145-6, 168
Rūm (see also Byzantium, Byzantines) 165
Ruṣāfah quarter of Baghdad 86, 87, 90, 95-6, 136, 189
Rūyān 135
Ruzayq, mawlā of Ṭalḥah b. ʿAbdallāh al-Khuzāʿī 164

S

sābiqah 140
Saʿd, Banū, of Tamīm 238-9
Ṣadaqah b. ʿAlī b. Ṣadaqah 144
Saʿdawayh al-Wāsiṭī 210, 218, 222
Ṣafā' 22, 32
al-Saffāḥ, Caliph 216
al-Safīniyyīn, al-Safīnatayn 18
Sahl b. Salāmah al-Anṣārī 2, 55, 57-60, 75-8, 90, 92
Saʿīd al-Allāf al-Qāri', *rāwī* 224
Saʿīd b. al-ʿĀṣ 101
Saʿīd b. al-Ḥasan b. Qaḥṭabah al-Ṭā'ī 47
Saʿīd b. Sājūr al-Kūfī 49, 51, 68-75, 81, 91-2
Saʿīd b. Ziyād, *rāwī* 234
Sajjādah, see al-Ḥasan b. Ḥammād Sajjādah
Salaghūs 197, 198, 237
Salamiyyah 163
Ṣāliḥ, *ṣāḥib al-muṣallā* 17, 66
Ṣāliḥ b. al-ʿAbbās b. Muḥammad, ʿAbbāsid 144, 167, 175
Ṣāliḥ b. Hārūn al-Rashīd 98, 137, 251-2
Sallām al-Abrash al-Khādim 134
Salm al-Khāsir, poet 64
Ṣanʿā' 28
Ṣaʿnabā 14
Sarakhs 80-1, 84
Ṣarāt, Ṣarāt Canal, Ṣarāt Bridge, of Baghdad 43, 70, 90
al-Sarī b. al-Ḥakam 106
sarīr 17
Sarūj 139
Sawād 59, 67, 70, 98, 99, 108, 161, 184
Shahriyār b. Sharwīn, Bāwandid ruler 64, 166
Shajarah 35
Shammāsiyyah quarter of Baghdad 184
Shirrīz 64
Shubayl, *ṣāḥib al-s.l.bah* 68
shuraṭ, sing, *shurṭah* 99
shuṭṭār 55
Simmar 69
Sind, India 106, 175, 179, 189
al-Sindī b. Yaḥyā b. Saʿīd al-Ḥarashī 17, 66, 214

Sirāj al-Khādim 39
Ṣiyādah, ? Ṣayyādah 75
sūdān ahl al-miyāh 33
Sulaymān b. ʿAbdallāh b. Sulaymān, ʿAbbāsid 93, 190, 197
Sulaymān b. Abī Jaʿfar al-Manṣūr 14, 234
Sulaymān b. Razīn al-Khuzāʿī, *rāwī* 248
Sulaymān b. Yaʿqūb, *ṣāḥib al-khabar* 221
Sundus 186
Sūra 70
Sūs, Susa 25
Syria 10, 134, 169, 175, 191, 192, 233-4, 237, 241

T

Ṭabaristān 64, 135, 136, 167, 175
Ṭāhir b. al-Ḥusayn 3, 10, 13, 48, 79, 95-6, 99-106, 110, 128, 131-5, 163
Ṭāhir b. al-Ḥusayn, Mosque of 58, 77
Ṭāhir b. Khālid b. Nizār al-Ghassānī, *rāwī* 169
Takrīt 184
Ṭalhaḥ b. Ṭāhir b. al-Ḥusayn 133-5
Ṭālibids (see also Ahl al-Bayt, ʿAlids) 19-21, 24, 26-7, 31, 34, 131, 169
Tamīm, Banū 237-8
Ṭarnāyā 75, 81
Tarsus 3, 185, 187, 221, 224, 231, 240
al-Taymī, ʿAbdallāh b. Ayyūb, poet 27
Ṭayyi', Banū 256n.
Thābit b. Yaḥyā, secretary 249
Theophilus, Byzantine Emperor 3, 144, 187-8, 194-5, 224
Thumāmah b. Ashras al-Numayrī 100, 138
Toghuz-Oghuz 107
Ṭūs 84-5, 240
Ṭuwānah, Tyana 188, 198-9

U

ʿUbaydallāh b. al-ʿAbbās b. Muḥammad, ʿAbbāsid 66
ʿUbaydallāh b. al-Ḥasan b. ʿUbaydallāh b. al-ʿAbbās 98, 107, 129
ʿUbaydallāh b. al-Sarī b. al-Ḥakam 3, 7, 159-60, 164, 171-3
ʿUbaydallāh b. ʿUmar al-Qawārīrī 210, 219, 220-2
ʿUjayf b. ʿAnbasah 166, 182, 186, 189, 192-4
ʿUmar b. Abī Rabīʿah, poet 244
ʿUmar b. Ḥafṣ al-Ballūṭī 165
ʿUmar b. al-Khaṭṭāb, Caliph 124, 210, 213, 219
ʿUmārah b. ʿAqīl, poet 244, 252, 255
al-ʿUmarī, judge of Raqqah 210, 213
ʿUmayr b. al-Walīd al-Bādhghīsī 181
Umayyads 140, 155, 243-4

Umm al-Faḍl bt. al-Ma'mūn 82, 185
Umm Ḥabīb bt. al-Ma'mūn 82
Umm Jaʿfar, see Zubaydah
Umm Jaʿfar, *qaṭīʿah* or fief of, in Baghdad 108
ʿUqayl, Banū 10
Urdunn 199, 223
ʿUsfān 34
Ushrūsanah 107, 135

W

Wahb b. Saʿīd al-Kātib 52
al-Walīd b. ʿUqbah 101
Warqā' b. Jamīl 27, 33-4
Wāsiṭ 16, 17, 23, 25, 46-9, 51, 74-6, 81, 147
al-Wāthiq, Caliph 234

Y

Yabrīn 257
Yaḥyā b. ʿAbdallāh, cousin of al-Ḥasan b. Sahl 59
Yaḥyā b. ʿAbd al-Raḥmān al-ʿUmarī 210, 219, 222
Yaḥyā b. Aktham 134, 182, 188, 230, 235
Yaḥyā b. ʿAlī b. ʿĪsā b. Māhān 53
Yaḥyā b. ʿĀmir al-Ḥārithī 45
Yaḥyā b. al-Ḥasan b. ʿAbd al-Khāliq, *rāwī* 109
Yaḥyā b. ʿImrān 166
Yaḥyā b. Muʿādh 78, 98, 106, 109
Yaḥyā b. ʿUmar b. Yaḥyā, ʿAlid 7
Yaʿlā b. Murrah, rebel in Azerbaijan 176
Yamāmah 108
Yaman, tribal group 178, 234
Yāsir, slave of al-Ma'mūn 102
Yāsiriyyah 18, 88-9
Yazīd b. Muḥammad al-Makhzūmī 39
al-Yazīdī, Abū Muḥammad Yaḥyā b. al-Mubārak 250-1
Yazīdī Shīrwān-Shāhs 147n.
Yemen 10, 28-9, 37-9, 130, 176, 180, 190
Yūnus b. ʿAbd al-Aʿlā; *rāwī* 165
Yūsuf b. Abī Yūsuf 219

Z

Zamzam 30
Zandaward 81
Zawāqīl 10
Zayd b. ʿAlī, Zayn al-ʿĀbidīn, Fourth Imām of the Shīʿah 15
Zayd b. Mūsā b. Jaʿfar, Zayd al-Nār, ʿAlid 26-8, 44
Zaydī Shīʿah 15n., 100
Ziryāb, mawlā of al-Mahdī and musician 244
Ziyād b. Abīhi 217
Zubaydah bt. al-Manṣūr, Umm Jaʿfar 154-7, 189
Zufaytā 159
Zuhayr b. Ḥarb, Abū Khaythamah 204
Zuhayr b. al-Musayyab al-Ḍabbī 14-15, 23, 43-4, 47-9, 50-1
Zuṭṭ 106, 108, 140